MICROECONOMICS

The Easy Way

Walter J. Wessels
Associate Professor of Economics
Department of Economics and Business
North Carolina State University

BARRON'S

All inquiries should be addressed to:
Barron's Educational Series, Inc.
250 Wireless Boulevard
Hauppauge, New York 11788

Library of Congress Catalog Card No. 96-53214

International Standard Book No. 0-8120-9601-0

Library of Congress Cataloging-in-Publication Data
Wessels, Walter J.
    Microeconomics the easy way / Walter J. Wessels.
        p.   cm. — (The easy way)
    Includes index.
    ISBN 0-8120-9601-0
    1. Microeconomics.   I. Title.   II. Series.
HB172.W47   1997
338.5—dc21   96-53214
                                                           CIP

PRINTED IN THE UNITED STATES OF AMERICA

9 8 7 6 5 4 3 2 1

TABLE OF CONTENTS

Chapter Eighteen
Poverty, Equality, and Economic Growth   297

Chapter Nineteen
International Trade   309

Preface

The goal of this book is help you understand microeconomics so you'll do better in class and in business. By the time you've completed this book, you should be better able to analyze and comprehend the complex economic world we all live and work in.

True to its title, *Microeconomics the Easy Way* is designed to make learning economics easier. Unlike most textbooks, we test your understanding throughout with examples and problems. By comparing your answer with the answer in the text, you can make certain that you understand each concept before going on to the next. If you're already in an economics course and have taken your first test, then you know by now the importance of frequently testing your understanding of economics, especially before a real test! By doing problems, such as those presented here, you can be sure you've learned the material correctly.

To help students learn faster, this book also features many problems that I have used as a teacher to help students understand the material better and with greater certainty. Also, this book uses a wide range of teaching methods, which help students with a wide range of learning styles.

Microeconomics the Easy Way is thorough. It can be used as a primary text, as a supplement, or as a study guide. It covers the microeconomic concepts found in most one- and two-semester introductory economics courses, whether presented at the master of business, college, and even the advanced high school level. It also will prove to be an invaluable aid for students taking intermediate microeconomics.

I suggest the following steps in using this book to learn microeconomics:

Step 1 Learn the Definitions

Economists use terms like *rent* and *profit* in ways that differ from their common usage. This is more by historical accident than by a devious plan to deceive unsuspecting students. Nevertheless, it is imperative that you learn the exact economics definition of these terms, because they have proven over time to be very useful for understanding economics events. The glossary contains the key terms—use it.

Step 2 Learn Marginal Analysis

Marginal analysis is an economic method of thinking that, if followed, allows firms to maximize profits and consumers to get the best deal. When you understand marginal analysis enough to use it, you'll have the basic key to understanding most of the material in the rest of the book. If you are buying this book to review just a few concepts, I suggest you review the material on marginal analysis in Chapter Two.

Step 3 Do all the Problems

Once again, don't assume you know the material just because you have read it. If that were true, I'd be the greatest golfer in the world. Do the problems and then compare your answer with the answer in the text.

Step 4 To Understand a Model's Results, Understand Its Assumptions

We will present many of the models used by microeconomists to understand the world. The key to using any model is to learn its assumptions. The purpose of assumptions is to simplify the analysis and focus on what is important to the situation. Any model's results flow directly from its assumptions.

Microeconomics the Easy Way embodies what I have learned from teaching economics and what I have learned from my students. I thank my many students for their questions and suggestions, which have made me a better teacher. For the same reason, I invite your suggestions and comments. My e-mail address is: Walt_Wessels @NCSU.EDU.

Walter J. Wessels
Raleigh, North Carolina
January, 1997

Chapter One

Exploring Economics

In June of 1842, Kit Carson and John Fremont embarked on the first of three expeditions that produced the maps that helped later settlers make their way across the western frontier. In front of them stood trees, rocks, and rapids. From these, they drew maps of forests, mountains, and rivers.

In the same way, you're about to embark on a trail of discovery. Most likely, you have seen the economy up close as a consumer and worker. You've seen the "trees, rocks, and rapids" of commerce. But to understand the economy, you need a map that guides you toward understanding how our economy works. This book provides the maps economists have found useful for understanding where our economy is going. This is a great adventure, an adventure in learning.

Economics is divided into two parts, microeconomics and macroeconomics. Microeconomics is like a close-up map of a city, whereas macroeconomics is like a map of the nation. Microeconomics maps up close how individuals make decisions and how these decisions affect the price and output of various goods and services. Macroeconomics maps the economy from afar, seeing not individuals but only aggregates of peoples and businesses. While microeconomics might study consumer spending on wheat, macroeconomics studies total spending on all goods combined. While microeconomics might study how a firm decides how many workers it hires, macroeconomics studies total employment in the United States. Microeconomics studies what determines the price of wheat and cars. Macroeconomics studies what determines the aggregate price level (such as the consumer price index). Microeconomics studies how technology and markets affect the income of individuals. Macroeconomics studies what causes aggregate output (such as the gross domestic product) to go up in expansions and down in recessions.

This book is about microeconomics, the study of how individuals and businesses make decisions and how these decisions affect the prices and output of goods and services. In contrast, macroeconomics is the study of aggregates of individuals, prices, and output. Modern macroeconomics is based upon the study of microeconomics.

Now let us look at one of the major topics in microeconomics.

MARKETS AND PRICES

Let us go back to the Middle Ages to what was one of the major centers of Western civilization at the time: Paris. As we watch, farmers bring their food products from the provinces into the bustling city. There, they trade these products for the goods produced by city craftsmen. Each day, the farmers bring to market what the city people want. Little is left unsold at the end of the day. Yet, no one tells farmers what these wants are. Amazingly, the city people also have ready for trade the goods the farmers want.

This same scene takes place today around the globe in all markets. Throughout time, the business of all markets has been trade. But there is one main difference. In medieval Paris, the farmers had to find buyers who wanted their crops and, in addition, had goods the farmer wanted in trade. Trade then was direct: goods for goods. Today, trade is indirect: goods for money and money for goods. Modern-day farmers sell their crops for money and then use the money to buy the goods they want. The persons they sell their crops to need not be the persons they buy from. Money eliminates the need for direct trade and facilitates indirect trade. Yet, ultimately, we all are traders, trading the goods and services we produce for the goods and services we buy.

Trading today is so indirect and so complex that no computer and no government, no matter how large, could trace all of its complex interactions. Do you know the people who made your car? Its windows? Do you know where the steel came from for its frame? Do you know who sewed the clothing you are wearing? Most of the goods you buy are from people you don't know. The beauty of money is that you don't have to know these persons, only the price of the goods they sell.

How does indirect trade—trade so complex that it is beyond the comprehension of any one person—take place? That is the main topic of this text. The simple answer is price. Everyone cares about price. Price to the consumer is *income* to the producer. Our income reflects the price of what we have to sell. Your wage, for example, is the *price* of the work time you sold to your employer (or to your customers, if you own your own business). Similarly, the prices you pay for groceries, housing, and all the other goods and services you buy become someone else's income. The power of this price system is that the better you are at producing what other people want, the higher the price you'll get and the more you'll earn. Price motivates people and allocates resources to where they are in demand.

Esperanto was developed in 1905 to be a universal language that all persons could easily learn and speak. Today, it is estimated that 100,000 people use Esperanto. Many of these persons feel that a common language would allow people to share information and knowledge worldwide. What they don't realize is that we already have a universal language: the price system. Prices allow people to communicate their needs and wants in a language all understand. In turn, the power of self-interest motivates people to respond to needs and wants expressed by prices.

The French government pays mothers to get prenatal care for their babies. As a result of this program, more pregnant women use the free medical facilities. Mothers and their children have benefited from this program. It is a testament to the power of self-interest over the power of love—even parental love—that many pregnant women had to be paid before they would obtain free medical care.

The following question illustrates how prices communicate the scarcity of goods and encourage people to adjust so as to offset changes in scarcity.

Thought Questions

To save the spotted owl, the government has restricted the harvesting of lumber from old-growth forests. The reduction in the supply of lumber caused lumber prices to go up. Higher lumber prices are expected to cost consumers $32 billion or about $330 per U.S. household.

How will the higher price of lumber affect home builders' use of lumber in building homes? How will this affect consumers' decisions to build new homes?

Higher lumber prices cause builders to use less lumber by using alternative materials and techniques. The higher prices of homes cause consumers to buy fewer homes or, alternatively, to buy homes using less lumber.

Did the higher price make people worse off?

No. It is the reduction in timber land that made people worse off. The higher price of lumber merely communicates the fact.

How did the higher price affect the impact of less timber land?

The higher price gave people the incentive to take steps to reduce the severity of the impact of less lumber on consumers. Without these adjustments, the impact of less timber land would have been even more costly.

GROWTH

Another key topic in microeconomics involves the question, What is the cause of economic growth? One could almost say economics began with this question, for it was in 1776, the same year as the American Revolution, that Adam Smith published his classic economic treatise *The Wealth of Nations*. In it, he asked the basic question of what determines the wealth and prosperity of a people. In today's terms, the question becomes, What determines the per capita income and its growth rate?

Consider the case of Germany. After World War II, its buildings, factories, and roads were in ruins. Germany probably had less in the way of physical means of production than India or Latin America at that time. Yet, within a few years, Germany's economy became one of the strongest in the world while India and Latin America remained relatively poor. Why and how? This is one of the questions that economists seek to answer.

NORMATIVE AND POSITIVE ECONOMICS

"Growth is good" or "Growth is bad" are assertions we often hear in the news. They are called *normative* statements because they reflect a subjective value judgment about what ought to be. One person could see new buildings rising and wages rising and find these events good. Another could see in the same events the destruction of old buildings and the greed of workers and find these same events bad.

In contrast, "Growth creates pollution" or "Growth gets rid of pollution" are called *positive* statements—assertions of fact that can be tested. In this case, studies have shown that economic growth increases pollution until per capita income reaches $4,000 and then, above that level, richer nations take actions to reduce pollution. The word *positive* comes from philosophy and has nothing to do with whether the statement is cast in a positive (e.g., "Growth causes pollution") or negative (e.g., "Growth does not cause pollution") mode. Both statements are positive, and as it turns out, both are true for different stages of growth.

Positive economics sets about to discover what is true about the economy; normative economics evaluates whether the facts found are good or bad.

It is important in economics to separate the positive from the normative. All too often, we believe to be true what we want to be true. Regrettably, the world is rarely accommodating. For example, many people wish that the poor did not have to live in substandard housing. Because of this wish, they believe that by outlawing substandard housing—by running landlords of substandard housing out of business—this problem will be solved. But is this assertion true? The answer is no. Substandard housing exists because that is all the poor can afford. Outlawing it without providing alternative shelter would only make the poor worse off; many of them would become homeless. Good intentions are wonderful, but without good policies, they often produce results opposite of those intended.

Thought Questions

Indicate whether these statements are positive or normative:
A. Slavery produced a 20% profit for slave owners.
B. Slavery is bad.
C. A sufficiently higher minimum wage will reduce employment.
D. The minimum wage is evil when it causes people to lose their livelihood.
E. The moon is made of green cheese.

A and C are positive statements. B and D are normative statements. E is a positive statement. A statement can be false and still be a positive statement. That's because a positive statement is an assertion that something is true. However, the facts may prove it to be false. Often, positive statements turn out to be factually wrong, but they remain positive and not normative statements.

A STRATEGY FOR LEARNING ECONOMICS

Remember when you were learning to add in grade school. You started out adding very small numbers such as 2 + 2. You may have been asked to combine two groups of two blocks to show how addition works. What if, on the very first day, you instead were faced with a complex problem like "Add 80.1344 to 5/6." Do you think you would have learned math? I don't think so!

We learn by simple examples. Even today, when I do my own economic analysis, I try to keep my numbers below ten. This makes my analysis easy to follow! In this text, most of my examples use small numbers. If you want real big numbers because they are more realistic, that's fine. But it's not the way to learn. First start out simple. Then, and only then, extend what you've learned to the more complex. That's the easy way to learn, and it is a key strategy for understanding economics.

KEY SKILLS IN MAKING ECONOMICS EASIER TO LEARN

The keys skills you need to learn economics are

1. The ability to see and manipulate visual pictures and
2. The ability to reason through an example.

How do you use your visual skills? While holding your head still, try this simple experiment, paying attention to where your eyes are looking (up or down, left or right). Close your eyes and imagine a pink elephant on its hind legs in a blue dress dancing and twirling around. You may see this picture clearly or only be vaguely aware that it's there. Now, ask yourself where you were looking. Most people look up when they visualize. Right-handed people tend to look up and to their right. If you had a hard time figuring out where you were looking, have a friend watch you imagine some made-up pictures with your eyes open. Or, hold your eyes in various positions and try to visualize the picture. Wherever it is easiest for you to see the dancing elephant is your visualization spot, which activates your brain to create and manipulate pictures. So when you are studying graphs, consciously visualize the graphs by looking at this spot.

The second skill, reasoning through an example, is generally done by talking to yourself. Your goal, when reasoning through an example, is to understand it. You should ask yourself why, given the assumptions, must the conclusion follow? Next, ask how, when one part of the example is changed, do the results change? Finally, ask what are the model's predictions and how would you show whether they are true or false?

Reasoning takes patience and time. Don't try to speed things up by just memorizing the results. Learn how and why they come about. In a math class I took in college, a group of students formed a cheating ring. They each took a chapter and memorized its results. Then, on the test, they each did the parts they memorized and then passed the answers among themselves. This worked well on the first test, but they did not realize that math is a sequential subject. It builds on itself such that you have to learn each step before going on. As a result, the cheaters flunked the course because none of them had learned all the previous steps.

Most students who fail to learn the logic and reasoning of economics use primarily their visual reasoning, seeing the results rather than talking through the problem. Seeing the results is very useful once you've become practiced at logic. But people who use their visual sense often jump to the wrong conclusion and, what is worse, tend to believe it. They often trick themselves into thinking they've learned something just by reading about it. As a result, multiple choice tests kill them! If this sounds like you, write out your answers to all questions. Test and retest yourself to be sure you really have learned the material.

PROBING TO LEARN ECONOMICS

I have found that students tend to use one of two learning strategies. One is the strategy of learning the procedures. For example, when learning a computer program, procedure learners break out the manual and methodically learn each keystroke. Procedure learners often say, "Just show me how it works—not why." They don't want to know why the program works and all the various ways a job can be done. This strategy is useful in first learning economics, but it won't take you very far. Some procedure learners memorize every page, every footnote, every problem, and every example, and yet, they still do poorly in economics!

Successful economics students have a strategy of learning by probing. In learning how to run a software program, they click the mouse all over the place and observe what comes up. They find out how the program works and then apply what they've learned to doing new things. In economics, they are interested in learning how many ways different economic concepts can be applied and what happens when they are modified. By probing assumptions and doing different variations of problems, they come to understand why each result follows from the logic of the analysis.

I was blessed with a poor memory. As a result, the only way I could learn economics was to understand it! It takes a bit longer at first, but it works better in the long run.

When you understand something, you then can recall and use it later. So if you come to a point in this text where you find yourself saying, "Well, I'll just memorize this so that I can move on," please stop, back up, and start again.

In one of the economics classes I taught, a girl was being tutored by her boyfriend. Yet, she was failing the class. She told me her boyfriend said to just read the text as everything was obvious. You see, her boyfriend was a genius. I told her to get a new boyfriend, one with average intelligence who was also making As in the course. A genius can make all sorts of mistakes and still get by. But average students getting good grades have to employ an efficient strategy to make full use of all their skills.

She didn't find a new boyfriend, but she did find a new study group that had an excellent strategy to learn economics. First, they read the text. Next, they tested themselves in several ways. First, they redrew all the graphs in the text while saying to themselves why each line had the shape it did. Second, they redid all the examples in the text to make sure they understood them. Finally, they did the problems (which I supply answers to) to be sure of their understanding. By testing and retesting their learning, they made sure they had a firm grasp of economics. Perhaps you should do the same!

An Example of How to Probe in Economics

We will now take a common observation and apply an economic model to it. I don't know if the model is true—it hasn't been tested.

Let's begin with the common observation that there are lot of bosses who are *mean*. I don't know whether this is true or not, but assume it is. We will define a *mean boss* as one who acts in a way that workers dislike.

Next, we want to create a model to explain how in a competitive economy mean bosses exist. So let's design a simple model. Assume the following:

1. There are many firms in competition with each other in the same industry, all producing essentially the same good, so that consumers buy from the firm with the lowest price.
2. There is easy entry into this industry, such that entering firms have similar costs and thus can compete on price.
3. Firms differ in only one aspect. Some have mean bosses whom workers dislike and some have nice bosses whom workers like.
4. Workers can easily change jobs and work for any of the firms.

Now let's begin probing.

Assumption one assures that all firms must sell the good at the same price. Why? Suppose one firm charges a higher price. Its customers will go elsewhere. If any firm charges less, it will get all the customers. But this violates the assumption of many firms. So all firms must charge the same price.

Assumption two assures that the price will be bid down to cost (cost here refers to the cost per unit of output and includes normal profits for being in business). Once again, why? If price exceeds cost (including a normal profit), firms will enter the industry and bid the price down. Entry will stop when price equals cost. So price equals cost.

Note that because price equals cost and because all firms are charging the same price, assumptions one and two imply that all firms have the same cost.

Assumptions three and four assure that workers working for the mean bosses must be paid a higher wage. Why? Because otherwise they would all work for the nice bosses. Thus, to get workers, mean bosses have to pay more.

So where are we? All firms have the same cost per unit output, yet mean bosses have higher labor cost. This leads us to the conclusion that mean bosses must do something to offset this cost disadvantage.

How can mean bosses make up for having higher labor costs? There are two ways. One way is that the bosses work for a lower salary—in effect, they pay for being mean! A second way is that some aspect of meanness makes them more productive, allowing them to offset the higher labor cost. Perhaps nice bosses are less efficient because they allow more slack on the shop floor or keep on workers who have lost their competitive edge.

Let us be clear as to what the model does and does not imply. It does not imply that simply being mean raises productivity. Rather, it implies that workers interpret practices that raise productivity as being mean. Other ways of being mean could lower productivity.

Let us also be clear about another point. The model could be totally false! This is an empirical issue for positive economics to examine.

SUMMARY

Economics is the study of how people make decisions in the face of scarcity and, in turn, how people coordinate their decisions through prices. It seeks to explain the mystery of how people who never directly communicate with each other, who may be living on the opposite sides of the world, and who may not even like each other if they met, still are able to produce and trade the goods that each wants. It seeks to examine how billions and billions of decisions are independently made and yet are brought together in the marketplace in a seamless and coordinated fashion.

Two of the key economic issues are how prices get determined in the marketplace and how economics prosper. These two issues are not separate. Those economies that seek trade are those that have grown.

To explain these billions and billions of decisions, economists seek the simplest explanations consistent with what we observe. Simple examples and simple models allow us to understand the complex. In learning about these models, you will need to learn how to use visualization and reasoning. The goal is not to memorize the results, but to learn them.

Your study strategy should be to read the text and to test your understanding continually. Work the problems spread throughout the text, redraw and try to understand all the graphs in this text, and finally, apply what you learn to the world around you.

CRIB NOTES

This section is a quick summary of the key points in the chapter.

Economics: Study of how people make choices in the face of scarcity.

Microeconomics: Study of individual persons, goods, businesses.

Macroeconomics: Study of aggregates (such as aggregate national income).

Normative statement: Makes moral judgment of good or bad.

Positive statement: Makes assertion of fact that can be tested. A statement need not be factually true to be a positive statement.

Review Questions

1. Is economics about finance and public policy?

2. Why can't government planners efficiently control the economy?

3. How are prices like language?

4. Why are prices an effective form of communication?

5. How can a negative statement such as "Poverty does not cause crime" be a positive statement?

6. Would it be a normative statement to say "It is bad that this section is about to end"?

7. Suppose you believe that all persons should be vegetarians and that you are ruler of the world. You could punish meat eaters, but you don't have enough police or jail cells to enforce your wishes. How might the price system be used to encourage people to not eat meat?

8. Which of the following statements are normative statements and which are positive statements?
   (A) Poverty should be widespread.
   (B) Poverty can't be abolished.
   (C) Governments can create prosperity by high taxes and waste.
   (D) Eating lots of cake will make you healthy.

9. Suppose the government banned the use of money and prices. Then people would have to trade goods for goods, finding people who have what they want and who want what they have. In such a world, which in each of the following pairs would be the better career?
   a. wheat farmer or specialist in genetic engineering of wheat plants
   b. doctor who is general practitioner or specialist in brain surgery
   c. electrician or electrical engineer

Answers

1. No. Economics studies how people make choices in the face of scarcity. Finance and public policy are some of the areas analyzed by economics, but they are not economics. Microeconomics studies the choices of individual persons and firms. Macroeconomics studies the choices and actions of aggregates of persons and firms.

2. Prices do the same job far more efficiently. Prices not only communicate information about changes in the scarcity of goods, but they also give people the incentive to respond to these changes in an efficient manner. In any case, why, given the history of mankind, would anyone believe that government planners want to be efficient, even if they could?

3. Prices communicate information about the demands of consumers and the availability of goods. Even if people don't know the many reasons for any given price change, they still get the message.

4. People have an incentive to respond to prices. Those who respond properly make money.

5. *Positive* here refers to whether the statement can be tested to see if and when it is true or false.

6. It is a normative statement if you feel it is morally wrong to end this section. It would be a positive statement if you said, "When this section ends, I will feel badly if I don't read more." This statement may be true or false—it is testable.

7. To use the price system, you could tax meat or, alternatively, subsidize vegetables. This would not make everyone a vegetarian, but it would move them in that direction. Sometimes, rulers of the world have to be satisfied with such results.

8. Normative: (A). Positive: (B), (C), (D). Note that positive statements can be true or false, while normative statements can be right or wrong.

9. Without a price system, the best choice is the career that produces something of value to most people. These actually are the least specialized careers: the first choice in each category. Prices enable people to specialize. Note how much lower our standard of living would be without the specialization allowed for by the price system.

Chapter Two

Scarcity and Choice

When Americans were asked how much annual income it would take to make them happy, most answered with a figure that was twice their current income. Those earning $20,000 a year said $40,000. Those making $40,000 said $80,000. And those making $80,000? $160,000! Few were happy with what they had.

Perhaps it's human nature to always want more. Interestingly, it is often the rich who want more the most! As the old joke goes, who is happier, the man with 12 children or the man with $12 million? The man with 12 children because the man with $12 million wants more.

Economics is based upon the proposition that our wants exceed the means to achieve them. This is called scarcity. A good is scarce when there isn't enough of it to satisfy all the wants we have for it. Scarcity faces rich and poor alike. In the preceding joke, the rich man faced more scarcity than the man with 12 children. Also, goods in small supply need not be scarce (such as records of me rap singing), and some goods in large supply can be scarce (such as fresh air in Los Angeles). The key is to note that it is the *excess* of people's wants for a good relative to its supply that creates scarcity.

SCARCITY

Scarcity means we can't satisfy all our wants. It forces us to choose which wants we satisfy and which we don't. So how do we choose which wants to satisfy?

Let us start with a simple example. In the 1930s, George Herriman created an anarchistic cartoon character named Krazy Kat. Krazy Kat's main passion in life was throwing bricks at people and things. The world was his arcade. Unfortunately for Krazy Kat, he didn't have enough bricks to throw at all the things he wanted to hit. How might he rationally go about choosing which objects he's going to heave a brick at? Consider the following economic method. He begins by putting the highest number on the object he most wants to hurl a brick at, a lower number on the next object he wants to hit, a still lower number on the object after that, and so forth, until all worthy objects are labeled from high to low. Now even though Krazy Kat may be crazy, he still wants most pleasure in the form of the highest score. How should he proceed? The economic strategy is that the first brick should be hurled at the object with the highest number, the second brick at the object with the second highest number, the third at the next highest number left, and so forth until all bricks are hurled. This will give him the highest score. If he chooses instead to throw a brick at any object left out by this strategy, he will get a lower score. (Make sure you understand this last point. If need be, write the numbers 1 through 10, cross out any three numbers, and your score equals the sum of the numbers you cross out. You should start with the highest number and go down . . . 10, 9, 8. Now try an alternative strategy. Which works best and why?)

Of course, as sophisticated and intelligent consumers, you and I don't face Krazy Kat's problem. Instead of throwing bricks at people and things, we just throw dollar bills. That is, we spend our dollars on the goods we put the most value (the highest score) on. The principle is the same: Our scarce resources should be allocated to their most valued uses.

MARGINAL ANALYSIS

Each day, Krazy Kat gets his supply of bricks and goes through the preceding analysis. But then he figures out a simpler strategy. First, he finds out the value of the target of the last brick he would throw using the preceding strategy. This is the least valued target from the set of targets he throws bricks at. It also has a higher value than any of the targets from the set of targets he didn't throw bricks at. We'll call this brick the *marginal* brick and the value of its target the *marginal value.*

This saves Krazy Kat a great deal of time. Instead of having to label each and every target, he merely compares any given target's value with the marginal value. If its value is the same or higher, he throws a brick at it. If it's lower, he doesn't waste his brick on it.

This is a form of marginal analysis. *Marginal analysis* focuses on the marginal unit only, comparing its value with alternatives and adjusting accordingly. It saves a great deal of time because the consumer does not have to put a value on all units, only those on the margin.

The Krazy Kat example can be made analogous to what consumers do with their money. Imagine for a moment that all objects (car, food, home, etc.) can be broken into units that cost one dollar each. Consumers each day are given a stack of dollar bills to spend on these units. They could spend the first dollar on the most valued object, the next dollar on the next highest value object, and so forth, until the last dollar is spent. They could then notice the marginal value of the last dollar spent. In subsequent days, they just compare an object's value with the marginal value. If it is greater or equal, they buy it. In this way, they can be assured that their dollars are reaping the highest total value.

The Use of Marginal Analysis at Coke

Most large corporations today use some form of marginal analysis to decide where to invest their capital. In the 1980s, Coca-Cola's CEO Roberto Goizueta found that his company had invested in a wide range of products besides soft drinks, including coffee, tea, and aquaculture. These investments had been made more or less randomly without any attempt to maximize the value of his company's investments. He found that his company could earn 16% by investing its money outside the company. Thus, 16% was the marginal return all internal investments should make; otherwise, the company would do better to invest the money outside the firm. Goizueta thus required that all internal investments make at least 16%. It turned out that a number of Coca-Cola's subsidiary businesses were earning far less than 16%—some only earned half this. So he sold off these divisions and invested the money elsewhere. In addition, all new investment projects must now show they earn at least 16% in order to get funded. In this way, he substantially increased the value of Coca-Cola's stock and decreased the chance that it would be the object of a takeover bid.

Stop right now and make sure you understand how this is the same strategy Krazy Kat used to maximize his brick score and the same strategy consumers use to maximize the total value of their dollar spending.

COST AND OPPORTUNITY COST

Accountants and economists are often pictured as dismal, grim, and joyless persons. Why do they have this grim reputation when in fact they are all party animals? I believe the main reason is that one of their major roles is to calculate costs. Few people like to be reminded that everything has costs. Consumers do not treasure the bills reminding them of the cost of their spending. Politicians do not cherish the advice of economists reminding them of the excessive cost of their projects.

Economics is so powerful because of its focus on cost. The cost of any resource (including money, time, energy, and goods) is what economists call its opportunity cost: the highest value of what the same resources could have produced elsewhere.

Thought Questions

Suppose there are three things you could do on some Sunday afternoon. You can only do *one* of these three things: (1) Do your homework, which you value at $50 (perhaps because education increases your future income). (2) Visit with your friends, which you value at $40. (3) Sleep, which you value at $30.

Now what is the opportunity cost of homework?
The answer is $40 because visiting your friends is the highest valued of alternative uses of your time.

Next, what is the opportunity cost of visiting your friends?
Be careful! It is $50, because if you visit your friends, you are giving up doing your homework (which is the highest valued use of the alternative uses of your time).

What is the opportunity cost of sleeping?
$50. If you sleep, once again the most valued activity you are giving up is doing your homework, which is worth $50.

How does this help you make your choice?
When you compare the value of any of these activities with their cost, only homework shows a profit.

Now let us consider a more complex example. Suppose that the government builds a canal costing $16 billion. According to economists, the $16 billion is a cost: It could have been used by the taxpayers to buy goods and services worth at least $16 billion. Yet politicians often declare the cost of their projects to be a benefit. Look, they will say, at the jobs created and the benefits brought into the communities where the money is spent! Ah, say the economists, look also at the jobs and the benefits destroyed where the money otherwise would have been spent! Further, economists would point out it would be better if the project created fewer jobs and used less resources! Why? Because then the unused workers and resources could be used elsewhere to increase national output even more. It would be the best of all worlds if all the government's output could be produced by one person and one dollar. We would have trillions of dollars left over to do other things. And although I don't know about you, I can think of a few things I could spend my share of those trillions of dollars on!

Henry Hazlitt in his excellent book *Economics in One Lesson,* called this tendency to call a cost a benefit the "broken window fallacy." He shows why this fallacy occurs. Imagine you observe a brick breaking a shop window. What do you see? You might see workers bringing materials in and fixing the window. Not only do window repair persons get jobs, but so do all the other persons involved in making and selling windows. Looking at what you see, and *only* at what you see, you might conclude that the way to create jobs is to break windows! But economics allows us to see the unseen cost of the activity—the opportunity cost of these resources. Had the window not been broken, the persons and resources could have been used to produce alternative goods that would add to our welfare.

Thought Questions

Show why a pill costing ten cents that cured all diseases would increase national output, even if it threw all doctors out of work.

Our nation would benefit from better health at less cost. In addition, it would benefit from the goods the doctors would produce in their new careers.

A hurricane wrecks havoc on a town. A newsperson states, "The storm has made our community better off because of all the jobs it has created in construction and clean up." Is the newsperson correct?

No. The unseen cost of the hurricane is that these workers could have been employed adding to the town's wealth rather than repairing it.

Let us note that in some macroeconomics models, government costs can become a benefit by stimulating the economy out of a recession. Once out of the recession, this benefit no longer exists. Nevertheless, the principle of opportunity cost still applies. The government has a wide variety of projects it can spend the money on. It is best to stimulate the economy with projects having the highest value. Thus, the use of opportunity cost to evaluate projects is still correct.

USE OF OPPORTUNITY COST IN BUSINESS

In the early 1900s, the Ford Motor Company estimated its costs by the following method: It took its bills, weighed them, and then multiplied the results by the average amount owed per pound of bills! The result was the near bankruptcy of Ford.

Fortunately, the calculation of cost has seen some advancements since Ford. Yet, some firms tend to ignore many hidden opportunity costs. For example, if they borrow money, they correctly record the interest they pay as a cost. Yet, if they use their own funds, they fail to record the interest they could have earned on that money as a cost. As a result, they may think they are making a profit on a project yielding 4%. But if the same money could have earned 10% elsewhere, they are losing 6% over what they could have earned.

Some of the highest costs businesses have is for the assets they already own outright such as land, buildings, equipment, and good will. Yet, many businesses ignore the potential value of renting these assets to others (or of selling them) as a cost of doing business. But this is folly. By using the opportunity cost of all their assets, these companies can then allocate their resources to their most profitable use. To not do so is a waste of resources.

In the past, lazy managers at many corporations wasted their company's capital by investing in low-yield projects when better yields existed elsewhere. This was a waste of the stockholders' money. In many cases, the result was a corporate takeover and the selling off of the company's unprofitable subsidiaries. As a result, the stock of these companies went up in value, often by billions of dollars. These billions of dollars reflect the capital that had been wasted by the previous managers and was now being put to better use.

TRADE-OFFS AND COSTS

People are always coming up with solutions to our nation's problems. The next time someone does this, spoil their afternoon by asking them, "What are the trade-offs?" This question is a spoiler of many a great scheme. That's because of scarcity! Due to scarcity, we can't do everything we want, nor can we solve all of our problems. To put it another way, we face trade-offs. We can do some things, but not others. Opportunity cost is a measure of what could have been done otherwise. It guides us in making the right trade-offs. I wish scarcity didn't exist. I wish we could spend more to cure all disease, but in our world of limited resources, spending more to cure cancer means spending less to cure heart disease. And while I'm at it, I wish every reader of this book would get a fleet of luxury cars, a beach home on each coast, a villa in France, and live forever. It sure would solve a lot of our nation's problems!

ECONOMIC DECISION MAKING: THE BENEFITS AND COSTS OF CHANGE

Every action we take creates changes. Buying a car, for example, changes the way you get around and changes the money you have left to spend on other things. Some changes are good and some are bad. We define *good* and *bad* from the perspective of the decision maker who took the action. The changes they want we'll call good changes. The changes they don't like we'll call bad changes. The value of the good changes are benefits of the action. The dollar value of benefit is the most one would be willing to pay to get the good changes. The value of bad changes are costs of the action: It is the most one would be willing to pay to get rid of the bad changes. Note that we said "willing to pay," and not "actually pay." In many cases, people get a good deal: They pay less for something than its value to them!

If the person is rational, he should take an action when its benefits exceed or equal its cost. Why the word *equal*? Because economists define cost to the minimum amount you have to be paid to do something. So if benefits just equal cost, by definition, you'll do it.

Points to Note

Point 1

We focus only on the changes that result from the action. If something doesn't change, we ignore it. That is, if something is the same whether or not we do something, then it shouldn't affect our decision. It's the same no matter what we do. Focusing on changes tells us what is relevant.

Alternatively stated, we should ignore sunk costs. *Sunk costs* are costs that are the same whether we take an action or not. Sunk costs do not change because we have already paid them or because we are committed to paying them no matter what (such as a mortgage).

Thought Questions

Last year, you paid a million dollars for a pair of running shoes (you were naive). The soles wear out and will cost $25 to fix. If not fixed, they are worthless. Alternatively, you can buy a new pair of running shoes exactly like your old ones for $10. Should you fix the old pair or buy the new one?

Buy the new one. It's cheaper ($10 versus $25). What about the million dollars? Tough luck! You've got to make the best of your current situation. To be sure you grasp this point, assume instead you got the first pair of running shoes as a gift. The answer is the same: Buy instead of fix.

Point 2

Good and bad are defined by whether we are willing to pay to get more of it (that is a good) or willing to pay to get rid of it (that is a bad). Hamburgers are a good to most persons but a bad to cows.

Point 3

The value of a commodity is the most we would pay to get it. Why *most?* Because most tells us how much you are willing to pay to get something. You may in fact pay less or get it for free. For example, if forced, you would probably pay up to $100 a day to have access to water. That's the benefit of water to you. Fortunately, water costs less than this. As another example, consider the person with the "I'd Rather Be Sailing" bumper sticker. Why aren't they out sailing if that's what they would really rather be doing? Evidently, they are unwilling to pay the price of sailing all the time (including lost job and no home life). The fact that they are not sailing says that at this moment in time it's not worth the cost. Driving is what they would truly rather be doing. I have an "I'd Rather Be Driving" bumper sticker. It states the simple economic truth and has the added advantage of spooking the drivers behind me.

APPLICATIONS OF ECONOMIC ANALYSIS

Application 1

Congratulations, you now have a vacation home on the beach. But, sorry, you can't be there during the summer because someone threw a brick at you, which landed you in the hospital. So you decide to rent the home out on a monthly basis. Whether you rent the house out or not, you have a monthly cost of $650, including mortgage payments and basic maintenance. If you do rent the house out, you have $200 a month in added wear and tear and utility costs. The questions is, What is the minimum rent you would accept instead of leaving the place empty?

Let us apply our tools. First, the action is to rent the home. Next, what is the cost of renting? This equals the bad changes due to renting compared to not renting. In this case, it's $200. So $200 is the lowest rent that will cover the cost of renting. Any less and we would be better off not renting. Any more, and we would be better off renting. At a rent of $200, we break even.

We ignore the $650 because it is a sunk cost—a cost already incurred and which must be paid no matter what we do.

The basic economic rule is to ignore sunk costs. To illustrate this point, suppose we paid attention to sunk costs. Let us show that they make no difference. Suppose the best market rate for our home is $500 a month. At this rate, when we rent, we lose $350 a month ($500 in revenue and $850 in total cost). If we don't rent, we lose $650 a month (no revenue and $650 in cost). We are better off by $300 by renting over not renting. Ignoring sunk costs gives us the same result: The benefit is $500 and the (change in) cost is $200, so the gain is $300 by renting.

Now let's up the ante. Instead of $650, let the sunk costs be $2,650 per month. Adding in sunk costs, we lose $2,350 by renting and $2,650 by not renting: We still are better off by the same $300 derived by ignoring sunk cost. True, we are worse off when sunk costs are higher. But what matters, given our situation, is what is our best course of action. The best course of action is the same, no matter what the sunk costs are! So, to save time and effort, it is best to ignore sunk costs. Paying attention to sunk costs should not change the answer of what to do!

Application 2

You're the CEO of Acme, Inc. The VP of marketing and the VP of production are competing to get $1 million in added funding. The VP of marketing argues that without marketing, the firm could not sell what it produces, especially in the current competitive environment. "Without marketing, we would be running huge losses." The VP of production says that the million dollars should go to buy new machinery that will save the firm $1,500,000 in energy costs. Which one should you give the million dollars to?

Only the VP of production gave a valid argument. She focused upon the changes the million dollars would bring and showed that the benefits of these changes more than cover its cost. The VP of marketing was talking about what his department was already doing, not what the million dollars would add. Most likely, in a competitive environment, more marketing would do little good. So, without better information from marketing, production should get the money.

Application 3

Three years ago you bought what was then a state-of-the-art computer for $3,000. Today, you are deciding whether to buy a new computer that costs $2,500. If you buy it, you can sell the old computer for $600 to your gullible cousin. The old computer's future service is worth $2,000 to you. The new computer's future service is worth $3,000 to you. Should you buy the new computer?

Calculate the changes in benefits (the good stuff) that would result from selling the old computer and buying the new one. There's the $600 from selling the old computer. Add to that the change in benefits from replacing the old with the new computer. This is the increase in the value of service: $1,000 (equal to $3,000 of future service from the new machine minus the $2,000 of future service from the old machine). So the benefits of the new machine are $1,600. Next, calculate its cost. It is $2,500. So the benefits are less than the cost. You should keep the old machine for now.

Notice that had you not owned the old machine, you would have bought the new machine. This leads to a very important point when marketing a good. There are usually two markets for most goods: new buyers and current owners. The second group is usually much more price sensitive as they can put off the purchase. The difference between these two groups also explains why software companies are willing to sell upgrades for a far lower price than what new buyers must pay, even though the two products are the same.

MARGINAL ANALYSIS

The core of microeconomics is marginal analysis. Marginal analysis breaks an action into small steps and evaluates the benefits and costs of each step. As long as the benefits of each step outweigh its cost, the step is taken. But once the step's cost exceeds its benefit, the step is not taken.

The following is the basic procedure of marginal analysis:

Step 1   Break an Action into Small Units

In most situations, the choice of doing more or less is available. What is being done is what I will call the *action variable*. This variable is broken into small units. To keep things simple, we'll let Q be the quantity of the action variable we are looking at. For example, Q could be the quantity of output the firm produces or the quantity of labor it hires.

The goal is to maximize the net benefit from taking the action:

Net benefit = Total benefits − Total cost

For example, the net benefit of being in business is its profits, such that

Profits = Total sales − Total cost

Step 2   Calculate the Benefits from Adding a Unit of Q

Calculate the value of the good changes. This is the marginal benefit of the step.

Marginal benefit = Change in total benefits (due to another unit of Q)

Step 3   Calculate the Cost of Adding a Unit of Q

Marginal cost = Change in total cost (due to another unit of Q)

Step 4   Take Step if its Marginal Benefits Exceed or Equal its Marginal Costs

That is, take step if

Marginal benefit ≥ Marginal cost

If this is the case, you are adding more to total benefits than to total cost, so the net benefits are going up by

Change in net benefit = Marginal benefit − Marginal cost

APPLICATIONS OF MARGINAL ANALYSIS

Application 1

Let us return to the Krazy Kat example. Suppose Krazy Kat can buy bricks for $5 a piece. Let the value of the most valued target be $10, the next most valued target be worth $8, the next, $6, the fourth, $4, and so forth. How many bricks should he buy?

Applying marginal analysis, the first brick has a marginal benefit of $10 and a marginal cost of $5. So Krazy Kat throws this brick. Notice how the first brick creates a net benefit of $5 ($10 − $5). The second brick has a marginal benefit of $8 and a marginal cost of $5, so it is thrown. This difference between marginal benefit and cost of $3 gets added to net benefits, bringing net benefits up to $8. The third brick's marginal benefit of $6 exceeds its cost of $5, thereby raising net benefits by $1. Net benefits now equal $9. If the fourth brick were thrown, its marginal benefit of $4 would be less than its cost, thereby reducing net benefits by $1. If it were thrown, Krazy Kat's net benefit would only be $8, which is one dollar worse than he did throwing three bricks. So three bricks is the optimum number of bricks to throw.

Application 2

Acme, Inc. sells its output at the market price of $8 a unit. Each plant has the costs shown in Table 2.1.

TABLE 2.1

Units of Output	Total Cost ($)
0	8
1	10
2	14
3	20
4	28
5	38

How much output should each plant produce? The marginal benefit of each unit of output is $8, the revenue it brings in. The marginal cost of the first unit of output is $2 (i.e., the increase in total cost is $10 − $8), the second unit's marginal cost is $4, the third unit's is $6, the fourth unit's is $8, and the fifth unit's is $10. Using marginal analysis, the first unit's benefit exceeds its cost, so it is produced. The second unit's benefit of $8 exceeds its cost of $4, so it is produced. The third and fourth units also cover their cost. (Producing the fourth unit is a toss-up, which we decide in favor of producing it.) But the firm would be worse off producing the fifth unit because its marginal cost of $10 exceeds its marginal benefit of $8.

Table 2.2 shows the total analysis. Notice how the change in profit equals the marginal benefit minus the marginal cost.

TABLE 2.2

Units of Output	Total Benefit ($)	Total Cost ($)	Marginal Benefit ($)	Marginal Cost ($)	Profit ($)
0	0	8	—	—	–8
1	8	10	8	2	–2
2	16	14	8	4	2
3	24	20	8	6	4
4	32	28	8	8	4
5	40	38	8	10	2

Application 3

What is the optimal level for a firm to spend on safety? The marginal cost of a dollar spent on safety is one dollar. But what are its marginal benefits? There may be several. First, workers may be willing to work for lower wages. If the company must pay for accident costs to workers, then the reduction in the expected level of these costs is also a benefit. Finally, there will be reduced down time as a result of a safer workplace. So the firm should continue to spend money on safety until, on the margin, the marginal benefit equals a dollar. Note that the optimal level of safety—the level that maximizes profits—is likely to be lower than the maximum attainable level of safety. An accident-free workplace is probably too costly to be worth achieving.

CRIB NOTES

Scarcity: Wants > means.
Rational action: Allocate resources to most valued uses.
Opportunity cost: The highest valued foregone use of a resource.
Focus on change: If action leaves X unchanged, ignore X in analysis.
Economic analysis: An action causes change. Compare value of all good changes with value of all bad changes. If value of good changes > value of bad changes, take action.
Net benefits: Total benefit – total cost.
Marginal analysis: Break action into small marginal steps.
  1. Measure increase in total benefits: Marginal benefit = Δ Total benefit
  2. Measure increase in total cost: Marginal cost = Δ Total cost
  3. Increase in net benefits: $MB - MC$
  4. Take step if $MB \geq MC$. Continue until $MB = MC$.

Review Questions

1. Don't only poor people face scarcity?

2. How do you tell if a good is scarce?

3. If a good is free, is it not scarce?

4. What is the essence of rational decision making?

5. How does marginal analysis help do this?

6. How is marginal value related to opportunity cost?

7. How can you make your decision making easier?

8. Why do we ignore sunk costs?

9. What is marginal analysis?

10. What are the most common economic errors people make in decision making?

11. "Water is scarce in these here parts," says Tom dryly. Which of the following observations would guarantee that water is a scarce good and not a free good?
    (A) It is costly to produce more water, as it must be drilled for in these here parts.
    (B) People have a need for at least some amount of water.
    (C) If water were free (sold at a zero price), demand would exceed supply.

12. Which of the following statements is consistent with economic logic?
    (A) We must resolve to win this war so that those who have already died will not have died in vain.
    (B) Our company is wasting away its capital by investing it at 8% when it could make 16% elsewhere.
    (C) Our city should build an art museum because without art, society would be worse off. (Assume "without art, society is worse off" is true.)

13. It has cost $16 billion for the government of Cimonoce to build a canal. If opened, it will generate $400,000 a year in benefits but at an annual cost of $500,000. Should it be opened? Wouldn't keeping it closed cause the $16 billion to be wasted?

14. Acme Grocery Store can sell its shelf space to outside vendors (like Campbell's Soup and Coke) for $40 per square foot per month. It can also stock some of the shelves with its own brand. The more shelf space it allocates to its own brand, the more it sells, but the sales per square foot go down. How should it allocate its shelf space between its own brand and those of outside vendors?

15. It costs money to make cars safer. Should you want a car that is totally safe? Should the government mandate that cars be made totally safe when anything less will result in some persons dying?

16. A CEO of a famous corporation proclaimed that his company was dedicated to achieving "zero defects" in their product lines. Is this in the customers' interest, assuming the costs of achieving zero defects is passed on to its customers?

17. You are on a desert island which, fortunately, has a natural spring that yields five gallons of water a day. You value the first gallon of water at $8, the second gallon at $6, the third at $4, the fourth at $2, and the fifth not at all.
    a. Is water scarce?
    b. If the spring only yields three gallons a day, how should you allocate it?

18. Why is water more valued in a desert than it is at a lake? After all, water is water!

19. Traditional accounting methods commit two sins: ignoring opportunity cost and counting sunk cost. For example, a manager proposed adding on a new shift of workers to meet increased demand. In costing these new workers, the accounting department adds in an overhead cost per worker, overhead costs reflecting the cost of the plant and managing it. When is this proper?

20. TV news shows are great for showing us the visible and obvious. What are the unseen costs or benefits ignored by the following news shows?
Show A. "Dangerous Prescription Drugs: Interviews with Victims"
Show B. "The Unsafe Workplace: The Dying Fields of Workers"
Show C. "How Pollution Is Poisoning the Air We Breathe"

Answers

1. Scarcity is the excess of wants over the means to provide for them. Scarcity forces us to make choices. Both rich and poor have wants exceeding their means and have to make choices.
2. Simple. If at a zero price, people want more of the good than exists, it must be a scarce good. Why? Because its use has to then be allocated because some uses must go unsatisfied. If at a zero price, there is more of the good than people want, it is not scarce. A good that is not scarce is sometimes called a free good.
3. No. *Free good* is a textbook term that means not scarce. A good given away for free can be scarce (for example, free tickets to a popular rock concert). Also, a good that costs a lot to make can still be a free good. For example, for a few billion dollars, I could develop and market a hair gel that renders people smelly, hairless, and impotent. My guess is that its supply would far exceed any demand for it even if I gave it away.
4. To maximize net benefits, allocate resources (this includes capital, time, and money) to their highest valued use.
5. If we know the value of the use the marginal unit of the resource is best allocated to, then we simply allocate a unit of the resource to any and all uses that have a value exceeding or equaling the marginal value.
6. When we rationally allocate the units of resource to their most valued use, the least valued use that gets satisfied is the marginal value. The highest value of the unsatisfied uses is the opportunity cost.
7. Focus only on the things that change as a result of your action. Put them into two columns: the changes you want and the changes you don't want. The value of the first column is the action's benefit; the value of the second column is the action's cost. The difference is the net benefit of the action: If it is positive, take the action.
8. A sunk cost is a cost that is the same whether you take an action or not. So it doesn't affect the value of the changes caused by an action; consequently, it doesn't affect which action is best. While it is true that higher sunk costs make you worse off, it is also true that they shouldn't change the best thing to do.
9. Marginal analysis just breaks a big decision into small steps and compares the benefits and costs of each step (these being called marginal benefit and marginal cost). Keep on doing something until marginal benefit equals marginal cost. Then stop!
10. The most common error is to pay attention to sunk costs. The second is to pay attention to total value instead of marginal value. For example, a politician might argue that because our nation's road system is so valuable, we should continue to build new roads. The correct criterion is whether the marginal benefits of the new roads—not the total value of all roads—are greater than their cost. A third com-

mon error is to ignore unseen opportunity costs. For example, many firms do not put their capital, land, and equipment to its best use because it has already been paid for and thus has no visible cost. But this does change the benefits of allocating these resources to their best use.

11. (C) is correct. (A) is wrong if current water supplies are more than ample. (B) is also wrong if water is plentiful.

12. Statement (B) is consistent with the economic logic of allocating resources to their most valued use. Statement (A) is wrong because it pays attention to sunk costs ("those who have died"). (C) is wrong because it confused total value of all art with the marginal benefit of another art museum.

13. It should not be opened as it can't cover its current cost. The $16 billion is a sunk cost: it has already been wasted, whether the canal opens or not.

14. It should allocate space to its own brand only as long as the last added square foot yields $40 or more. If the marginal square foot allocated to its own brand adds less, it's better utilized by renting it to outside vendors.

15. You should only want added safety if the benefit of the added safety is worth its cost to you; otherwise, you are worse off. Most people are not willing to pay for complete safety because it costs too much. After reaching some level of safety, they'd rather have the money. For example, you could be safer by buying a tank, but most people find the added safety not worth the cost. If the government forced them to do so, they would be worse off. They would rather take the risk.

16. The customers' interest is only being served if the benefits of reduced defects are higher than the costs of reducing defects. The best level of defects, from the customers' point of view, is where the marginal benefit of reducing defects equals the marginal cost of reducing defects. Going any further (where the marginal cost exceeds the marginal benefit) makes them worse off.

17. a. No. Its supply (five gallons) exceeds the wants for it if the price were zero (four gallons). b. Now the water is scarce and is best allocated to the three most valued uses (worth $8, $6, and $4).

18. Water is more scarce in a desert than it is at a lake. Thus, its marginal value is higher in a desert.

19. The overhead expense should be added only if it truly reflects the change in overhead cost due to adding the shift of workers: otherwise, it should be ignored.

20. Show A: Unseen are the benefits of the drugs. Even though most drugs are dangerous to some people, they help others. The issue is whether their potential benefit outweighs their cost. Show B: Unseen is the cost of making the workplace safer. The issue is whether workers prefer higher wages or higher safety. Show C: Unseen are the costs of reducing pollution. The issue is whether the benefits of reducing pollution are worth the cost.

Chapter Three

The Economic Way of Thinking

A couple was very happy when they had a little boy whom the doctors pronounced as being very bright. But their happiness turned to worry when the child never spoke. They took him to doctors and speech therapists, but none could help. One day, when he was five, the boy looked up from his breakfast and said, "This toast is burnt and the eggs are simply not up to the usual standards." The parents were incredulous. They asked, "You can speak beautifully! Why, oh, why haven't you spoken before?" The boy responded, "There's been no need to speak. Up to now, everything has been fine."

This story illustrates the essence of economic models. Everything is fine. Then something occurs that gives people an incentive to change. They change. And then everything is fine again.

Let us begin small with squirrels.

SQUIRRELS IN THE BACKYARD

My neighbor Phil had a bird feeder that was periodically ransacked by squirrels. He went to the hardware store where he bought birdseed, and they advised him to buy extra birdseed and put it out for the squirrels. In this way, they reasoned, the squirrels would leave the bird feeder alone. So Phil tried this, and it worked for a while. But within a few months, he found his bird feeder being raided twice as often as before. He was befuddled and tried even more birdseed. Once again, this worked for awhile, but then his bird feeder was practically dismantled by squirrel work crews.

What happened? Why didn't the extra birdseed work?

To answer this, let me propose a very simple model, one that has proved useful in describing the migration patterns of other animals. The model goes like this:

Assumption: Squirrels are constantly looking for more food.
    Result 1: Barring any obstacles (such as a cat in the yard), squirrels will move to areas offering more food per squirrel than other areas.
    Result 2: This movement will continue until all areas offer the same amount of food per squirrel.

Note how the results follow from the assumption. If result 1 were not true, we would have to conclude that squirrels are not looking for more food. But how would we know if result 1 were correct? The main way would be to observe the migration and distribution of squirrels across an area. If one area suddenly offers more food, we would expect to see squirrels moving there. Result 2 would have to emerge.

So what about Phil? The model says that by putting out extra birdseed, he was attracting more squirrels to his yard. All he was doing was increasing the chance his bird feeder was going to be raided.

Let's put a little more precision in our predictions. Suppose squirrels within a few miles of Phil's neighborhood currently get about two pounds of food a week. If Phil suddenly puts out four pounds of food, then we can predict that eventually Phil will see two new squirrels living in his yard. Eight pounds would mean four new squirrels.

But note something else. After all the squirrels have moved, each will be getting two pounds of food. Each squirrel seeking more has the result that no squirrel gets any more.

BUILDING CONTRACTORS AND NEW HOME PRICES

What determines the price of new homes? There are many factors, but let us focus on one: the cost of building the home. To focus on building costs, we'll subtract out the price of land from the new home price and focus on the price of the home net of land cost. Second, to keep the example simple, we'll assume the cost of building each home is $50,000. This is the cost to builders and includes enough to pay them for their time and trouble. So here's our model:

Assumption: There are many builders, each seeking to make the highest profit (the difference between the selling price and $50,000).

Result 1: Barring obstacles (such as zoning restrictions), builders will move to areas where the prices of homes exceed $50,000.

Result 2: This movement will continue until the price of all homes is $50,000.

What will happen if the price exceeds $50,000? Builders will build more homes, and the added supply will cause their price to fall. But builders will keep coming until the price falls back to $50,000. Now suppose Builder A reads about a new method that reduces building costs to $40,000. What will happen initially? The builder will earn a large profit of at least $10,000 a home. What will happen as other builders copy the profitable builder? More homes will be built, and this added supply will cause the price of homes to fall to $40,000. Who benefits from the new method of home construction? Initially, the builder benefits in the form of higher profits. Ultimately, the consumer benefits in the form of lower prices. Competition shifts the profits of doing things in a better way from businesses to consumers.

Is the model true? The model's main prediction, that building prices eventually match buildings costs, appears correct. Consider what would happen if home prices always exceeded costs: There would be no bankrupt builders. Because bankrupt builders are plentiful, the model is essentially correct. Where it is wrong, and this is easily remedied, is in assuming a home's cost stays the same as more homes are built. Instead, in a building boom, costs rise rapidly. As a result, home prices rise rapidly in building booms.

WELFARE AND MIGRATION

This type of model has recently been applied to welfare recipients. It asks, what happens when a state, say New York, offers higher welfare payments?

Let us begin with the simplest model and see how it works:

Assumption: People on welfare are constantly looking for higher welfare payments.
  Result 1: Barring any obstacles, people on welfare will move to the states offering higher welfare payments.
  Result 2: This movement will continue until welfare payments are the same.

To make result 2 work, there needs to be some mechanism that causes welfare benefits per person to go down as more welfare recipients move to a state. One such mechanism might be as follows. Suppose New York voters want to allocate 10% of their income to welfare payments. That's the limit of their generosity. So as more welfare recipients move to New York, each will get less. Movement into New York will continue until all states pay the same welfare benefits per person.

To keep the numbers small, suppose New York has $100,000 to allocate to welfare recipients. How much will each get if there are 10 of them? If there are 20?

If there are 10, each gets $10,000 ($100,000 divided by 10). With 20, each gets $5,000. How many will there eventually be if other states pay $4,000 in benefits per recipient? Twenty-five recipients reduce the benefits in New York to $4,000 each (let N be the number of recipients, then solve $\$100,000/N = \$4,000$).

What if New York raises the amount it pays out in total to $200,000? What will happen eventually to the welfare benefits each recipient gets? Nothing—it will still equal what other states pay ($4,000). Initially, it will be higher ($8,000 = $200,000/25), but eventually another 25 recipients will move in until the total is 50 ($200,000/50 = $4,000). Greater generosity has little effect on each recipient's benefits.

What would happen in this model if New York persisted in offering higher benefits than other states? All welfare recipients would live in New York.

How would you test to see if this model is true? Welfare benefits should eventually be the same across states and, in the meantime, should be coming closer together. Migration of welfare recipients should be toward states with higher benefits.

The last question raises a problem with this model: It's not true! Its prediction of equal benefits is certainly not true, nor have benefits been getting more equal.

So how can we modify the model to improve its predictions? What it needs is a reason for welfare recipients to stop moving into a state even when it pays more in benefits. Let us propose the following reason: Assume all welfare recipients do some work and what they care about is the sum of their welfare benefits and their work income. Assume also that as more welfare recipients move into an area, they compete for a limited number of jobs such that each gets a lower work income. Thus, a state can be offering higher benefits than others, but this mechanism will stop more recipients from moving into the area.

What does this model predict will happen in the long run? In the long run, recipients will move until welfare benefits plus work income will be the same across states.

How will work income compare to welfare benefits across states? States with better benefits will have worse work income. To put some numbers to this problem to illustrate how this model works, suppose that all states have a total of welfare plus work income of $10,000 per recipient. Thus, the recipients in a state with welfare benefits of $6,000 will have work income of $4,000. Those in states offering $3,000 will have work income of $7,000.

How will New York's increasing its benefits affect its welfare recipients in this model? The welfare rolls will increase until work income goes down so much that there is no longer any net advantage to move to New York. For example, an increase in benefits from $6,000 to $8,000 will cause work income to eventually fall from $4,000 to $2,000.

If some welfare recipients work more than others, how will recipients who initially worked more be affected by better benefits? Initially, they will be better off; higher benefits and the same work income. But eventually, they could be made worse off. In the preceding example, work income fell 50%. For the average recipient, work income fell from $4,000 to $2,000, just offsetting the $2,000 increase in benefits. But for someone earning more, say $6,000, he will lose $3,000 in work income and only gain $2,000 in benefits: he is worse off by $1,000. Those who work more could actually lose by New York's offering higher benefits: They have the most to lose from the added competition for jobs.

Once again, we ask the key question: Is the model true? Even though the model explains the direction of migration of welfare recipients, the actual level of migration is far smaller than would be consistent with the model. The degree of migration comes nowhere near to equalizing income across states. However, it does illustrate why welfare recipients complain about losing jobs to the new immigrants to this country.

THE NATURE OF ECONOMIC MODELS

How are these models similar?

1. People act to be better off. People seek the highest income. Businesses seek the most profit. More generally, people seek the highest level of satisfaction.
2. Incentives cause people to change and move in new directions. If some area offers more, people move. People move to areas offering better jobs and to careers offering more satisfaction; businesses move to markets offering better profits and to ways of building things that lower cost.
3. As more people seek the incentives, the incentives disappear. If incentives do not disappear, people will keep on changing and changing. An ever-increasing number of homes would be built so that each one of us would have not one, not two, but many, many homes. All welfare recipients would move to one state. To avoid these absurd results, and to make the models consistent with what we observe, each model needs someone or something that says, "Stop!" In the home-building case, the reason was that the price was bid down to cost. Similarly, in most economic models, the stop comes from falling prices or rising costs or both.

WHAT MAKES A GOOD MODEL

A good model has the following characteristics:

1. It focuses our attention on only a few factors, keeping things simple.
2. It has precise predictions.
3. Its predictions can be tested.
4. The outcomes it predicts can be validated.

The preceding models focused upon the effects of incentives and the competition they produce. Their predictions were very precise (for example, equal welfare benefits). Their predictions, being precise, can be tested. The first two models have performed well (the distribution of animals and the tendency for home costs to reflect costs); the third, not so well. But that is information also; it gives us insight into how important welfare benefits are in people's decisions to move.

So what makes a model bad? Here's a good bad one: It sounds good but is totally useless. The price of cheese will change with changes in consumer preferences. The model certainly focuses our attention on a factor that affects cheese demand: consumer preferences. But it's a very bad model because it is impossible to make predictions with it! First, how would we know if tastes change? If you say, "by the changing price of cheese," then it's too late! I want to know how the price will change ahead of time! The model gives us no way to predict how preferences will change. It's a really bad model. Sounds good! Acts bad!

Here's a good test to see if a model is useless. If the model can explain how anything can happen, then it is useless for predicting what will happen. For example, if events A, B, or C could all happen and a model can explain why each could occur, it is useless for telling you which will occur. It is not falsifiable. The bad example is Marxism. With its many vague and imprecise explanations of everything, it is a pretty but useless model capable of predicting anything.

SOME KEY RESULTS FROM ECONOMIC MODELS

For their models, economists have gathered several key insights. Let's look at the main ones.

Key Insight 1: People Change to Be Better Off

One of the hardest points to get across in economics is that people do things to be better off. For example, in any exchange, both the buyer and the seller are better off. Both benefit from the trade; otherwise, they would not have made it. And in particular, one does not gain at the other's expense.

Thought Questions

Susan buys a Chevrolet from Mean Charley, the only dealer in her area, who has a monopoly on car sales. Is she worse off?

No! She would not have bought the Chevrolet if it wasn't worth more than what she could have otherwise bought with the money. Would she have been even better off if there had been more competition? The answer is yes, but this doesn't change the fact that she bought the car to be better off.

Do slumlords exploit the poor by supplying lousy housing?

No. If the poor could find a better deal, they'd go for it. The fact that they rent from the slumlord means the slumlord is offering them the best deal possible.

Will getting rid of slumlords help the poor?

Getting rid of slumlords will leave the poor with the worse alternatives they passed up to live in the slumlord's housing. Only by providing them with alternative better housing will they be better off.

Key Insight 2: The Key Issue Is How Much

In all models, there has to be a reason people do something up to a point and then stop. In economic models, people stop when there is no longer any incentive to do more.

Marginal analysis says the same thing in another way. It reminds us that decisions should be made in terms of how much, not all or nothing. Too much is when the marginal cost exceeds marginal benefit. Too little is when the marginal benefit exceeds marginal cost. Just right occurs when marginal benefit equals marginal cost.

It is one of the major human foibles to frame arguments in terms of all or nothing. Consider these examples. You are either for safe roads or for killing motorists. You are either for economic growth or for massive poverty. Yet, most human activities can be framed in terms of how much. How safe should our roads be? How clean should our air be? How much growth do we want?

Key Insight 3: Equilibrium Is Where Things Are Going

Equilibrium in physics is when a system is in balance with no tendency for further change. For example, when a ball has come to rest at the bottom of a bowl, it is in equilibrium. In economics, equilibrium takes place when, barring obstacles, all possible mutually beneficial trades have taken place. If there is any way in which any two people could both benefit from buying and selling (trading) with each other, then we're not in equilibrium. They can and will change (by trading with each other) to become better off.

Let us apply this. The government imposed a number of safety standards on cars such as seat belts and air bags. The rationale given is that consumers want these products but the car makers don't want to supply them. But if consumers' value for these products is more than the cost to make them, equilibrium theory tells us that car makers would benefit by supplying them. Certainly, many consumers do want these products and get them because it is profitable for auto makers to supply them. It represents a mutually beneficial trade. But this is not true for all consumers. Many with low incomes do not want these products because they cost more than they are willing to pay for them. This forces low-income persons to buy older and often more dangerous cars. With the mandated safety standards, they are often made less safe because they are prevented from buying the level of safety they could afford.

Thought Questions

What would happen if safety standards were mandated for all cars, old and new? How would the poor be affected?

This would make cars safer. But if the poor don't want to pay for the added safety, this would leave them worse off. They would then have to give up owning a car, or they would have to take a car with a lesser net benefit.

How do we know the new car has less net benefit than the old car?

If it did not have less net benefit, the poor, in the absence of safety standards, would choose to buy the new car instead of the old. Because they choose the old, it must supply more net benefit.

Let us now examine another car problem. When a new car leaves the showroom, it immediately depreciates in value by several thousand dollars. It is the same car, yet suddenly it is worth less. How can this be? There appears to be a missed mutually beneficial trade. For example, buyer A is willing to pay $20,000 for a new car. Buyer B just paid $20,000, left the showroom, and suddenly wants to sell it for $18,000. But the market for used cars values it at $15,000. Result: no trade. Yet both buyer A and buyer B would be better off by $1,000 if B sold her car to A for $19,000.

So why don't we observe this type of trading? Why instead do we see new car prices fall so fast after they are bought? Because this has been going on for so long, there must be some obstacle to this type of trade. One of the prime candidates is what is called the lemon effect. Most new cars sold soon after being bought are lemons. Because buyers can't easily tell a good car from a bad car, they're only willing to pay the price for a lemon. As a result, those owners with good new cars can't find buyers willing to pay the price that the good cars are worth.

Key Insight 4: Equilibrium Results Need not Be the Results People Wanted to Achieve

Squirrels seeking more food resulted in each getting the same. States paying higher welfare benefits may make some welfare recipients worse off. Builders seeking profits bid profits down.

Looking just at what people intend is not adequate for predicting what the outcome will be. The same is true for government laws. For example, electricians in most states must pass stringent tests in order to get a license to do electrical work. The goal of state licensing is to protect the public safety. Yet, a recent study showed that the more stringent the state licensing standards are, the greater the percent of people who die in electrical accidents. Why?

First, stricter licensing means fewer electricians. Fewer electricians mean higher prices. Some people can't afford these higher prices. They select the alternative of doing the electrical work themselves. Most do an adequate job. Unfortunately, some do not, and let me tell you, they're real burned up about this! They are victims of one of the unintended consequences of government laws.

CRIB NOTES

The **economic forces of competition** occur because people respond to incentives and continue until the reason for the incentive disappears.

A **good model** (1) Focuses on essential factors; (2) gives precise predictions; (3) gives predictions that can be tested; (4) provides outcomes that validate the model's predictions.

People act to become better off.

Equilibrium tells us where things are going.

Review Questions
---

1. What are some of the impediments to all mutually beneficial trades taking place?

2. Why is equilibrium important? How does it explain change?

3. Why do people pollute when the cost is far in excess of any benefits?

4. Mary had the electricity cut off at her restaurant by a storm. A passerby sells her a bag of ice for $100. The bag of ice allows Mary to save $400 of food that would have otherwise rotted. Was she a victim of price gouging if ice normally sells for $10 a bag?

5. We observe that when it rains, fewer people go to amusement parks. How does this illustrate the equilibrium principle?

6. In recent years, car manufacturers have been producing safer cars with such devices as air bags, seat belts, and crumple zones. With more safety features, will drivers be safer? To answer, consider how these devices affect how fast people drive and the resulting death toll on the highway.

7. More on lemons. Suppose brand X cars are either very good, worth $20,000 new, or very bad, worth only $10,000. Ten percent of Xs are bad. If new car buyers are willing to pay the average worth, what are they willing to pay for a new X? Suppose that then, after a month, they can tell if the car is bad or good. What will a one-month-old X sell for?

8. Assume there are two types of towns: clean towns and dirty towns. Assume also that all people have the same preferences and want to live in clean towns. Finally, assume there are no obstacles to living in either type of town. What would an economic model predict about the cost of living in clean and dirty towns?

9. Suppose one of the dirty towns, Grimy Gulch, cleans up. What will happen?

10. Suppose that the only two traits that drivers value in tires is durability and traction. Why is it that, at a given price, we would expect no tire to be the best in both categories?

Answers

1. The lemon problem gives the prominent reason: lack of good information. Because buyers can't know which cars are lemons, lemon owners have the incentive to offer their cars at the same price as good cars. This drives the price of all used cars, good and bad, down. Thus, there may be some owners of good cars who would like to trade their cars to buyers who would pay a good price if they knew for sure it was a good car. But the lack of information prevents this. Lack of information results in lots of good trades not taking place. Consider unemployment. Those who are unemployed want to trade pay for their efforts. If employers have complete information about all workers and if workers had complete information about all jobs, unemployment would be unnecessary.
2. Equilibrium describes how people achieve the best they can with what they have. Once this is achieved, there is no need for further changes in what they are doing.

New information, new products, and new technology are just some of the events that can create new opportunities for new trade. To predict the effects of these new things, we simply compare the *before* equilibrium with the *after* equilibrium. The resulting changes are what the new things can be predicted to eventually bring about.

A second role for equilibrium analysis is to work out the full impact of events, especially new government laws. Often, these laws achieve the opposite of what they intend. Equilibrium analysis demonstrates this and shows better ways to achieve what is intended.

3. If someone has the incentive to pollute, then the benefit of the pollution (say profits from making something) must exceed the cost of pollution to them. But these costs may not include pollution's cost to others. So people pollute, even when its costs exceed its benefits, when they don't bear the full cost of pollution.

4. She is better off; otherwise, she would not have bought the ice. It is true that the seller probably made $90 on the ice. But it is also true that Mary made $300 by buying the ice ($400 − $100). So she is also guilty of price gouging. She paid way less than what the ice is worth. However, the concept of price gouging assumes someone loses by the amount the other gains. As we have seen, both parties of this trade are made better off!

5. When it rains, amusement parks are less fun. So no one would go on rainy days unless there were some offsetting benefit. This offsetting benefit is fewer people at the parks. When there are fewer people, each person waits less time in line for amusement rides and has less disutility of fighting crowds. So attendance falls on rainy days until, for the marginal person going to the park, the cost of being rained on just offsets the benefit of fewer people. For this person, it doesn't matter when they go.

6. Using marginal analysis, people increase the speed of driving until the marginal benefit of added speed just offsets its added cost. One of these added costs is the cost resulting from the higher likelihood of being in an accident. Safer cars reduce the cost of being in an accident. Thus, they reduce the marginal cost of driving faster. The result will be that people will drive faster, resulting in more accidents. On the other hand, because cars are safer, there will be fewer deaths per accident. So the net effect on the death toll is uncertain. One study suggested that seat belts increased the number of accident-related deaths by causing drivers to drive faster, with the result that more pedestrians were killed in auto accidents than lives saved by the seat belts.

This leads me to the following modest proposal. Pass a law requiring that all drivers be seated on the front bumper. I predict fewer accidents. Of course, even a fender bender will likely result in the driver's death. But hey! They were following too close! They deserved it!

7. The average worth is $19,000 (90% chance of $20,000 plus 10% chance of $10,000). So the new X sells for $19,000. If a buyer gets a good car, it's worth $20,000, so they're not about to sell their car or even trade it for another new one. But if it is bad, it is only worth $10,000. The used price will be $10,000. All cars offered are lemons, and they sell for what they're worth.

8. If the cost of living were the same, everyone would live in a clean town. But as more people seek to live in a clean town, land prices would go up, making the cost of living higher there. Eventually, the value of cleanness would be offset by the higher cost of living. At that point, there is no longer any incentive to move into a clean town. People would not care, at that point, which town they lived in!

9. We've now created an incentive for people to move into Grimy Gulch: a clean town at dirty town prices. But as more people move in, land prices and other re-

lated costs will rise, until there is no longer any net advantage of being in Grimy Gulch. Landowners in Grimy Gulch will be better off. Renters will not be better or worse off.

10. If one tire were best in both categories, people would only buy that tire. If more than one type of tire is available, we would expect to find some trade-offs. For example, if one tire has more durability, the other gives better traction. Of course, at a higher price, you may be able to get more of both. However, within the highest price category, one would again expect to find similar trade-offs.

Chapter Four

Demand and Supply

INTRODUCTION

Even though I have never met a demand and supply diagram I didn't like, I can't say that's true for my students. But anyone can master demand and supply analysis. I know. I have worked with many students having trouble and found they lack a certain key distinction and a key skill necessary to learn this amazing technique of analyzing markets. The key distinction they need to be able to make is to identify *cause* and the resulting *effect*. The key skill they need is to be able to link cause and effect to the demand and supply diagram. This is not something to be vague about. You must be clear on these points. If you are, demand and supply analysis will be easy! So let us begin.

A SHORT FABLE ABOUT DEMAND AND SUPPLY

In a mythical country, all the buying and selling of shoes took place once a year in the central plaza. Imagine as you came upon this plaza that there were two large buildings. In the far left-hand corner of the plaza was the hall of shoe buyers, Demanders' Hall. In Demanders' Hall were all the persons wanting to buy shoes, or, for people who couldn't make it to town, their representatives. The demanders fortunately all wanted exactly the same kind of shoe. So they gathered once a year in individual stalls throughout Demanders' Hall to bid for shoes. In the far right-hand corner of the plaza was Sellers' Hall. Here were all the shoemakers. Each came to get orders for shoes to take back home to make and ship to demanders. The Guild Board of Sellers' Hall made sure all shoes were the same as what demanders wanted and met their exacting standards.

Over the years, buyers and sellers of shoes met to set the year's price for shoes. There evolved a custom that ensured no waste. The town crier stood in the courtyard between the two great halls and sent two pages out, one to each hall. Each page carried a list of prices. In Demanders' Hall, the page went to each demander and asked how many shoes he wanted at each price. The page recorded the answers, noted who made them, and when finished, added up the total for each price. Similarly, the other page at Sellers' Hall roamed its vast corridors going to each seller and asking how many shoes each would make at each price on the list. The page recorded the answers, noted who made them, and added up this total.

The pages then ran to the courtyard. The town crier compared the two lists. Then, he announced a price at which the shoes would be sold for the year. What amazed the citizenry is that the crier always settled at a price where the total number of shoes wanted by demanders at that price equaled the number of shoes sellers wanted to sell at that price. As a result of his skill, the town crier commanded such a huge fee that he was the richest man in the country.

The day came when the town crier passed his skills onto his child. He reminded his child that what he was about to pass on was secret and not to pass out of the family as it was the source of their wealth. On a piece of parchment, he drew a vertical line upon which he wrote the prices he had on his list, going from low prices at the bottom to higher prices up the line. On the horizontal line, he wrote the quantities of shoes, going from low to higher quantities from left to right. "Now what I do," he told his child, "is plot from the Demanders' Hall list each price and its total. I connect these points and call this the demand curve. Next, I plot each price and its total from the Sellers' Hall list. Then, I connect the dots for these points and call this line the supply curve. Finally, I go to where the lines meet and use that price to settle all trades. That is the market clearing price. At that price, all buyers get to buy the shoes they were willing to buy and all sellers get to sell the shoes they were willing to make."

"Why not settle at a higher price than where the lines meet?" the child asked.

The father smiled and said, "Once I did that out of curiosity. I found that at the higher price, the totals of the sellers exceeded the total demanders wanted. There was excess supply. Now the sellers who got orders at the higher price were quite happy. Ah, but the other sellers were very mad at me when I told them there were no orders for them. The abuse and criticism was immense. I learned my lesson well and never did that again!"

"Then," asked the child, "why not settle at a lower price than where the lines meet?"

"Well," the father said, "At the lower price, the totals of demanders exceeds the totals of sellers. There is excess demand. I reasoned that if I settled at the lower price, I could not fill the orders of all the demanders such that some would go shoeless. Could you imagine the criticism I would get then? Letting people go shoeless! Oh no. Not even I would attempt such foolhardiness."

The child, and his children, and their children lived happily ever after. That is, until an economist pointed out that the town crier was unnecessary because the open posting of prices would do the same job for free. Then the family became destitute, existing only by selling old demand and supply diagrams.

Key Points

That's enough storytelling. Here are some questions.

Suppose the town crier got a list of prices and quantities but it didn't say which hall it came from. How could he tell? If the quantities go up as the price goes down, then it is from Demanders' Hall. People want to buy more at lower prices. On the other hand, if the quantities go down as the price goes down, then it is from Sellers' Hall. Sellers want to sell less at lower prices.

How would the town crier know if he accidentally tried to settle trade at a price that was too high? Supply would exceed demand. Some shoes would be left unsold. And if the price were too low, what would happen? Demand would exceed supply. There would be unfilled orders. So when do we get to the right price? We get there when everyone—buyers and sellers—actually gets exactly what they want, no more, no less. Buyers buy all they want at the right price and sellers sell all they want at that price. This price is called the *market clearing price* because everyone's orders are completely filled. The order slate is cleared. No one is disappointed.

Suppose the market clearing price is $14. Who'll be disappointed if the town crier tries to set the price at $18? At a higher price, some of the sellers will be disappointed. At $14, the quantities demanded and supplied are the same. As the price goes up, the quantity demanded goes down while the quantity sellers want to sell goes up. Obviously, with supply exceeding demand, demanders are going to be able to buy all they want at $18. But some sellers will be disappointed because they can't sell all they want. Now show that at a lower price, say $10, demanders will be disappointed.

GRAPHING DEMAND AND SUPPLY CURVES

For the first time in publishing history, the charts and graphs from the town crier are now available to the public. To see a facsimile of the chart, just look at Table 4.1. It shows the combined lists from Demanders' and Sellers' Halls.

TABLE 4.1

TOWN CRIER'S LIST OF BIDS FOR SHOES

Price ($)	Total Number of Pairs Wanted by Demanders' Hall	Total Number of Pairs Offered by Sellers' Hall
20	18	42
18	22	38
16	26	34
14	30	30
12	34	26
10	38	22
8	42	18

At $20, demanders want to buy 18 pairs while sellers want to sell 42 pairs: Supply exceeds demand. Should $20 be chosen as the price, there will be 24 unsold pairs of shoes. This is an excess supply or surplus of shoes.

The unhappy sellers who were short-shrifted will push to lower prices. As the price falls to $18, the excess supply falls to 16 unsold pairs (38 − 22) but it still exists, so the price will be pushed lower by unhappy sellers. At $16, the surplus falls to 8 pairs (34 − 26). The pressure to lower prices still exists until at $14, there is no excess supply and all sellers find a buyer for each of the 30 pairs they offer.

Starting from the bottom, what happens if the price is $8? Demanders want 42 pairs, but sellers are willing to offer only 18. If $8 were the price, there would be 24 pairs demanded but not supplied (42 − 18). This is an excess demand or shortage of 24 pairs. The unhappy demanders would want a higher price. What happens to the excess demand as the price goes up? As the price goes up, the excess demand falls. At $10, it falls to 16 pairs (38 − 22). At $12, it falls further to 8 pairs (34 − 26).

What happens at $14? There is no excess demand for shoes: Those wanting shoes get them. Also, as we have seen, there is no excess supply of shoes: Those offering shoes get to sell them. We say the market clears.

At what price does the most trade take place? At the market clearing price of $14 with 30 shoes. To see this, go to any other price. The smaller of the two numbers (demand or supply) will be the amount actually bought and sold. At $14, the amount actually bought and sold is largest. Why the smaller number? The demand number at each price represents the most quantity demanders want to buy; they'll buy no more. The supply number is the most quantity sellers want to sell; they'll offer no more. So the smaller of the two numbers is the most that will be bought and sold.

Now, Figure 4.1 is a graph of the above chart. To see how the graph is constructed, imagine the town crier calling out one of the prices. At that price, he records on the chart the quantity demanders say they want as well as the quantity the sellers say they're willing to supply. For example, at $18, he plots a point on the graph for 22 pairs for demanders and a point for the 38 pairs offered by sellers. He does this again and again for every price. Then he connects the demanders' points and gets the demand curve. And when he connects the sellers' points, he gets the supply curve.

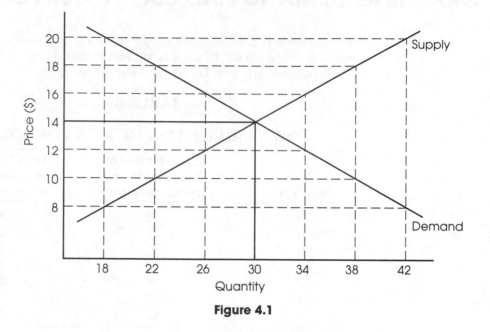

Figure 4.1

WHAT THE DEMAND CURVE SHOWS

The demand curve shows how changes in price cause people to change the amount they want to buy. Price is the cause. Quantity demanded is the effect.

Logically, to understand how this cause and effect works, you have to understand the following point. The demand curve shows marginal benefit of the good to consumers. For example, in Figure 4.1, the 38th pair of shoes has a marginal benefit of $10. That is, the marginal value and price of the 38th pair is $10. This is how much consumers gain from having 38 rather than 37 pairs. The more pairs consumers have, the less they value added pairs. For example, the 42nd pair has a lower marginal benefit of $8.

Visually, when we look at the height of a demand curve, it shows the marginal benefit of each unit. As we move to the right along the demand curve, we also move down: Its height falls because marginal benefit of the added units falls. As a result, the demand curve has a negative slope: quantity up, price down; quantity down, price up. Price and quantity move in opposite directions.

The logical link is this: Because each added unit of a good is put to less valued uses than the previous units, the marginal benefit falls as quantity goes up. Price reflects marginal benefit. So the price on the demand curve falls as quantity goes up.

DIAMONDS AND WATER

Here is a famous puzzle that stumped economists for years. We all know that water is more valuable than diamonds. Without water, we would die. Without diamonds, some may cry, but few would die. Yet, a pail of diamonds sells for a much higher price than a pail of water! How can this be? Doesn't price reflect value? So why doesn't the more valuable good command a higher price?

The puzzle was solved by noting the difference between marginal and total benefit (or marginal and total value). Marginal benefit is the addition to total benefit. As we get more of something, the marginal benefit of an added unit is less (Why? because it will be put to less valued uses). If we have a whole lot of something, the marginal benefit from more of it may be very, very small. We have lots of water; the marginal benefit of another pail is small. We have few diamonds; the marginal benefit of another pail of diamonds is high. On the other hand, the total benefit of water—the total value of all the water in the world—is much higher than that of diamonds!

Total benefit is what you would lose if you lost all of something. Marginal benefit is what you would lose if you lost just one unit of something. Going the other way, marginal benefit is the addition to total benefit.

The confusion between total and marginal benefit leads to many poor purchases. Salespersons for good *X* will point to good *X*'s total benefit. However, the correct decision rule is to only buy good *X* when its marginal benefit is higher than (or equal to) its cost. For example, a salesperson of a burglar alarm system points out how important security is. "Most of us would pay anything to avoid being robbed and killed, so isn't this burglar system a good deal at $5,000!" This is fallacious. The correct question is What is the marginal benefit of the burglar alarm? Might not the same money be better spent on a steel door, a sign saying (falsely) you have a burglar alarm, and a 200-pound dog that hates strangers? What does the burglar alarm add? It may still be worth it (I have one). But to make the correct decision, compare alternatives, shop around, and most of all, focus on added value (that is, on marginal benefit).

CAUSE AND EFFECT ALONG THE DEMAND CURVE

When the price goes down (cause), the quantity bought goes up (effect). Why?

First, let's examine the logical explanation. We assume that people will buy a unit of a good if its marginal benefit exceeds (or equals) its price.[1] At lower prices, more units of the good meet this criterion. So, as price goes down, the quantity demanded goes up.

In Figure 4.1, at a price of $18, 22 pairs had a marginal benefit of $18 or more and so are demanded. But at a lower price of $14, 30 pairs have a marginal benefit that exceeds (or equals) the price and so are demanded.

Second, we have the visual link to cause and effect. Draw a price line from left to right from the vertical axis to the demand curve. This tells us how many units people want to buy at that price. Now look at the units people don't want to buy at that price (those for which the price line you drew is vertically above the demand curve). Con-

---

[1]Why "equal"? If it is equal, one is actually no better or worse off buying the last unit. As a way of breaking this tie, we say that if the price equals marginal benefit, the unit will be bought. This has the advantage of matching our logic to our graphs.

sumers aren't willing to buy these units because the price on the price line exceeds their marginal benefit from these units.

CAUSE AND EFFECT ALONG THE SUPPLY CURVE

The supply curve shows that a higher price causes sellers to want to supply more. Price is the cause, and the quantity supplied is the effect.

To understand how cause and effect works, you have to understand this key point: The supply curve reflects marginal cost. For example, when the price was $10, sellers offered 22 pairs of shoes. The 22nd pair must have a cost of $10 (this is called marginal cost as it is the cost of the last of 22 pairs). As long as the price exceeds (or equals) the marginal cost of another pair of shoes, sellers will offer that pair.

How does the marginal cost of the 23rd pair compare with the marginal cost of the 22nd pair? It must cost more than $10. If it costs less, it would have been offered for sale at $10.

The visual link to this logic is this: Draw a horizontal price line from the vertical axis to the supply curve. This tells us how many units sellers would like to sell at that price. All these units cost the same or less than the price to make and so are gladly supplied. The units to the right of this intersection are not supplied because the marginal cost of producing them exceeds the price on the price line. For these added units to be produced, the price must go up. Thus, the supply curve slopes upward because marginal costs go up. It has a positive slope: price up, quantity up; price down, quantity down. Price and quantity move together, in the same direction, along the supply curve.

THE MARKET CLEARING PRICE

Demand equals supply at the market clearing price. This is the price where both demanders and sellers give the same number of pairs of shoes to the town crier (this is $14 in Figure 4.1). At any other price, their answers differ. At a higher price, sellers want to supply more pairs; demanders, less. This is called a surplus. At $18, for example, sellers would like to sell 38 pairs, but buyers only want to buy 22 pairs. There is a surplus of 16 pairs of shoes (38 − 22).

At a lower price than the market clearing price, demanders want more pairs than sellers want to sell. This is called a shortage. At $10, for example, demanders want to buy 38 pairs but sellers only want to sell 22 pairs. There is a shortage of 16 pairs here (38 − 22).

If the price is $18, how many shoes will be sold? Twenty-two pairs. Above the market clearing price, buyers determine how much will be bought. Sellers, if they could, would sell more, but they can't because buyers don't want more.

At $18, sellers are stuck with a surplus of shoes. How will they likely change the price? They will lower the price.

At $10, how many pairs will be sold? Twenty-two pairs. Below the market clearing price, sellers determine how much will be sold. Buyers, if they could, would buy more, but they can't because sellers don't want to sell any more.

At $10, there is a shortage of shoes. How are buyers likely change the price? They will bid the price up.

When will the price stop changing? The price will stop changing when demand equals supply: no shortage; no surplus. Buyers buy the amount they want. Sellers sell the amount they want. And these amounts are the same. That's why the market clearing price is also the equilibrium price—price stays there until the demand or supply curves shift.

Are there any tricks to help us? Yes. Notice that at each price, as you go from the vertical axis to the right, you hit either the demand curve or supply curve first. The first curve you hit determines how much will actually be bought and sold at that price. As you do this for all prices, you'll trace out the locus of trade. Starting at a high price, the locus of trade is first the demand curve as price falls to the market clearing price, and then switches to the supply curve. That's trick one. The second trick is that the most trade takes place where the demand and supply curves cross. Only a government subsidy could cause more trade to occur. But barring this, trade is maximized where demand and supply are equal.

A STORY

After the town crier had been ousted from his job by the roving economist, he opened a shoe store. If he sold shoes for $20 a pair, he noticed that he had a hard time moving his stock, having lots of shoes left unsold. So he held a sale, selling shoes for $10 a pair. At that price, his shelves were emptied, with customers begging him for more pairs. As he kept adjusting the price, he eventually came to the equilibrium market clearing price.

Keeping track of inventories is an excellent market strategy for narrowing in on the correct price to charge.

Strangely, many firms do not do this. Go to a dress store during sales time. You will likely find lots of very large and very small sizes but few average sizes. Why? Because most stores only stock one of each size. Stores, by doing this and charging the same price for all sizes, ensure they'll have a surplus of extreme sizes and a shortage of average sizes. Go to any sale and see what sizes are offered: lots of very large, lots of very small, and only a few in-betweens.

MINIMUM WAGES

The most famous of price floors is the minimum wage. It is the quintessential economic metaphor for good intentions leading to bad results. Sincere people, wanting to help the poor, propose raising the minimum wage. The higher wage, they argue, will give a better living. So the minimum wage is increased. But something happens. Employers don't want to employ so many people at the higher wage. Some poor people lose their jobs. So instead of getting a better living, they get none at all. Here we see good intentions but the opposite results.

This point can be reemphasized in several ways. Why not, it might be asked, raise the minimum wage even more? How about to $50,000 a year? Think how most families would then be better off! Of course, this would create massive layoffs and poverty.

Most studies suggest that every 10% increase in the minimum wage results in a decrease in employment of about 1 to 3%. They also suggest that few of the poor actually work for the minimum wage. Instead, most minimum-wage jobs serve as starting jobs for new workers, most of whom go on to earn more. Making the minimum wage higher makes it harder for most of these persons to get started.

Remember that the issue is not assuring poor people a living wage. The issue is assuring poor people a hiring wage—a wage they'll be hired at! The market wage does that very well!

PRICE CONTROL AND QUALITY

Price ceilings and price floors keep people from making mutually advantageous trades. Thus, it is not surprising that buyers and sellers conspire to evade price controls. One major way is the black market—the illegal sale of goods at illegal prices. For example, in World War II, the government put a price ceiling on food ("to protect the public from price gouging"). A shortage of food resulted. The government used ration coupons to distribute foods. To get around these price controls, it became a somewhat common practice for customers to go to farmers and buy the food they wanted at the official government price and to, in addition, buy the farmer's dog. As they left with the dog and food, they let the dog go, who then returned to the farmer.

A second major method of evasion is to vary the quality of the product. How quality is varied depends on whether the government-fixed price is too low or too high. At too low of a price, there is a shortage. Buyers normally are willing to bid up the price, but this is illegal with a price ceiling. Instead of the price being bid up, the quality of the product is bid down. For example, food is delivered less often to grocery stores (thus saving money but resulting in food being less fresh). In Argentina, where there were once price controls on bread, bread was delivered as uncooked bread dough! It is not surprising that landlords of rent-controlled apartments are some of the meanest and stingiest landlords. Poorer service, fewer improvements, fewer options; all are ways of reducing the quality of the products. Its effect is to raise the real price paid. In fact, the effective price can turn out to be higher than in the absence of price controls!

If the government sets the price too high with a price floor, it will be sellers who seek buyers. Instead of lowering the price, they will try to raise the quality of the product. This has the impact of effectively lowering the price of the good by giving more for the money. For example, when airline fares were set by the government, airlines competed by offering wider seats, better food, and better service. This may sound good, but recall that these are extras that people would not want to pay for in the absence of the price controls. Indeed, since airlines have been deregulated, many of these services have disappeared because consumers were not willing to pay for them. Some low-fare airlines even charge for meals, if they serve them!

A good case to illustrate the impact of price floors on quality is the minimum wage. Minimum wages create a surplus of applicants who are willing to bid the wage down. But because they can't do this, they bid down the quality of the job. Employers respond by supplying less training. One study suggests that workers lose more from less training in the form of future wage increases than they gain from the minimum wage increase. Other adjustments include working workers harder and requiring them to work off the clock. My own work suggests that minimum wages may well decrease the full wage of workers, the full wage including the value of training and the quality of the job in addition to the money wage being paid. The evidence suggests minimum wages increase the quit rates of workers and, in addition, reduce the number of persons wanting to seek and hold jobs.

CRIB NOTES

Demand curve: Shows maximum Q demanders are willing to buy at each P. Slope is negative. Demand price = Marginal benefit of good to buyers.

Supply curve: Shows maximum Q suppliers are willing to supply at each P. Slope is positive. Supply price = Marginal cost of good to supplier.

Market clearing price: Q demanded = Q supplied.

Price > Market clearing price $\longrightarrow$ surplus ($Q^S > Q^D$)

Surplus $\longrightarrow$ lower price

Price < Market clearing price $\longrightarrow$ shortage ($Q^S > Q^D$)

Shortage $\longrightarrow$ higher price

Locus of trade: Amount actually bought/sold is smaller of Q^D and Q^S at each price. Max Q at market clearing price.

Price floor (if effective: P_{floor} < Market clearing price): shortage.

Price ceiling (if effective: $P_{ceiling}$ > Market clearing price): surplus.

Review Questions

1. Take each quantity, both demand and supply, in Table 4.1 and double it. What will the new equilibrium price be? The new equilibrium quantity?

2. Now triple each number. What happens?

3. Returning to Table 4.1, add eight units to each number in the demand column but leave the supply column unchanged. What will the new equilibrium price be? What would happen if the price stayed at $14?

4. Returning to Table 4.1, add 16 units to each number in the demand column and eight to each number in the supply column. What will happen?

5. Returning to Table 4.1, suppose the government wants to buy enough shoes to keep its price at $20. How many pairs will the government have to buy?

6. Draw the following demand curve.

$$P^D = \$10 - Q$$

where P^D is the demand price and Q is the quantity. How many Q will consumers demand if the price is $8? $6? $4? $2?

7. Draw the following supply curve:

$$P^S = \$2 + Q$$

where P^S is the price and, now, Q is the quantity supplied. What is the supply when $P = \$4$? $6? $8?

8. Using the equations in questions 7 and 8, what is the equilibrium market clearing price?

9. How many units will be bought and sold if the price is $8? Will there be a shortage or surplus of the good?

10. How many units will be bought and sold if there is a price ceiling of $4? Will there be a shortage or surplus of the good?

11. The following chart shows the value of the various uses Mary can put widgets to. Derive her demand curve for widgets[2]. (Each use uses one widget.)

Use	Value of Use ($)
A	10
B	2
C	8
D	6
E	4
F	0

12. Marilyn is a maker of widgets. She calculates the total cost of making widgets as follows. Fill in the marginal cost of making an added widget. Derive her supply curve.

Quantity	Total Cost ($)	Marginal Cost ($)
1	2	
2	6	
3	12	
4	20	
5	30	

13. Suppose there are ten Marys and ten Marilyns in a marketplace. What will the market demand and supply curves look like? What will the market clearing price be?

14. In question 13, if there is a $2 price ceiling on widgets, how many will be bought and sold? Will Mary be happy?

15. Suppose there are six demanders, each of whom wants one widget. Each writes on a piece of paper the highest price she is willing to pay for one widget. Similarly, there are six suppliers of widgets, each of whom is willing to supply one widget. Each writes on a piece of paper the minimum price at which he is willing to supply one widget. Each is put into a separate pile and then mixed up. Recollect these pieces of paper and decide what the market price should be.

Demand pile: $10 $8 $9 $5 $6 $7

Supply pile: $5 $9 $7 $4 $6 $8

---

[2]Economists, including me, have an inordinate fondness for widgets. The reason is that we are quite expert in the demand and supply conditions of mythical products. Widgets allow us to use simple numbers that are easy to manipulate. Using real goods requires large numbers (billions of gallons) and strange prices ($1.99).

16. There was once a town called Oldville. The town was full of old people living in apartments. One day, young people starting moving into Oldville. They bid rents up. This made the old people of Oldville mad. They proclaimed, "How dare they raise rents! We've lived in these apartments for years. We fought in the war! We're good people! The world owes us cheap rent! So we demand rent controls to keep us from being exploited."
    a. Who caused the rents to go up? the landlords? Who is being hurt by rent controls?
    b. Oldville depends upon property taxes. What will happen over time?

17. Suppose there are 100 persons with the following daily demand curve for gasoline and 100 stations with the following supply curve:

Gallons	Demand Price ($)	Supply Price
1	3	0.50
2	2	0.75
3	1	1.00
4	0.50	2.00

    a. In the absence of price controls, what will the market price of gasoline be? How much will be sold?
    b. Suppose a price ceiling of $0.50 is imposed upon gasoline. How many gallons will be bought? Will there be a shortage or surplus? How much?
    c. Each station now rations out one gallon per visit to each customer. To get gasoline, people now have to wait in line. Thus, in addition to the price of gasoline, there will be a time cost of getting gasoline. What is the highest time cost (per gallon) that demanders will be willing to wait? What will this do to the full price of gasoline?

18. Why do shortages mainly occur when price controls are in effect?

19. The National Organ Transplant Act of 1984 makes it illegal to buy and sell human organs. What are the likely effects of this act?

20. College sports put a price ceiling on the wages of college athletes. The price ceiling is a wage of zero. These athletes are often worth millions to the school in extra ticket sales at college sporting events. Does an individual college have an incentive to try to evade this price control?

21. Draw the demand and supply diagrams for the following goods:
    a. A free (nonscarce) good.
    b. A good that is so costly no one can afford it.
    c. What people mean when they say, "I wouldn't give an owl's hoot for . . ." Are they taking about its demand price or supply price? Show its demand and supply curve.

Answers

1. It will still be $14. To see this, note that at $14, the quantity demanded and supplied was initially 30. Now both are doubled (both to 30). So they are still equal at $14.
2. The equilibrium price stays the same. As long as demand and supply quantities go up by equal amounts, it will not change.
3. Demand equals supply at $16, where demand equals supply at 34 pairs. If the price

stayed at $14, there would be a shortage of shoes. Demand would exceed supply by eight pair.

4. We'll get the same results as in question 3 because, at the original equilibrium price, in both questions, demand now exceeds supply at eight units.

5. At $20, supply exceeds demand by 24 pairs (42 − 18). So the government would have to buy up this surplus of 24 pairs of shoes.

6. The demand curve starts at $P = \$10$ (its vertical intercept), slopes down with a negative slope of −1, and then intersects the horizontal axis at $Q = 10$ (as at $P = 0$, $Q = 10$). At $8, Q is 2 (plug 8 into where P is and solve $8 = 10 - Q$ for Q). At $6, Q is 4. At $4, Q is 6. At $P = \$2$, $Q = 8$.

7. The supply curve has a vertical intercept of $2 and slopes up with a positive slope of +1. At $P = \$4$, $Q = 2$ (plug $4 in for P and solve $4 = 2 + Q$ for Q). At $P = \$6$, $Q = 4$; at $8, it equals 6.

8. $6. At $6, the quantity demanded is four units, and the quantity supplied is four units. Because both are equal at $6, that is where the market will clear.

9. At $8, the quantity demanded will be two units. The quantity supplied at $8 will be six units. Since demanders will buy no more than two units while suppliers want to supply still more, the actual amount bought and sold will be two units. There will be an unsold surplus of four units.

10. At $4, the quantity demanded will be six units; the quantity supplied at $4 will be two units. Because suppliers will supply no more than two units while demanders want more (six units), the actual amount bought and sold will be the smaller of the numbers: two units. There will be a shortage of four units that demanders want but can't buy.

11. She will demand widgets in the order of their (marginal) value:

Price ($)	Quantity	Uses Widgets Put To
10	1	A
8	2	A and C
6	3	A, C, and D
4	4	A, C, D, and E
2	5	A, C, D, E, and B
0	6	A, C, D, E, B, and F

Note why the demand curve has a negative slope: at lower prices, she is willing to buy more widgets for the lower valued uses.

12. The marginal cost is the addition to total cost needed to produce the added unit. For example, the fourth unit has a marginal cost of $8. A price of $8 will cause Marilyn to supply four units because it covers the marginal costs of the first four units. Her supply curve will be as follows:

Price ($)	Quantity
2	1
4	2
6	3
8	4
10	5

Note that her supply curve is also her marginal cost curve.

13. At each price, sum the demands for all ten Marys and get the demand curve. Do the same for the ten Marilyns. The equilibrium price will be $6, with the quantity demanded and supplied being 30 units.

Demand and Supply in the Land of Ten Marys and Ten Marilyns

Price ($)	Quantity Demanded	Quantity Supplied
10	10	50
8	20	40
6	30	30
4	40	20
2	50	10

14. Ten units (the smaller of demand and supply at $2). If this all goes to two Marys, they will be very happy. But the other eight Marys will be quite contrary because they get none! They are willing to pay a higher price rather than have none at all.

15. Order from the highest price and calculate what demand and supply will be at each price. This is shown in the table below. The market price will be $7 and the market quantity will be four units.

Demand and Supply: Usual Form

Price ($)	Quantity Demanded	Quantity Supplied
10	1	6
9	2	6
8	3	5
7	4	4
6	5	3
5	6	2
4	6	1

16. a. The new young people moving into town bid the rents up. The landlords, by raising rents, ensure that apartments go to those who most value them (that is, those who are willing to pay the highest rent for them). Rent controls hurt the landlords and the young people, who are denied the right to bid apartments away from old people.

b. Over time, property values will go down because rents (and thus the value of the apartment) are held down. Landlords will have no incentive to keep their apartments up, so they will deteriorate.

17. a. $1 and 300 gallons a day (three gallons per person).

b. What suppliers are willing to supply at $0.50: 100 gallons. There is a shortage of 300 gallons (400 gallon demand minus 100 gallon supply at $0.50).

c. For each demander, the demand price for the first gallon is $3 and the price ceiling price is $0.50. So people are willing to pay $2.50 extra in waiting time to get that one gallon. The effect of the price ceiling will be to raise the effective price of gasoline. Each customer gets one gallon per visit to the gas station. Note how the waiting time discourages them from going back on the same day to buy a second gallon.

18. In the absence of price controls, shortages are short-lived because higher prices eliminate the shortage. But with price controls, the shortage remains. That's why the only time in our nation's history that we experienced long lines for gas was when there were price controls on gasoline (during the oil crisis).

19. The act has created a shortage of organs. In 1993, for example, almost 3,000 people died waiting for transplants. The act reduces the supply of organs and, hence, the number of people that can be saved. In addition, people seek very costly ways to get around the intent of the act. For example, hospitals have some discretion to

offer organs from local patients. As a result, rich patients sign up on many hospitals' waiting lists and have a better chance of getting transplants.

20. Yes. Demanders face a shortage of athletes. So they will be willing to pay athletes in other forms: better living accommodations, employment for the family of the athlete (provided by grateful alumni), and hiring coaches that have a reputation of being able to recruit good players.

21. c. People are talking about the demand price for a hoot, which is worthless. The cost of getting an owl to hoot on demand is high, especially when it is the spotted owl.

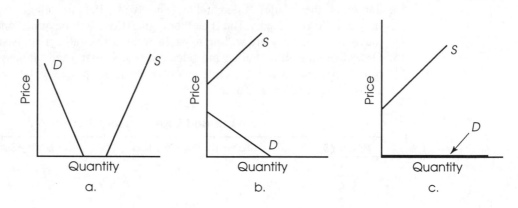

Chapter Five

Elasticity

HOW MUCH?

So far, we have used demand and supply curves to predict how price and quantity change. We know that if the price of fish goes up, the demand for fish will fall. But by how much?

How much? is a very important question! It determines the fate of industries. If a higher price results in demand falling a great deal, an industry could be wiped out. But if it falls only a little, the total dollar sales of the industry could actually go up, enhancing its profits.

ELASTICITY: THE ANSWER

To answer How much?, economists use elasticities. There are many types of elasticities. But all involve the same elements. First, they measure the percent change in the quantity (for example, the percent change in the quantity of fish demanded). Second, some variable caused this change: The percent change in this variable is measured (for example, the percent change in the price of fish). Third, we divide the first by the second: The result is an elasticity for this event. It is the ratio of the effect (the percent change in quantity) divided by the cause (measured in percent terms)[1]. (Note: The ratio of A to B means A divided by B, or A/B). Elasticity measures how responsive quantity is in percent terms.

Example 1

Suppose the quantity demanded of fish goes up 10% due to a 5% decrease in the supply price. The price elasticity of demand is equal to 2. (Note: Price elasticities are always stated as a positive number.) This number is derived by dividing the percent quantity response, 10%, by the percent change in price, 5% (2 = 10%/5%).

Example 2

Suppose, instead, the income of fish consumers goes up 20% and their demand for fish (at any given price) goes up 10%. We say in this case that the income elasticity of

---

[1]Remember: quantity effect on top, cause on the bottom. Memory Peg: "Getting to the bottom of things tells us the cause": bottom—cause.

demand is 0.5. The number 0.5 is derived by dividing the percent quantity change, 10%, by the percent change in income, 20% (0.5 = 10%/20%).

Economists use elasticities because they work. That is, if the price demand for a good is 0.3 in 1960 for the United States, it often turns out that it will be close to 0.3 in other nations, in other years, and in the various regions of the nation.

THE PRICE ELASTICITY OF DEMAND

The price elasticity of demand (which we denote as *Ed:P*) is the percent change in quantity demanded due to a 1% change in the price, stated as a positive number. It is calculated as follows:

$$Ed.P = \frac{\textbf{Percent change in quantity demanded}}{\textbf{Percent change in price}} \quad \textbf{stated as positive number}$$

If the price of widgets goes up 5% and the quantity demand of widgets goes down by 15%, then *Ed:P* = 3 = 15%/5%.

If the price of electricity goes up 10% and the quantity demanded of electricity goes down 3% the *Ed:P* = 0.3 = 3%/10%.

If the *Ed:P* for electricity equals 0.3, what will happen if the price of electricity goes up 20%? If, for every 1% increase in the price, the quantity demanded falls 0.3%, then a 20% increase in the price will cause the quantity demanded to fall 6% (= 0.3 times 20%).

In general, we have the following.

Equation 1

Percent change in quantity demanded = – *Ed:P* × Percent change in price

or

$$\%\Delta Q^D = -\ Ed:P \times \%\Delta P$$

Note the minus sign: This reflects the result that price and quantity demanded move in opposite directions along the demand curve.

Ed:P can be expressed in terms of the formula as

$$Ed:P = -\ \%\Delta Q^D/\%\Delta P$$

For example, if shoe prices go up 10% and the quantity demanded falls 5%, *Ed:P* for shoes equals 0.5 (= –[–5]/10) And if movie tickets go up 20% in price and movie attendance falls by 40%, *Ed:P* for movie tickets equals 2.0 (= –[–40]/20).

The bigger the price elasticity of demand is, the more elastic demand is. By elastic, we mean the quantity demanded responds more to price. A 10% increase in price will lower quantity demanded by 1% if *Ed:P* = 0.1 but will decrease it by 10% if *Ed:P* is larger and equal to 1.0 (be sure to work this out!).

Price is the cause: The bigger the effect—the more quantity changes—the more elastic the demand. If I throw a brick at a brick wall and it doesn't bounce back much, then it is inelastic. If I throw a rubber ball at a brick wall and it bounces back a lot, it's elastic. I have been told that mimes are very elastic in their movement, but let me tell you that, using the brick wall test, they fall short of being elastic.

Here are some useful ranges:

$Ed{:}P < 1$: Demand is inelastic
$Ed{:}P = 1$: Demand is unitary elastic
$Ed{:}P > 1$: Demand is elastic

We are often interested in total revenues (or total sales, $P \times Q$). If the price change leaves the demand curve unchanged, we can calculate the impact of the event on total sales using the following approximation.

Equation 2

Percent change in total revenue =
Percent change in quantity demanded + Percent change in price

or

$$\%\Delta(P \times Q) = \%\Delta Q^D + \%\Delta P$$

For example, if a 10% increase in the price caused the quantity demanded to fall 6%, then total sales will rise by about 4% (=10% + [−6%]). On the other hand, if a 10% fall in the price caused the quantity demanded to rise 17%, total sales will rise by about 7% (=[−10%] + 17%).

Equation 2 combined with equation 1 allows us to use the price elasticity of demand to solve for the impact on total sales.

Equation 3

Percent change in total sales = $(1 - Ed{:}P) \times$ Percent change in price[2]

or

$$\%\Delta(P \times Q) = (1 - Ed{:}P) \times \%\Delta P$$

If $Ed{:}P = 1.2$, then a 10% increase in the price will reduce the quantity demanded by 12% and thus reduce total revenue by 2% (−2% = (1 − 1.2) × 10%). If demand is elastic, total revenue goes down when the price goes up.

If $Ed{:}P = 0.8$, then a 10% increase in the price will reduce the quantity demanded by 8% and thus increase total revenue by 2% (+2% = (1 − 0.8) × 10%). If demand is inelastic, total revenue goes up when the price goes up.

If demand is unitary elastic ($Ed{:}P = 1$), total revenue is the same at all prices: Every percent increase in P is met by an equal percent decrease in Q, leaving total revenue ($P \times Q$) unchanged.

If demand is inelastic ($Ed{:}P < 1$), a higher price increases total revenues and a lower price decreases total revenues: Price and total revenues move together. On the other hand, if demand is elastic ($Ed{:}P > 1$), then a higher price will decrease total sales while a lower price will increase total revenues: Price and total revenue move in the opposite direction.

---

[2]Substitute for the Percent change in Q the term $- Ed{:}P \times$ % change in P.

SOME APPLICATIONS

Application 1

If the demand for subway rides is inelastic, what will happen to ridership and total revenues if the subway raises its fares? A higher price reduces the quantity demanded so ridership will fall. But because demand is inelastic, total revenues will go up. With fewer riders, the subway system will have lower total costs. This, combined with higher revenues, will cause profits to go up (or, more typically, reduce losses).

Application 2

How will this result differ if demand is elastic? Ridership still falls when the price goes up. But now it falls so much that total revenues also fall. The smaller ridership will likely reduce profits because most of a subway's costs are the same no matter how people ride. For public transportation, the price elasticity of demand equals 3.5 over the long run so higher fares mean less revenue.

Application 3

The demand for farm goods is highly inelastic ($Ed:P = 0.2$). If bad weather reduces the amount of food harvested by 10%, will farmers as a group be better or worse off?

As a group, they will be better off because total revenues for farm goods will go up. First, the price of farm goods must rise to cut back demand to match the 10% reduction in supply. As $Ed:P = 0.2$, the price must rise by 50% (plug the 10% quantity reduction and $Ed:P = 0.2$ into equation 3 and solve for the percent change in price). Total farm revenues will rise by 40% (use equation 3). Those farms losing most of their crops will be worse off. But others will be better off such that, on the whole, farmers as a group will earn more. This is why farmer collectives sometimes purposefully destroy part of their crops.

WHAT MAKES DEMAND MORE ELASTIC?

The more elastic the demand for the good is, the more its quantity demanded responds to price changes. Suppose the price goes up. Demand is inelastic if the quantity demanded only goes down a little. But if it goes down by a large amount, demand is very elastic. Remember: Quantity goes down in both cases. Elastic or inelastic tells us by how much.

There is one key factor that determines how elastic the demand for a good is. That key factor is the availability of substitutes. More substitutes $\longrightarrow$ more elastic! The more elastic the demand for good X is, when the price of X goes up, consumers find it easy to find substitutes for good X and so they buy a lot less of good X.

All the following factors make demand more elastic; they make the quantity demanded more responsive to price changes. They all work by making more substitutes available.

Factor 1: More Time

The more time consumers have to adjust, the more substitutes they can find, and the more elastic demand will be.

Factor 2: More Narrowly Defined Good

The more narrowly defined the good, the more substitutes there are for it, and, usually, the more elastic its demand will be. For example, Bill's Shell gasoline is a more narrowly defined good than Shell gasoline, and, in turn, Shell gasoline is more narrowly defined than gasoline. Suppose Bill's Shell gasoline goes up in price, but the price of all other gasolines stay the same. We would expect people to go elsewhere and the demand for Bill's gas to fall dramatically. Now suppose Shell gas raises its price at all its stations: we would expect some people to switch to other brands, but the decrease in demand will not be as dramatic as it was for Bill. The elasticity of demand for the more broadly defined good (Shell gas) is smaller than it is for the narrowly defined good (Bill's Shell gas) because there are more substitutes for Bill's gas. Now suppose all gasoline prices go up. We would expect the quantity demanded of gas to fall, but not as much as demand for Shell's gas fell (in percent terms) when only Shell raised the price of its gas. That's because there are fewer substitutes for gas than there are for Shell gas.

Exceptions to this rule are those goods that people have a fierce loyalty to. For example, the demand for ice cream is far more inelastic ($Ed{:}P = 0.1$) than the demand for food ($Ed{:}P$ is 0.3).

Factor 3: The Easier It Is to Find About Substitutes

The more information available, the more easily consumers will find substitutes for a good whose price has gone up. Advertising is a major source of information about the prices and the availability of goods. Consumer magazines also assist buyers in finding about the quality and value of alternatives. All these make demand for any particular good more elastic.

Factor 4: The Larger the Good's Share of Income

The larger the good's share of income, the more important the good's price is to the consumer's welfare. Thus, the bigger the share, the more likely it is that consumers will be willing to look around for substitutes. This rule doesn't always work because sometimes there are no substitutes! But it works in most cases.

For example, older persons who spend a large share of their budget on drugs are far more likely to look around for a cheaper source of drugs. Compared to younger persons, their demand for drugs from a given drug store is far more elastic than that for younger persons. That's why drug stores offer discounts to senior citizens—if they didn't, they would go elsewhere! On the other hand, most people will not search hard to find cheaper salt.

ELASTICITY AND STRAIGHT-LINE DEMAND CURVES

A favorite true–false question is, "True or false: The price elasticity of demand is the same along a given straight-line demand curve." Most students answer this true, when it is false (that's why it is a favorite). It is true that the slope ($\Delta P/\Delta Q$) is the same along a straight-line demand curve. But elasticity equals the following equation.

Equation 4

$$Ed{:}P = \frac{1}{|\text{slope}|} \cdot \frac{P}{Q}$$

The denominator of the first term on the right-hand side is the absolute value of the slope (that is, the slope stated as a positive number). This keeps $Ed{:}P$ a positive number. While the slope is the same along a straight-line demand curve, P and Q are different at each point. Starting on the vertical axis, $Q = 0$ and $Ed{:}P$ is infinite (any number divided by 0 is infinite). As we move right, Q goes up and P goes down, so $Ed{:}P$ falls. When it hits the horizontal axis, the demand curve's price elasticity equals 0, as $P = 0$.

There is a very simple relationship to calculate the elasticity of a demand curve at any particular point. In Figure 5.1, the price elasticity of demand at point X equals the length of B divided by the length of A, or the length of b divided by the length of a, or the length of b' divided by the length of a'.

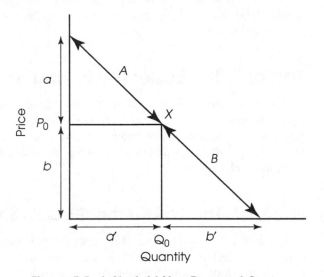

Figure 5.1 A Straight-Line Demand Curve

$$Ed{:}P = B/A = b/a = b'/a'$$

For example, halfway down a straight-line demand curve (where $A = B$), the elasticity always equals 1.0. Starting at $Q = 0$ and before reaching halfway (so that $B > A$), demand is elastic (as $B/A > 1$). More than halfway, (where $B < A$), it is inelastic (as $B/A < 1$).

In Figure 5.2, the demand curve is $P^D = 10 - 0.5Q$. Its slope is constant and equals -0.5. But its elasticity varies at all points. Because we are interested in total revenue, this is plotted in the bottom graph.

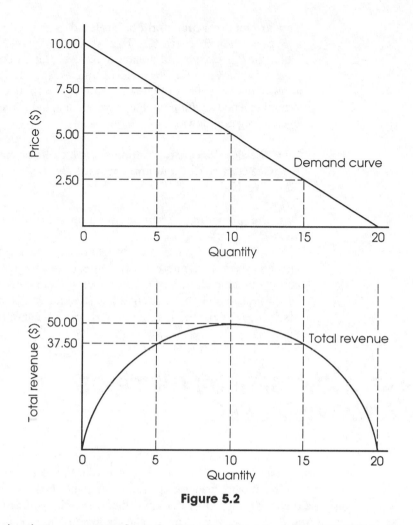

Figure 5.2

Notice that, as we move from $Q = 0$ to $Q = 20$, total revenue ($P \times Q$) begins at 0 (as $Q = 0$), rises, peaks at $Q = 10$, and then falls back to 0 at $Q = 20$ (as $P = 0$ at this point). Moving up to halfway (from $Q = 0$ up to $Q = 10$), demand is elastic so total revenue rises as P goes down. At the halfway point, $Ed{:}P = 1$ and total revenue remains unchanged (the slope of the total revenue curve is 0 at $Q = 10$). Then past $Q = 10$, demand becomes inelastic and so total revenue falls as P goes down.

Thought Questions

How were the total revenues calculated for $Q = 5$? $Q = 10$? $Q = 15$?

At $Q = 5$, it's $P \times Q$ or $\$7.50 \times 5$ or $\$37.50$. At $Q = 10$, $P \times Q$ equals $\$5 \times 10$ or $\$50$. This is the maximum total revenue. At $Q = 15$, it's $\$2.50 \times 15$ or $\$37.50$.

What is the elasticity of demand at $Q = 5$, 10, and 15?

At $Q = 5$, using the b'/a' formula, we have $Ed{:}P = 15/5 = 3$. At $Q = 10$, $Ed{:}P = 10/10 = 1$. At $Q = 15$, we have $5/15$ or $Ed{:}P = 1/3$. Using the b/a formula, we have at $Q = 5$, $Ed{:}P = 7.50/2.50 = 3$; at $Q = 5/5 = 1$; at $Q = 15$, we have $Ed{:}P = 2.50/7.50 = 1/3$.

How are total revenue and *Ed:P* related?

See equation 3 where %Δ Total revenue = (1 − *Ed:P*) × %Δ*P*. When *Ed:P* is elastic and greater than 1, as *P* goes down, total revenue goes up. When *Ed:P* is inelastic and less than 1, as *P* goes down, so does total revenue. In Figure 5.2, up to *Q* = 10, demand is elastic, so total revenue is going up. Past *Q* = 10, demand is inelastic, so total revenue is going down.

Since the slope is constant along a straight-line demand curve, is the price elasticity of demand constant also?

No. No. No!

Can the preceding formulas be applied to curved demand curves?

No. However, if you draw a straight line that is tangent to the point on the curve you're interested in (*tangent* means just touching and having the same slope as the curve does at that point), then calculate *Ed:P* for that point on the straight line (treating it as a demand curve), this will be the elasticity of the curved demand curve at that point!

APPLICATION: SETTING THE PRICE FOR A MOVIE TICKET

In many cases, a business wants the highest total revenues possible. This occurs when total costs do not go up when more is sold. For example, the total cost of showing a movie in a movie theater is the same, no matter how many people see the movie. Suppose the movie theater owner knew that if she charged $14 a ticket, no one would come. And if she gave tickets away, she could sell 500 tickets a show. If the demand curve is a straight line, then it starts at *P* = $14, has a slope of − 14/500 (going from *Q* = 0 to *Q* = 500, a run of 500, the price falls from $14 to $0, a rise of −$14, so rise over run is −14/500), and hits the horizontal axis at 500 (where *P* = $0). The theater would maximize its total revenue at a ticket price of $7 (halfway between $0 and $14), selling 250 tickets (halfway between 0 and 500). Its maximum total revenue would be $1,750 per show ($7 × 250). Even if the theater sat 1,000 people, it would be better to have empty seats rather than to try to fill it by cutting the price below $7. So with the vertical axis intercept (the price that empties the theater), the theater owner can set her price by taking one-half of that price. With the horizontal intercept (the quantity when the good is free), she can predict how many people will come by taking one-half that quantity. This assumes the demand curve is a straight line. It also assumes the theater has enough seats to accommodate the estimated quantity (here, 250).

Here is another method for business persons to estimate the price elasticity of demand for their product: Take the current price (P_1). Estimate what price will cause customers to stop buying your good (call this P_2). *Ed:P* is approximated by $P_1/(P_2 − P_1)$.

TWO EXTREMES

There are two extreme types of demand curves. A perfectly elastic demand curve is a horizontal line: The demand price is unaffected by the quantity sold. A small farmer, for example, over the range of output, can sell all output without affecting the market price for the output. So Farmer Jones' wheat has a perfectly elastic demand curve, at least over the range Farmer Jones can produce. The other extreme is a perfectly inelastic demand curve: This curve is represented by a vertical line. No matter what the price is, people buy the same amount. Only a few goods come close to this type of demand curve. Addictive drugs and vital medical procedures probably come close to being in perfectly inelastic demand.

MEASURING THE PERCENT CHANGE

There are several ways to measure the percent change in a variable. For example, suppose the price rises from $10 to $12. The change in price is $2. To get the percent change, we need to divide this change by some base price and multiply by 100 (to change the decimal into a percent):

$$\%\Delta P = \frac{P_{new} - P_{old}}{P_{base}} \bullet 100$$

One choice is the old price ($10). In this case, the percent change in the price is 20% (= 2/10 × 100). Another choice is the average price ($P_{new} + P_{old}$ divided by 2). In this case, the percent change is 18.2% (= 2/11 × 100).

When the base is the average of the old and new and the result is used to calculate elasticity, the result is called an arc elasticity. Most texts prefer the arc method[3].

As an example, suppose the price goes from $9 to $11 and the quantity goes from 25 to 15. What is the arc price elasticity of demand? The arc percent change in price is 20%. The arc percent change in quantity is −50%. The elasticity of demand is 2.5 (=|50/20|).

If you know the equation for demand, then it is possible to calculate the point elasticity at any given point. The point elasticity is

$$Ed{:}P = \frac{1}{|slope|} \bullet \frac{P}{Q}$$

For example, if $PD = 20 - 2Q$, what is its point elasticity when the price equals $6? Solving this equation at $P = $6 gives $Q = 7$. The slope, stated as a positive number, is 2. So the point elasticity is 0.4286 (= 1/2 times $6 / 7). We can also use the length method, using the price segments: $Ed{:}P = $6/$14 = 0.4286$.

---

[3]Memory Peg: Noah's ark (arc) had two of every animal to form the base of the future animal population.

INCOME ELASTICITY

An increase in consumer income typically increases the demand for a good. That is, when income goes up, the demand curve shifts right. Holding the price constant, we measure the increase in the quantity demanded in percent terms. The income elasticity of demand for the good equals the percent increase in quantity demanded divided by the percent increase in income (which caused demand to shift up). Alternatively, the income elasticity is the percent increase in the quantity demanded due to a 1% increase in income. It is calculated as follows.

Equation 5

$$Ed{:}Inc = \%\,\text{Change in } Q^D \,/\, \%\,\text{Change in income}$$

Once again, the effect is on the top; the cause is on the bottom. Memory aid: things work from bottom up.

For many goods, income elasticity is more important than its price elasticity of demand. That is because while their prices, after taking account of inflation, haven't changed much, consumer income has gone up with gross domestic product (GDP), growing on average between 1% and 3% a year, year after year, doubling every two or three decades.

If $Ed{:}Inc = 1$, the good's demand grows with income. The good's share of income stays the same. However, if $Ed{:}Inc < 1$, the good's demand rises but not enough to keep pace with the growth in income. Its share continually falls, creating a declining industry. The prime example is farming. On the other hand, when $Ed{:}Inc > 1$, then as income rises, the good's demand rises faster than income and its share rises. There is an expanding industry. The fate of many industries is in their income elasticities!

Equation 6[4]

$$\%\Delta\text{Good's share of income} = (Ed{:}Inc - 1) \times \%\Delta\text{Income}$$

Various ranges for income elasticities have been identified:

$$Ed{:}Inc < 0 \text{ inferior good}$$
$$Ed{:}Inc > 0 \text{ normal good}$$
$$0 < Ed{:}Inc < 1 \text{ necessity}$$
$$Ed{:}Inc > 1 \text{ luxury or superior good}$$

There are two types of normal goods: necessities and luxury goods.
If income goes up:

Inferior goods	Q goes down	share goes down
Necessity	Q goes up	share goes down
Superior good	Q goes up	share goes up
Normal good	Q goes up	need to know more

---

[4]This is derived from the approximation (assuming P is fixed): $\%\Delta\,(P \times Q\,/\,\text{Income}) = \%\Delta Q - \%\Delta\text{Income}$.

Application

Here are the income elasticities for several goods: furniture 2.6, automobiles 2.5, restaurant meals 1.6, tobacco 0.6, electricity 0.2, margarine −0.2. What will happen to these goods' share of income as the economy grows? Furniture and auto shares will grow dramatically, followed by restaurant meals. On the other hand, tobacco's share and electricity's share will fall. Worst of all, margarine's share will fall as will the amount sold!

CROSS-ELASTICITIES

Now we introduce cross-elasticities. And let me tell you, they're really mad! This is the effect of the price of good Y on the quantity demanded of good X (both measured in percent terms, of course).

Equation 7

$$EdX{:}PY = \%\Delta \text{ in } Q^D \text{ of } X \ / \ \%\Delta \text{ in } P \text{ of } Y$$

Goods X and Y are substitutes if $EdX{:}PY > 0$. For example, if the price of Hondas goes up, people may buy more Saturns (that is, the demand curve for Saturns shifts right). Or if the price of hot dogs goes down, people may buy fewer hamburgers.

Goods X and Y are complements if $EdX{:}PY < 0$. For example, if the price of gasoline goes up, the demand for Cadillacs may go down. Or if the price of mustard goes up, the demand for hot dogs may go down.

SUPPLY CURVE ELASTICITIES

Guess what! The price elasticity of the quantity supplied equals

$$Es{:}P = \%\Delta \ Q^S \ / \ \%\Delta \ \textbf{Price}$$

The higher the elasticity of supply, the more the quantity supplied goes up for a given rise in price. As before, if the supply curve is a straight line, it need not have the same elasticity at all points[5]. However, around a given price and quantity, the flatter the supply curve, the more elastic it is. Figure 5.3 shows some of the possibilities.

---

[5]The only exception is a straight-line supply curve that emerges from the origin (where P and $Q = 0$). For this curve, at all points, $Es{:}P = 1$.

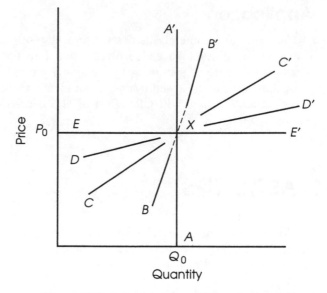

Figure 5.3 Supply curves through Point X

Supply curve AA' is perfectly inelastic. An example would be the supply of Vincent van Gogh's paintings. There are no more to be had, no matter how high the price is. Quantity is totally unresponsive to price! Supply curve DD' is more elastic than supply curve CC', which in turn is more elastic than supply curve BB'. To check this out, draw a horizontal price line slightly above P_0 and trace out the effect of the higher price. You should get the respective quantities supplied as having this relationship: $qd > qc > qb > q_0$. A given price increase increases Q^S more along curve D than curve C and more along C than curve B. Check this out in Figure 5.4.

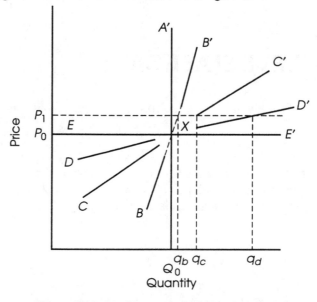

Figure 5.4 Supply curves through Point X

Supply curve EE' is perfectly elastic. The quantity response is so great it is essentially infinite. An example would be a good whose each added unit cost exactly the same to produce as the one before, no more or no less.

What makes a supply curve more elastic? That is, what keeps the marginal cost from rising as Q goes up? What keeps MC constant?

Factor 1: More Time

The more time a firm has, the easier it is to find the added resources it needs to produce additional units. This makes cost rise less. On the other hand, if the firm has to respond quickly to an unexpected increase in demand, it won't be able to expand its plant and equipment easily and instead will have to work at, near, or even above capacity. This causes marginal costs to escalate quickly, as in supply curve BB'. But over time, the industry can add to its workforce and its plants and equipment, so that in the long run (that is, over a period of several years), supply becomes more elastic, as in supply curve DD' or even EE' (which characterizes many industries in the long run).

Factor 2: The Good's Inputs Are in Elastic Supply

As the industry expands to increase supply, it must buy the various inputs (such as labor, plant, and equipment). If these inputs' prices stay the same and do not rise, the producers will be able to add new output at a marginal cost that is the same, or not too much higher, than that of previous units. The supply will be elastic. On the other hand, they may be a major purchaser of one of the good's inputs. For example, they could be one of a few buyers of a certain type of machinery, or they may be a large employer in their labor market. In these cases, buying more inputs may cause their prices to go up (for example, the industry may need to raise wages to get added workers). This raises costs and makes supply less elastic.

Factor 3: The Industry Is Below Capacity

If the industry is operating below its capacity, it can usually supply more output at the same or slightly higher marginal cost: The supply will be elastic. After capacity is hit, though, costs tend to rise dramatically as workers go on overtime, machines are overused, and inventories are depleted.

Factor 4: The Good Is Easy to Store

This rule applies to seasonal fluctuations in supply. If the good is easily stored, the industry can produce at a steady rate without taxing its capacity. Instead, it adds to inventories in low-demand periods and sells from inventory in high-demand periods. In this way, it keeps costs down and can meet spikes in demand at a low cost.

APPENDIX: MATH OF PERCENTS

Elasticity is the $\%\Delta Q$ divided by $\%\Delta$ in cause. The Δ term means change in. So $\%\Delta Q$ means percent change in Q where Q is quantity.

The math of percents follows.

First, the percent change in the product of two numbers (A times B) approximately equals the sum of the percent change in each number:

$$\%\Delta A \times B = \%\Delta A + \%\Delta B$$

For example, if prices go up 10% and output goes down 6%, then total sales ($P \times Q$) go up by 16%. If prices go up 10% and output falls by 14%, then total sales go down by 4%.

Second, the percent change in the ratio of A to B (A/B) approximately equals the percent change in A minus the percent change in B:

$$\%\Delta A/B = \%\Delta A - \%\Delta B$$

For example, if your wage goes up 10% but prices go up an average of 6%, your real wage (W divided by P) goes up by 4%.

CRIB NOTES

Elasticity: $\%\Delta Q$ divided by $\%\Delta$ in cause Δ = change in
Price elasticity of demand: $|\%\Delta Q^D/\%\Delta P|$ (|x| means make it a positive number).

Elastic if *Ed:P* > 1	**TR and P move opposite.**
Unitary elastic if *Ed:P* = 1	**TR constant no matter what P is.**
Inelastic if *Ed:P* < 1	**TR and P move together.**

Extremes: *Ed:P* = 0 **perfectly inelastic (curve vertical line).**
Ed:P = ∞ **perfectly elastic (curve horizontal line).**

Straight-line demand curve:

Ed:P = **Length of bottom segment/Length of top segment.**

More substitutes ⟶ more elastic.
More substitutes when (1) more time to adjust; (2) more information about substitutes; (3) good more narrowly defined; (4) larger share of income; (5) purchase can be put off (such as on durable goods like cars).

Income elasticity of demand: $\%\Delta Q^D/\%\Delta$Income

Ed:Inc > 1 **Superior**	**Share of income goes up when income up.**
1 > *Ed:Inc* > 0 **Necessity**	**Share goes down when income up.**
Ed:Inc > 0 **Normal**	**Q up when income up.**
Ed:Inc < 0 **Inferior good**	**Q (and share) down when income up.**

Cross-elasticity of demand for good X: *EdX:PY* = $\%\Delta Q^D x/\%\Delta Py$.

If *EdX:PY* > 0 X and Y **substitutes** (*Py* up, $Q^D x$ **up).**
If *EdX:PY* < 0 X and Y **complements** (*Py* up, $Q^D x$ **down).**

Price elasticity of supply: $\%\Delta Q^S/\%\Delta P$
Supply more elastic when (1) more time; (2) inputs in more elastic supply to industry; (3) industry more below capacity; (4) good easily stored (3, 4 applies to short term).

Extremes: Vertical supply line: *Es:P* = 0.
Horizontal supply line: *Es:P* = ∞.

Review Questions

1. Widget makers raise widget prices. Total widget sales go up. What can we conclude about the price elasticity of demand for widgets?

2. The elasticity of demand for electricity is 0.3 in the short run and 1.9 in the long run. Many utilities have invested in nuclear power, hoping they could lower their

costs. Instead, nuclear power turned out to be far costlier than expected. To pay for these higher costs, these utilities have raised their rates. Will raising rates help them? Answer for the short run and long run. To illustrate your answer, assume rates (i.e., price) went up 10%.

3. For the following demand curve, calculate the price elasticity of demand when the price falls from $5 to $4 and when it falls from $4 to $3. Calculate the elasticity using the old amount as the base and using the arc method. Also, use the point elasticity method (assuming the slope remains the same over this region) to calculate the elasticity at $5, $4, and $3.

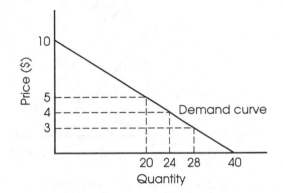

4. Employment (L) in an industry equals output (Q) times the workers per unit of output (wu). In percentage terms, $\%\Delta L = \%\Delta Q + \%\Delta wu$. An increase in productivity by 10% reduces wu by 10% (that is, 10% fewer workers per unit of output are needed). A 10% increase in productivity will reduce the cost and price of each unit of output by 10%. The lower price should cause output demanded to go up. How will increases in productivity affect employment when demand is elastic? When it is inelastic? Illustrate these answers by examining an elastic case ($Ed{:}P = 1.5$) and an inelastic case ($Ed{:}P = 0.5$).

5. How will the following events affect the elasticity of demand for beer?
Event one: at 8 P.M. on Friday night, beer prices at bars rise temporarily all over the nation until the next Sunday.
Event two: Beer spending as a fraction of income rises.
Event three: Consumers of beer come to regard white zinfandel wine as a fine substitute for beer.
Event four: State law prohibits advertising the price of beer.

6. For each group, indicate whether they are likely to be complements or substitutes. Indicate the likely sign of the cross-elasticity of demand.
Group A: Tires and cars
Group B: Cars and public transportation
Group C: Hondas and Toyotas
Group D: Mustard and hot dogs

7. When 25% of the Brazilian coffee harvest was wiped out by a cold wave, coffee bean prices went up 50%.
   a. What is the price elasticity of demand for Brazilian coffee beans?
   b. Using this price elasticity, what happened to the total dollar sales of Brazilian coffee beans?
   c. Why does Brazil sometimes destroy part of their coffee crop?

8. Richer persons buy more suits made out of natural fiber and spend a larger share of their income on them than do the rest of the population. On the other hand, they buy fewer suits with polyester in them. What is the income elasticity of demand for natural-fiber suits? For polyester suits?

9. Use the following graph to answer the question. It shows two demand curves, both with the same slope.

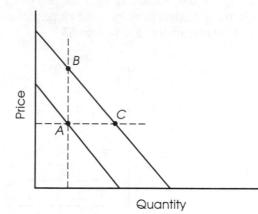

Between the following pairs of points select which has the higher elasticity:
(A) *B* or *C*
(B) *A* or *B*
(C) *A* or *C*

10. "I see in this textbook that the elasticity of demand for newspapers is 0.5. That means that it is inelastic. So, we at the *Gonzoville Gazette* should raise our prices to increase our total revenues." What is wrong with this statement?

11. If the demand curve for widgets is $P^D = 20 - 2Q$, what is the elasticity of demand at $P = \$12$?

12. Tony sells his pizza at \$10. He would get no business if he raised his price to \$15. If he gave away pizzas, he would give away 600 of them a day. If he faces a straight-line demand curve, what is his elasticity of demand?

13. What is the elasticity of the demand curve: $P^D = 200/Q$?

Answers

1. Demand must be inelastic. Total sales would only go up if the quantity went down less, in percent terms, than the price went up.
2. In the short run, the demand for electricity is inelastic: Higher rates will generate more revenues. But in the long run, the demand for electricity is elastic: The higher rates will cause total revenues to fall! They will be worse off than before (and will probably raise rates again!). For a 10% rate increase:
   When $Ed{:}P = 0.3$, Q will go down 3% and total revenue will go up 7%.
   When $Ed{:}P = 1.9$, Q will go down 19% and total revenue will do down 9%.
3. For \$5 to \$4: old *P* or *Q* as base $Ed{:}P = 20\%/20\% = 1.0$
   arc elasticity $Ed{:}P = 18.18\%/22.2\% = 0.818$

For \$4 to \$3: old P or Q as base $Ed{:}P = 16.7\%/25\% = 0.667$

arc elasticity $Ed{:}P = 15.38\%/28.57\% = 0.538$

Point elasticity: $Ed{:}P$ at \$5 = 1, $Ed{:}P$ at \$4 = 0.667, $Ed{:}P$ at \$3 = 0.429

4. Using the formula, we can see that output (Q) must go up by more than 10% if employment is not to fall. If demand is elastic, the quantity demanded will go up more (in percent terms) than the price goes down. Thus, output will go up by more than 10%, which more than offsets the reduction in *wu,* and thereby increases employment. If demand is inelastic, output will go up less than 10%, and employment will fall. In the elastic case when $Ed{:}P = 1.5$, output demanded will go up 15%, workers per unit output will go down 10% and, thus, summing these effects, employment will go up 5%. On the other hand, when demand is inelastic such that $Ed{:}P = 0.5$, output demanded will go up 5% while workers per unit output will go down 10%, with the result that employment will fall 5%. Fortunately, for most industries, demand is elastic (around 1.1) with the result that increases in productivity expand employment.

5. Event one: Less time to adjust $\longrightarrow$ more inelastic.

   Event two: Larger fraction of income $\longrightarrow$ more elastic.

   Event three: More substitutes $\longrightarrow$ more elastic.

   Event four: Less information $\longrightarrow$ more inelastic.

6. A and D: Complements, sign is negative.

   B and C: Substitutes, sign is positive.

7. a. $Ed{:}P = 25\%/50\% = 0.5$.

   b. Total revenue went up 25%.

   c. As long as demand is inelastic, cutting output will increase the price and, this, in turn, will raise total revenue. You might ask why Brazil doesn't always destroy part of its crop. The reason is that if coffee prices were permanently higher, more countries would begin to grow coffee beans, and there would be more substitutes for Brazil's beans. This, in turn, would make the demand for Brazil's beans more elastic. By rarely and randomly destroying the crop, Brazil discourages this from happening.

8. Natural-fiber suits are a luxury good as their share of income goes up. Polyester suits are an inferior good as fewer of them are bought.

9. Recall that $Ed{:}P = (1/|slope|) \times (P/Q)$. a. Demand is more elastic at point B than it is at point C because P/Q is bigger at B (and the slope's the same).

   b. Point B is more elastic than point A (Q is the same but P is higher at B).

   c. Point A is more elastic than point C (P is the same but Q is smaller at A).

10. The 0.5 figure means that when all newspapers raise their price by 1%, the demand for all newspapers goes down 0.5%. If only one newspaper, the *Gonzoville Gazette,* raises its price, its subscribers are likely to find many substitute newspapers elsewhere. This makes the price elasticity of demand for the *Gazette* much more elastic than the price elasticity for all newspapers together.

11. Solving the demand curve equation at $P = \$12$, $Q = 4$. Using equation 5, $Ed{:}P = (1/2)(12/4) = 6/4 = 1.5$. One can also divide the segments of the vertical axis: The top segment is \$8 (= \$20 − \$12), the bottom is \$12. So we have $Ed{:}P = 12/8 = 1.5$.

12. His demand curve is $P^D = 15 - 0.025Q$. Note that −0.025 is rise over run (or −15/600). At \$10, $Q = 200$. Using equation 5, $Ed{:}P = (1/.025)(10/200) = 2$.

13. $Ed{:}P = 1$ at all points. Just multiply both sides of the demand equation by Q and you get $P \times Q = 200$. No matter what the price, total revenue is \$200.

Chapter Six

The Theory of Demand

INTRODUCTION

A beggar asked me, "Can I have some change?" I shot back, "Why can't you accept things as they are!" But change is all that we as scientists can know. We can never really know things as they are, except to the degree that we can observe how things change in response to different changes.

Similarly, economists take consumers' taste as a given. Some people travel hundreds of miles to the beach only to swim in the motel pool. Some people put purple tile in their bathrooms. Some people eat and even like liver. I can't explain why, nor do I try. But there are two things we can observe. First, we can observe how consumers respond to changes in their income. Second, we can observe how consumers respond to changes in prices. Next, we can combine this information to predict the impact of various events, as all events can be broken down into two types of impacts: those due to income changes and those due to price changes. We add the effects up, and presto! We get our prediction! And we add, in small print, "assuming tastes don't change."

That is what this chapter is about. Breaking up events into these two changes to get predictions.

Now, here's a taste of the future. Remember that a higher price should reduce the quantity demanded. This is not always true. What happens to the gasoline purchases of an oil well owner when oil (and gasoline) prices double? Do they go down? Or, maybe, just maybe, do they go up? Stay tuned. In the meantime, use these fine examples to irritate your teacher.

PRICE

As Yogi Berra said, "It's getting so that a dime isn't worth a nickel anymore." Similarly, inflation makes the use of the actual price of a good meaningless when adjusted for inflation. After all, a good that cost $5 in 1890 cost more in a real sense than a $5 good in 1990.

To measure the real price of a good, we measure its price in comparison to other prices by dividing by an index of prices. Usually, the real price of a good is derived by dividing the good's dollar price by the Consumer Price Index (CPI) (which reflects the price of a basket of most consumer goods).

Another measure of the price of any good is its opportunity cost (recall that opportunity cost is the value of the best foregone alternative). For example, the price of a new TV set is the utility you would have gotten with the money had you spent it elsewhere. Similarly, the price of going to a free concert is the utility you would have gotten from what you would have done otherwise.

The real price of a good is its opportunity cost. To illustrate why, suppose we have the following prices for a can of beans:

		CPI as a price (Consumer Price Index/100)
Year	Price of beans	
One	$2.40	1.20
Two	$3.60	2.00

I've converted the CPI into a price by dividing it by 100[1]. In year one, for example, a basket of the consumer goods cost $1.20; in year two, the same basket cost $2. The real price of beans is $2.00 in year one ($2.40/1.20) and 1.80 in year two ($3.60/2.00). This also reflects the opportunity cost of beans. In year one, one could have had one can of beans or two baskets of consumer goods. In year two, one could have had one can of beans or 1.8 baskets of consumer goods. Now, I know you can't buy little baskets of consumer goods. These consumer baskets are an imaginary construct designed to make it easy for you to visualize our concepts. Relax and just go with it. Imagine there really are little baskets and that the CPI (divided by 100) is their price. Actually visualize these little baskets, with little appliances, miniature homes, tiny little groceries, and whatever. And see a price tag hanging over the side of the basket; on it is the consumer price index.

THE LAW OF DEMAND

The law of demand states that an individual will buy more of a good when its real price (or relative price) falls. A fall in a good's price brings about two changes that affect consumers:

Change 1: Income Effect

The fall in the good's price increases the real income of consumers. The resulting rise in the consumer's income has an income effect: they buy more of the good.

Now let's go through this slowly. Mr. Consumer is sitting in his kitchen when he reads that bread prices have fallen. Even though his money income is unchanged (as we assume he doesn't sell bread), the fall in the price of bread means his real income is now higher. His real income is the purchasing power of the money income. It is calculated by the money income divided by the consumer price index. For the average consumer, we use the Consumer Price Index. But each consumer has, in effect, their own price index. The bigger the share of the good in a consumer's spending, the more his own price index will be changed (%ΔPrice index = Good's share in spending × %ΔGood's price). Mr. Consumer calculates how much his real income has gone up and then decides how much of this he'll spend on bread. If bread is a normal good, he'll buy more. If it is inferior, he'll buy less. But sorry, Mr. Consumer! You aren't finished yet. Next, you have to add in the substitution effect.

---

[1]The Consumer Price Index is a price index of the goods consumed by an urban family of four. Its value in 1984 was 100; since then, due to inflation, its value has risen. In 1995, it had risen to 151. In ten years, prices had risen by 51%.

Change 2: The Substitution Effect

The substitution effect is the change in demand resulting from the change in the good's relative price, holding real income constant. When we say "holding real income constant," we mean that the income effect has been accounted for. The good's real price (its price divided by the Consumer Price Index) or its relative price (its price relative to other goods) has changed. When the good goes down in price while other goods' prices remain unchanged, it is now cheaper to buy, so people will buy more of it.

Mr. Consumer realizes that the 10% decrease in bread's price means he gives up 10% less now to get another loaf of bread. That is, the opportunity cost of bread has gone down since he has to give up less of other goods to get a loaf. What a deal! So he substitutes bread for other goods. (Hint: That's why we call it the substitution effect.)

To summarize, a lower price has two effects. First, it raises the consumer's real income. This leads to the income effect (more income, more of the good). Second, it lowers the real price of the good. This leads to the substitution effect (lower real price, more of the good). The change in the quantity demanded is the sum of these effects.

Table 6.1 summarizes these effects.

TABLE 6.1

Price Change	Type of Good	Income Effect (1)	Substitution Effect (2)	Net Effect on on Quantity (3) = (1) + (2)
Up	Normal	–	–	–
	Inferior	+	–	?
Down	Normal	+	+	+
	Inferior	–	+	?

Note the question mark in Table 6.1. This refers to a special case called the Giffen paradox. In this case, the good is an inferior good and the income effect is stronger than the substitution effect. A higher price reduces real income and if the good is inferior and the income effect is very, very strong, the higher price could lead to more of the good being bought. (Note: More refers to the quantity bought, not the dollar amount!) This case has rarely, if ever, been observed. In general, the substitution effect dominates when the good is inferior.

The law of demand will also be wrong if the consumer is also a seller of the good. In that case, the increase in the price of the good will increase the consumer's income and, if strong enough, cause him to buy more. For example, the owners of an oil well will have more income if the price of oil goes up. This income effect is likely to be strong enough to cause them to buy more oil (and products made from oil) despite their higher price and the substitution effect's impact.

So why do we call it the law of demand when it is sometimes violated? First, the law is really referring only to the substitution effect. Second, since when is a law always obeyed?

MEASURING THE CHANGE IN REAL INCOME

One way to measure the change in real income due to a change in a price is to calculate the change in real income (dollar income divided by a price index). A second way, which gives a slightly different answer, is to calculate the difference between the consumer's actual income and the income he would need to have to buy the same goods as he did before but at the new price. This difference is the change in real income due to the price change that is used to calculate the income effect.

Thought Questions

Suppose Mr. Consumer spends all his $100 weekly income on bread and on other goods. He buys 10 loaves of bread at $3 a loaf and buys $70 of other goods. The price of bread falls to $2. If he spends 40% of any new income on bread (in absence of a substitution effect), then what is the income effect for this price decrease?

At $2 a loaf, he needs to spend $20 to get the same ten loaves plus $70 to buy the same amount of other goods as before. This adds up to $90. So the change in real income is $10 (equal to $100, his current income, minus $90, what money he would now need to buy the same goods). With this $10, he would spend $4 on bread, which, at $2 a loaf, would buy two more loaves. So the income effect of the price decrease is plus two loaves.

Do the same for a price increase from $3 to $4.

Now he needs $40 to buy ten loaves plus $70, or $110. The change in income is −$10 ($100 − $110). So he'll spend $4 less on bread, which at $4 a loaf, means the income effect is minus one loaf.

USING INCOME AND SUBSTITUTION EFFECTS

Now that we have seen how to measure the change in real income, let us solve a few problems using income and substitution effects.

Thought Questions

Joe spends $100 a week. He spends $25 on bread, which costs $2.50 a loaf and the rest on orange juice, which costs $5 a bottle. How much of each is he buying? What is the relative price of bread? Its opportunity cost?

He is buying 10 loaves of bread ($25/$2.50) and 15 bottles of orange juice ($75/$5). The relative price of bread is 1/2 (= $2.50/$5.00). Bread's opportunity cost is one-half bottle of orange juice (the $2.50 spent on a loaf of bread would have bought half a bottle of orange juice). Both have to be the same number.

If the price of bread falls to $1, and he continues to buy the same quantities as before, how much money will be unspent? How is this like getting more income?

He was spending $2.50 × 10 on bread. In this hypothetical case, he would now be spending $1 × 10 on bread. That's a saving of $15. The decrease in the price of bread is like getting $15 in more income.

If he gets $1 more in income, he spends 50 cents of this on bread and 50 cents on orange juice. What is the income effect of the lower bread price?

He would spend $7.50 on bread, which at $1 a loaf, would buy 7.5 more loaves. The income effect is +7.5 loaves.

What is the new opportunity cost of bread? Suppose that for every 10% decrease in the price of bread he buys 5% more loaves than he did originally (this is in addition to the income effect you calculated previously). What is the substitution effect?

The new opportunity cost is $1.00/$5.00 or 0.2. Now he only has to give up one-fifth (or 0.2) of a bottle of orange juice to get a loaf of bread. The price has decreased by 60%, which means there will be a 30% increase in his bread demand because of the substitution effect. The substitution effect will be +3 loaves.

How many more loaves will he buy?

The income effect (+7.5) added to the substitution effect (+3) gives a net effect of +10.5. He'll now be buying 20.5 loaves of bread a week.

If gasoline prices go up 100%, how will the change in demand for gasoline differ between Alaska and North Carolina? One of Alaska's major industries is oil production, the profits of which are heavily taxed by Alaska and spread over its citizens. North Carolina has no oil industry.

The higher price of gasoline will make Alaskans richer and North Carolinians poorer. So the income effect in Alaska is likely to be positive while it is negative in North Carolina. Both states are likely to have similar substitution effects. Thus, the demand for gasoline is likely to go down by a larger percent in North Carolina.

Jacob only consumes two goods, hot dogs and hot dog buns. Both cost $1 each and he has $60 a day to spend on both. They are perfect complements: He consumes them in the fixed ratio of one hot dog to one hot dog bun, no matter what their relative price. What is the income effect and substitution effect of an increase in hot dog prices to $2 (buns still cost $1)?

Before the price increase, he consumed 30 hot dogs and 30 rolls. After the price increase, the pair costs $3 and so he buys 20 pairs ($60/$3): 20 hot dogs and 20 hot dog rolls. This is a pure income effect. There is no substitution effect because the ratio remains unchanged. The income effect can also be calculated as follows. The dollar increase in the price of hot dogs is like losing $30 in income if he continued to buy the same amount as before (30 dogs times $1 higher price). At the new price, he will cut back consumption of both by 10 ($30/$3) and consume 20 of each.

Mary has $8 to spend on cola (which costs $1 a bottle) and chips (which cost $2 a bag). With the $8, she buys four colas and two bags of chips. One week, she only has $6 to spend but is surprised to find that chips have gone down in price to $1 a bag. Note that she could, if she wants, still buy four colas and two bags of chips. If chips and colas are substitutes, will she? (Assume she can buy fractions of bottles or bags if she wants).

Whenever you see a problem like this, where income and some price both go down (or up) such that the person can buy the same quantities as before, be on alert! There is no income effect! If they could buy the same as before, their real income is unchanged! There is no change in real income and no income effect. This leaves only a substitution effect. Chips are now relatively cheaper, so she'll buy more chips and fewer colas. She'll substitute chips for colas.

Inflation increases every price by 10% and all incomes by 10%. How will this affect the demand for cars (the price of which has also gone up 10%).

Real income is unchanged so there is no income effect. The relative price of cars is unchanged so there is no substitution effect. The demand for cars will remain unchanged. This reflects the famous macroeconomics theory that if inflation is fully reflected in prices and income, it will have no real effect on the economy.

TOTAL AND MARGINAL UTILITY

Assume that a person's level of satisfaction can be measured in units of *utils*[2]. The person's goal is to get the highest number of utils as possible. *Total utility* measures a consumer's total satisfaction. When the consumer consumes another unit of a good, the total utility goes up: This addition to total utility is *marginal utility*. If 10 units of food provide 30 utils of satisfaction and if 11 units provide 35 utils, then the 11th unit's marginal utility is 5 utils (35 − 30).

The law of diminishing marginal utility states that as a person consumes more of a good in a given period, the total utility goes up but each added unit adds less to total utility than the previous unit did. So if the 11th unit of food adds 5 utils, the 12th unit of food will add less than 5 utils to total utility.

Note that as more is consumed, total utility goes up! What's diminishing is the addition to total utility.

Restated, the law of diminishing marginal utility says that as one consumes more of a good in a given period, the marginal utility of each added unit declines.

---

[2]In fact, there is no way we can directly measure utility or compare it between people. Nor can we measure how much it changes for someone else. On the other hand, all of us have some subjective sense of the relative utility we get from alternative goods. Assuming there are utils is more of an analogy used to illustrate how consumers maximize their net benefits.

THE LAW OF EQUIPROPORTIONAL MARGINAL BENEFIT

The consumer wants to get the highest total utility possible. So she must allocate her dollars between goods wisely. How to do this? First, we'll look at the rule and then a set of examples that show how the rule works.

First, calculate the marginal utility from each added unit of each good, divide this by the good's price: the resulting ratio is the marginal utility per dollar (called *MU/P*). Second, spend each dollar on the good with the highest marginal utility per dollar. (Note: That's marginal utility per dollar, not just marginal utility!)

Example 1

Marvin has $9 to spend on food and clothing. Each unit of food costs $1. Each unit of clothing costs $1. Marvin's total utility is the sum of the utility he gets from food and clothing. Table 6.2 shows his utilities. Be sure you can derive the marginal utility column where it is left blank. Show how much of each he should buy to maximize his utility.

TABLE 6.2

Food Units	Total Utility of Food	Marginal Utility	Clothing Units	Total Utility of Clothing	Marginal Utility
0	0	—	0	0	—
1	6	6	1	12	12
2	11	5	2	22	10
3	15	4	3	30	8
4	18	3	4	36	6
5	20	2	5	40	4
6	21	1	6	42	2

Divide the marginal utility by $1 for both food and clothing. In this case, the marginal utility per dollar is the marginal utility column in Table 6.2. Since *MU/P* for the first unit of clothing is highest (12 utils), the first $1 should be spent on clothing. The second dollar should also be used to buy clothing as the second unit has the highest marginal utility per dollar (10 utils). Similarly, the third $1 is best spent on clothing. The *MU/P* for the fourth unit of clothing equals the *MU/P* of the first unit of food (6 utils). So Marvin would be equally well-served by buying either. Let us, for illustrative purposes, choose food whenever there's a tie. So the fourth dollar is spent on unit 1 of food and the fifth dollar goes to unit 4 of clothing. The sixth dollar goes to the second unit of food (which now has the highest *MU/P* of 5 utils). The seventh and eighth dollars go to the third unit of food and the fifth unit of clothing (both provided 4 utils per dollar). The ninth dollar is best spent on the fourth unit of food (having 3 utils per dollar). Marvin will buy 4 units of food and 5 units of clothing. You should show that any change from this will make Marvin worse off (assuming he spends $9 and no more).

Example 2

Repeat the preceding example, but with the price of clothing being $2 a unit (food still costs $1 a unit). You should derive the *MU/P* columns now!

Table 6.3 shows the *MU/P* for both goods. Just go down each column in order of the highest *MU/P*. Stop when all $9 are spent. (Be careful: each unit of clothing costs $2.)

TABLE 6.3

Food Units	Marginal Utility per Dollar for Food	Clothing Units	Marginal Utility per Dollar for Clothing
0	—	0	—
1	6	1	6
2	5	2	5
3	4	3	4
4	3	4	3
5	2	5	2
6	1	6	1

Marvin will buy 3 units of food and 3 units of clothing, spending $3 on the food and $6 on clothing. His total utility is 45 utils (see Table 6.2). If he buys any other combination with his $9, he will be worse off. For example, with 5 units of food and 2 units of clothing (costing $9), his total utility will be 42. With 1 unit of food and 4 of clothing (costing $9), his total utility will be 42. In both cases, he gets a lower utility (42 instead of 45 utils).

Example 3

Let's change the price of food and clothing so that Marvin's real income is the same as in Example 2. (That is, he can, with his $9, still buy 3 units of each.) Why are we doing this? To eliminate the income effect and show why the substitution effect occurs. Let the price of food be $2 and the price of clothing be $1. The result should show more clothing being bought than in Example 2. You should be able to derive the *MU/P* columns from Table 6.2.

Here's the new *MU/P* table (Table 6.4). Go in order of the highest *MU/P* (perhaps crossing the highest off) until all $9 is spent.

TABLE 6.4

Food Units	Marginal Utility per Dollar	Clothing Units	Marginal Utility per Dollar
0	—	0	—
1	3	1	12
2	2.5	2	10
3	2	3	8
4	1.5	4	6
5	1	5	4
6	0.5	6	2

The result is Marvin will buy 2 units of food and 5 units of clothing. He spends $4 on food and $5 on clothing. This is a pure substitution effect: The higher price of food reduces the units bought in Example 2 from 3 to 2. His total utility is 51 (see Table 6.2). He would have been worse off staying where he was in Example 2 (3 and 3) where his total utility was 45. You should show that any other mix of goods that costs a total of $9 yields a lower utility than 51 (gotten with 2 and 5).

What results do these examples illustrate? First, total utility is maximized by buying goods with the highest marginal utility per dollar. The last unit of a good bought should have the highest or the same MU/P as any other good not yet bought.

The preceding example used discrete units of goods. If the units of goods can be divided up such that fractional amounts can be bought, the consumer will buy each good so that on the margin, they get the same marginal utility per dollar from all goods. Any shift, no matter how small, can make them worse off. Hence, the law of equal marginal benefits per dollar (or the law of equiproportional marginal benefits, where the proportional marginal benefit is marginal utility per dollar).

Thought Questions

Jodi spends all her income on two goods: clothing and food. The marginal utility from the last unit of clothing is 10 utils. The last unit of food increases her utility by 20 utils. Clothing costs $5 per unit. Food costs $8 per unit. Is she spending her money wisely? How should she shift?

Set up Table 6.5 to solve this type of problem.

TABLE 6.5

Food	Clothing	Food
Marginal Utility	10	20
Price ($)	5	8
MU/P	2	2.5

Look at the last row. It is the first divided by the second. Food has the higher marginal utility per dollar: It's a better deal. By reallocating one dollar away from clothing (which reduces total utility by 2 utils) and spending on food (which increases total utility by 2.5 utils), Jodi is better off (by 0.5 units). So she should buy more food and less clothing. Special warning: Multiple choice trap answer is "buy more food and more clothing to be better off." This answer is wrong, wrong, wrong. She already is spending all her money. If she buys more of one, she must buy less of the other. This type of question always calls for more of one and less of the other.

A grocery store has a fixed amount of shelf space, which it measures by square feet. If the last square foot of shelf space allocated to milk adds $20 a month to its profits and the last square foot of shelf space allocated to cola adds $50 to its profits, how should the store reallocate its shelf space?

It should allocate more space to cola and less to milk. On the margin, the last square foot added to each should yield the same (or close to the same) addition to profits. Note: We do not look at average profit per square foot or the total profit per item. We focus on the margin and what it adds to profits! This is the law of equiproportional benefit applied.

How should you allocate your time among questions on a test? Should you spend more time on the questions with the highest points?

The last minute spent on each question should yield the same addition to your total score; otherwise, you should reallocate your time. (This is equivalent to what we already derived: The last dollar spent on each good should add the same to total utility.) You should not necessarily spend more time on the questions with the highest points. Suppose you have 3 minutes to take a quiz. Question 1 is worth 90 points. The first minute on this question adds 60 points to your score; the second minute adds 1 point. Question 2 is worth 10 points. The first minute adds 6 points; the second minute, 4 points. Using the marginal points per minute rule, you should spend 1 minute on question 1 and 2 minutes on question 2, giving you a total score of 70 points. Any other allocation lowers your score.

THE LAW OF DEMAND AND MARGINAL UTILITY

As we've seen, consumers who want to maximize their utility will allocate their spending on all goods such that the last dollar spent on each good yields the same increase in utility. If this were not the case, they could be better off by reallocating the dollars with low marginal utility uses toward higher valued uses. For example, if the last dollar spent on good X produces 3 utils and the last dollar spent on good Y produces 7 utils, then by taking the last X dollar and spending it on Y will increase utility by a net of 4 utils ($= 7 - 3$).

Therefore, the consumer should have equal MU/P for all goods:

$$\frac{MU_X}{P_X} = \frac{MU_X}{P_Y}$$

To show the law of demand, let the price of X fall. We now have

$$\frac{MU_X}{P_X} > \frac{MU_X}{P_Y}$$

Now, the last dollar spent on good X yields more than the last dollar on good Y. The consumer can now increase the utility by redirecting dollars toward good X. As this happens, the MU_X falls and the MU_Y rises (both as a result of the law of diminishing MU). This continues until all goods once again have the same MU/P.

CONSUMER SURPLUS

Recently, I went to buy a hard disk for my computer. I was willing to pay up to $1,000 for it. But to my surprise, it only cost $300. I was better off by $700. This $700 reflects the net benefit I got from buying the hard disk. It is a measure of how much better off I was as a consumer. Now we turn to consumer surplus, which is a similar measure we can use for all goods.

Consumer surplus is the dollar net benefit a consumer gets from consuming a good:

Consumer surplus = Total benefit − Total cost,

where benefits and costs are measured in dollars.

Since consumer surplus is the same as the consumer's net benefit, the consumer uses marginal analysis to maximize consumer surplus. This goes step by step, adding one unit of the good. Each added unit increases total benefit: This is that unit's marginal benefit. The marginal benefit of the good is its demand price (defined as the most the person would pay for another unit of the good). Each unit adds to total cost: This is the unit's marginal cost. In most cases, each unit of the good costs the same. So its marginal cost equals the actual price paid. The consumer buys another unit as long as

Demand price (= Marginal benefit) ⩾ Price paid

as

Increase in consumer surplus = Demand price − Price paid

The consumer stops buying when the demand price equals price paid (or as close to this as possible without the price exceeding the demand price).

Example 1

Ms. Consumer is willing to pay up to $10 for the first unit of food, $9 for the second unit, $8 for the third, and so forth (each consecutive unit worth $1 less than the previous unit). Food costs $4 a unit. How many units will Ms. Consumer buy? What is her consumer surplus?

She will buy 6 units. The sixth unit's marginal benefit is $4 and its cost is $4, so she'll buy it (we assume if the benefit covers the cost, it will be bought). The total benefit is $49 ($10 + $9 + $8 + $7 + $6 + $5 + $4)[3]. The total cost is $24 ($4 × 6 units). The consumer's net benefit or consumer's surplus is $25 ($49 − $24).

Example 2

What is the consumer's surplus in the graph shown in Figure 6.1?

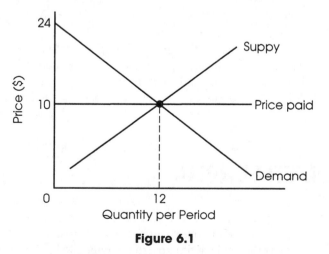

Figure 6.1

---

[3]Whenever you get a sequence like this, add the first and last number (here, their sum is 14). The next "end" pair, as you go in one, sums also to 14. Keep going. There are 3 such pairs here plus the middle 7. So the total sum is 3 × 14 + 7.

The height of the demand curve reflects marginal benefit of the unit on the horizontal axis. Ten dollars is the price paid per unit. This will buy 12 units at $10. So total cost is $120 ($10 × 12). But what is the total benefit? It is the area under the demand curve. If we sum the demand prices, we get total benefit. Summing the demand prices on this graph is equivalent to calculating the area under the demand curve (just as the area under the $10 line shows the total cost to the consumer). Now, let us return to high school geometry, which I know you loved and remember. The area under the demand curve forms what is widely known as a trapezoid with a base of 12 and a height on the left side of $24 and a height on the right side of $10. Let's turn it into a rectangle. Its average height is $17 (the average of $24 and $10). Its base is 12 units. So its area is base times average height or 12 × $17 or $204. This gives a consumer surplus of $84 (= total benefit minus total cost or $204 − $120).

The consumer surplus also equals the area between the demand curve and the $10 line. See the shaded area in Figure 6.2. This area is a triangle with a base of 12 and a height of $14. A triangle is half a rectangle, so its area is half that of a rectangle:

Area of triangle = 1/2 × 12 × $14 = $84

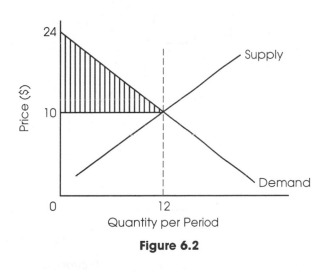

Figure 6.2

MARKET DEMAND IS SUM OF DEMANDS

So far, we have focused upon one consumer. Once we have the demand curve for one consumer, we get the demand curves for all consumers by adding these curves up in the same way the town crier did for the Demanders' Hall: At each price, you find out how much each demander wants to buy and then add these numbers up to get how much the market wants at that price. If we were using graphs, we would have the demand curves together horizontally. So if at $P = \$4$, Mr. A wants 6 widgets and Mr. B wants 2, the market demand curve for Mr. A and Mr. B together is a demand for 8 widgets at $4.

APPENDIX: INDIFFERENCE CURVE ANALYSIS

Some texts use indifference curves to present the theory of demand. An indifference curve shows the various combinations of goods that yield the same level of utility to a consumer. The name *indifference* refers to the fact that the consumer doesn't care which combination of goods he or she gets if they are all along the curve. That's because they all yield the same utility. These curves are sometimes called utility curves.

An Indifference Curve

Figure 6.3 shows one indifference curve.

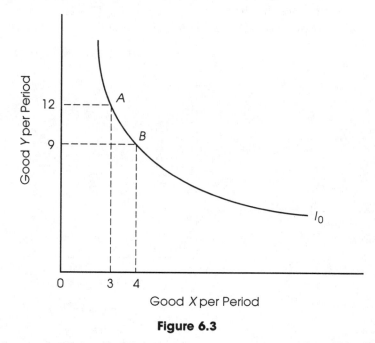

Figure 6.3

Points to note:

The consumer gets the same utility at point A (12 Ys and 3 Xs) that they do at point B (only 9 Ys but 4 Xs).

They are indifferent between point A and point B.

All points above I_0 make the consumer better off.

All points below I_0 make the consumer worse off.

A consumer who is at point A is willing to trade 3 units of Y to get the fourth unit of X (moving from point A to B).

At point A, the consumer's demand price for 1 more X is 3 Y: A lower price would make them better off; a higher price, worse off.

The slope of I_0 between points A and B is (approximately) -3.

The demand price for X equals the positive value of the slope (i.e., 3). The demand price is not in dollars but in units of Y.

As you move to the right on I_0, the slope becomes flatter. This reflects the law of demand. The demand price for X falls as the consumer has more X.

Many Indifference Curves

For every level of utility, there is a separate and distinct indifference curve. Several of the curves are shown in Figure 6.4.

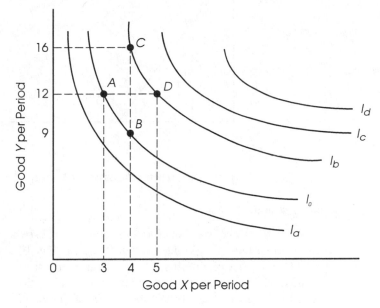

Figure 6.4

Points to note:

Indifference curves are like height lines on a map: A given line shows a given height, and higher lines show the consumer reaching greater heights of satisfaction.

Curve I_a shows a lower level of utility than curve I_0.

Curve I_b shows a higher level of utility (as do I_c and I_b).

Point C shows a higher level of utility than point B because the consumer has more Y (16 instead of 12 units) and the same amount of X (4 units).

Point D shows a higher level of utility than point A because the consumer has more X (5 units instead of 3) and the same Y (12 units).

Indifference curves do not cross or touch: Higher curve must always show a higher utility.

Crossing curves is a no-no! A definite no-no. I mean it! If you do, I'll tell Mom!

Budget Constraint

The budget constraint shows the combinations of goods the consumer can buy with his current income. It's a constraint because the consumer could buy less than his income but not more! That is, no borrowing! We assume he spends all his income on goods X and Y. These assumptions keep the analysis simple and give reasonable predictions.

Figure 6.5 shows the budget constraint for a consumer who earns $100 a day, where the price of Y is $10 and the price of X is $20.

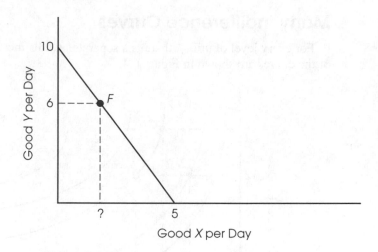

Figure 6.5 Budget Constraint Facing Consumer

Points to note:

At any point on the budget constraint, the consumer is spending $100.

If the consumer buys only good Y and no X, he can buy 10 units of Y (= income divided by the price of Y): This is the vertical intercept.

If the consumer buys only good X and no Y, he can buy 5 units of X (= income divided by the price of X): This is the horizontal intercept.

The slope of the budget constraint is –2 (a rise of –10 as X runs 5 units from 0 to 5).

The consumer must give up 2 units of Y to get 1 more unit of X.

The supply price of X is 2; this price is in units of Y, not in dollars.

The supply price equals the price of X divided by the price of Y.

How many units of X can the consumer buy if he is at point F? To solve this, solve for how much he is spending on good Y (6 units cost $10 each so she is spending $60 on Y). Subtract this from income to get $40 being spent on good X. Good X costs $20 per unit, so this $40 buys 2 units of X. So the question mark can be replaced with 2.

An increase in income would move the whole budget constraint up and to the right without changing its slope.

An increase in the price of X would leave the vertical intercept unchanged but would cause the curve to become steeper, moving the horizontal intercept to the left.

An increase in the price of Y would leave the horizontal intercept unchanged but would cause the curve to become flatter, moving the vertical intercept down.

Utility Maximization

The indifference curves show what the consumer wants: The higher the better. The budget constraint shows what the consumer can get. So given that they are on budget constraint, the consumer tries to get to the highest indifference curve possible. Figure 6.6 shows the results. Point E shows the highest level of utility the consumer can achieve given his income and the prices of goods X and Y. The consumer is said to be in equilibrium at point E: He doesn't want to move because any move off point E along the budget constraint makes him worse off. Figure 6.6 shows the consumer demanding 3 units of good X.

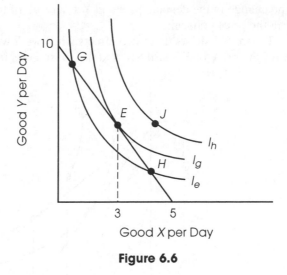

Figure 6.6

Points to note:

I_g is the highest indifference curve the consumer can get.

The consumer would prefer to be at point J, but he does not have enough income to reach that point.

The consumer could be at point G or point H, but these have a lower utility than he can achieve at point E.

If, at any point on the budget constraint, the indifference curve cuts through the budget constraint (such as at point G or H), the consumer can move to a higher curve.

At point E, where the highest achievable utility is reached, the indifference curve does not cut through the budget constraint. Instead, it is tangent (that is, it just touches the curve once)[4].

At point E, the demand price for good X (the positively stated slope of the indifference curve) equals its supply price (the positively stated slope of the budget constraint). The consumer is in equilibrium.

At point G, the demand price exceeds the supply price: The consumer moves toward more X.

At point H, the supply price exceeds the demand price: The consumer moves toward less X.

Showing the Effects of Lower Price

The income and substitution effects of a lower price can be illustrated in various ways with indifference curve analysis. We will choose one of the more common ways. The substitution effect is shown by changing the slope along a given utility curve. The change in slope is due to the change in price. The substitution effect is now defined as the change in the demand for good X due to a change in the price of X, holding the consumer's utility level constant. The income effect is shown by changing utility curves such that one is at the same slope on each curve. The income effect is now defined as

---

[4]There are two exceptions to this tangency condition. First, the indifference curve may not be nice and smooth as we show it. It may be jagged. At point E, it may not be tangent, but the highest curve will still touch the budget constraint once while lower curves will cut through the budget constraint. Second, the consumer may be in a corner, such that he buys all of one good and none of the other. For example, if the demand price for X exceeds the supply price of X at all points, the consumer will buy all X. Tangency will not be achieved. But the not-cut-through condition will hold.

the change in the demand for good X as a result of the resulting change in utility, holding the price constant.

Figure 6.7 shows these two effects when we lower the price of good X from $20 to $10; the price of Y is still $10 and the consumer's income is $100.

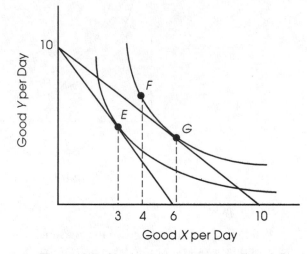

Figure 6.7 Slope same at points *E* and *F*

Points to note:

Total effect of lower price: Point E to point G, demand for X up 3 units.
Income effect: Point E to point F, income effect increases X demanded by 1 unit.
Substitution effect: Point F to point G, substitution effect increases X demanded by 2 units.

Special Case

If an event changes prices but lets the consumer still buy what she bought before, we say there is no income effect. That is, if the consumer does not change, she will have the same utility as before. But the new prices, no matter what they are, will allow her to move to a higher utility. The direction and extent of the move will be mainly determined by the substitution effect (although there is a small, very small, income effect). In Figure 6.6, the consumer had $100 in income and the price of X was $20 a unit and the price of Y was $10 a unit. The consumer bought 4 units of Y (show this) and 3 units of X. Figure 6.8 shows the effect when the price of good X falls to $10 but income falls by $30. With $70, the consumer can still buy 3 units of X (costing $30) and 4 units of Y (costing $40).

The new budget constraint goes from point $X = 0$, $Y = 7$ to point $X = 7$, $Y = 0$. The consumer can still be, if she wants, at point E. But now the old indifference curve cuts through this new budget constraint. So we know the consumer can move to a higher utility. In this case, anyplace along the line segment between E and K will yield a higher utility than before. Exactly where depends on where the new tangency point will be (not shown). But we see in Figure 6.8 that when the consumer moves to segment EK, more X will be demanded. This is a substitution effect.

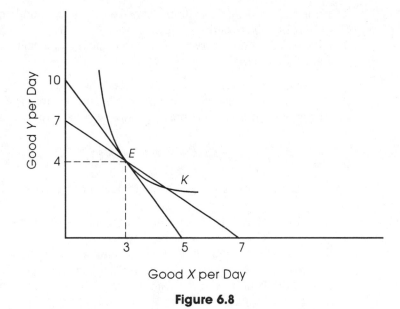

Figure 6.8

The Easy Case

To make the use of indifference curves easier, here's a simple trick. Suppose we are interested in good X only. We assume the consumer spends all his income on good X and on other goods. Now here's the trick: Define each unit of other good so that each unit costs $1. Now let's look at what this does for us. Mr. Consumer spends $200 a week on X and other goods. The price of X is $40 a unit. Figure 6.9 shows the results.

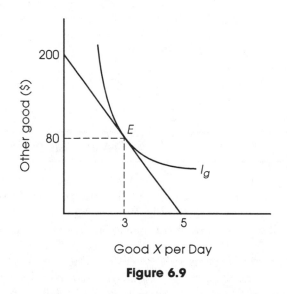

Figure 6.9

Points to note:

The vertical intercept is his dollar income. Why? Because $200 buys 200 units of other goods.

He buys 80 units of the other goods. Why? He's spending $120 on good X (3 × $40) so he's spending $80 on the other good.

The difference between the vertical intercept and $80 is the amount he's spending on good X ($120).

The slope of the budget constraint, stated as a positive number, is the supply price of good *X* in dollars (here, it's 40).

The slope of the utility curve (stated as a positive number) is the demand price for good *X* in dollars!

By using the convention that other goods cost $1, we've gotten rid of the relative price and can substitute the actual price. This makes this type of graph much easier to use. I suggest you repeat the previous two sections, letting good *Y* be all other goods.

CRIB NOTES

Change in Price: Has two effects on Q^D: Income effect + Substitution effect.

Income effect: Due to the change in real income = ($Income/Price index).

If normal good: Lower price, higher real income, demand up.

If inferior good: Lower price, higher real income, demand down.

Substitution effect: Due to change in relative price (Price of good/Other prices).

Higher price, reduction in demand.

Giffen good: Inferior good plus strong income effect leads to lower price decreasing demand.

Marginal utility: Per dollar determines how dollars allocated. Allocate to highest *MU/P* good yet unbought. On margin, all goods yield same *MU/P*.

Law of equiproportion marginal benefit: Allocate resource to alternative uses until that marginal unit adds same total benefit in each use. If unit = $, spend income until get same *MU/P* on all goods.

Consumer surplus: Dollar net benefit of good to consumer

Consumer surplus = Total benefit − Total cost = Area of triangle

Total benefit = Sum of demand prices = Area under demand curve

Total cost = Price paid × Quantity = Area under price paid line.

Review Questions

1. Mad Max has $100 a week to spend, and at $2 a bottle, he buys 20 bottles of beer. If you gave Max another $20, he would spend $10 of it on beer. The price of beer then falls to $1 a bottle. What is the income effect of this price increase? What is the substitution effect if he then consumes 35 bottles of beer?

2. Mad Max earns $500 a week, of which he spends $100 on having fun and $400 on other goods. A unit of fun costs $20. Then the price of fun goes up to $40 a unit. At the same time, and as a result of totally unrelated reasons, he gets a raise and his income goes up to $600 a week. So, if he wants to, he can still buy 5 units of fun and $400 of other goods. But will he? What effect, the income or substitution effect, is in effect here?

3. Salt today represents a very small fraction of a consumer's budget. But prior to modern times, salt was used to preserve meat and feed cattle and as an important

spice. Wars were fought over salt mines, and revolutions were fomented by taxes on salt. Describe the income effect of a higher price of salt in today's world and in premodern times. When will it be bigger?

4. The government increases the tax on food. It takes the proceeds and returns it to the citizens in the form of valued goods and services (assume, for this example, that every dollar of government goods and services is valued by the public at $1). What is the likely income and substitution effect of this event?

5. Joe spends all his income on beer and pretzels. The marginal utility from beer is 12 utils. The addition to total utility from the marginal bag of pretzels is 15 utils. Beer costs $3 a bottle. Pretzels cost $5 a bag. Is Joe maximizing his utility? If not, how can he do better?

6. True or false: If the consumer is maximizing utility such that the MU/P for all goods is equal, then if a unit of good X costs twice as much as a unit of good Y, then X's marginal utility should be twice that of good Y.

7. True or false: If the consumer is maximizing utility such that MU/P for all goods is equal, then if good X costs twice as much as a unit of good Y, good X's total utility should be twice that of good Y's.

8. The government mandates various safety standards, all of which cost money and save lives. Holding the amount being spent on safety constant, how should safety standards be set? Assume the only goal is to save lives. That is, to make this a simpler question, we are purposely ignoring the value of reducing accident injuries and lost work time.

9. Mary is CEO of a large corporation. She allocates her time between marketing and production. Assume she works a nine-hour day. The following table shows the total product of her hours spent in each activity. Which activity is more important (in terms of total product). Which should she spend more hours on?

Hours on Marketing	Total Productivity of Marketing Hours (millions)	Hours on Production	Total Productivity of Production Hours (millions)
0	—	0	—
1	12	1	8
2	20	2	14
3	24	3	18
4	25	4	20
5	25.5	5	21

10. The average consumer values going to the park at $10 for the first hour, $8 for the second hour, and so on (decreasing in increments of $2 for each added hour). Going to the park is free (its price is $0 per hour). How many hours will the consumer go to the park? What is the consumer surplus? If a town is building a park, how does it put a value on the benefits when the price is free?

11. The demand curve for widgets is $P^D = 20 - 2Q$. The price is $8. What is the consumer surplus for widgets?

12. Bill's demand price for a box of widgets is $10 for the first box and $5 for a second box. If he can buy one box for $8 or two boxes for $6 each, how many boxes will he buy?

13. Mary values one golf game a month at $50, a second game at $40, a third at $30, a fourth at $20, a fifth at $10, and a sixth at −$10 (she would pay $10 to not play a sixth game in a month's time). The golf course is the only one Mary can play at. It is private and charges monthly dues, but members can play for free. What is the maximum monthly dues it can charge Mary?

14. Assume utility can be measured in utils. If the last dollar spent on good X has a marginal utility of 5 utils and the last dollar spent on good Y yields 3 utils, then how can the consumer make themselves better off? By how much?

15. Assume utility can be measured in utils. Both good X and good Y have the following utility:

Units of Good	Marginal Utility
1	9
2	6
3	4
4	3
5	2.5
6	2

   a. The consumer has an income of $12. The price of X and the price of Y are both $2. How many units of each will the consumer buy?
   b. If the price of X and the price of Y both fall to $1, how many units of both good will the consumer buy? Is this an income or substitution effect?
   c. Starting with part a., assume instead that the price of X rises to $3 but the price of good Y falls to $1. How many units of each will the consumer buy? Is this an income or substitution effect?

16. Mary's goal is to maximize her lifetime income, which equals her current income plus all future incomes. She is in school and has to decide whether to spend her time studying or working. But her time is limited. How should she make this decision, given her goal?

17. The following shows the cost per premature death averted for various regulations. Given the cost of imposing these regulations on the economy, how could the money be better spent if the goal is to reduce the number of premature deaths?

Regulation	Cost per Premature Death Averted ($)
EPA Arsenic Emission Standards	13.5 million
EPA Dichloropropane Drinking Water Standards	653 million
OSHA Formaldehyde Occupational Exposure Limit	82.2 billion
EPA Wood Preserving Chemical Standards	5.7 trillion

Answers

1. If he continued to buy 20 bottles, he would save $20. This is like getting $20 in added income, of which he'll spend $10 on beer. At $1 a bottle, the income effect is +10 bottles. The substitution effect is the remainder: +5 bottles. These add up to +15, the increase in beer consumption (from 20 to 35).

2. Because Mad Max can buy the same amount of fun and other goods as before, his real income is unchanged. So there is no income effect. But there is a substitution effect. The higher price of fun will cause him to buy less fun and more of the other goods. His spending on other goods will increase above $400.

3. It will be bigger, and much more negative, in premodern time. The larger the good's share in income, the more its higher price will reduce real income. Recall the equation %Δ Price index = Good's share × %Δ Good's price. For a given price increase, the bigger the share, the more the price index goes up. The more the price index goes up, the more real income falls.

4. People's income will not be dramatically changed, if at all. They are paying more taxes, but they are getting them back in the form of more government goods and services (by assumption, at least). So the income effect is zero (or very small). On the other hand, the substitution effect still exists. This will cause people to buy less food. Most taxes involve mainly substitution effects, not income effects.

5. Construct the following table:

Good	Beer	Pretzels
Marginal Utility	12	15
Price ($)	3	5
MU/P	4	3

He is not maximizing his utility. The last dollar spent on beer gives him more utility. He should buy more beer and fewer pretzels.

6. True. If $\dfrac{MU_X}{P_X} = \dfrac{MU_Y}{P_Y}$, then, solving for P_x/P_y, we have $\dfrac{P_X}{P_Y} = \dfrac{MU_X}{MU_Y}$

Thus, if X's price is twice that of Y's, then, at the optimal level of consumption, X's marginal utility will be twice that of Y's. Note that this relationship holds only at the optimal level of consumption and assumes X and Y are easily divisible. If they come in discrete units, this relationship will likely be an approximation.

7. False. Total utility need not be proportional to marginal utility. For example, for good X, unit 1 may have a marginal utility of 9 and the second unit a marginal utility of 8. For good Y, unit 1 has a marginal utility of 4. If X costs $2 a unit and Y costs $1 a unit and the consumer has $5 to spend, he will buy 2 units of X and 1 of Y (prove this!). The total utility from X is 17 utils; from Y it is 4. This refutes question 7's assertion.

8. On the margin, the last dollar cost mandated by each safety standard should yield the same reduction in deaths. (To make this more realistic, the last million dollars mandated by each standard should yield the same reduction in deaths.) To illustrate, using this lives saved standard, fewer restrictions should be put on pollution and more money spent on providing ambulances to rural communities.

9. You need to first calculate the addition to total product (called the *marginal product*) of each hour as shown in the following table:

Hours on Marketing	Marginal Product of Marketing Hours (millions)	Hours on Production	Marginal Product of Production Hours (millions)
0	—	0	—
1	12	1	8
2	8	2	6
3	4	3	4
4	1	4	2
5	0.5	5	1

Next, starting with the first hour, allocate each added hour to the most productive use. The first hour goes to marketing, the next two are split between marketing and production, and so forth. When all nine hours are allocated, she should be spending four hours on marketing and five hours on production. In total dollars, marketing is worth more (25 million versus 21 million for production). But she spends more on production because it is marginal product, not total product, that determines where each added hour should be spent. The process of going from highest and then down the list is for expositional purposes and does not imply any particular time line. She can do all marketing for four hours and then spend five hours on production, or do production first, or mix them up in any order she finds useful.

10. The consumer will spend six hours in the park (an acceptable answer is five hours, but we assume someone does something if its value covers its cost, which the sixth hour does). The consumer surplus is the total benefit in this case as the total cost is zero. It equals $10 + $8 + $6 + $4 + $2 + $0 = $30. This is how much the consumer would pay as an entry fee to go into the park. Using this consumer surplus (times the number of annual visits) is a way the town can put a value on the benefits of building the park. Consumer surplus is used to value many public projects when there is no price.

11. Solve for Q. $8 = 20 - 2Q$, so $Q = 6$. Next, calculate the area of the following triangle: $1/2 \times \$12 \times 6 = \$36$. This is the consumer surplus shown in the following figure.

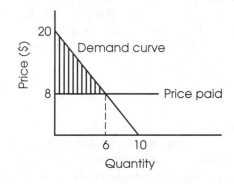

12. He'll buy two boxes. He'll take the offer with the higher consumer surplus (or net benefit). The consumer surplus of the first offer is $2 ($10 − $8). The consumer surplus for the second offer is $3 ($15 − $12). Marginal analysis can also be used. The marginal benefit of the second box is $5. Its marginal cost (the increase in total cost) is $4 ($12 for 2 − $8 for 1) so he will buy the second box.

13. If each game is free, she will play five games a month. Her total benefit from playing would be $150 ($50 + $40 + $30 + $20 + $10). So the dues could be as high as $150 a month and she would still join. Her consumer surplus would be reduced to zero in this extreme case. Note that if the club charged a per game fee instead of dues, they would get less per month.

14. Take the last dollar spent on good Y. This reduces utility by 3 utils. Next, spend it on good X. This increases utility by 5 utils. On net, the consumer's utility goes up 2 utils.

15. a. The consumer will buy 3 units of X and 3 units of Y, the last dollar spent on each having an MU/P of 2 utils per dollar. The full income of $12 will be spent.
    b. Now the consumer will buy 6 units of both goods, the last dollar spent on each having an MU/P of 2 utils per dollar. This is a pure income effect because the relative price of good X (P_X/P_Y) is unchanged.
    c. The consumer will buy 6 units of good Y and 2 units of good X, the last dollar spent on each having an MU/P of 2 utils per dollar. There is no income effect as the consumer is still able to buy 3 units of X and 3 units of Y with their $12. So the increase in demand for Y is a substitution effect.

16. She should use the rule of equiproportional marginal benefit. She should allocate her limited resource (time) to her activities (studying and working) so that the last hour of each increases her lifetime income the same amount. So the increase in her income from working should equal the increase in her income from studying (which increases her future income due to passing and getting better grades). For example, if her current wage is $12 an hour, her last hour of studying should increase her future income by $12.

17. Total deaths could be reduced by shifting regulations from the more expensive to the least expensive per death. These figures suggest that there is a serious misallocation of resources, with the result that more people are dying than need be.

Chapter Seven

Short-Run Output and Costs

INTRODUCTION

Most texts present this material in two chapters, separating the output material from the cost material. As a result, most students are left in a complete fog as to why they are studying output until they get to the next chapter. Instead, we'll combine output and how it affects cost. This chapter will cover output and cost over a short period (the *short run*). The next chapter covers output and costs when the firm has plenty of time to adjust to any changes (the *long run*).

But why study output and costs? Because we want to predict how events affect the supply price of goods. The supply price reflects the marginal cost of the good. In turn, marginal cost is determined by the productivity of inputs and the cost of inputs.

We also want to know how costs change with output. The faster they rise, the steeper the supply curve.

The next three chapters each contain lots of material. I suggest the following approach. Read it through quickly pretending that you understand it. Then reread it carefully, redrawing the graphs and redoing the various tables. Then check your knowledge by doing the problems at the end of each chapter. I also suggest you keep mentally separate the short-run material from the long-run material.

TIME AND COST

The more time a producer has to plan and acquire the best mix of inputs, the lower the unit cost will be. On the other hand, the less time a producer has to adjust, the higher the unit cost will likely be. There is a rather famous office cartoon showing a roundish character bouncing all over the page, laughing, with the caption, "You want it WHEN?" Haste does make waste—and higher costs.

To focus on the important element of time, we will break time into two extremes: the short run and the long run.

1. Short run is the period of time when the firm increases some but not all of its inputs to produce more output (or decreases some but not all of its inputs to produce less). Usually, a firm will meet a temporary increase in demand for output by paying their workers to work overtime. But most likely, it will leave plant size and equipment unchanged.
2. Long run is the period of time when the firm increases all inputs in the most efficient manner possible to produce more outputs. Labor, materials, plant size, the number of plants, equipment, advertising, training, staff, and managers can all be changed in the long run.

In this chapter, we will focus on short-run outputs and short-run costs. The next chapter will cover the long-run relationships. This will help keep the short-run material separate from the long-run material in your mind. This, in turn, will reduce your confusion.

To avoid the confusion between total cost and the cost per unit, we'll use the term *unit cost* to refer to the cost per unit. Total cost is the cost for all the units produced.

SHORT-RUN OUTPUT AND COSTS

The rest of this chapter focuses on short-run costs. We assume the firm's plant and equipment is in place along with any other inputs that would prove too costly to change for a temporary increase in output.

Since the supply curve reflects marginal cost, we focus on marginal cost. Marginal cost (*MC*) is the increase in total cost due to increasing output by one unit. If five units have a total cost of $50 and six units raise total costs to $59, then the marginal cost of the sixth unit is $9.

Variable inputs are the inputs the firm changes in the short run to change its output. To keep our analysis simple, we will assume that labor is the only variable input. All other inputs are fixed in that they do not change as output is increased. These are called fixed inputs. Fixed inputs remain unchanged when output goes up or down in the short run. Labor is usually measured in hours. Most of the time, we'll measure labor in terms of the number of workers hired. This makes the results more visual and tangible but assumes in effect that each worker works the same number of hours.

As the firm hires more labor, output (*Q*) goes up. The marginal product of labor (*MP*) is the increase in output due to an additional unit of labor. If 12 workers produce 50 units and 13 workers produce 60 units, the 13th worker's marginal product is 10 units.

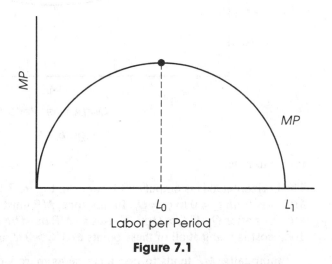

Figure 7.1

Figure 7.1 shows the usual pattern for *MP*: It rises then falls as *L* goes up. From 0 to L_0, each added worker adds more and more to output. From L_0 to L_1, each added worker adds to output, but less and less. The L_1th worker adds nothing to total output. Between 0 and L_1 workers, output goes up with each added worker. Thus, at L_1 workers, total output is highest. Beyond, L_1 workers, the *MP* is negative, meaning added workers reduce total output.

Why does *MP* rise and then fall? Think of a factory floor and imagine workers walking in, one by one, trying to produce output. The first few workers will likely not be able to do much. However, as employment approaches a critical mass, each added worker increases output dramatically. Think of the last worker added to an assembly line: That worker allows the whole assembly line to work! So *MP* first rises. However, as more workers enter, the firm approaches its capacity and each added worker begins to add less. *MP* falls.

Marginal cost is related to marginal product in the following way.

Equation 1

$$MC = \frac{W}{MP}$$

where *W* is the wage per unit labor[1]. For example, if one worker costs $400 a week and she increases output by 10 units, then each unit's marginal cost is $40. That is, each unit took 1/10 of a worker to produce and this added $40 to total cost. Hence, its marginal cost is $40. What if *MP* = 2? Then *MC* = $200. And if, instead, *MP* = 40? Then *MC* = $10.

The higher the *MP*, the lower the cost. The lower the *MP*, the higher the cost. Figure 7.2 shows the usual pattern for *MC*.

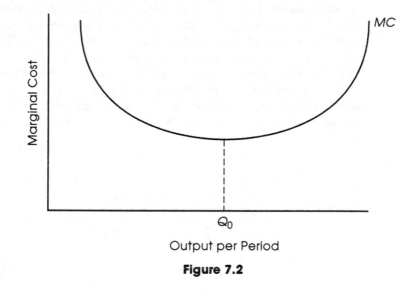

Figure 7.2

Points to note:

The horizontal axis is output, not labor as in Figure 7.1
MC falls from $Q = 0$ to $Q = Q_0$. In this zone, *MP* must be rising.
MC rises after Q_0. If $Q > Q_0$, *MC* rises so *MP* must be falling.
Total cost is rising at all of these points as $MC > 0$ at all points.

Empirically, *MP* tends to first increase as more workers are hired and then, after some point, it begins to fall. The point where it begins to fall is called *the point of diminishing returns*. Figure 7.1 shows the typical pattern of *MP*. It first rises as more *L* is hired until L_0 is reached. From 0 to L_0, each added worker adds more to total output than did the previous worker. The point of diminishing returns is L_0 workers. After L_0, each added worker add less to total output than the previous worker.

---

[1]The *wage* includes all fringe benefit costs and all other costs associated with employing the worker.

Because *MP* rises and then falls, it follows that *MC* must first fall then rise! (See equation 1.) Figure 7.2 shows this pattern. Note that the horizontal axis is output, not labor as in Figure 7.1. Q_0 is the output produced by L_0 workers. Up to Q_0, *MP* is rising and so *MC* is falling. At L_0, workers' marginal productivity is at its highest so marginal cost is at its lowest. Beyond Q_0, *MP* begins to fall; this reduction in marginal productivity is reflected in rising marginal costs. Marginal costs begin to rise because of diminishing returns.

THE LAW OF DIMINISHING MARGINAL RETURNS

The law of diminishing marginal returns states that at some point, as the firm hires more of a variable input while other inputs stay unchanged, the variable input's marginal product will begin to fall, such that successive units add less to output than did the previous units. *Marginal returns* is an old term for marginal product. In Figure 7.2, the point of diminishing returns occurs at L_0. Some points to remember: This law applies only in the short run and only when some inputs remain unchanged. It need not apply in the long run[2].

The proof of this law goes as follows. Assume the law does not apply. Then *MP* would be continually increasing and *MC*, falling. Thus, given this assumption, we should see only one factory producing each good. Adding another factory would split output and raise marginal costs. So only one factory will be in each industry as that is the cheapest way of producing all its output. For example, all the world's steel would be produced in one factory if the law of diminishing returns did not apply. Clearly, this is not the case. Thus the assumption is wrong. Instead, *MP* must begin to decline at some point! This completes the proof.

An Example Illustrating Figure 7.1 and Figure 7.2

Acme Tool Works was recently sued by Wiley Coyote (*Canis latrans*) for producing products that defy the laws of physics in a perverse and injurious manner. We are fortunate that the lawsuit produced the following documents allowing us to see how marginal product and marginal cost are related. Table 7.1 shows the firm's employment, total output, and marginal product.

TABLE 7.1

Workers Hired (*L*)	Total Output (*Q*)	Marginal Product
0	0	—
1	2	2
2	5	3
3	9	4
4	12	3
5	14	2
6	15	1

---

[2]What does apply in the long run is the following: As one input is increased relative to other inputs, at some point, its relative marginal product will begin to decline.

Be sure to verify that the sum of the marginal products equals total output. One worker adds 2 units to output, making output equal to 2. The second worker adds 3 more units, making output equal to 5, so 5 equals the sum of the marginal products of the first 2 workers: $5 = 2 + 3$. Similarly, the total output of 3 workers, 9, equals the sum of their successive marginal products $(2 + 3 + 4)$.

Acme, during the period under litigation, paid each worker $24. This allows us to calculate the marginal costs ($= W/MP$) in Table 7.2. The first unit of output has a marginal cost of $12 as does the second unit. The next 3 units have a marginal cost of $8. Marginal cost (at $6) is lowest for units 6 through 9. Units 10 through 12 cost more: $8 each in added cost. The point of diminishing returns sets in with the fourth worker.

TABLE 7.2

Workers Hired (L)	Total Output (Q)	Marginal Product	Marginal Cost ($)
0	0	—	—
1	2	2	12
2	5	3	8
3	9	4	6
4	12	3	8
5	14	2	12
6	15	1	24

FIXED AND VARIABLE TOTAL COSTS

In the short run, there are two types of inputs: variable inputs and fixed inputs. Similarly, there are two types of total costs: total variable cost (the cost of the variable inputs) and total fixed cost (the cost of fixed inputs).

Stop right now and reread the preceding paragraph. If you understand it and commit it to memory, you will avoid one of the major areas of student confusion: having no idea which costs are variable and which are fixed. But you are smarter. Fixed costs are the costs of fixed inputs! Variable costs are the costs of variable inputs! If the input doesn't change when output goes up, it is a fixed input, and its cost is a fixed cost. If more of the input is needed to produce more output in the short run, then it is a variable input, and its cost is a variable cost.

Fixed and variable refer to the input, not to the cost itself. For example, suppose a firm finances its fixed inputs, plant, and equipment with a variable-interest-rate mortgage. With this type of mortgage, the annual payments the firm makes go up and down with some key interest rate such as the treasury bill rate. Now suppose the interest rate goes up. What happens to the annual cost of the plant and equipment? It will go up! Yes, it will vary. But this cost is still a fixed cost because it is the cost of a fixed input. If you still don't get it, every time you see the term *fixed cost,* rewrite it as the *cost of fixed inputs,* and every time you see the term *variable cost,* rewrite it as the *cost of variable inputs.* Now it may seem like I've spent a lot of words on this, but I've known students who've taken a whole course in managerial accounting where these concepts are repeatedly used and yet know not what they mean.

Thought Questions

When output goes up in the short run, what happens to total variable cost?

In the short run, the firm hires more variable inputs to produce more output. With more variable inputs, the total cost must be higher. Total variable cost must be higher (translation: The total cost of variable inputs must be higher).

When output goes up in the short run, what happens to total fixed cost?

In the short run, the firm leaves the number of fixed inputs unchanged. With the same number of fixed inputs, the total fixed cost will be the same so more output will leave total fixed costs unchanged. Other events might increase the total costs (such as the increase in interest rates in the preceding example) but not an increase in output.

How can we tell what the total fixed cost is?

Find out what total costs are when output is zero. That's total fixed cost, the only cost that can exist at $Q = 0$ because no variable inputs have yet to be hired. Only the fixed inputs are in place. All added costs, due to producing more Q, are variable costs.

Are fixed costs sunk costs?

Yes, because we assume the firm has already purchased its fixed assets. In the long run, as we will see, fixed costs are no longer sunk.

TOTAL COSTS AND MARGINAL COSTS

Since there are two types of inputs, variable and fixed, the sum of their costs add up to the total cost of producing the good.

Equation 2

Total cost = Total variable cost + Total fixed cost
or
$$TC = TVC + TFC$$

TC is the cost of the total inputs being used to produce output (Q).

Marginal cost (MC) is the increase in total cost due to one more unit of output.

Equation 3

$MC = \Delta TC$ due to one more unit of output.

Because total fixed costs do not change as more is produced, we have

$$\Delta TC = \Delta TVC = MC$$

where Δ refers to change due to one more unit of Q.

Graphically, marginal cost is the slope of the total cost curve in Figure 7.3. The vertical distance between the *TC* curve and the *TVC* curve equals *TFC*.

Up to Q_0, the slope of the *TC* curve is becoming flatter, reflecting the falling *MC* in Figure 7.2. After Q_0, the slope of the *TC* curve becomes progressively steeper, reflecting the rising *MC* in Figure 7.3.

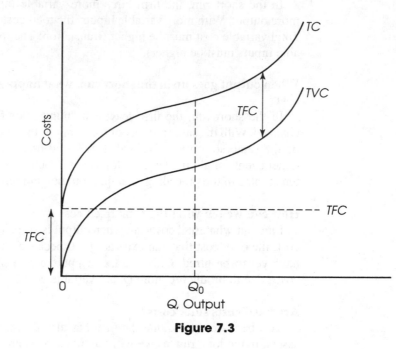

Figure 7.3

Be sure to note in Figure 7.3 that at $Q = 0$, $TC = TFC$. This is true because, by definition, $TVC = 0$ at $Q = 0$. All costs above *TFC* are variable costs! For example, Table 7.3 shows these relationships.

TABLE 7.3

Output	Marginal Cost ($)	Total Variable Cost ($)	Total Fixed Cost ($)	Total Cost ($)
0	—	0	24	24
1	12	12	24	36
2	8	20	24	44
3	4	24	24	48
4	8	32	24	56
5	12	44	24	68

Note the following:

$$TC = TVC + TFC$$

TFC is the same at all Q.

$$TC = TFC \text{ at } Q = 0$$

MC is the increase in TVC.

$$MC = TVC \text{ at } Q = 1$$

MC is the increase in TC.

Also, no matter what number *TFC* is, the change in *TC* as output goes up is the same and equal to *MC*. Verify this by letting *TFC* equal $240 and recalculating the *TC* column.

AVERAGE COSTS

There are two average costs, one for each type of input, average variable cost (AVC) and average fixed cost (AFC).

Equation 4

$$AVC = \frac{TVC}{Q}$$

and

$$AFC = \frac{TFC}{Q}$$

In addition, there is an average of all costs. Because the sum of total variable costs and total fixed costs equals total cost, it follows that their averages have the same relationship.

Equation 5

$$ATC = AVC + AFC$$

where ATC is the average total cost (ATC = TC/Q). Some texts call this *average cost,* but I find it helps to add the T to make clear that it is the average cost of the total inputs being used. To derive equation 5, take equation 2 and divide each term by Q.

MARGINAL COSTS, TOTAL VARIABLE COSTS, AND AVERAGE VARIABLE COSTS

All these costs are related. But remember that all of them are derived from the key cost, marginal cost. Marginal cost is the leader: The rest are just other ways of keeping tabs on it. Table 7.4 shows how they are related to each other. The marginal cost column is the key column. It equals *W/MP* and is determined by the wage and the technology the firm is using. The next two columns are derived from the *MC* column.

TABLE 7.4

Output	Marginal Cost ($)	Total Variable Cost ($)	Average Variable Cost ($)
0	—	0	0
1	8	8	8
2	6	14	7
3	4	18	6
4	6	24	6
5	8	32	6.40
6	10	42	7

Total variable cost is the sum of the *MC*. Recall that *MC* is the addition to *TVC* for each added *Q*. So we add up the *MC*s to get the *TVC*. It's like finding out how high up a staircase one has gone by measuring how high each step is and then adding up the heights of all the steps. For example, the *TVC* of 3 units is $18 and is the sum of $8 + $6 + $4.

Equation 6

$$TVC = \text{sum of } MC$$

Average variable cost is *TVC* divided by *Q*. But because *TVC* is the sum of *MC* (up to the current *Q*), *AVC* is also the average marginal cost. For example, at *Q* = 4, the *AVC* is 6: This is also the average of the *MC* ($8 + $6 + $4 + $6 divided by 4).

Equation 7

$$AVC = \text{average } MC$$

Finally, since *AVC* = *TVC/Q*, we can solve for *TVC* and get

Equation 8

$$TVC = Q \times AVC$$

For example, at *Q* = 6, the *AVC* is $7, so we could figure out that *TVC* is $42 (6 × $7).

A COMMERCIAL BREAK

Marginal cost is used in marginal analysis. If producing and selling a good adds enough to total revenue to cover its marginal cost, then the good should be produced. Knowing marginal cost allows us to maximize profits. It tells us how much output to produce. It is a very useful number to know!

How about the total variable cost? It helps determine if the firm should be up and running or whether it should shut down. The firm will be up and running when *TR* ≥ *TVC*. The firm should be covering its variable costs; if not, it should go out of business.

Average variable cost can also be used for this purpose. Taking the up-and-running condition, *TR* ≥ *TVC*, and dividing both sides by *Q*, we have

$$P \geq AVC$$

So if the price, which is the *average revenue,* covers average variable costs, the firm should be up and running.

What about fixed costs? Ignore them. They're sunk. They don't affect *Q*.

MARGINAL AND AVERAGE COSTS

For review: Marginal cost is the addition to total variable cost. Total variable cost is the sum of marginal costs. Average variable cost is the average marginal cost.

Rule: The average always moves toward the marginal.

The reason for this is the marginal is what's added to the total. If what's added on (that is, the marginal) is bigger than the average, the average moves up (toward the marginal). If what's added on is smaller than the average, the average moves down.

For example, the average height of students in a classroom is 5 feet 10 inches. Bob, the center of the basketball team, comes in. His height is 6 feet 6 inches. The average height of students in the classroom will go up. Next, Bill who is a three-year-old prodigy going to college, enters the room. His height is 3 feet 2 inches. The average height of students in the classroom goes down.

Here's another example. The average marginal cost of a quantity of output is $40 (this is also the average variable cost). A new unit of output "enters the room" and its marginal cost is $50. The average marginal cost will go up.

Consider also this example. Your average test grade is 85. Because you've read this book, studied it diligently, and urged your friends to buy not one but two copies, on the next text you make a 95 (think of this as a marginal addition to your total score). Your average grade goes up.

Equation 9

So we have:

Marginal > average   **then average up**
Marginal < average   **then average down**
Marginal = average   **then average unchanged**

Now we just add variable and total in along with cost, and we have, as output goes up one unit:

Marginal cost > average variable cost   *AVC* **goes up**
Marginal cost < average variable cost   *AVC* **goes down**
Marginal cost = average variable cost   *AVC* **unchanged**

and

Marginal cost > average total cost   *ATC* **goes up**
Marginal cost < average total cost   *ATC* **goes down**
Marginal cost = average total cost   *ATC* **unchanged**

Some students have trouble with the > and < signs. On the big side of the symbol is the bigger number, on the smaller side, the smaller number. So

Big number > Smaller number
Small number < Bigger number

The > symbol points to the smaller number.

These rules also imply that marginal cost equals average variable cost at the minimum average variable cost. Suppose the minimum *AVC* occurs at 10 units of output. Before this, $MC < AVC$ so the average variable cost is falling. At $Q = 10$, $MC = AVC$ and average variable cost stays unchanged. After $Q = 10$, $MC > AVC$ so average variable cost starts rising again. So the smallest *AVC* occurs at $Q = 10$. Before that, as Q increased, it was falling from a greater height. After that, it rises again as Q increases.

The same is true for average total cost. However, the minimum *ATC* must occur at a greater Q than does the minimum *AVC*. This is because total cost starts out as a larger number (as fixed costs are added into total costs) and so needs more Q to drag it down to its minimum.

So we have

Minimum *AVC*	**where** *MC = AVC*
Minimum *ATC*	**where** *MC = ATC*

What about average fixed cost? Does it have a minimum? No! It equals total fixed cost (an unchanging number as *Q* goes up) divided by *Q*. It just gets smaller and smaller and smaller.

The graph in Figure 7.4 shows the *MC* curve, the *AVC* curve, the higher *ATC* curve.

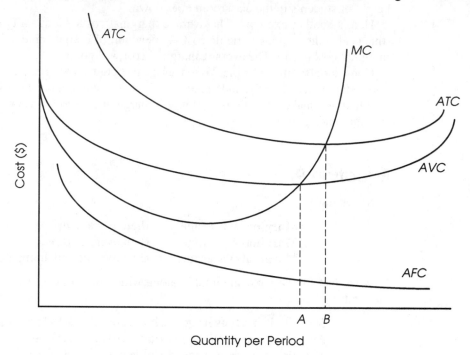

Figure 7.4

Points to note:

At *Q* = 0, *MC* = *AVC* and *AFC* is infinite (any number divided by zero is infinite).
At *Q* = *A*, *MC* = *AVC*, so the minimum *AVC* is at *Q* = *A*.
At *Q* = *B*, *MC* = *ATC* so the minimum *ATC* is at *Q* = *B*.
Output *B* > output *A*.
As *Q* goes up, *MC* curve rises before *AVC* and *ATC* start to rise.
AFC is always falling.
The vertical distance between the *ATC* curve and the *AVC* curve equals *AFC* since

$$ATC = AVC + AFC \text{ and, thus, } ATC - AVC = AFC$$

Because *AFC* is falling, the *ATC* curve gets closer to the *AVC* at higher *Q*.

ANOTHER AVERAGE-MARGINAL RELATIONSHIP

As the firm hires more labor, each laborer adds her marginal product to total output. So the total output is the sum of the marginal products (added over the workers hired). The average product of labor is

Equation 10

$$\text{Average product of labor} = \frac{Q}{L}$$

The average product of labor (AP_L) is the average of the marginal products (since Q is the sum of the MPs). So we can use the same average, marginal rules:

$MP > AP_L$	AP_L is rising
$MP = AP_L$	AP_L is unchanged
$MP < AP_L$	AP_L is falling
$MP = AP_L$	AP_L is at its maximum

For example, see Table 7.5.

TABLE 7.5

Labor	Output	MP	AP of Labor
0	0	—	—
1	4	4	4
2	12	8	6
3	24	12	8
4	32	8	8
5	35	3	7
6	36	1	6

Note the following: AP_L is the average MP; Q is the sum of MP; maximum AP_L is at $Q = 4$ where $AP_L = MP$; and the average moves "slower" than the marginal as L goes up. Figure 7.5 shows the marginal product and average product relationship graphically.

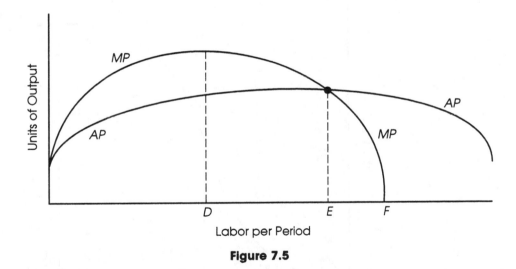

Figure 7.5

Points to note:

Labor, not output, is on the horizontal axis.
Point of diminishing returns starts at $L = D$.
Maximum AP_L at $L = E$ where $AP_L = MP$.
Total output is maximized at $L = F$ (after that, $MP < 0$ and Q falls).
AP_L is still positive after MP becomes negative after $L = F$.

Firms would never hire beyond $L = F$.
AP_L and MP start out the same at $Q = 0$.
Hold it. There's more! The following equation links AP to AVC:

Equation 11[3]

$$AVC = \frac{W}{AP_L}$$

Further points to note:

Maximum AP_L corresponds to minimum AVC.
Minimum AVC occurs at $L = E$.
Similarly,
Maximum MP corresponds to minimum MC.
Minimum MC occurs at $L = D$.
$MP = AP_L$ where $MC = AVC$.

APPENDIX: GEOMETRY OF SHORT-RUN PRODUCTION

Total Output and Labor

Some texts use the following diagram to motivate the rise and fall in MP and AP. It shows total output (Q) and labor inputs (L), assuming capital and other inputs are fixed. Figure 7.6 shows the typical total output curve.

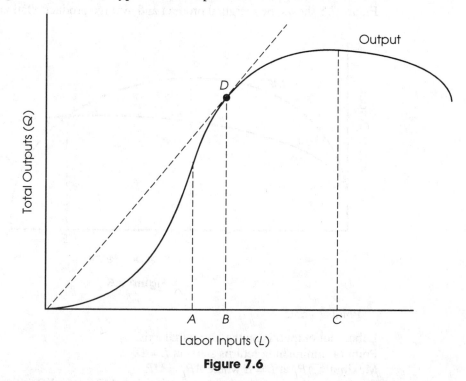

Figure 7.6

---

[3]The proof is as follows. Plug in Q/L for AP. Multiply top and bottom of right side of the equation by L. Multiply both sides of the equation by Q. We get $AVC \times Q = W \times L$ or $TVC = WL$, which is correct, because the only variable input is, by assumption, labor so its cost is the only variable cost.

The slope of the total output line is the marginal product. The slope equals rise over run: here, the run is one worker and the rise is the increase in Q due to adding this worker. Hence, the slope $= MP$, the increase in output due to adding one more worker. The MP is rising—the slope is getting steeper—as labor (L) increases from 0 to worker A. After this, the slope begins to become less and less steep as we move along it to the right: MP begins to decline. At the maximum output, at worker C, $MP = 0$. After that, MP and the slope of Q become negative.

A *ray from the origin* is any line drawn from the zero where the horizontal and vertical axes meet (ray $0D$ is an example). Let us look at a ray going to the output line (such as ray $0D$). Its slope equals the average product of labor (AP_L). That's because the run is employment (measured from $L = 0$) and its rise is output: $AP_L = Q/L$. Ray $0D$ is a very special ray: It has the highest slope. It is the only ray that's tangent to the output line (it just touches the output line once). When the firm employs B workers, it has the highest average product possible. Note that at $L = B$, the slope of the ray from the origin and the slope of the output curve are the same: $AP_L = MP$. For fewer workers, the ray's slope will be less than the slope of the output line: $MP > AP_L$. So, as we move from $L = 0$ to $L = B$, AP_L rises (the ray from the origin to the Q curve gets steeper). Increasing employment beyond B results in the ray from the origin having a larger slope than the slope of the Q curve: $MP < AP_L$, so we observe AP_L falling as we move right along the output curve.

Total Cost and Output

The same analysis applies to the graph in Figure 7.7, which shows the total cost curves and output. The slope of the total cost and total variable cost curves is marginal cost: The rise is the increase in cost due to the run of one more unit of output. Any ray from the origin to the TVC curve has a slope equal to the AVC. Any ray from the origin to the TC curve has a slope equal to ATC.

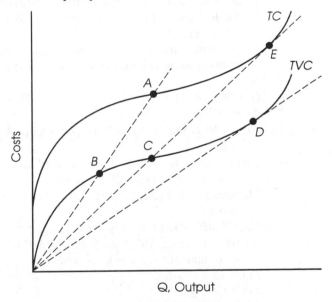

Figure 7.7

Let's examine several points on this graph.

Point A: Slope of ray > Slope of TC curve so

$ATC > MC$ and ATC is falling

Point *B:* Slope of ray > Slope of *TVC* curve so

$$AVC > MC \text{ and } AVC \text{ is falling}$$

Point *C:* Same as point *B* (note how ray's slope is less than at *B,* showing *AVC* is falling over this range).

Point *D:* Slope of ray = Slope of *TVC* curve

$$AVC = MC$$

Lowest *AVC* occurs here.

At higher *L,* Slope of ray < Slope of *TVC* curve

$$AVC < MC$$

so *AVC* is rising as it moves to higher *L* beyond point *D.*

Point *E:* Slope of ray = Slope of *TC* curve

$$ATC = MC$$

Lowest *ATC* occurs here.

At higher *L,* Slope of ray < Slope of *TC* curve

$$ATC < MC$$

so *ATC* is rising as it moves to higher *L* beyond point *E.*

CRIB NOTES

Short run: Period when only some inputs (but not all) are increased when the firm wants to increase output.

Long run: All inputs increased to produce more.

Variable inputs: Inputs that are increased to produce more in the short run.

Fixed inputs: Inputs not increased in short run to produce more.

Marginal product: Increase in Q due to one more unit of input (here, L).

Q = Sum of *MP.*

$AP = Q/L.$

$AP = MP$ at maximum *AP.* As Q goes up, *AP* approaches *MP. MP* leads.

Total cost: Total variable cost (cost of all variable inputs) + Total fixed cost (cost of all fixed inputs). $TC = TVC + TFC.$

Marginal cost: Increase in *TC* due to one more $Q = \Delta TVC$ due to one more $Q.$

MC: W/MP when L is only variable input.

As *MP* goes rises, *MC* goes down. As *MP* falls (after reaching point of diminishing returns), *MC* rises.

TVC: Sum of *MC.*

AVC: $TVC/Q.$

$AFC = TFC/Q.$

AVC: W/AP when L is only input.

ATC: $AVC + AFC.$

TFC: $Q \times AFC.$

TVC: $Q \times AVC.$

TC: $Q \times ATC.$

Review Questions

1. Solve the following quick questions:
   a. If average total cost is $12 and output is 10 units, what is total cost?
   b. If $TVC = \$200$ at $Q = 10$ and the MC of the 11th unit is $25, what is the TVC at $Q = 11$?
   c. If $TC = \$300$ and $TVC = \$200$, what is TFC?
   d. If $AFC = \$24$ at $Q = 2$, what is AFC at $Q = 4$ and at $Q = 10$?
   e. If at $Q = 10$, $AFC = \$20$ and at $Q = 20$, $TVC = \$500$, what is TC at $Q = 20$?
   f. If $TVC = \$400$ and $AVC = \$40$, what is Q?
   g. If $ATC = \$40$ and $AVC = \$35$ at $Q = 20$, then what is AFC? TFC?
   h. If $W = \$24$ and $MP = 6$ and $AP_L = 2$, what is MC? AVC?

2. Indicate in the following whether the average cost is going up, down, or remaining unchanged as Q is increased.
   a. $MC = \$12$ and $AVC = \$15$.
   b. $MC = \$15$ and $AVC = \$10$.
   c. $MC = \$20$ and $ATC = \$25$.
   d. $MC = \$12$ and $AVC = \$10$ while $ATC = \$20$.
   e. $W = \$24$, $MP = 6$ and $AP_L = 4$. What is happening to AVC? to AP_L?
   f. $AP = MP$. What's happening to AVC? to AP_L?

3. True or false?
   a. ATC never, ever falls below AVC.
   b. AVC only falls when MC falls.
   c. ATC only falls when $MC < ATC$.
   d. AVC will rise if $MC > ATC$.
   e. AFC is at a minimum when $AFC = MC$.
   f. $AP_L > 0$ when $MP = 0$.
   g. Output is largest when AP_L is largest.
   h. AP_L begins to fall when MP falls.

4. Acme has the following costs:

Output	Total Costs
0	$ 500
1	$1,400
2	$1,800
3	$2,400
4	$3,600

   What is its fixed cost? What is its lowest ATC? Its lowest AVC?

5. Fill in this table. The wage for each unit of labor is $120.

Labor Input (L)	1	2	3	4	5	6
Output (Q)	2		9		19	23
MP				5		
MC of 1 Q ($)		40				
AP_L						
AVC of 1 Q						

6. Fill in this table.

Q	MC ($)	TVC ($)	TFC ($)	TC ($)	AVC ($)	AFC ($)	ATC ($)
0	—				—	—	—
1	16						
2					15		71
3		42					
4				160			

7. A study of health care expenditures that took account of the many factors that affect health concluded that health spending per person varies across cities by a factor of 2 with virtually no difference in health outcomes. That is, cities with twice the spending per capita on health had the same mortality rates and the same degree of health, after taking into account differences in age, gender, income, and race. What does this suggest the marginal product of medical care is? Why is this so?

8. The production of aluminum takes an extraordinary amount of electricity to produce.
   a. If the price of electricity goes up, how does this affect an aluminum maker's MC, AVC, AFC, and ATC?
   b. Assume that, instead, the firm has to pay more on its mortgage that was used to build its plant. How will this affect its MC, AVC, AFC, and ATC?

9. Suppose that fertilizer has a constantly rising marginal product. That is, when we add another pound of fertilizer to an acre of wheat, it raises output more than the previous pound did. If the smallest farm has an acre of land, what is the optimal farm size; that is, what farm size has the lowest ATC? How much will this farm produce?

10. "Mr. Jones," says the salesman, "this machine will do half your work for you!"
    "Good," replies Mr. Jones, "I'll take two and retire."
    What is wrong with Mr. Jones's logic?

Answers

1. a. $120 (using $ATC = TC/Q$).
   b. $225 ($\Delta TVC = MC$).
   c. $100 (using $TC = TVC + TFC$).
   d. $TFC = \$48$ (using $AFC = TFC/Q$). So $AFC = \$12$ at $Q = 4$ and $\$4.80$ at $Q = 10$ (using same equation and the fact TFC is the same at all Q).
   e. $TFC = \$200$ (using $AFC = TFC/Q$). $TC = \$700$ at $Q = 100$.
   f. $Q = 10$ (using $AVC = TVC/Q$).
   g. $AFC = \$5$ (using $ATC = AVC + AFC$). So $TFC = \$100$ (using $AFC = TFC/Q$).
   h. $MC = \$4$ (using $MC = W/MP$) and $AVC = \$12$ (using $AVC = W/AP_L$).
2. a. AVC is falling.
   b. AVC is rising.
   c. ATC is falling.
   d. AVC is rising while ATC is falling.
   e. $MC = \$4$, $AVC = \$6$ so AVC is falling. AP_L is rising.
   f. $MC = AVC$ so AVC remains unchanged. AP_L is unchanging. This works for any wage so W does not need to be specified.
3. a. True ($ATC = AVC + AFC$ and $AFC > 0$ at all Q).
   b. False (AVC only falls when $AVC > MC$; MC can be rising but must be below AVC).
   c. True.

d. True (as $MC > ATC > AVC$).

e. False. AFC is always smaller at larger Q.

f. True (AP_L only equals 0 when $Q = 0$, but Q is at its maximum where $MP = 0$).

g. False. (Output is largest where $MP = 0$. When AP_L is largest, $MP = AP_L > 0$.)

h. False (AP_L falls when $AP_L > MP$; MP can be falling while AP is rising if $MP > AP$).

4. $TFC = \$500$ as $TC = TFC$ at $Q = 0$. We have:

Q	TC	TVC	ATC	AVC
1	1,400	900	1,400	900
2	1,800	1,300	900	650
3	2,400	1,900	800	633
4	3,600	3,100	900	775

The minimum ATC is $800. The minimum AVC is $633.

5.

Labor Input (L)	1	2	3	4	5	6
Output (Q)	2	5	9	14	19	23
MP	2	3	4	5	5	4
MC of 1 Q ($)	60	40	30	24	24	30
AP_L	2	2.5	3	3.5	3.8	3.83⅓
AVC of 1 Q	60	48	40	34.29	31.58	31.30

6.

Q	MC	TVC	TFC	TC	AVC	AFC	ATC
0	—	0	112	112	—	—	—
1	16	16	112	128	16	112	128
2	14	30	112	142	15	56	71
3	12	42	112	154	14	37.33	51.33
4	6	48	112	160	12	28	40

In doing this type of problem, fill in what you know. You know if AVC is \$15 at $Q = 2$, then $TVC = \$30$. Similarly, $TC = \$142$. Next, you can solve for TFC from these two numbers and fill in the TFC column. You also know that $TVC = \$0$ at $Q = 0$. This should get you started.

7. It suggests that the marginal product of more medical care is zero. This most likely occurs because medical care is free to most patients (because of health insurance) so they buy it until its MP is reduced to zero.

8. a. This affects variable costs. MC, AVC, and ATC will go up. AFC will stay the same.

   b. This affects only the fixed cost. MC and AVC will stay the same. AFC and ATC will go up.

9. Because fertilizer has a constantly rising MP, this means the MC on a one-acre farm will be constantly falling. Similarly, its AVC and its ATC will be constantly falling. If we add another acre and split the fertilizer between the farms, MC and ATC will be higher! So the optimal farm size is one acre. It will produce all the wheat in the world at a lower cost than having the same amount of fertilizer spread over many farms. Since we observe more than one farm in existence, we can conclude that fertilizer has, beyond some point, a declining marginal product. That is why farmers everywhere spread the fertilizer around!

10. He ignores the law of diminishing marginal product. The second machine will do less than the first. He'll still have work to do.

Chapter Eight

Long-Run Output and Costs

LONG RUN

The story so far: Demand goes up. In the short run, firms meet this increase in demand by hiring more labor, even if this means output exceeds the efficient capacity of its plants and equipment. But if the increase in demand persists, and if nothing else happens, then over time the firm will expand its productive capacity to efficiently meet the higher demand. The time it takes to do this is called the *long run*. The long run is defined as the time it takes firms to fully adjust their output level in the most efficient manner possible. By "efficient," we mean at the lowest unit cost.

What is interesting about this long-run concept is that computers and new production and managerial techniques are making the long run progressively shorter. The firms that survive in today's markets are those that meet changes in demand quickly and efficiently. In many cases, the long run is less than a year!

THE LAW OF SCIENCE AND CONSTANT RETURNS TO SCALE

The scientific method is based upon a very fundamental assumption: If we do something again in exactly the same way as it was done before, we should get exactly the same results. This assumption's important corollary is that if we vary just one thing while doing everything else exactly the same way as before, then any change in results must be due to the one thing we changed. This corollary is the basis of scientific inquiry and, also, of economic analysis.

The law of science has an important economic implication. If a firm duplicates everything it does, it should get the same results again. So if it were to double all of its inputs, it should get twice the output it had before.

More generally stated, if the firm expands all inputs by X%, output should go up X% This is called *constant returns to scale*. "Scale" means the number of workers, plants, machines, and all other inputs. If the scale goes up X% and output goes up X%, then the firm has constant returns to scale. What remains constant is the ratio of output to inputs (for example, the output per worker).

Besides constant returns to scale, there are two other possibilities.

INCREASING RETURNS TO SCALE

A firm has increasing returns to scale if, when it increases all inputs by $X\%$, output goes up by more than $X\%$. What increases as the firm makes its scale larger is the ratio of output to inputs.

One reason for increasing returns to scale is that many physical production processes require a large scale to be run efficiently. For example, there is a certain size of furnace needed to smelt ore into iron or steel. Building two furnaces half the size will not give the same output as the one big furnace. In the cultural revolution in China, Mao Tse Tung tore down the big steel mills and had every household build a little steel furnace in the backyard. This was done to show that "Communist will is superior to Western science." How did this experiment turn out? Western science won.

A second reason is that a larger scale of operation may afford certain economies not available to smaller firms. A larger firm can have managers, staff, and workers performing specialized tasks to the degree that they become expert in doing them. This division of labor makes these personnel more efficient at what they are doing.

DECREASING RETURNS TO SCALE

A firm has decreasing returns to scale if, when it increases all inputs by $X\%$, output goes up by less than $X\%$. What decreases as the firm makes its scale larger is the ratio of output to inputs.

Suppose we observe a firm increasing all its inputs 25% yet its output only goes up 20%. This violates the law of science. So how can this occur? For some reason, the firm has become less efficient than before. Why?

One of the main reasons is that as firms grow, they become harder to manage efficiently. While all the inputs we observe double, there is one input that stays the same: the entrepreneurial input of the owners of the firm. To illustrate, suppose Joe owns one restaurant. He's there every night to make sure the chef prepares the food well, to make sure the customers are happy, and to be sure the staff doesn't steal too much. He decides to buy another restaurant exactly like his current one and hires enough staff to double his current capacity. But now he must divide his time between both restaurants. Even if he puts a new manager in charge of the new restaurant to do the same things he did at the old restaurant, the new manager may not have the same incentives as Joe did to run the restaurant efficiently. Joe might make the new manager a part owner and this might cure the problem. If not, any successive restaurants he adds are likely to be less and less efficient as the bureaucratic conflicts and inefficiencies grow. Decreasing returns to scale will set in.

What is the return to scale in these firms?

	Labor	Capital	Output	Labor	Capital	Output
Firm A	10	20	30	20	40	60
Firm B	30	6	3	45	9	6
Firm C	2	2	4	4	4	7

Firm A has constant returns to scale. Inputs double (go up 100%) and output doubles (goes up 100%). Firm B has increasing returns to scale. All inputs go up 50% and output goes 100%. Firm C has decreasing returns to scale. All inputs increase 100% while output only goes up 75%.

SCALE AND COSTS

To illustrate how economics of scale affect the unit cost of goods, I am going to assume the firm has a basket of inputs (such as labor, capital, land, and management) that can be treated as a unit of input. I'll label these units of inputs with my own made-up term, *inputium*. Each unit of inputium costs $10.

Let us now describe a typical firm. It starts out small, employing 24 units of inputium and producing 8 units of output. Thus, its cost per unit output is $30. The $30 figure is derived by taking total cost (24 units of inputium times $10) and dividing this by output ($30 = $240/8). Alternatively, $30 can be derived by taking the $10 times the inputium used per unit output (3). In general,

Equation 1

$$\text{Unit cost} = P_I \cdot \frac{I}{Q}$$

where P_I is the price of 1 unit of inputium; I is the number of units of inputium; Q is output; and I/Q is the ratio of inputs to output.

Table 8.1 shows the firm as it grows.

TABLE 8.1

Inputs (I)	Output (Q)	I/Q Input Output Ratio	Cost per Unit ($)
24	8	3	30
48	24	2	20
96	48	2	20
192	60	3.2	32

The firm first experiences increasing returns to scale as it doubles its inputs (from 24 to 48 units of inputium) and output triples (from 8 to 24). Because output increases more than inputs, the firm's input/output ratio falls (from 3 to 2) as does its unit cost (from $30 to $20). When the firm doubles in size again (from 48 to 96 units of inputium), it experiences constant returns to scale as output also doubles (from 24 to 48 units of output). Because the ratio of inputs to output stays the same (at 2), its unit costs are the same (still $20). Finally, when the firm doubles its inputs once again (from 96 units to 192), it experiences decreasing returns to scale as output only goes up 25%. Its ratio of inputs to output goes up (from 2 to 3.2) as does its unit cost (from $20 to $32).

Figure 8.1 shows the long-run average cost (average cost is the same as unit cost) for a typical firm. Unit costs fall from 0 to *A;* in this zone, it is has increasing returns to scale. Then unit costs are the same from output *A* to output *B;* in this range, it has constant returns to scale. Finally, from *B* on, its unit costs go up as it runs into decreasing returns to scale.

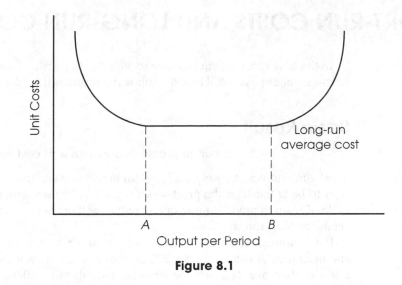

Figure 8.1

Points to note:

From 0 to output *A*, the firm has increasing returns to scale, reduced ratio of inputs to output, and, thus, a lower unit cost (= long-run average cost).

From outputs *A* to *B*, the firm has constant returns to scale, a constant ratio of inputs to output, and, thus, a constant unit cost.

From output *B* on up, the firm runs into decreasing returns to scale, a rising ratio of inputs to output, and, thus, a rising unit cost.

Empirically, most firms have increasing returns to scale as they grow (from 0 to *A)*, and then constant returns to scale from then on. Few are observed having decreasing returns to scale. What this implies is that after firms reach the highest level of efficiency at output *A*, they are able to duplicate and sustain this level of efficiency as they expand. Beyond this point, future gains in profits come from expanding their market for their output and not from economies of scale.

At output *A*, the firm has reached its *minimum efficient scale*. The minimum scale of output is important because if it is relatively large to the market the good is sold in, then only a few firms will coexist in an industry.

DECREASING RETURNS TO SCALE AND DIMINISHING RETURNS

Students often confuse decreasing returns to scale with diminishing returns. Diminishing returns is the decline in marginal productivity due to increasing variable inputs when other inputs are not increased. Logic tells us that all inputs, when increased while others are not increased, will eventually hit the point of diminishing returns. On the other hand, decreasing returns *to scale* occurs when all inputs are increased but output fails to increase in proportion with the inputs. There is no logical reason to expect decreasing returns to scale to occur.

SHORT-RUN COSTS AND LONG-RUN COSTS

In the long run, the firm has time to adjust to any scale of production in the most efficient manner possible. Thus, the following result will hold at all levels of output.

Basic Result

Long-run unit cost ≤ short-run unit cost for all Q

Short-run unit cost only equals long-run unit cost when the short-run output just happens to be at the scale the plant was designed to be most efficient at. Using that same scale of plant to produce more or less output will result in a short-run unit cost that exceeds the long-run costs.

For example, Acme has constant returns to scale. It has only two inputs, workers and machines. A machine costs $20 an hour to use and each worker costs $20 an hour. Some of the ways it can use the 1 machine are shown in Table 8.2.

TABLE 8.2

Machine Hours	Workers Hours	Output	Cost per Unit Output ($)
1	1	2	20
1	2	4	15
1	3	5	16

At these costs, the most efficient combination is 1 machine and 2 workers (costing $60 and producing 4 units of output, resulting in per unit cost of $15; be sure you calculate the other unit cost figures in the last column).

Suppose demand is such that the firm's output has held steady at 20 units. It has had time to adjust by employing 5 machines and 10 workers so that unit costs are $15. Then, suddenly, output demanded goes up to 24 units. In the short run, it is stuck with 5 machines because the firm in Italy that makes the machines is on back order. However, it can add a third worker to 4 of its machines (bringing employment to 14 workers) to increase output to 24. However, this raises its unit cost to $15.83 ($100 for capital and $280 for labor, for a total cost of $380, which we divide by 24 units to get a unit cost of $15.83). This is its short-run unit cost. However, in the long run, it can expand its machines to 6, reduce its workforce back[1] to 12, and produce output at $15 a unit again. If output expands again, we once again get a short-run adjustment of more workers and higher unit cost. But, as the firm adjusts, unit costs come back to their long-run level of $15.

Figure 8.2 illustrates how short-run and long-run costs compare for a typical firm. The long line is the long-run average cost curve. Three of the many possible short-run cost curves are shown. Curve A is the short-run cost curve for a plant that achieves maximum efficiency at output level Q_a. Note that at a higher level of output, it could produce at a lower short-run average cost. But the firm could still do better by increasing the scale of the plant. As a result, this size of plant would be used to produce Q_a in the long run but not more than Q_a. The bottom of the short-run cost curve does not tell

---

[1]Over the business cycle, firms initially increase their labor by employing their current workers more hours rather than by hiring more workers. Over time, they expand their number of workers while cutting back on overtime. Changes in weekly hours of work tend to precede increases in output while changes in employment tend to take place after increases in output have taken place.

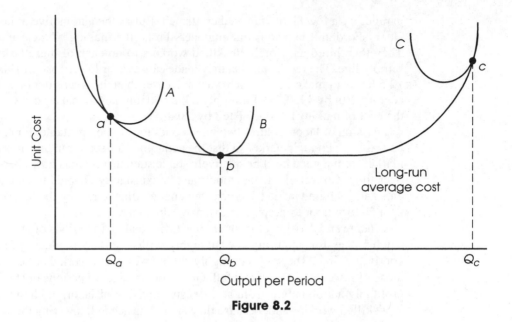

Figure 8.2

you what output the scale of the plant is appropriate for! Curve B's efficient scale happens also be its lowest short-run cost. But curve C's most efficient scale is at Q_c, which is above curve B's lowest short-run cost.

Sometimes, students draw the long-run curve through the bottom of the short-run cost curve as in Figure 8.3. But this violates Result 1: Short-run unit costs are never lower than long-run costs. In this case, the short-run cost curve should be drawn tangent to the long-run cost curve, just touching the long-run curve on the short-run cost curve's left-hand side.

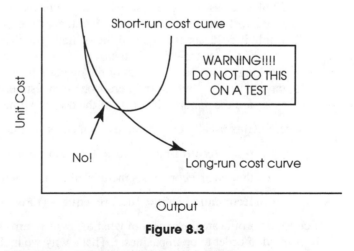

Figure 8.3

DIVISION OF LABOR AND CHANGE

One of the main reasons for increasing returns to scale is the division of labor that larger scales of production make possible. Division of labor is the specialization of workers in doing one or only a few tasks. Specialization has two main advantages. First, it allows the worker to learn fully the best way to do the task. Second, in many cases, it allows the firm to hire unskilled workers and train them quickly because each has few tasks to do. To illustrate, at one time automobiles where made one by one in garages by a few highly talented craftsmen. But as the automotive industry expanded, Henry Ford and his industrial engineers broke the making of a car into many tasks. They then hired and taught unskilled workers to do each of these tasks along an assembly line. The result was that they made cars at a far lower cost. In 1909, it took Ford 12.5 hours to make a car, which was far shorter than the weeks it took at the turn of the century. But by 1920, Ford was only taking 90 minutes to make a car. Over these years, the cost of making a Model T fell by a half.

Division of labor requires two main conditions to be profitable. First, the good must have a large enough market so that the economies of scale can take place. Second, the market for the good must be relatively stable such that there is little change in the good over time. Conversely, if the good must be constantly adapted to changing technologies and changing markets, there is not enough time to recoup the huge costs of setting up a factory floor to support an extensive division of labor.

Change and division of labor are inversely related. In periods of change, firms adopt batch processing, requiring few but highly skilled workers producing a few specialized goods at a time. The wages of highly skilled workers in periods of change rise, while those of lower skilled workers fall. On the other hand, in periods of stability, firms can profitably adopt and invest in an extensive division of labor, bidding up the wages of low-skilled workers and, because they are not as needed, lowering the wages of higher skilled workers. Periods of stability tend to be periods of greater equality in earnings. Conversely, the 1970s and the 1980s were periods of change and periods of rising inequality.

PROFITS AND COSTS

Each business has two types of costs:

1. Explicit costs are those costs paid for inputs, including wages for employees, material cost, and depreciation and maintenance on plant and equipment.
2. Implicit costs are the costs of the owner's time and investment in the firm. The cost of the owner's time is measured by what the owner could have earned by working elsewhere. The cost of the owner's investment is what the owner could have earned elsewhere in interest on an investment of equivalent risk. Together, these are the opportunity costs of the owner's time and capital.

Accountants usually only count explicit costs, so that the profits they report are

Accounting profits = Total revenue – Explicit cost

On the other hand, economists include all costs, whether explicit or implicit, so that

Economic profit = Total revenue – (Explicit + Implicit cost)

Economic profits are the excess of what the owner earns over and above what he needs to be paid in order to be in business[2]. That's why we include all costs.

Economic profit is what determines how people act. If economic profits are positive or even if they equal zero, the owner will remain in the current business. In addition, economic profits measure how much the owner is better off in his current business than he would have been elsewhere. On the other hand, accounting profits might be positive and yet the owner could be worse off.

---

[2]An equivalent definition of economic profit is this: Economic profit is the largest amount of money that could be consumed by the owners and not reinvested such that the firm's future earnings are not reduced. This requires that all costs be fully accounted for, including the true cost of depreciation and obsolescence of plant and equipment.

Thought Question

Jennifer has started a computer software company. She invested $100,000 of her own money and gave up a $60,000 a year job to run the company. She could have earned 9% had she invested the $100,000 elsewhere. In the first year, her company has revenues of $500,000 and explicit costs (wages for employees other than Jennifer, rent, etc.) of $450,000. What is her accounting profit? What are her implicit costs? Her economic profit?

Her accounting profit is $50,000 (= $500,000 − $450,000). Her implicit cost is $69,000, which is the sum of foregone wages ($60,000) and foregone interest earnings ($9,000). So her economic profit is − $19,000 (= $500,000 − 450,000 − $69,000). That is, she has an economic loss of $19,000: She would have been better off by $19,000 by being elsewhere. Of course, she might stay in business because she anticipates making positive profits in the future.

HOW TO OVERSTATE ACCOUNTING PROFITS

Some firms have even been known to juggle the books to misstate their accounting profits. They try to exaggerate profits to shareholders (to push the value of their stocks up) and then understate their profits to the government (to push taxes down).

Suppose a firm wants to overstate its profits. Here are some of the main ways some firms do this.

1. Overstating sales. Some firms lend money to buyers to get them to buy their goods. Sometimes these loans are made at below-market interest rates, thereby overstating the value of the sales. Sales will also be overstated if the firm does not take into account the likelihood that these buyers may default on the loans.

2. Overstating the value of increased inventories. Firms often count the value of unsold output put into inventory as part of sales. This is legitimate if the output is expected to be sold. But sometimes, the presence of unsold output indicates that the firm is facing a declining market. In the latter case, the goods added into inventory should not be counted as current sales.

3. Understating depreciation. Plant and equipment tends to wear out over the years and also to become obsolete. Depreciation is the annual cost of this wear-and-tear and obsolescence. Because it cannot be directly observed, the firm has to estimate the cost. And of course, a firm that understates this cost will be able to overstate its profits.

4. Understating future liabilities. Firms often incur obligations that entail costs, but because they do not occur in the current period, they go unreported. For example, until recently, firms did not report the cost of their promises to employees to provide them with health care after retirement. When forced by the accounting standards board to include these costs, this unreported cost wiped out the profits of many firms. Another unrecorded cost is the value of stock options given as compensation to top management. These obligations have a potential cost whose value can be easily estimated, yet this pay goes unrecorded.

CRIB NOTES

Long run: Firm has time to adjust all inputs so it produces a given level of Q at the lowest possible cost.

$LRAC \leq SRAC$ at all Q. $LRAC$ curve forms envelope below the $SRAC$ curves.

Returns to scale: Let I = inputs and Q = output.

Constant returns to scale: $\%\Delta I$ = resulting $\%\Delta Q$ such that Q/I constant.

Increasing returns to scale: $\%\Delta I < \%\Delta Q$ such that Q/I rises as Q rises.

Decreasing returns to scale: $\%\Delta I > \%\Delta Q$ such that Q/I declines as Q rises.

$LRAC = P_I \times I/Q$. Falls with increasing returns to scale, is constant with constant returns to scale, and rises with decreasing return to scale.

Economic profit = Total revenue – Explicit costs – Implicit costs, where implicit costs include foregone cost of owner's time and capital.

Review Questions

1. It takes 20 workers and 30 machines to make 50 widgets. It takes 30 workers and 45 machines to make 80 widgets. What economy of scale does the firm have over this range?

2. The following production functions show how output (Q) is related to the number of labor inputs (L) and the number of capital inputs (K). Indicate whether the production function has increasing, constant, or decreasing returns to scale.
   Production function A: $Q = 3\,L$
   Production function B: $Q = L \times K$
   Production function C: $Q = 2L + 3\,K$
   Production function D: $Q = L^{\frac{1}{2}} K^{\frac{1}{2}}$
   Production function E: $Q = L^A K^B$

3. Acme lays a railroad track between Apex and Base City. If it runs one train a day, it produces 2,000 ton miles a day. If it buys and runs a second train each day, it produces 4,000 ton miles a day. Over this range, does it have increasing, constant, or decreasing returns to scale?

4. In the developing country A, all its production processes are characterized by increasing returns to scale. In mature country B, all its production processes are characterized by constant returns to scale. If both countries are experiencing the same growth in population and capital investment, which is likely to have the higher rate of growth in per capita income?

5. Bill bought a time share for $10,000. He pays $300 a year in maintenance fees and gets a week's vacation, which he values at $500. "What a deal," Bill says. If he could earn 8% on his money elsewhere, do you agree with Bill?

6. The firm currently has a plant whose scale is such that its average cost curve is shown by curve A in the following graph. Curve B shows the long-run minimum average cost a firm can have should it vary all inputs, including the scale of the plant. If the firm had to produce X units in the short run, what would its unit cost be? In the long run? Will it be using the same scaled plant whose average cost is curve A?

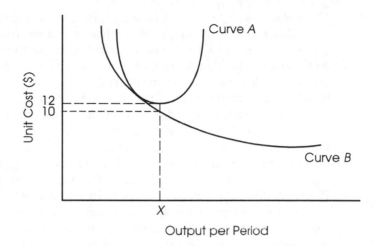

Output per Period

7. "Marxists for years have complained about capitalism creating assembly-line jobs that alienate workers. Yet, the problem for low-skilled workers today is that there are too few alienating jobs." In what sense is this quote correct?

8. If the world economy is characterized by constant returns to scale in terms of all inputs (including land, air, and water) and if the population of the earth doubled along with capital, what would happen to per capita income?

9. How does international trade foster increasing returns to scale?

Answers

1. Increasing returns to scale. All inputs increased by 50% while output increased by 60%. The ratio of output to inputs increased.
2. Use the following easy way to solve this type of question. First, let L and K equal 1 and solve for Q. Then double all inputs by letting L and K both equal 2. Check to see if output is 2 times what it was before (then we have constant returns to scale), less than 2 times what it was before (decreasing returns to scale), or greater than 2 times what it was before (increasing returns to scale).
Production function A:
Q when $L = 1$: $Q = 3 \times 1 = 3$
Q when $L = 2$ $Q = 3 \times 2 = 6$
6 is twice 3 so we have constant returns to scale.
Production function B:
Q when $L = 1$ and $K = 1$: $Q = 1 \times 1 = 1$
Q when $L = 2$ and $K = 2$: $Q = 2 \times 2 = 4$
4 is more than twice 1 so we have increasing returns to scale.
Production function C:
Q when $L = 1$ and $K = 1$: $Q = 2 \times 1 + 3 \times 1 = 5$
Q when $L = 2$ and $K = 2$: $Q = 2 \times 2 + 3 \times 2 = 10$
10 is twice 5 so we have constant returns to scale.

Production function D:

Q when $L = 1$ and $K = 1$: $Q = 1^{1/2}1^{1/2} = 1$

Q when $L = 2$ and $K = 2$: $Q = 2^{1/2}2^{1/2} = 2$

2 is twice 1 so we have constant returns to scale.

Production function E:

Q when $L = 1$ and $K = 1$: $Q = 1^A1^B = 1$

Q when $L = 2$ and $K = 2$: $Q = 2^A2^B = 2^{A+B}$

If $A + B = 1$, new $Q = 2$ so we have constant returns to scale.

If $A + B < 1$, new $Q < 2$ so we have decreasing returns to scale.

If $A + B > 1$, new $Q > 2$ so we have increasing returns to scale.

3. Acme doubled the number of trains but it didn't lay a second track. Thus, it was able to double output without having to double all inputs. So it has increasing returns to scale over this range. Projects with huge up-front capital costs often have economies of scale over a wide range of output and only reach the minimum efficient scale at very high levels of output.

4. Country A. The same increase in inputs causes its output to grow at a faster rate than in country B. The output to labor ratio is increasing in country A. So its per capita income (which is equivalent to output per person) will grow faster than in B. Eventually, its growth rate will slow down to B's rate as its economy becomes mature and its economies of scale have been fully utilized.

5. No. The accounting profit is $200 (counting the $500 as a form of revenue). But the implicit cost of the time share is the $800 a year he could have earned annually had he invested the $10,000 elsewhere. So his full cost is $1,100 ($300 + $800) and his economic loss is −$600. But don't tell Bill. He'll just get mad at you and at all economists.

6. Short-run cost would be on curve A: $12 a unit. Long-run cost is on curve B: $10. The long-run cost of $10 was not achieved in the plant whose scale is shown in curve A. Instead, it was achieved in a larger plant.

7. The division of labor increases the productivity and wages of low-skilled workers. The division of labor may also create boring, alienating jobs (although studies show that it is mainly workers with white-collar parents that find these jobs boring). Most low-skilled workers would gladly trade off being alienated for higher wages.

8. If all inputs doubled (available land, labor, and capital), output would double, and output per person would stay the same. Output per person must equal the income per person (this has to be true by definition for the whole population but is not necessarily true for any particular individual). But if one input is fixed (say land), then doubling all the other inputs must result in less than twice the output. So population (labor) doubles but output less than doubles: income per person must go down. Fortunately, in recent centuries, new inventions, better educated workers, and increasing returns to scale have resulted in this not occurring.

9. International trade allows for wider and larger markets. Goods that were previously produced in each nation in small quantities can now be produced in one or a few nations at a great savings due to the economies of scale allowed by the division of labor and large-scale production. Each nation will have its own specialty goods and will trade these for some of the goods it previously used to produce inefficiently. To see this point more clearly, imagine that the city you live in required that all goods bought and sold in that city be built in that city: cars, planes, homes, medical goods, and so forth. Everything must be locally produced! What would happen to per capita income? It would dramatically fall.

Chapter Nine

Perfect Competition

WHERE WE ARE GOING

The question this chapter seeks to answer is How is the market price determined? It divides the answer to this question into two periods: the short run and the long run. That's the same way we separated the previous two chapters.

Right now, I'm going to give away the answer. In the short run, price is determined by marginal cost. In the long run, price is determined by the minimum average cost. In both runs, the price is bid down to cost. That's where the word *competition* in our chapter title comes in: Competition is what causes the price to be bid down to cost.

PERFECT COMPETITION

There are two extremes in markets. At one extreme is a monopoly, where only one firm sells a good for which there are no close substitutes. At the other extreme is perfect competition where many firms sell goods that are perfect substitutes for one another. Most markets fall somewhere between these two extremes. By analyzing each extreme, it is possible by mixing the results to get predictions about where any given market is going.

Perfect competition is characterized as a market having:

1. A standardized good. Consumers regard the goods from each firm as a perfect substitute for the goods from other firms.
2. Many firms producing the good. How many? Enough to make collusion (that is, getting together and acting like a monopoly) impossible. How many is that? In simulation games where each player acts as a firm, it takes around 8 to 15 players to get the competitive result.
3. No barriers of entry to the market. Barriers to entry include patents, licensing agreements, and government restrictions that keep competition out.
4. Consumers and firms fully informed. All are informed about prices and the quality of the goods available.
   The next assumption is not necessary for perfect competition. It does, however, keep things simple:
5. All firms are identical. They all have exactly the same costs and cost curves.

The result of these assumptions is that each firm takes the market price of the good as something it cannot affect. If it produces more or less, within its current range of output, the market price stays the same. For example, one farmer's wheat crop, whether it's large or small, has no effect on the market price of wheat.

EQUILIBRIUM TO EQUILIBRIUM

We start with an industry fully in equilibrium. In our theoretical world, there have not been any changes in technology or demand for a long time. So each firm has fully adjusted to its long-run optimal scale, and no firm wants to enter or leave the industry. Everyone is in equilibrium.

Next, some event occurs. For example, demand might increase. First, there will be a short-run response. And then, if nothing else changes, the industry will in the long run fully adjust to this change, returning to equilibrium again. After the industry reaches equilibrium, all firms will once again be at their optimal scale, and no firm will want to leave or enter the industry.

So the industry starts in equilibrium and ends in equilibrium.

RUNS

There are actually two short runs and two long runs, but most textbooks do not make this clear.

The first set of runs is for the firm. In the firm's short run, it can only change its variable inputs to meet a change in demand. In the firm's long run, it can change all its inputs to meet a change in demand.

The second set of runs is for the industry. In the industry's short run, no new firms can enter the industry nor can any existing firms exit the industry. The number of firms is fixed in the industry's short run. In the industry's long run, firms can freely enter and exit from the industry until no more want to enter (or leave).

The two runs are linked because we assume that whatever existing firms do can be copied by new firms. In the short run, existing firms cannot increase their plant and equipment. Thus, a potential new firm also can't get new plant and equipment! Thus, they cannot enter the industry in the short run. Similarly, in the long run, an existing firm can add plant and equipment as needed to produce output efficiently. Similarly, new firms can copy the existing firms by entering into the industry by adding all the plant, equipment, and variable inputs they want. This continues until the long run is reached: No one wants to enter or leave and no one wants to produce more or less.

FIRM'S SHORT RUN

The firm follows three rules to get the highest profits it can.

Rule 1: In the short run, ignore sunk costs.
Rule 2: Add output as long as price covers marginal cost.
Rule 3: In the short run, produce output only if price covers average variable cost.

All three rules follow from marginal analysis.

Rule 1: In the Short Run, Ignore Sunk Costs

Rule 1 is that the firm ignores sunk costs. In the short run, these are the firm's fixed costs, which we assume the firm has already paid for. Fixed costs are the same no matter what the firm does, even if it shuts down! So they shouldn't affect what the best level of output is.

Thought Question

Acme can produce one widget a year or none at all. Its fixed costs are $100,000 for its plant and equipment. Its variable cost is $40,000. A widget sells for $70,000. Should it produce one widget or none at all?

It should produce one widget. Ignore the fixed costs! The marginal benefit of one widget is $70,000. Its marginal cost is $40,000. Hence, its net benefit is $30,000. Since its net benefit is positive, Acme is better off producing the one widget. To verify this, compare the profits of zero and one widget. If it produces no widget, its profit is −$100,000. If it does produce the widget, its profit is −$70,000. It is better off by $30,000 by producing the widget. The same would have been true if its fixed costs were $10 or $1 million!

Rule 2: Add Output as Long as Price Covers Marginal Cost

Rule 2 tells us how much output the firm should produce (assuming rule 3 says it should produce output). Using marginal analysis, the firm sets its level of output (Q) to maximize:

Profits = Total revenue − Total cost

To maximize profits, it compared the marginal benefit of increasing output by a unit (the resulting increase in total revenue) with its marginal cost (the increase in total cost).

The marginal benefit is the market price of the output: that's how much producing and selling one more unit of output adds to total revenue $(TR = P \times Q)$.

Marginal benefit of Q = Market price

For example, if the market price is $12 and the firm increases output from 4 to 5 units, the fifth unit adds $12 to its total revenues, which increases from $48 (= $12 × 4) to $60 (= $12 × 5).

The marginal cost is the increase in total cost due to producing one more unit of output. This is called the *firm's marginal cost*. So

Marginal cost of $Q = MC$

The increase in profits due to one more Q equals

Δ Profit = Marginal benefit − Marginal cost

or

Δ profit $= P - MC$

Finally, the firm, seeking the highest profits, increases Q as long as $P > MC$, thereby adding more and more to profits. It stops where $P = MC$. We have at optimal level of Q

$$P = MC.$$

When the optimal Q has been reached, the firm stops at that Q! Note that this is where profits are highest, not where output is highest.

Thought Question

Acme has a marginal cost of $1 for its first unit of output, a marginal cost of $2 if it adds a second unit of output, a marginal cost of $3 for its third unit of output, and so forth, each added Q having an MC that's a dollar higher than the previous Q's MC. If the market price is $6, how many units of output will it produce? What will its profit be, assuming it has a fixed cost of $5?

Using marginal analysis, we could generate Table 9.1. Marginal benefit equals marginal cost $(P = MC)$ at 6 units of output. So 6 is the optimal level of output, producing the highest profit possible.[1]

TABLE 9.1

Output	Marginal Benefit ($)	Marginal Cost ($)	Total Revenue ($)	Total Cost ($)	Profits ($)
0	—	—	0	5	–5
1	6	1	6	6	0
2	6	2	12	8	4
3	6	3	18	11	7
4	6	4	24	15	9
5	6	5	30	20	10
6	6	6	36	26	10
7	6	7	42	33	9
8	6	8	48	41	7

Points to note:

Marginal benefit is the price.
Total revenue increases by P.
Total cost increases by MC.
The $P = MC$ rule applies only in the zone where MC is rising. If MC is falling, higher profits may be had by increasing output as $P > MC$ for added output.
The increase in profits is $P - MC$. For example, going from $Q = 3$ to $Q = 4$, $P - MC$ for $Q = 4$ is $2 ($6 – $4). Similarly, profits go up by $2 (from $7 to $9).
The goal is to make the highest profit. It is not to make a profit.
Changing the fixed cost (here, it's $5) does not change the optimal Q. For example, if the fixed cost is $50, all the numbers in the total cost column go up by $45 and all the numbers in the profit column go down by $45. But the highest number is still at $Q = 6$. It's a profit of – $35 (a loss of $35). Any other level of output will make the loss bigger! So please, ignore fixed cost!

---

[1]The same is true for $Q = 5$. But recall that we use the tiebreaker of assuming that when the price covers the cost, the good will be provided.

Rule 3: In the Short Run, Produce Output only if Price Covers Average Variable Cost

Rule 2 says a unit of output should be produced if its price covers its marginal cost. Rule 3 says output should be produced only if its price covers its average variable cost. If not, the firm should shut down. Suppose we use rule 2 to find the optimal level of output. If, at this optimal output,

$$\text{Price} \geq AVC$$

then the firm should stay in business. To see why, multiply both sides by Q. We have

$$\text{Total revenue} \geq \text{Total variable cost}$$

This means the total benefit of being up and running ($= TR$) exceeds or equals the cost of being up and running ($= TVC$). It should be up and running. Note that we focus on variable costs because sunk costs don't matter.

On the other hand, if at its best Q,

$$\text{Price} < \text{Average variable cost}$$

the firm should shut down. To see why, multiply both sides by Q to get

$$TR < TVC$$

Here the firm should shut down because its revenues do not cover its variable costs. For example, this firm can sell all its output at a price of $6. Apply rule 2 to determine its optimal level of output. Then apply rule 3 to see if it should be up and running or if it should shut down. Its fixed cost are $5. (See Table 9.2.)

TABLE 9.2

Output	Marginal Benefit ($)	Marginal Cost ($)	Total Revenue ($)	Total Variable Cost ($)	AVC ($)	Total Cost ($)	Profit ($)
0	—	—	0	—	—	5	– 5
1	6	12	6	12	12	17	–11
2	6	6	12	18	9	23	–11
3	6	2	18	20	6.67	25	– 7
4	6	6	24	26	6.50	31	– 7
5	6	9	30	35	7	40	–10
6	6	11	36	46	7.66	51	–15
7	6	15	42	63	9	68	–21

Rule 2 says produce at $Q = 4$. Why not $Q = 2$? Because the next unit has $P > MC$. Marginal analysis is applied in the zone where MC is rising. The firm should shut down as $P < AVC$ at $Q = 4$.

Points to note:

The profit at $Q = 0$ (–$5) is bigger than any other profits in the profit column.
At no Q does total revenue cover the firm's total variable cost.
$P = MC$ rule applies only in the zone where MC rises with Q.

Quick Summary

Marginal analysis of firm's output decision:
marginal benefit of added Q is P;
marginal cost of added Q is MC;
increase in profit from added $Q = P - MC$.
increase Q if $P > MC$.
optimal Q^* where $P = MC$.
Stay in business in short run if at optimal Q^*, it is covering its variable cost
    If $P \geq AVC$ at Q^*, stay in business
    If $P < AVC$ at Q^*, better to shut down

FIRM'S SHORT-RUN SUPPLY CURVE

We now will use these three rules to construct the firm's short-run supply curve. If you go back to Sellers' Hall, you will recall that each seller would write down for each price how many pairs of shoes he would supply. That is what a supply curve does: It tells us at each price how many units sellers are willing to supply.

Thought Question

For the following firm, use the three rules to determine how many units the firm will supply at $1. At $2. Do this through $7. The firm's fixed cost is $1 trillion. (Note: You should be able to derive the AVC column from the MC column, using the fact that TVC equals the sum of MCs.)

TABLE 9.3

Q	MC ($)	AVC ($)
1	6	6
2	1	3.50
3	2	3
4	3	3
5	4	3.20
6	5	3.50
7	6	3.86

First, ignore the sunk cost in determining what output to produce. If $P = \$1$, rule 2 says, if you produce, Q should be 1. Rule 3 says don't produce because $P < AVC$ at $Q = 1$. So if $P = 1$, $Q = 0$. The same holds true at $P = \$2$, $Q = 0$. At $P = \$3$, rule 2 says, if you produce, Q should equal 4. Rule 3 says the firm should produce as $P = AVC$. So if $P = \$3$, $Q = 4$. For all prices higher than $3, rule 3 is satisfied. Once the price equals or exceeds the smallest AVC, the firm should produce. So we proceed with rule 2 and get the firm's short-run supply curve:

Price	Firm's Supply
$1	0
2	0
3	4
4	5
5	6
6	7

Points to note:

The firm should produce when the price equals or exceeds the minimum *AVC.*
Once $P \geq$ minimum *AVC,* the *MC* curve becomes the supply curve. That is, for each
given price, find the Q for which $P = MC$ and that is Q the firm will supply

What is the firm's short-run supply curve in Figure 9.1?

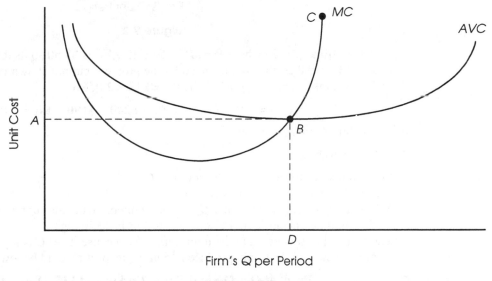

Firm's Q per Period

Figure 9.1

The firm's short-run supply curve is the *MC* curve above the minimum *AVC* of *A.*
In Figure 9.1, the supply curve is *B* to *C* (and higher if it were shown).

If the price is below *A,* it shuts down and supplies nothing. If the price equals *A,* it
supplies $Q = D$ units of output. To see how much it supplies at a higher price, take a
ruler and draw a horizontal line from the price on the left-hand axis to the *MC* curve
and then down a line straight to the Q-axis. That's the Q it will supply at that price.

The firm's shut-down price is the price below which the firm shuts down. If the price
is at or above the shut-down price, the firm should operate. As the preceding two examples show, in the short run:

Short-run shut-down price = Minimum average variable cost

Note that at the shut-down price the firm is still open! It only shuts down when the
price slips below the shut-down price.

How many units will this firm supply at a price of $12? If its fixed cost is $40, what
is its profit? What is its shut-down price? Refer to Figure 9.2.

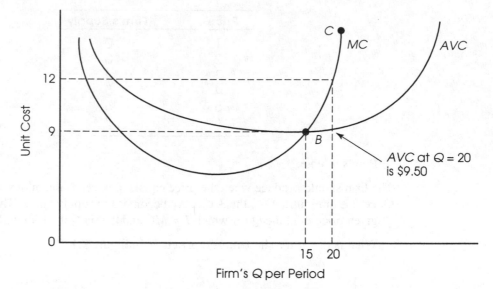

Figure 9.2

The optimal $Q = 20$ where $P = MC = \$12$. Its AVC is \$9.50 so its total variable cost is \$190. Its fixed cost is \$40, as given by the problem but not shown in Figure 9.2. Finally, its total revenue at $Q = 20$ is \$240 (= \$12 × 20). So

$$\text{Profits} = TR - TVC - TFC = \$240 - \$190 - \$40 = \$10$$

Its shut-down price is \$9.

Points to note:

Short-run shut-down price = Minimum AVC.
$MC = AVC$ at the minimum AVC.
MC is rising (going up at higher Q) on the segment that is the supply curve. Thus, the firm will be operating in the zone where MP is declining.
The firm is not producing at the minimum AVC because its AVC is higher for Q greater than 15. If it only produced 15 units, its profit would be lower:

$$\text{Profit at } Q = \$15 \text{ and } P = \$12 = \$180 - \$135 - \$40 = \$5$$

Sometimes an example will add in the average total cost curves and the average fixed cost curves. Remember to ignore sunk costs. So ignore these two curves because they both include fixed cost. Output is going to be determined by marginal cost and shut down is going to be determined by variable costs. These two curves, and only these two curves, determine what short-run supply will be. The only thing total cost adds is to tell us what profits are as:

$$\text{Profit} = (P - ATC) \times Q$$

where $P - ATC$ is the firm's average profit per unit.

What is the optimal Q in Figure 9.3 when the market price is \$15? What is the firm's profit?

The firm should produce 100 units, where $P = MC$. At $Q = 100$, $ATC = \$12$ so it is making a profit of \$3 a unit, so total profits are \$300 (\$3 times a Q of 100). Why not produce where ATC is at a minimum? Because $P > MC$ at $Q = 93$; consequently, it can add to its profits by producing more, even if this means its ATC goes up.

Points to note:

Q where $P = MC$ in rising portion of MC curve.
$MC = AVC$ at the minimum AVC.

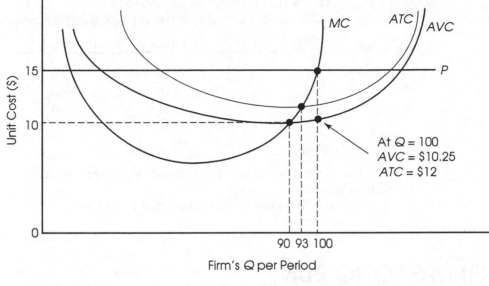

At $Q = 100$
$AVC = \$10.25$
$ATC = \$12$

Figure 9.3

$MC = ATC$ at the minimum ATC.
If $MC > AVC$, then firm's AVC exceeds its minimum AVC.
The shut-down price is \$10.
$TFC = \$175$ (at $Q = 100$, $ATC = \$12$ and $AVC = \$10.25$).
Profits are highest at $Q = 100$.
Fixed costs could be so high that $ATC > P$ and the firm is making a loss, yet the optimal Q would still be $Q = 100$!

SHORT-RUN INDUSTRY SUPPLY

In the short run, by definition, firms can neither leave nor enter the industry. Thus, the number of firms is fixed. So, to get the industry supply, we just sum the supplies of each firm in the industry.

We have assumed that all firms have the same cost curves. So if one firm will supply 3 units of output at a price of \$12, and if there are 100 firms in the industry, the industry supply will be 300 units at \$12.

Note that the industry supply curve still reflects marginal cost!

Thought Question

There are 200 firms in the widget industry. All firms are identical. One firm's supply curve is as follows, where q is the firm's supply.

P (\$)	q
4	0
5	5
6	9
7	11
8	12

(Minimum $AVC = \$5$)

What is the industry's supply curve?

Just multiply each *q* by 200 to get the industry's supply *(Q):*

P (\$)	Firm's q	Industry Q
4	0	0
5	5	1,000
6	9	1,800
7	11	2,200
8	12	2,400

Points to note:

The industry's short-run supply curve will be positively sloped.
It rises because *MC* goes up.
Its rise is due to the law of diminishing marginal returns.

FIRM'S LONG RUN

Let us once again distinguish two concepts that get confused in many texts. First, there are sunk costs: These are costs that the firm has already committed to up front. For example, if it bought its plant and equipment, these costs have to be paid whether the firm is up and running or if it shuts down. Second, there are inputs that do not increase with output. These are fixed inputs, and their cost is fixed cost. In the short run, we assumed the firm has already paid for all its fixed inputs. Thus, in the short run, fixed costs (the cost of fixed inputs) were also sunk costs.

In the long run, there are no sunk costs. All plant and equipment depreciate over the years and eventually the firm can decide whether to replace them or close the plant. At that point, the cost of new plant and equipment that will replace the old has not yet been sunk.

We also assume that, in the long run, all inputs are variable. That is, increasing any of the inputs will increase output, and, conversely, increased output will be achieved efficiently in the long run by increasing all inputs.

When all inputs are variable, the rules that apply in the short run still apply.

Rule 1: The firm should ignore sunk costs—but this is easy in the long run as there are no sunk costs in the long run!

Rule 2: Price should cover the variable cost of adding another unit of output.

The only change is that marginal cost includes the cost of increasing all inputs, not just a few. Note that the marginal cost due to increasing all inputs to produce another unit of output need not be higher than the marginal cost of increasing only a few inputs. That's because it is often cheaper in the long run to increase all inputs a little rather than to increase a few inputs a lot.

Rule 3: The firm should operate and produce output when

$$P \geq ATC$$

as $ATC = AVC$ and $AFC = 0$.

There are no fixed inputs and, thus, no fixed costs in the long run. Nevertheless; we'll continue to identify certain inputs as fixed and show their costs as fixed costs. The *fixed* means fixed in the short run. In the long run, we really mean *formerly fixed.*

Figure 9.4 shows the firm's long-run supply curve going from point *B* to *C* (and higher if we had drawn the *MC* line higher). The long-run shut-down price is \$*A*.

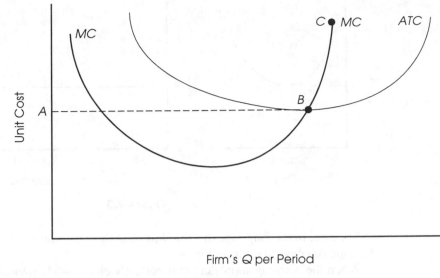

Figure 9.4

INDUSTRY LONG-RUN SUPPLY CURVE: CONSTANT COST INDUSTRY

Let us begin with the simplest case. We have already assumed that all firms are equally efficient and face the same costs. In addition, in the long run, we've assumed that firms can freely enter and exit the industry. Now let us add a third assumption: The price of inputs stays constant as the industry expands. Alternatively stated, all inputs are in perfectly elastic supply to the industry.

Given these assumptions, there is only one long-run result. Firms will enter the industry until the price is bid down to the lowest unit cost possible.

Long-run result: Price = Minimum *ATC*.

Why is this the only result possible? Suppose we observe $P >$ Minimum *ATC*. This means each firm is making an economic profit. Can this be a long-run equilibrium? No! Because as long as economic profits are to be made, new firms will enter the industry (recall that economic profits are the excess of revenues over the cost necessary to get someone to operate in the industry). So new firms will enter. In turn, this increases the quantity supplied. In turn, this reduces the price.

Entry continues until economic profits are bid to zero and $P =$ Minimum *ATC*.

We have $P >$ Minimum *ATC* $\longrightarrow$ profits being made $\longrightarrow$ new firms enter $\longrightarrow$ increase in supply $\longrightarrow$ price falls $\longrightarrow$ entry continues until $P =$ Minimum *ATC*.

On the other hand, suppose we observed the opposite; $P <$ Minimum *ATC*. Now, all firms are making a loss! In the long run, some firms will leave the industry. In turn, supply is reduced. In turn, the price goes up. This continues until the price goes back to minimum *ATC*.

We have: $P <$ Minimum *ATC* $\longrightarrow$ losses being made $\longrightarrow$ old firms leaving $\longrightarrow$ decrease in supply $\longrightarrow$ price rises $\longrightarrow$ exit continues until $P =$ Minimum *ATC*.

In the long run, firms will enter or exit, thereby changing the supply of Q until $P =$ Minimum *ATC*. Given free entry and the assumptions we made, the industry's long-run supply curve is shown in Figure 9.5. On the left, the firm's minimum *ATC* is A. On the right, the industry's supply curve is perfectly elastic at price A. Firms will enter and exit to make this true.

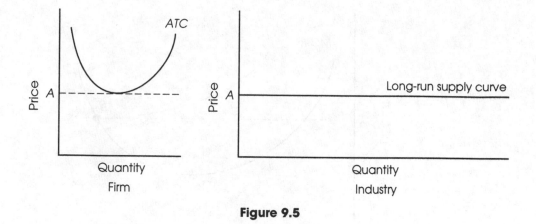

Figure 9.5

Because, in the long run, all firms will be at their minimum *ATC,* they all will be in the zone of constant returns to scale.

When the long-run supply curve is perfectly elastic—a horizontal line—we say the industry is a constant-cost industry. To make predictions is very easy for constant-cost industry. Just calculate what the most efficient way of making a good is (i.e., its minimum *ATC*). That's what the price will equal in the long run.

Thought Questions

All firms have the following long-run costs:

q	MC	TC
1	10	10
2	6	16
3	10	26
4	20	46

If industry demand is $P^D = 100 - 0.05Q$, what will the long-run price be? The long-run industry Q? Each firm's output? Profit? How many firms will there be in the industry?

First, you need to find the minimum *ATC*. It's $8 at $q = 2$. Next, solve for industry Q, using this price and the demand curve: $8 = 100 - 0.05Q$. $Q = 1,840$. Each firm will have an economic profit of zero (because P = Minimum *ATC*). As each firm has a $q = 2$ at the q where it achieves its minimum *ATC,* there are 920 firms in the industry (Number of firms = Industry Q/firm $q = 1,840 / 2$).

A researcher for Wiley Widgets discovers a way to make widgets 30% more valuable to customers and, at the same time, reduce the cost of making them by 10%. Unfortunately, Wiley Widgets forgets to patent this technique so it is available to all. The widget industry is a constant-cost industry. In the long run, how will this discovery change the price of widgets?

It will reduce the price by 10%. Yet, widgets are more valuable, but competition bids their price down to their new lower cost. This is shown by the move from A to B in Figure 9.6. In Figure 9.6, it is assumed the initial long-run price of widgets was $10. Because of its 30% increase in value, the value of the Q_0th unit of the good jumps to

$13 while its unit cost falls to $9. A $4 per unit profit is being made. But new firms will copy this technique, enter the industry, and bid the price down to the new long-run supply curve at $9. The demand curve is shown to be shifting up because widgets are more valuable to customers after this discovery. Notice how the shift in the demand curve does not change the long-run supply price.

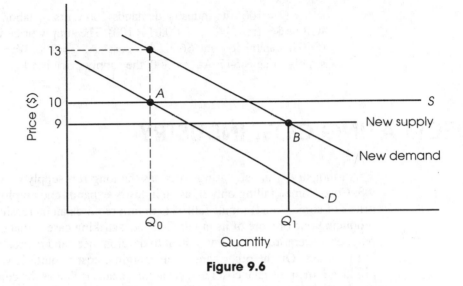

Figure 9.6

INCREASING COST INDUSTRY SUPPLY CURVE

An increasing cost industry has a long-run supply curve as shown in Figure 9.7. It is positively sloped. For an industry to have increasing long-run costs, we must modify the third assumption by assuming, instead, that the price of all (or some) inputs goes up as the industry expands.

All firms have the same costs but the price of inputs goes up as the industry expands. Why does this raise costs? Because as the industry expands, the price of inputs goes up with the result that all firms now have a higher minimum *ATC*.

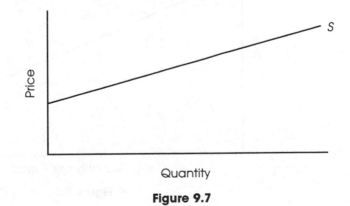

Figure 9.7

Thought Question

Each widget takes 2 units of capital and 1 unit of labor to produce. Capital costs $20 per unit, no matter how many units the industry demands. Labor's supply curve is $W^S = \$5 + 0.01L$. What will the long-run supply price be when $Q = 100$? When $Q = 200$? 300?

At $Q = 100$, the industry demands 100 units of labor. The wage will be $6 (from $W^S = \$5 + 0.01 \times 100$). The supply price will be $46 ($40 in capital cost and $6 in labor cost). At $Q = 200$, $W^S = \$7$ and the supply price is $47. At $Q = 300$, the supply price is $48.

DECREASING COST INDUSTRY

An industry with decreasing costs has the long-run supply curve shown in Figure 9.8. Costs can be falling only if, as an industry expands and employs more inputs, the prices of some (or all) inputs fall. This in turn requires an increasing return to scale in producing one or more of its inputs. The most striking case is that of computers. Computer chips require a large investment to develop them and to create their manufacturing facilities. On the other hand, their marginal cost is quite low. Thus, as more are produced, their average cost falls. What this means is that as the computer industry expands, the companies can buy chips at a cheaper price. If they sold only a few computers a year, each computer would cost in the millions to cover the cost of developing and making the chips. However, if they sold millions of computers, the cost of chips would become very low, which, in turn, would reduce the price of computers.

Decreasing-cost industries have the unusual characteristic that an increase in demand results in a lower price. Similarly, a tax of X dollars per unit increases the price by more than X dollars.

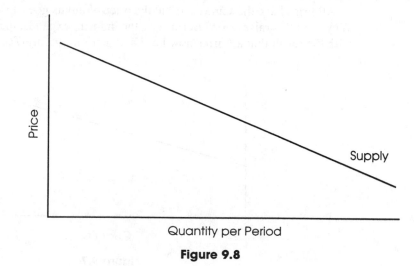

Figure 9.8

Thought Question

Suppose the government imposes a $100 tax on each computer to help finance its censorship of the Internet. If each computer originally costs $2,000, show graphically that the price will go up by more than $100 if computers are a decreasing-cost industry. (Assume all computers are identical and produced by many firms.)

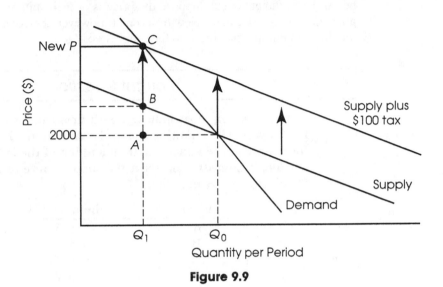

Figure 9.9

Before the tax, $P = \$2,000$ at Q_0. The tax shifts the supply curve vertically up by $100, as shown by the arrows: distance B to C is $100. In addition, the higher price reduces demand to Q_1. The decrease in Q raises the cost of computers to suppliers from $2,000 to price $= B$. Add to this increase in cost (from A to B) the $100 tax and we have the result: New price $= \$2,000 + (B - A) + \$100$ and so, new price $> \$2,000 + \$100$.

WHY DOES COST GO UP?

Why does the price go up when demand goes up? There are three reasons:

1. Short run for firm: Diminishing marginal productivity.
2. Long run for firm: Decreasing returns to scale.
3. Long run for industry: Rising price for inputs.

Each of these reasons is different from the other. In particular, consider the long run for an industry. Rising costs are *not* due to diminishing marginal product because, in the long run, all inputs can be increased so as to avoid the consequences of diminishing *MP*. Similarly, all firms will be at their minimum *ATC* and so, all will have constant returns to scale. The main cause of unit costs going up in the long run is rising input prices. However, if the industry is relatively small in the input markets from which it buys, it will face a constant input price as it expands: It will be a constant-cost industry.

Diminishing *MP* applies in the short run. Decreasing returns to scale apply in the intermediate run as the industry expands, but before the price is bid down to the minimum *ATC*. Finally, rising input prices apply in the long run (if they apply!).

ANOTHER REASON FOR RISING LONG-RUN COSTS

Costs will rise in the long run if the new entrants to the industry are not as efficient as the current firms in the industry. Go back to the shoe example and suppose that the town crier starts with a low price and slowly goes up. Which firms are likely to supply shoes when shoe prices are low? The efficient firms or the inefficient firms? Obviously, the efficient firms, as they have lower costs. So if new firms enter the industry, they will be the less efficient ones. Suppose the price is at their minimum *ATC*. Now demand goes up and the price rises. New firms enter; however, they don't bid the price back to its old level but, instead, bid it to their higher cost!

Thought Question

In the really big boat industry, each firm can only produce one boat a year. The following shows the minimum *ATC* of one boat for several of these firms, both in and out of the industry. These are long-run costs. Construct the supply curve to the industry. Dollar figures are in millions.

Firm	Minimum ATC
A	$ 8
B	$ 5
C	$ 7
D	$ 6
E	$10

Start at the bottom with the lowest price and work your way up:

Supply price	Quantity	Firms supplying boats
$10	5	B, D, C, A, E
$ 9	4	B, D, C, A
$ 8	4	B, D, C, A
$ 7	3	B, D, C
$ 6	2	B, D
$ 5	1	B
$ 4	0	none

One of the largest industries characterized by this difference in efficiency is agriculture. For a given amount of work and fertilizer, some land is more productive than others. As the demand for food expands, farmers have to move to less productive land to raise more crops. This causes the supply price of food to go up, even in the long run.

SHORT TO LONG RUN: AN INCREASE IN DEMAND

To trace the effects of events on price and output, we use the following sequence:
Start: long-run equilibrium
Event
Short-run equilibrium
Intermediate run
End: long-run equilibrium

Figure 9.10 shows the start: the initial long-run equilibrium. On the left side is the firm's equilibrium and on the right side is the industry's equilibrium. We will assume that the industry is a constant-cost industry, so that if costs don't change, the industry will return to the price shown in this initial diagram.

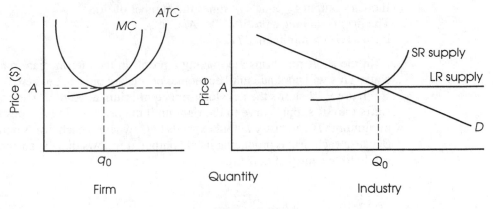

Figure 9.10

Points to note:

The firm's output is at q_0, the q which has its minimum ATC.
$MC = ATC$ at q_0.
Q_0 equals the number of firms times q_0.
The industry's short-run supply curve (SR supply) equals the number of firms times the q along the firm's MC curve.
The industry's long-run supply curve (LR supply) is a horizontal line whose height is the firm's minimum ATC.
Economic profit $= 0$.

Now, let us go to the event. Let demand go up. Figure 9.11 shows the short-run effects of this event. The equilibrium goes from point a to point b, the price from A to B, firm output from q_0 to q_b, and industry output from Q_0 to Q_b.

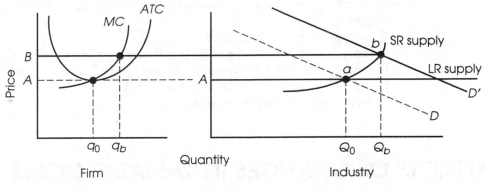

Figure 9.11

133

Points to note:

New demand curve shown by D'.
Firm produces where new price $B = MC$ at q_b.
Price is determined where demand equals SR supply at point b.
Industry output Q_b equals q_b times the number of firms.
The firm is making a profit as $P > ATC$ at q_b.
Firm's $ATC >$ minimum ATC.

In the short run, firms are making a profit. In the intermediate run, new firms will enter. This will continue until economic profits are bid back to zero.

Figure 9.12 shows the new long-run equilibrium at point c. The entry of new firms shifts the SR supply curve to the right until the price is bid back down to price A, the minimum ATC. Industry output expands to Q_c whereas each firm's output returns to q_0. Because each firm is producing its old output, it follows that expansion in output is due solely to the entry of new firms.

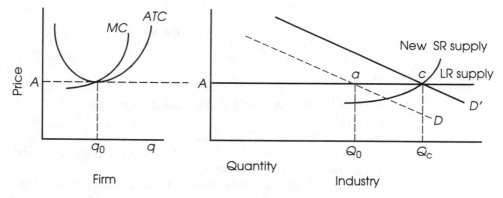

Figure 9.12

Points to note:

Price returns to original price A.
Firm output q_0 where $MC = P =$ minimum ATC.
SR supply curve $(Q =$ firm's q times number of firms) shifts right as number of firms goes up.
$Q_c =$ New number of firms times q_0.
Industry equilibrium at point c. No firm is making a profit as $P =$ minimum ATC.
In constant-cost industry, change in demand leaves P unchanged in long run.
In increasing-cost industry, new price $>$ price A.
In decreasing-cost industry, new price $< A$.

EFFECTS OF CHANGES IN VARIABLE COSTS

Industries often face increases in costs. Suppose that the price of oil goes up and the industry we are examining uses oil in its production process. Also, to isolate the impact of this higher cost, assume that demand stays the same (that is, the demand curve does not shift).

Figure 9.13 shows the full effects of this event:

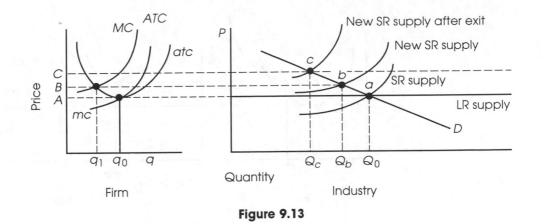

Figure 9.13

Points to note:

The industry starts at point *A,* where *P* = minimum *ATC* along the old cost curves (shown by *mc* and *atc).*

The effect of the higher cost shifts the *MC* and *ATC* cost curves vertically up (the *q* at which *ATC* reaches a minimum can also change, but we assume it stays unchanged).

The short-run effect is that the new price is established where demand equals the new SR supply at point *b*, output Q_b and price *B*.

In the short run, each firm produces q_1 where price *B* = new *MC*. Firms are making a loss at price *B* < new *ATC*.

Firms leave the industry, shifting SR supply curve to left until point *c* is reached. At this point, *P* = new minimum *ATC,* each firm produces q_0 units of output, and industry supply (Q_c) equals number of firms × q_0 (or whatever *q* is associated with firm's new minimum *ATC).* Main source of reduced supply: few firms.

New SR supply curve after exit = Number of firms (now fewer) × firm's *q* along its new higher *MC* curve.

EFFECTS OF INCREASE IN FIXED COSTS

Up to this point, we've assumed that no input is fixed in the long run. In fact, in many cases, industries have fixed inputs in the long run. For example, the cost of setting up an organization is effectively a fixed input—that is, they are the same no matter how much output goes up. Land in many countries is a fixed input that cannot be easily increased for farming. Whereas an input may be fixed (that is, it does not increase with output), its cost need not be sunk. Instead, fixed costs in the long run—if they exist—can change!

Now let's examine what happens if fixed costs go up.

If fixed costs go up, marginal costs (the cost of the variable inputs) will be unaffected. Thus, in the short run, nothing happens! The firm's marginal costs are the same. Price equals the same *MC* at the same *Q*. The number of firms is unchanged. So industry supply is the same in the short run.

What *has* happened is that firms are now taking a loss. So, after the short run is over, firms leave the industry. In the intermediate run, firms leave the industry, causing the supply to fall. The price goes up until it covers the new minimum *ATC*. Figure 9.14 shows the results. The industry starts and, initially, stays at point *a* when fixed costs go up. The firm's *MC* is unchanged but its *ATC* jumps up from *atc* to *ATC*. Eventually

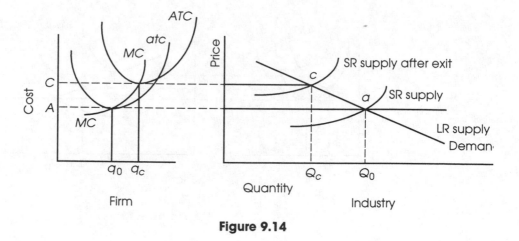

Figure 9.14

firms leave the industry until the price rises from *A* to *C* and the industry moves to point *c*.

Points to note:

MC curve stays the same.

Price rises to *C* in the long run as firms exit the industry until *P* = minimum *ATC*.

Each firm's output *(q)* goes up from q_0 to q_c as the price rises up the *MC* curve. Remaining firms will be larger than before. The greater size is needed to cover the bigger long-run fixed costs.

Since *Q* goes down and *q* goes up, the percent of firms exiting the industry must be greater than the percent reduction in *Q;* the industry is left with fewer but larger firms.

Thought Question

Los Angeles recently required all dry cleaners to add very extensive pollution control equipment to reduce the emissions due to the use of dry cleaning chemicals. This equipment was very expensive (around $50,000) and was so large that most dry cleaning stores only needed one unit. Even if their output expanded dramatically, that one unit would be sufficient to clean their emissions. So here is a long-run fixed cost, and because it was not yet in place, it was not a sunk cost even in the short run. What would be the effects of this law?

Unlike the case above, where the fixed inputs are already paid for, the firm can avoid buying the fixed input of pollution equipment by going out of business. Thus, this law will cause some of the dry cleaners to immediately leave the industry. The remaining firms will be larger, selling their output at a higher price. However, they will not be making a profit, because the higher price reflects the higher cost of doing business.

ALLOCATIVE EFFICIENCY

Competitive markets are allocatively efficient, in that they maximize the net benefits to society of supplying the good. We can use marginal analysis to show this result. Suppose we want to maximize the net benefit to society by optimally setting the quantity (Q) of good X.

We want to set Q to maximize net benefit = total benefit – total cost. As Q increases by 1 unit, total benefit goes up by X's marginal benefit. But the demand price (P^D) for the good reflects its marginal benefit (MB) to consumers, so

$$\Delta TB = MB = P^D$$

Total cost goes up by X's marginal cost (MC). But the supply price (P^S), in both the short and long runs, reflects the marginal cost to suppliers of producing the good, so

$$\Delta TC = MC = P^S$$

Q should be increased as long as net benefit of X goes up. But

$$\Delta NB = MB - MC = P^D - P^S$$

At the optimal Q,

$$MB = MC, \text{ and } P^D = P^S$$

In Figure 9.15, the shaded area reflects the net benefit to society of producing good X. Note that this area reflects the vertical difference between the demand price and the supply price up to the optimal Q, Q^*. This is the same result that competitive markets produce. A key result is that competitive markets are socially efficient! In equilibrium, the demand price equals the supply price, and the social net benefit of the good is maximized. This result requires that the demand price reflect the benefit of goods to consumers (for example, that they are not fooled or misled) and that the supply price reflects the cost of the good to suppliers (for example, that they pay the full cost of the pollution they produce).

Another way competitive markets are efficient is that firms in the long run produce at the lowest cost possible (that is, at the minimum ATC). Competition forces managers to be efficient. If they aren't, their business will be bid away from them. From a social point of view, this means that society is getting the output it enjoys at the least cost in its scarce resources. Studies suggest that economies that protect their industries grow more slowly and are less productive.

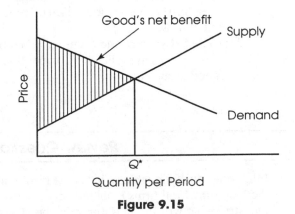

Figure 9.15

A CHALLENGE

Return to Chapter Three. Notice how the models presented in that chapter are similar to the model of perfect competition. Squirrels compete until all get the same food per squirrel, builders compete until their economic profit is reduced to zero, and welfare recipients move until all get the same net utility. All these results are similar to the long-run result of no economic profit. The model applies to many areas of life. For example, when I go shopping for shrubs and flowers, I want plants that grow fast and are easy to care for. So I shop for the cheapest plant I can find. Why? Because I know that competition will cause the cost of the plant to reflect its cost. And the plants that grow fastest and are the easiest to care for will also have the lowest cost! Price reflects cost, not value (except for the marginal unit of the good). As another example, I advise my students to avoid careers that everyone likes. Why? Because if lots of people like a career, they will be willing to go into it even when it pays a low money wage. Lots of people like the idea of being a forest ranger. So it is not surprising then that forest rangers earn little. Few people like being an economist. Hey, so where are my big bucks?

CRIB NOTES

Perfect competition: Many firms producing standardized good, no entry barriers produce Q if $P \geq MC$ and $P \geq AVC$.

Firm short-run supply curve: MC curve above minimum AVC.

Industry short-run supply: Number of firms × firm's q where $P = MC$. Number of firms fixed in short run.

Long-run supply: P^S = Minimum ATC, Q where P^D = Long-run P^S.

Constant-cost industry: Minimum ATC stays the same as Q goes up.

Increasing cost industry: Minimum ATC rises as Q goes up (due to input prices rising).

Decreasing cost industry: Minimum ATC falls as Q goes up (due to input prices falling).

Event: Demand up $\longrightarrow$ price up $\longrightarrow$ firm q up along MC curve $\longrightarrow$ $P > ATC$ and firm's profit > 0 $\longrightarrow$ firms enter industry $\longrightarrow$ price down till P = Minimum ATC.

Event: Variable cost up $\longrightarrow$ MC curve up, firm q cut $\longrightarrow$ reduction in industry supply $\longrightarrow$ $P \leq$ Minimum ATC, firms making loss $\longrightarrow$ firm exit $\longrightarrow$ price rises more until P = new higher minimum ATC.

Triangle between D and S curve: = Net benefit to society of good. Area = 1/2 base × height. Competition maximized net benefit of good to society.

Review Questions

1. Fill in the following table. What is the firm's shut-down price in the short run? In the long run? If all firms in an industry are like this one, and it is a constant-cost industry, what will the long-run price be? (Assume this also shows its long-run costs.)

Output	Marginal Cost ($)	Total Variable Cost ($)	Total Cost ($)	AVC ($)	ATC ($)
0	—	—	10	—	—
1	12				
2	6				
3	3				
4	3				
5	6				
6	8				
7	11				
8	17				

2. How many units will the firm supply in the short run if the price is at $3, $4, $6, $8, $11, $15, and $7?

3. Using the data from question 1, what will the industry Q and P be and how many firms will there be if the demand curve is $P^D = 80 - 0.02Q$?

4. If there are 600 firms in this industry, what is the industry's short-run supply curve?

5. Assume the industry is in equilibrium as described in question 3. Then consumers are willing to pay $15 more per unit than they were before: Demand jumps up so that now $P^D = 95 - 0.02Q$. What will the short-run price be? How much will each firm produce? (Note: Solve this by adding a column to the table in question 1 that shows the demand at price). What will the long-run price be and what will output be?

6. A constant-cost industry firm is in long-run equilibrium. Then demand goes up. Indicate which of these events will occur in the short run and which in the long run (if they occur in both, put both down).
   Event A. The price goes up.
   Event B. Industry output goes up.
   Event C. Firm output goes up.
   Event D. Firm makes a profit.
   Event E. More firms enter (or have entered) the industry.

7. An increasing-cost industry firm is in long-run equilibrium. Then demand goes up. Indicate which of these events will occur in the short run and which in the long run (if they occur in both, put both down).
   Event A. The price goes up.
   Event B. Industry output goes up.
   Event C. Firm output goes up.
   Event D. Firm makes a profit.
   Event E. More firms enter (or have entered) the industry.

8. A decreasing-cost industry firm is in long-run equilibrium. Then demand goes up. Indicate which of these events will occur in the short run and which in the long run (if they occur in both, put both down).

Event A. The price goes up.
Event B. The price goes down.
Event C. Industry output goes up.
Event D. Firm output goes up.
Event E. Firm makes a profit.
Event F. More firms enter (or have entered) the industry.

9. Describe the short-run and the long-run effects on the firm and industry of a decrease in demand. Assume the industry is a constant-cost industry.

10. The following are the demand and long-run supply curves for a decreasing-cost industry:

$$P^D = 200 - 2Q$$
$$P^S = 120 - Q$$

a. How can we tell that this is a decreasing-cost industry?
b. What is the equilibrium price and output?
c. Suppose a $10 per unit tax is imposed: how much will the price go up?
d. Suppose instead a $10 subsidy is given: how much will the price fall?

11. A competitive firm's $MC = \$8$, $ATC = \$12$, $AVC = \$6$, and $P = \$7$. Should it expand output, contract output, stay where it is, or shut down?

12. The widget industry is international and highly competitive. The world price for widgets is $10. Suppose the United States imposes a $1 per unit tax on U.S. widget makers (foreign suppliers go untaxed). What is the likely long-run consequences of this tax? Give your answer assuming widgets are a worldwide constant-cost industry. Assume before the tax is imposed that the industry is in a long-run equilibrium.

13. How would you predict the price of personal computers in the year 2005 (after adjusting the price to reflect changes in quality and power)? Assume you know the price of personal computer parts in the year 2005.

14. If demand is $P^D = 21 - Q$ and supply is $P^S = 3 + 2Q$, what is the maximum net benefit society can get from this good? How does this compare to competitive result? What is the social net benefit (in $)?

15. People in grocery stores usually try to get into the shortest line. If all clerks are equally efficient at getting people through, what does this imply about the average length of line for each clerk? If a store owner observed one clerk having a line that is longer than average, and the store owner believes her customers know the relative efficiency of clerks, then what can she conclude about that clerk's efficiency?

16. Which is more competitive, a football game or taking a test to qualify to get into college?

Answers

1. You should have the following:

The short-run shut-down price is $6 (the minimum AVC). The long-run shut-down price is $8 (the minimum ATC). The long-run supply price will also be $8 (the minimum ATC).

Output	Marginal Cost ($)	Total Variable Cost ($)	Total Cost ($)	AVC ($)	ATC ($)
0	—	—	10	—	—
1	12	12	22	12	22
2	6	18	28	9	14
3	3	21	31	7	10.33
4	3	24	34	6	8.50
5	6	30	40	6	8
6	8	38	48	6.33	8
7	11	49	59	7	8.43
8	17	66	76	8.25	9.50

2. Using the rules, at $3 or $4, it will shut down. Only when the price reaches $6 will it begin operating: At $6, $q = 5$ (where $P = MC$). At $8, $q = 6$. At $11, $q = 11$. But what about $P = \$15$? There is no MC of $15. Using the rules, the firm adds output as long as $P > MC$. It stops at $q = 7$ (if it went on to produce the eighth unit, its profits would fall by $2). Similarly, at $P = 7$, $q = 5$.

3. The long-run price is $8 (the minimum ATC). Next use the demand curve to solve for Q: $\$8 = 80 - 0.02Q$, so $Q = 3{,}600$. Each firm has a q of 6 when $P = \$8$. So the number of firms equals 600 (= 3,600/6).

4. It is the short-run supply curve times 600:
   Shut-down price = $6

Price	Firm's q	Industry Q^S
$5	0	0
$6	5	3,000
$8	6	3,600
$11	7	4,200
$17	8	4,800

What about in-between prices? They are the same as the short-run prices. For example, if $P = \$16$, $q = 7$, and $Q = 4{,}200$.

5. The new table will be as follows:

Price	Firm's q	Industry Q^S	Quantity Demanded
$5	0	0	4,500
$6	5	3,000	4,450
$8	6	3,600	4,350
$11	7	4,200	4,200
$17	8	4,800	3,900

Demand equals supply at $11. Each firm will produce 7 units of output. In the long run, the price will return to $8 (the minimum ATC). Solving for Q in the demand equation gives $Q = 4{,}350$. There will be 725 firms (up from 600), each producing 6 units.

6. Event A: short run
   Event B: short and long run
   Event C: short run
   Event D: short run
   Event E: long run

7. Event A: short and long run
   Event B: short and long run
   Event C: short run (long run is uncertain)

Event D: short run
Event E: long run

8. Event A: short run
   Event B: long run
   Event C: short and long run
   Event D: short run (long run uncertain)
   Event E: short run
   Event F: long run

9. Short-run firm: Output is down, making a loss.
   Short-run industry: Lower demand equals supply at lower price. Output is down. Price falls but can fall no further than shut-down price.
   Long-run firm: Output is back to initial level, economic profits are zero, price equals minimum ATC.
   Long-run industry: There are fewer firms (as they exit, output falls, price rises until $P = $ Minimum ATC). Price returns to long-run level.

10. a. The sign of the coefficient on Q in the supply equation is negative, telling us that a higher output reduces the supply price.
    b. $Q = 80$, $P = \$40$.
    c. We have $P^D = P^S + $ tax or $200 - 2Q = 130 - Q$. Solving this gives $Q = 70$ and $P = \$60$. The \$10 tax has raised the price by \$20!
    d. We have $P^D = P^S - $ Subsidy or $200 - 2Q = 110 - Q$.
       $Q = 90$ and $P = \$20$. A \$10 subsidy has reduced the price by \$20!

11. Because $P < MC$, it should contract output. Because $P > AVC$, it should operate and not shut down.

12. In the long run, the price of widgets will be \$10 because that reflects the cost of making widgets to foreign firms. Because the cost of making widgets in the United States is now \$11, the whole U.S. widget industry will disappear over time. Foreign widget makers (or U.S. firms relocating overseas) will replace them. The extent of this devastation will be less if it is an increasing-cost industry: then those firms in the United States that are efficient enough to produce widgets at \$9 or less (excluding the tax) will survive. The same logic applies to states applying their own taxes to industries that are competitive nationally.

13. Personal computers is a very competitive industry in that it takes little capitalization to set up a firm to put together and market computers. Thus, one can predict that the price of personal computers in 2005 will equal the price of their parts plus a small premium reflecting the cost of the labor and capital of their owners.

14. $MB = P^D = 21 - Q$. $MC = P^S = 3 + 2Q$. Added Q causes social net benefit to go up when $MB \geq MC$, till $MB = MC$. This occurs at $Q = 6$. If produced competitively, market Q would be 6 as $P^D = P^S$ at $Q = 6$ (and $P = \$15$). Competition maximizes net benefit to society. Draw graph. Area of triangle between demand and supply curve equals \$54 ($= 1/2 \times 6 \times \$18$).

15. Competition will keep the lines, on average, equal in terms of the expected time of staying in line. If customers have full information and one line is extra long, it must mean that clerk is extra fast. The long line for the fast clerk keeps the expected waiting time in line the same between all clerks!

16. The test. Football has only two firms with a winner-take-all result. The test has many players, and many will win. Here's one test of the degree of competition in a market: how much are firms willing to help each other? The more they help each other, the more competitive they are. Farming is highly competitive and farmers often help each other. Why? If Farmer Jones helps Farmer Smith, Farmer Jones is not hurt as neither affects the market price. On the other hand, if GM helps Ford, it could seriously hurt GM's market share. You won't see GM and Ford sharing marketing or production data!

Chapter Ten

Monopoly

INTRODUCTION

Australia is the world's oldest continent and as a consequence, it is also one of the flattest. Over the eons, water brought by the rains has slowly eroded what once were its majestic mountains. In only a few million years, the sea will cover Australia and the land down under will be down under. In much the same way but in far shorter time, competition erodes away monopoly. The life cycle of most industries can be written like this: The first person with a new product has a monopoly and makes huge profits, then other firms enter seeking profits, until we have the long-run competitive results of normal profits (and no economic profits).

WHAT IS A MONOPOLY?

A firm is a monopoly when it is the only firm selling the good such that (1) the good has no close substitutes, and (2) the firm has no current or potential rivals.

All firms, in some sense, produce unique goods. Wheat from a farm in Iowa differs in some way from the wheat grown across the road. But consumers are only willing to pay a premium for the goods of some firms. If they are willing to pay a premium, the firm has a monopoly. Thus, if consumers regarded flowers grown in my backyard as a must-have item, I'd be rich. But, they don't and I'm not. As I tell my students, "Remember, each of you is a unique individual, just like everyone else." Consumers determine if a good is unique.

The absence of rivals means the monopoly can set its price at whatever level it wants and not have to worry about rivals undercutting its price. In the next chapter, we'll see what happens when firms do have to worry about what the others will do.

WHY DO MONOPOLIES PERSIST?

Competition doesn't always wear away monopolies. Monopolies persist when there are *barriers of entry* that keep competing firms from entering into the industry. Protected behind their barriers of entry, a monopoly can make profits even in the long run without worrying about new rivals. Some of the main barriers to entry include the following.

1. Legal barriers: The government limits entry into many industries (such as electricity and cable TV) and occupations (for example, by the licensing of medical doctors). Similarly, the FDA makes it so costly to introduce new drugs to the United States that our drug prices are twice the world average.
2. Patents and copyrights: Patents protect inventors and copyrights protect writers and artists from having others freely copying their ideas for a certain number of years. This is a form of monopoly but one that most people regard as being beneficial.
3. Control of strategic resources: A strategic resource is a resource that must be present to produce a particular good. No resource, no good. For example, DeBeers controls 90% of the world's diamond production, giving it considerable monopoly power.
4. Large economies of scale: Economies of scale exist when a firm expands output and finds its average cost is lower. Suppose the economies of scale are sufficiently large, such that just one firm can produce all the output of the industry and still have falling average cost. That firm can then cut its price enough to drive any potential rival out of the industry and still make a profit. Cement is an example. The fixed costs of building a cement plant are so large that most areas can only support one cement plant. The area of each cements plant's market is determined by how far a cement truck can travel before its cement dries. This is usually less than 100 miles. As a result, most cement plants are monopolies within their 100-mile neighborhood.

Monopolies that exist because their economies of scale allow them to produce all a market's output at a lower average cost are called *natural* monopolies.

Other barriers to entry include brand names, high up-front costs (important in less developed capital markets where investment capital is hard to obtain), and technological superiority maintained through research and development.

MARGINAL REVENUE FOR MONOPOLY

The key test for monopoly power is this: Can the firm raise the price of its good and still keep at least some of its customers? If the answer is yes, then it has some monopoly power.

Stated another way, the demand curve facing a monopoly slopes downward. Figure 10.1 shows the demand curve for a monopoly firm. It is the same demand curve as in our usual demand and supply diagrams: It shows the demand by the whole market for a single good! However, in this case, only one firm sells this good!

In contrast, the demand curve facing one perfectly competitive firm would be perfectly horizontal and flat at the market price. In the extreme case of perfect competition, when the competitive firm charges a penny over the market price, it loses all of its customers.[1]

Remember this one key point, which will make learning about monopolies easier: The monopoly price will always be on the demand curve. It can't charge more, and it would be stupid to charge less. So a higher price means a lower quantity sold!

We assume, unless stated otherwise, that the monopoly sells all its output at the same price. For example, if it charges $10 in Figure 10.1, it will sell 20 units. In Figure

---

[1]Recall that perfect competition and monopoly are two extremes. Most firms fall in between. Thus, most firms can raise their prices a small amount—but not a large amount—and still keep some of their customers.

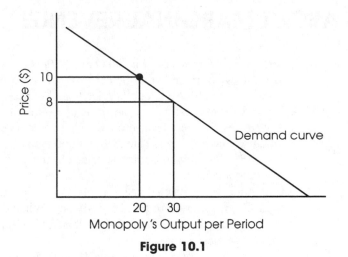

Figure 10.1

10.1, why doesn't the monopoly charge more for the 20 units? Because it is on the demand curve. If it raises the price above $10, it can't sell all 20 units. At a price above $10, it must sell less!

Marginal revenue *(MR)* is the addition to total revenue from selling one more unit of output (within a given time period). In terms of marginal analysis, marginal revenue is the marginal benefit to the firm of producing that unit. For a competitive firm, marginal revenue equals that unit's price. But for a monopoly, its marginal revenue is below its price. Why? Because it has to lower its price on all units to sell more. That is,

**Marginal revenue for *K*th unit = Price – Loss
from price cut on prior *K* – 1th units**

Thought Questions

Acme can sell 50 widgets at $100 and 51 units at $99. What is the 51st unit's marginal revenue (or, how much does it add to total revenue)?

$49. The 51st unit sells for $99. But to sell it, we have to cut the price on the previous 50 units by $1. So the 51st unit brings in only $49 in net new revenues ($99 – $50). Alternatively, just calculate

**Marginal revenue for 51st unit = Addition to total revenue =
Total revenue for 51 units – Total revenue for 50 units =
$5,049 (= $99 × 51) – $5,000 (= $100 × 50) = $49!**

If Acme can sell all its output for $100 because it is a competitive firm in a much larger market, what is the marginal revenue of the 51st unit?

$100! It has no loss in revenue from having to cut the price because it does not have to cut the price to sell more! It faces a horizontal demand curve.

FACTS ABOUT MARGINAL REVENUE

1. $MR = P - |\Delta P|Q$ where Q is old Q and $|\Delta P|$ is the absolute value of the price cut.
2. $MR < P$ when price has to be cut. $MR = P$ for a perfectly competitive firm because it doesn't have to cut its price to sell more.
3. $MR = P$ for the first unit of output as $Q = 0$ in number 1.
4. The firm will never, never produce where MR is negative. A negative MR means total revenue is falling! That's not a good idea.
5. $MR = P \cdot (1 - \frac{1}{\eta})$ where η is the price elasticity of demand (expressed as a positive number).
6. Using number 5, when demand is inelastic, $\eta < 1$ and so $MR < 0$. When demand is elastic, $\eta > 1$ and $MR > 0$. Memory peg: When demand is **In**elastic, more output means **In**ferior revenues. When demand is **EL**astic, more output means **ELe**vated revenues.
7. Total revenue is maximized where $MR = 0$. TR goes up as long as $MR > 0$, and it falls when $MR < 0$.
8. When the demand curve is a straight line sloping downward[2]:

The MR line starts at the same P on the vertical axis.
The MR line falls twice as fast as the demand curve.
The MR line hits the horizontal axis at half the Q as the demand curve does.
The MR line is always halfway between the vertical axis and the demand curve.

Figure 10.2 shows an example: The demand curve is also the average revenue curve (because the demand curve shows the price and the average of total revenue $(P \times Q)$ is P). So the average revenue follows the marginal revenue curve, using the average/marginal relationships we've learned.

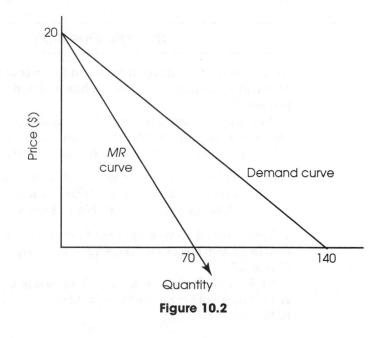

Figure 10.2

---

[2]In this case, the demand curve's equation is $P^D = a - bQ$. The marginal revenue's equation is $MR = a - 2bQ$. This is derived as follows. Total revenue $= P^D \times Q$ so we multiply the PD equation times Q, given $TR = aQ - bQ^2$. By definition, $MR = dTR/dQ = a - 2bQ$.

MARGINAL ANALYSIS APPLIED TO MONOPOLY

The monopoly selects the level of output *(Q)* to get the largest profit possible. At each *Q*, it will set the highest attainable price possible. That means its price for that *Q* must be on the demand curve. That implies more $Q \longrightarrow$ lower *P!*

Here's the marginal analysis of finding the profit-maximizing *Q*.

Step 1. Increase *Q* by one unit.

Step 2. Measure marginal benefit of increasing *Q* by one unit:

MB = Marginal revenue

Step 3. Measure marginal cost of increasing *Q* by one unit:

MC = Marginal cost

Step 4. Increase *Q* as long as $MR \geq MC$ because

Δ Profit = MR − MC

Step 5. Optimal *Q* (highest profit) where $MR = MC$.

Next, we apply the monopoly shut-down rules:

Short run: Shut down if at *Q* where $MR = MC$ the $AVC > P$.

Long run: Shut down if at *Q* where $MR = MC$ the $ATC > P$.

Thought Questions

Acme is a monopoly. At 20 units of output, its marginal revenue is $20 and its marginal cost is $15. The price it is selling output at is $30. Its average variable cost is $25. In the short run, should it shut down, expand its output, contract it, or remain at its current level of 20?

$P > AVC$, so it shouldn't shut down. At the current level of output, it is covering its variable cost. As $MR > MC$, it will increase its profits by expanding its output.

Fill in Table 10.1. At what level of output will Acme maximize profits?

TABLE 10.1

Output	Price ($)	Total Revenue ($)	Total Cost ($)	Profit ($)	Marginal Revenue ($)	Marginal Cost ($)
0	9		6			
1	8		9			
2	7		11			
3	6		12			
4	5		14			
5	4		17			
6	3		21			

See Table 10.2. The monopoly will produce 4 units of output where $MR = MC$ and profits are maximized at $6.

TABLE 10.2

Output	Price ($)	Total Revenue ($)	Total Cost ($)	Profit ($)	Marginal Revenue ($)	Marginal Cost ($)
0	9	0	6	−6	—	—
1	8	8	9	−1	8	3
2	7	14	11	3	6	2
3	6	18	12	6	4	1
4	5	20	14	6	2	2
5	4	20	17	3	0	3
6	3	18	21	−3	−2	4

Points to note:

MR is the increase in TR due to one more unit of Q.
MC is the increase in TC due to one more unit of Q.
The change in profit equals $MR − MC$.
The firm maximizes profits, not total revenue (which is largest at $Q = 5$).
The price goes down $1 for each added Q; when the price falls by a constant amount for each added Q, MR falls twice as fast (here, $2 for each added Q).

Thought Question

In Figure 10.3, draw a line showing what output the firm will produce and what price it will charge.

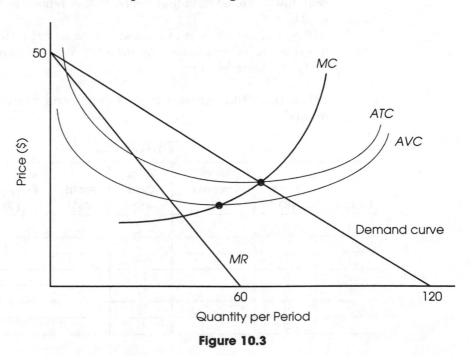

Figure 10.3

The firm will produce at that Q where $MR = MC$. The price will be that on the demand curve for that Q as shown in Figure 10.4.

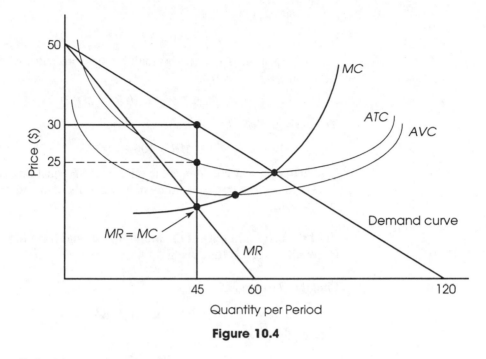

Figure 10.4

Points to note:

Find where MR crosses MC. Draw a line down to the horizontal axis to find the Q and draw a line vertically up to the demand curve to find the price.

Because the demand curve is a straight line, the MR curve falls twice as fast and, on the horizontal axis, has half the Q the demand curve does (60 versus 120).

P is on the demand curve, not the MR curve!

Profit equals $(P - ATC) \times Q$ or $\$5 \times 45$ or $\$225$.

Thought Question

(**Advanced! Skip if you have not had calculus.**):

A monopoly faces the following demand curve:

$$P = 100 - 2Q$$

It has the following total cost schedule:

$$TC = 10 + 2Q + 1.5Q^2.$$

Derive the TR equation, take its first derivative to get the MR equation, and take the first derivative of the TC schedule to get the MR equation.

The first derivative of Y with respect to X is the change in Y due to a change in X. Thus, the first derivative of TR with respect to Q is MR, and the first derivative to TC with respect to Q is MC. In general,

$$\frac{d(aX^b)}{dX} = abX^{b-1}$$

and for most problems you only need to know

$$\frac{daX}{dX} = a \text{ and } \frac{daX^2}{dX} = 2aX$$

So we have

$$MC = 2 + 3Q$$

The *TR* equation is derived by multiplying both sides of the price equation by *Q*

$$TR = P \times Q = 100Q + 2Q^2$$

The derivative of *TR* with respect to *Q* is

$$MR = 100 - 4Q$$

Notice that the *MR* equation is the same as the *P* equation except that it has twice the slope (this holds only when the demand curve is a straight line).

Find the price and output the monopoly should have to maximize its profits. What is that profit?

Find the *Q* where *MR = MC*:

$$100 - 4Q = 2 + 3Q.$$

Solving for *Q*, we have

$$98 = 7Q$$
$$Q = 14$$

Using the demand equation, $P = 100 - 4(14) = \$44$.
Total revenue is $\$44 \times 14 = \$616$.
Total cost (using the *TC* equation) $\$332$ *(TC = 10 + 2 × 14 + 1.5 × 14 × 14)*.
Profits = $TR - TC = \$616 - \$332 = \$284$.

MONOPOLY: LONG RUN AND SHORT RUN

The only change in going from short to long run for a monopoly is that it goes from short-run costs to long-run costs. Unlike a competitive firm, there's no entry into the industry. Thus, a monopoly does not face any long-run competitive pressure that will bid its price down to cost.

The shut-down rules compare price with *AVC* in the short run and price with *ATC* in the long run. Graphically, the monopoly should shut down when its demand curve is completely below the appropriate average cost curve (*AVC* for short run and *ATC* for long run). Figure 10.5 shows a monopoly that should stay open in the short run (producing *Q**) but shut down in the long run.

Points to note:

AVC curve goes under the demand curve so stay open in the short run (because at some *Q*, *P > ATC*).
ATC curve is always above the demand curve so shut down in the long run (because at all *Q*, *P < ATC*).

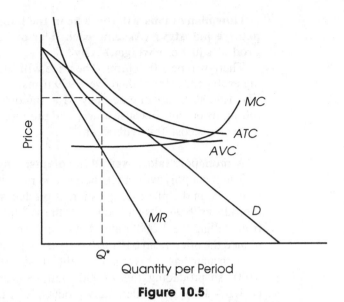

Figure 10.5

WHAT DOES MONOPOLY THEORY PREDICT?

Monopolies produce where $MR = MC$. What does this imply?

Result 1: Monopolies will not charge the highest price possible. The highest price comes with producing just one unit. But at $Q = 1$, $MR > MC$ so the monopoly will lower its price to sell more and increase more profit. Remember: The monopoly is constrained by the demand curve from charging too high a price!

Key point to remember: A monopoly is on its demand curve: It can't charge anything it wants and, at the same time, sell what it wants! So a higher price for a monopoly means a lower quantity sold.

Result 2: Monopolies need not produce at the lowest average cost. A monopoly produces where $MR = MC$. Only by chance will this occur at the same Q that minimizes ATC! It may produce at a lower Q or a higher Q.

Result 3: The monopoly does not have a supply curve.

The supply curve is a schedule of prices that tells us how much will be supplied at each price. The monopoly only quotes one price so there is no supply curve for a monopoly.

Result 4: Price exceeds marginal cost. Since $P > MR$ and $MR = MC$, it follows that $P > MC$.

Result 5: Monopolies produce less than a competitive industry would when costs are the same. Because $MR < P$, each added unit of output is worth less to a monopoly than to a competitive firm. So even if it faces the same marginal costs as do the competitive firms in an industry, it will produce less because it has a lower marginal benefit.

Thought Question

Each plant in an industry produces one widget. Each widget costs $100 to make. The demand curve for widgets is such that the demand price falls $1 for each added unit of output. In addition, at $Q = 1,000$, the demand price equals $100.

How many firms will there be in the long run if this is a competitive industry? (Assume each firm owns just one plant and produces just one widget.) Why?

There will be 1,000 firms. The price will equal the cost of producing each unit, $100. If there were 999 firms, the price would be $101. The 1,000th firm can enter, pay $100 in costs, and collect $100 by selling its output. Because a firm will produce a unit of output when it covers its cost, this will occur.

A monopoly takes over all the plants; why will it cut output?

The monopoly will cut its output and raise its price. Unlike a firm discussed in the previous question, it produces all units of output. If it produces 999 units and now adds the 1,000th unit, it (1) adds $100 from selling the 1,000th unit, but (2) it loses $999 because it had to reduce the price from $101 to $100 on the previous 999 units. So the 1,000th unit has a marginal benefit of –$899! Its marginal cost is $100, so producing the 1,000th unit reduces its profits by $999 ($= MB - MC$). It will definitely produce less. In fact, it will produce only 500 units in this case![3]

Result 6: Monopolies need not make a profit. The $MR = MC$ rule says nothing about whether the monopoly should shut down or stay open. It is possible that it is just breaking even! Of course, should the monopoly find that it is making a loss in the long run, it will go out of business.

Result 7: Monopolies will produce in the elastic portion of the demand curve. Since $MC > 0$, it will be true for the marginal Q, $MR > 0$. If $MR > 0$ for the firm, then $MR > 0$ for the whole market as the monopoly is the whole market. If $MR > 0$ for the monopoly and for the market, then demand is elastic.

Thought Question

Acme makes widgets. Acme's marginal revenue is positive. We can conclude the market demand for widgets is elastic. True or false?

False. If Acme is a competitive firm, then we only know that the demand facing Acme is elastic. We know nothing about the elasticity of market demand. However, if Acme is a monopoly, then we do know that the market demand is elastic because Acme's demand is the market demand!

MONOPOLY: A SIMPLE CASE

There is a special case for monopoly that is easy to solve. This is the case where:

1. *MC* is a horizontal line. This corresponds to long-run constant returns to scale and a constant-cost supply curve.

---

[3]The demand curve is $P^D = 1,100 - Q$ and the marginal revenue curve is $MR = 1,100 - 2Q$. $MR = MC$ at the MC of 100. You'll get $Q = 500$ and $P = \$600$.

2. The demand curve is a straight line.

In this case, the price should be halfway between *MC* and the demand curve's vertical intercept. Output should be halfway between zero and the *Q* where marginal cost intersects the demand curve. It's as easy as cream, that is, half and half. Figure 10.6 illustrates a simple case.

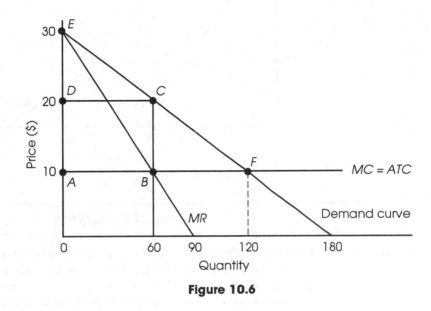

Figure 10.6

Points to note:

$P = \$20$ is halfway between $30 and $10.
$Q = 60$ is halfway between 0 and 120.
Profit $= (P - ATC) \times Q = \$10 \times 60 = \$600$.
A competitive industry would produce at $Q = 120$ and $P = MC = \$10$.
The price elasticity of demand is 2 (using the ratio of bottom over top on the price axis). Demand is elastic.

Why does this rule work? Profits equal the area of rectangle *ABCD* in Figure 10.6. To get the biggest profit, we want the biggest rectangle inside triangle *AEF*. To draw the biggest rectangle inside the right-angled triangle *AEF*, just go halfway on each of its legs that make the 90 degrees and form the rectangle.

To make the preceding case more applicable, suppose the *MC* curve slopes upward. Draw a horizontal line where *MR* = *MC*. Then using this line, use the preceding information to solve for the price! Figure 10.7 shows such a case.

Points to note:

Because $MC = MR$ at the same *Q* and *MC* as in Figure 10.5, both firms have the same optimal price ($20) and output (60).
We can't calculate the profits because we don't know what the *ATC* is.

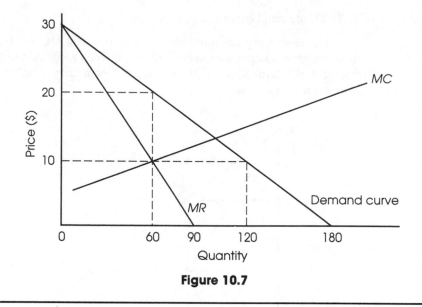

Figure 10.7

Thought Questions

A monopoly faces the following demand curve: It can sell one unit at $10, two units at $9 each, three at $8 each, and so forth (each added Q reducing P by $1). Its average and marginal cost for all units is $4.50. How many units should it produce? What price will it charge and what profit will it make? Assume it can only produce discrete units of output.

The marginal revenue of the first unit is $10, the second unit adds $8 to total revenue, the third unit has a marginal revenue of $6, and the fourth, $4. Using marginal analysis, the first three units have an MR that exceeds their MC and should be produced. Producing the fourth unit reduces profits by $0.50 ($MR - MC = -\$0.50$). So $Q = 3$, $P = \$8$, and profit is $10.50.

A monopoly faces the following demand curve:

$$P = 20 - Q$$

so its MR curve is $MR = 20 - 2Q$. It has a constant marginal cost of $8 ($MC = ATC = \$8$ at all Q). How many units will it produce? At what price? What is its profits?

Use the $MR = MC$ equality to solve for Q:

$$20 - 2Q = 8 \text{ or } Q = 6.$$

Use the price equation to solve for P: $P = 20 - 6 = \$14$. Profits equal $\$6 \times 6 = \$36$.

The government imposes a $2 per unit tax on the monopoly in the above question. What will its new price, quantity, and profits be? How much does the price go up relative to the tax?

Using $MR =$ new MC, we have $20 - 2Q = 10$, or $Q = 5$. The new price is $15. The new profit is $\$5 \times 5 = \$25$. Although the tax raises the monopoly's cost by $2, its price only goes up by $1. In general, for straight-line demand curves, monopolies pass only a fraction of a cost increase onto consumers in the form of a higher price (and similarly, they only pass along a fraction of cost cuts onto consumers). This need not be true for other types of demand curves!

Water flows freely from a spring in Gulch Valley. Farmers freely use this water. Then a monopoly buys the rights to the spring. If farmers would pay at most $50 a gallon for water and if, when water is free, they use 1,000 gallons a day, what price will the monopoly charge for the water? Assume the demand curve for water is a straight line.

Because $MC = 0$, the monopoly will sell water where $MR = 0$. This occurs at a price halfway between $50 and zero dollars: $P = \$25$. Q equals half of 1,000 or $Q = 500$.

THE STATIC SOCIAL COST OF MONOPOLY

If a monopoly faces the same costs as a competitive firm, then it will produce less and charge more. Economists measure the social loss of the reduced output by measuring the net benefit to society that's lost as a result. The net benefit of a unit of output is equal to its price (reflecting its marginal value to consumers) minus its marginal cost (reflecting its cost). For example, suppose a monopoly cuts output by one unit that would have sold for $100 and had a marginal cost of $80. The net benefit of that unit to society (not the monopoly!) is $20. So by not producing this unit, the monopoly denies society $20. This is the social loss from not producing this unit. If it cuts output by another unit, which would have sold for $105 and would have cost $75, the added social loss is $30. The total social loss is $50 ($20 plus $30).

In general, the social cost of a monopoly is each unit's $P - MC$ summed over the reduced Q. The reduced Q is measured by the difference between (a) What a competitive firm would have produced (such that $P = MC$ on the margin) and (b) what the monopoly produces.

Thought Question

A monopoly faces the following demand curve: One unit of output sells for a price of $10, two units for $9, three for $8, four for $7, and so forth (each added Q selling for $1 less). Its marginal cost is $4 for all units. What is its social cost, assuming a competitive firm has the same cost?

The monopoly will produce four units while the competitive Q is seven units. So units 5, 6, and 7 are the reduced Q not produced by the monopoly but which would have been produced in a competitive industry. The lost social net benefit from unit 5 is its $P - MC$ or $6 - $4 or $2. For unit 6, it's $1. For unit 7, $0. The total social loss is $3.

Graphically, the lost net benefit is the area between the demand curve (P) and the marginal cost curve, measured between the monopoly's Q and the competitive Q. Figure 10.8 illustrates a case. The monopoly will be at point E_m on the demand curve, charging $23 and selling 28 units (and $MR = MC = \$16$). The competitive firm will be at E_c, charging $19.50 and selling 42 units. The area between the demand curve and the MC curve form a triangle whose left side rises from $16 to $23 and whose length is 14 units (from 28 to 42). The area of a triangle is ½ base × height or ½ × 14 × $7 or $49. So the social loss from the monopoly is $42.

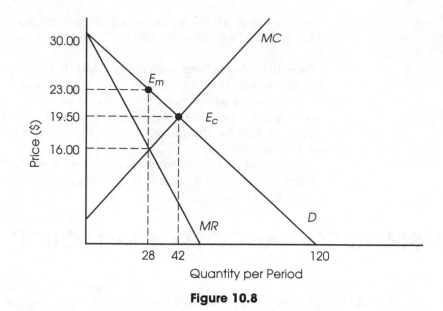

Figure 10.8

There is one aspect of this calculation that many students find troubling. The social cost of monopoly does not include the loss to consumers from having to pay a higher price! In Figure 10.7, this loss to consumers equals $3.50 more for the 28 units the monopoly sells (for a total loss of $98). Why don't we count this as part of the monopoly's social loss? The reason is that the monopolist is a member of society. While consumers lose $98 due to the higher price, the monopoly gets the $98! One person gains, the other loses. On net, economists call it a wash so we don't count this. We only count the losses that no one gets any benefit from: the lost net benefit from the units not produced!

To illustrate this point, suppose you are willing to work for your employer for a wage of $10 and the employer values you at $25. If you push your wage from $10 to $22, you are better off by $12, and the employer is worse off by $12. Because the same output is produced in either case, the measured net benefit to society should be the same in either case. Such a shift of income from one group to another that leaves output unaffected is called a *transfer payment*. Transfer payments do not get counted in social benefits or costs. Using a similar logic, economists ignore the impact of the higher price for those units still produced because this is merely a transfer of money from consumers to monopoly.

The preceding analysis is called the *static* cost of monopoly to society because it ignores some of the possible dynamic benefits of some monopolies. In free markets, most monopolies arise from innovation and creativity. Others arise because consumers want a monopoly. For example, most people are very particular about their brand of aspirin and soft drinks. Similarly, every major movie star—from Shirley MacLaine to Clint Eastwood—is a form of monopoly created by the public. These monopolies make a profit because they make better use of resources than would have otherwise existed.

DIFFERENCES BETWEEN MONOPOLIES AND COMPETITIVE INDUSTRIES

Difference 1

A lump-sum tax will not affect price as long as it doesn't cause the monopoly to shut down. A lump-sum tax in a competitive industry will raise the price.

A lump-sum tax is a tax the firm must pay, no matter how many units it produces. In a competitive industry, in the long run, a lump-sum tax will drive some firms out of business and cause prices to rise. Because the lump-sum tax leaves MC unaffected, the taxed monopoly will produce the same output (at the Q where $MR = MC$) and thus charge the same price (on its demand curve). As long as the lump-sum tax is less than its profits, it will stay in business in the long run.

Difference 2

An increase in demand need not cause a monopoly to supply more. In a competitive industry, supply will always increase.

In a competitive industry, an increase in demand always results in more output being supplied. But a monopoly does not have a supply curve. The quantity it supplies depends on the shape of the new higher demand curve: If the shape changes enough, it could supply less!

For example, a monopoly faces the following curve:

Quantity	Price
1	4
2	3
3	2

It has a constant cost of $1.50. How many units will it supply?

Now suppose the demand curve shifts up to

Quantity	Price
1	8
2	4
3	2.50

What Q will it supply?

Initially, it will supply two units (because the second unit adds $2 to its revenues and only $1.50 to its cost). But with the new higher demand curve, it supplies only one unit! The second unit adds nothing to revenues and adds $1.50 to costs. It will not be produced.

Difference 3

The competitive firm in the long run will produce at its minimum average total cost; only by chance would a monopoly do so.

Competition, in the long run, forces firms to charge the lowest average cost or be driven out of business. A monopoly, of course, does not face such forces. It will produce where $MR = MC$, and this may or may not be where its average costs are lowest. But rest assured, it will be where profits are highest!

Difference 4

A price ceiling, correctly placed, can increase the quantity supplied by a monopoly. It will always decrease the quantity supplied in a competitive industry.

A price ceiling placed between a monopoly's P and MC will increase output. The most output possible occurs when the price ceiling is placed at the same price a competitive firm would charge (that is, the P where $P = MC$).

A price ceiling (up to the point it hits demand curve) becomes, in effect, the new demand curve facing the firm. This new demand curve is perfectly horizontal, just as a competitive firm's demand curve is perfectly horizontal. As a result, the monopoly now has $MR =$ the ceiling $P!$

Thought Question

In Figure 10.9, what Q will the monopoly produce in absence of a price ceiling? When the ceiling shown is imposed, what will its new Q be? What price ceiling would maximize its output?

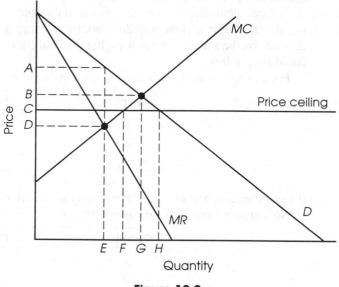

Figure 10.9

When there is no price ceiling, the monopoly will produce E units of output and charge price A. Any price ceiling between its price (A) and its marginal cost (D) will increase output. A price ceiling at price C will cause the monopoly's MR to also equal C, so it will produce where its new $MR = MC$ or F units of output. Why not H units (a common wrong answer!)? Because $MC > C$ at $Q = H$. If the price ceiling is set at price B (where the demand $P = MC$), output will be maximized at G units of output. A higher price ceiling results in the new $MR > MC$: The monopoly wants to produce more but consumers want to buy less! So the monopoly will move up the demand curve when the price ceiling exceeds price B. A price ceiling of price A, for example, will cause the monopoly to supply E units. A still higher price ceiling (above price A) is above the price the monopoly wants to charge and so is ineffective.

PRICE DISCRIMINATION

Price discrimination is the practice of selling the same goods at different prices. Two units of a good are the same when they have the same quality and have the same cost. An example of price discrimination is selling seats in a movie theater at two different prices, a low price to children and a higher price to adults. Both adults and children take up the same amount of space (one seat) and cost the same to show the movie to. On the other hand, if a car's higher price in Hawaii reflects the added shipping cost, it is not a case of price discrimination.

Why would a monopoly practice price discrimination? That is, why would it want to cut its price for some, but not all, of its customers? Recall that when it charges just one price

One price monopoly: $MR = P -$ Loss from price cut on previous Q

If the monopoly can avoid cutting its price on all its Q, it can raise its marginal revenue! For example, if it could cut its price only on the new output it could sell, but keep the old higher price on its previous Q, it is better off!

A monopoly can only practice price discrimination under certain conditions. The conditions for price discrimination follow.

Condition 1

Buyers cannot resell to each other. If those buying for a low price can easily resell to those who would otherwise have to pay a higher price, the monopoly will find all its output being sold at the low price. For example, most luxury European cars sell for a lot less in Europe than they do in the United States. Many persons buy these cars in Europe, ship them here, then sell below the U.S. price, and still make a profit. To discourage this, these car companies refuse to repair the cars not bought from dealers.

Condition 2

The monopoly can tell which customers will pay more and which will only buy for less. If movie theaters couldn't tell the difference between kids and adults, they'd have a harder time charging a higher price to adults. Having no shame, I would buy the kid's ticket at a movie if I could. But, perhaps fortunately, I don't look like a 12-year-old (the fortunate one is the 12-year-old!).

Let's illustrate these points with an example. Suppose I am the only seller of soft drinks on a beach. There are only two customers on this lonely beach. They are Sweaty Sam who would pay $2 for a cola and Tightwad Teddy who would pay $1 for a cola. Each only wants one cola. My cost per drink is 75 cents. If I charge only one price, I would be best off charging $2 and selling just one drink (to see why, work out my profits if I charge less, all the way down to 75 cents). However, I could make a larger profit if I could price discriminate, charging $2 to Sam and $1 to Teddy. Condition 1 is met if I can keep Sam away from Teddy; otherwise, Sam will get Teddy to buy two drinks for $1 and resell one to him. Condition 2 is met if I can tell which customer is Sam! That is, can I tell which customer is willing to pay the higher price? If yes, great. If no, then I might cut Sam's price and raise Teddy's and be worse off!

If a monopoly can price discriminate, it will charge the higher price to the customers who have the most inelastic demand for their product and the lower price to the customers who have the most elastic demand.[4] For example, drug stores give senior discounts because senior citizens are more willing to shop around for the lowest price. That is, they have a more elastic demand for a given store's drugs. Similarly, movies sell tickets to kids at lower prices because children tend to have a more elastic demand for tickets.

If the monopolist faces two demand curves, it will set its prices so that both markets have the same marginal revenue (assuming it has the same MC in both). If one market had a higher MR than the other, it would pay to shift output from the low MR market to the higher MR market. In that way, the monopoly gets more revenue for that unit. It will continue to do this until the last unit in both markets has the same MR.

Thought Questions

A monopoly has a U.S. demand curve where it can sell one unit at $6, two at $5, three at $4, and so forth (each added unit lowering the price by $1). It has a Canadian demand curve where it can sell one unit for $3, two for $2, and three for $1. It has a constant marginal cost of $1. What price will it charge in the United States? In Canada?

Treat this as two separate problems, except you're using the same MC. In the United States it will charge $4 and sell three units (unit three's MR is $2 and unit four's is 0, so it stops at three). In Canada, it will charge $2 and sell two units (unit two's MR is $1, which covers the cost of producing it). Note that the MRs are not equal in this case because this problem involves discrete jumps in quantity. One tries to get as close to equality as one can without going beyond it (as $MR < MC$ means a lower profit). Equality would be reached if it could sell fractions of a unit.

A monopoly has a constant marginal cost of $4 and faces these demand curves:

United States: $P = \$20 - Q$
Brazil: $P = \$16 - 2Q$
What price will it charge in each market?

We have the following MRs (by doubling the slope):
United States: $MR = \$20 - 2Q$
Brazil: $MR = \$16 - 4Q$

Setting each to $4, the best U.S. Q is 8 and $P = \$12$. The best Brazilian Q is 3 and $P = \$10$. Using the bottom over top method of calculating elasticities for straight-line demand curves, in the United States, the price elasticity of demand at $12 is 1.5 ($= \$12/8$), and in Brazil, it's 1.67 ($= \$10/6$): The lower price market has the higher elasticity.

---

[4]Be careful! This does not say it charges the higher price to customers whose demand is inelastic and the lower price to customers whose demand is elastic. It says it charges the higher price to the customer with the most inelastic demand. If customer A has an elasticity of demand of 2 and B has an elasticity of demand of 3, then the monopoly will charge the higher price to customer A. Both have elastic demands, but A has the least elastic (or the more inelastic) of the two demands.

CRIB NOTES

Monopoly: only firm producing goods with no close substitutes.

$MR = P - |\Delta \text{Price}| \times \text{Previous } Q$

$P > MR$ for monopoly.

Produce where $MR = MC$ if $P \geq AVC$ in short run and $P \geq ATC$ in long run.

Shut down in short run: Demand curve below AVC curve at all points.

Shut down in long run: Demand curve below ATC curve at all points.

Social cost $= P - MC$ summed over Q not produced by monopoly but produced by competitive industry.

Event	Monopoly	Competitive Firm or Industry
Lump-sum tax < profits	$\Delta P = 0$	P up in long run
Supply curve	No	Yes
Price ceiling	Q up for some P	Q down (or unaffected)
Practice price discrimination	Yes, if can	No

Price discrimination: Different prices for same good.

Charge more to those with more inelastic demands.

Charge less to those with more elastic demands.

If several separate markets, set P so same MR in each market.

Conditions for price discriminations: (1) Buyers can't resell goods; and (2) monopoly knows which customers have more inelastic demand.

Review Questions

1. a. Fill in the following table.
   b. How do we know this firm is a monopoly?
   c. Indicate what output the firm should produce and what price it should charge.
   d. What would a competitively acting firm charge?

Output	Price ($)	Total Revenue ($)	Total Cost ($)	MR ($)	MC ($)
0	—	0	5	—	—
1	7		6		
2	6		8		
3	5		11		
4	4		15		

2. The government imposes a $2 a unit tax on the firm in question 1. How much will its price go up?

3. What is the largest lump-sum tax the government could impose on the firm in question 1 without driving it out of business in the short run? In the long run? Assume it doesn't have to pay the per-unit tax in question 2 and that the lump-sum tax is only paid if the firm is up and running.

4. What's wrong with the following statement? "If all farmers cut their output by half, crop prices would soar. Therefore, all farmers are monopolists."

5. Mary inherited two widgets and, because these are the only widgets in existence, she has a monopoly on them. There are only two customers, each who'll buy one (and no more) widgets. Sam will buy one widget for $20 and Tim will buy one widget for $5. Mary cannot price discriminate between Sam and Tim and so must charge the same price for both. What will she charge? What is the social cost of her monopoly (assume her MC is zero).

6. Mary's Wrench Shop has a monopoly on Mary's Easy-To-Use Power Wrench. Mary's marginal cost is $10, and she sells her wrenches for $40. Is she exploiting her customers (that is, is she making them worse off)? Where is the social cost in her monopoly?

7. A monopoly faces the following demand curve:

$$P = 40 - Q$$

It has a constant marginal cost of $10.
   a. What price will it charge?
   b. If the government imposes a $6 tax on each unit, what will the new price be?
   c. If, instead, the cost per unit goes up to $6 due to higher wages, what will the new price be?
   d. If, instead, the demand per unit goes up by $6, such that the new demand curve is $P = 46 - Q$, what will the new price be?

8. Dixieland is a theme park that has a monopoly. Each and every patron has the following demands for rides (where Q is the number of rides per day):

$$P = 10 - 0.5Q$$

The marginal cost of each ride is $2.
   a. If Dixieland charges an admission to each ride, what is the optimal price per ride? What are its profits per customer?
   b. Instead, it charges an admission fee plus a price for each ride ticket. What is the optimal combination of admission fee and ride ticket price?
   c. Most theme parks just charge an admission fee. What does this imply about the marginal cost per ride?

9. Mom's Cooking Restaurant is located 20 miles from the nearest restaurant, Wife's Place Restaurant. It has 100 potential customers evenly spread along the road from Wife's to Mom's. The customers regard the two restaurants' cooking as equal in quality and choose the restaurant based upon the full price of the meal:

Full price of meal = Cash price + Travel price

where the travel price is $1 per mile traveled. Wife's cash price for a meal is $20. Because of the nature of area, no restaurant can ever locate closer to Mom. Does Mom have a monopoly? Assuming that it cost Mom $8 to make a meal, what price should Mom's charge and how many customers will it get?

10. A monopoly sells in two different markets. In market A, the price elasticity of demand is 2; in market B, it's 4. Its marginal cost is $42. What price should it charge in each market, assuming it can price discriminate?

11. A monopoly's price is $10, its marginal revenue is $0, its marginal cost is $2, and its average variable cost is $12. In the short run, should it expand, contract, or go out of business? Or do we need more information?

12. What is wrong with the following statement: "A monopoly seeks to maximize its profit per unit of output"?

13. Every customer of Dux Soap is willing to pay $5 a week for one box of Dux and a second box a week for an additional $1. Each box costs Dux 50 cents to make. Assume Dux only sells to its current customers.
    a. If it sells all boxes at the same price, what price will it set?
    b. What prices would it set if it could price discriminate between the first and second box?

14. Assuming sellers can practice price discrimination, pick which of the following pair is likely to be charged the lower price. State briefly why.
    Pair A: Kids and adults at movie theaters.
    Pair B: Business persons and tourists on airlines.
    Pair C: Drinkers and teetotalers at restaurants.

15. A monopoly has the following prices and marginal costs:

Q	P	MC
1	10	2.5
2	9	3
3	8	3.5
4	7	4
5	6	4.5
6	5	5

    a. How many units will it produce and at what price?
    b. What is the social loss from the monopoly?
    c. What price ceiling would cause it to produce the socially optimal level of output?

16. Art is an artist. He loves painting and is willing to paint for free. He would, however, not be willing to pay to paint. The monthly demand for his paintings is

$$P = \$1{,}000 - 100Q$$

How many paintings should he paint per month?

17. State whether the following statements are true, false, or uncertain for (1) a monopoly and (2) a competitive firm.
    a. The firm will produce where $MR = MC$.
    b. The firm's $MR = P$.
    c. The market demand will be elastic.
    d. A price ceiling can increase output.
    e. The firm produces at the minimum ATC in the long run.

f. The firm's supply curve is positively sloped.
g. The firm maximizes profits.

Answers

Output	Price ($)	Total Revenue ($)	Total Cost ($)	MR ($)	MC ($)
0	—	—	5	—	—
1	7	7	6	7	1
2	6	12	8	5	2
3	5	15	11	3	3
4	4	16	15	1	4

1. a. See above table.
   b. You can tell it is a monopoly because the price falls as Q goes up. If this were a competitive firm, all the numbers in the price column would be the same.
   c. The monopoly will produce where $MR = MC$ at $Q = 3$. Its price will be $5 and its profits will be $4.
   d. A competitive firm takes P as its MR and will produce $Q = 4$ at $P = \$4$.
2. Its price will go up $1. To see why, add $2 to each number in the MC column. The firm will choose to produce two units (with an MR of $5 and an MC of $4); adding the third unit will decrease profits by $2. Its price will be $6, up from $5 in the previous problem. The answer would be the same if the question was "Suppose the MC goes up by $2 a unit."
3. In the short run, $9. In the long run, $4. It will produce three units as the lump-sum tax leaves the optimal output unaffected (assuming the firm stays in business!).
   In the short run, its total revenue is $15, and its total variable cost is $6 ($TVC$ equals its total cost of $11 less its fixed cost of $5, where $TFC = TC$ at $Q = 0$). A tax higher than $9 would make it better off shutting down because it couldn't cover its variable cost plus the tax.
   In the long run, the biggest lump-sum tax is $4, equal to its profit at $Q = 3$.
4. If only one farmer cuts output by half, farm prices would remain the same. So each farmer is a perfect competitor, able to sell all output at the same price. Each farmer is too small to influence the market price.
5. She can sell one for $20 or two for $5 each. She is better off selling one for $20 and throwing the other away. The social cost is $5, the $P - MC$ for the second unsold unit. Society is worse off because the net benefit from what could have been a mutually beneficial trade is foregone because Mary can't charge a lower price to Tim.
6. First of all, let me salute all makers of power tools. I want power and they give it to me! Next, no, Mary is not making her customers worse off. They are only buying her tools because they value them over and above their price. So where does her social cost come from? Her social cost comes from the fact that if she priced the tools competitively, the social net benefit from her tools would be even greater. Alternately stated, the unsold tools have a price that exceeds their marginal cost, so it would be profitable for society to reallocate resources (whose alternative use value is reflected in their MC) to making Mary's tools (where their marginal benefit to society is reflected in the price on the demand curve). But it's not profitable to Mary because she values the added tools not at their price but at their marginal revenue, which is lower!

7. a. $25. One can use the simple case formula of going halfway between cost ($10) and the demand price on the vertical axis ($40). Or one can convert the price equation into a marginal revenue equation by doubling the slope ($MR = 40 - 2Q$) and solve for Q and then P by setting $MR = MC$.

   b. and c. $28. In the simple case, the price goes up half of the cost increase, no matter what the cause.

   d. Again, the answer is $28. The price goes up half of the demand increase (measured vertically), in the simple case.

8. a. The optimal ticket price is $6 (use the $MR = MC$ equation). Each customer will buy eight ride tickets so its TR will be $48 per customer. Its total cost will be $16 (= $2 × 8) so its profits will be $32.

   b. To get the most from customers, it should sell tickets at the marginal cost of each ride and charge an admission fee equal to the customer's consumer surplus (the area between the demand curve and the ticket price). Each ticket will sell for $2. Customers will ride 16 rides (using the demand equation). The admission fee equals the consumer surplus. This area forms a triangle that is $8 high on its left side (going from $2 up to $10) and is 16 rides long, so its area equals 1/2 × $8 × 16 or $64. This is also Dixieland's profits because the ride ticket's price covers the cost of the rides. This is an example of price discrimination.

   c. If rides are free, then the marginal cost of another ride must be zero. Alternatively, having free rides may save enough in selling and collecting ride tickets to make this the more profitable option.[5]

9. Mom is a monopolist, or perhaps, in this case, a momopolist! She can raise her price and not have all her customers leave. She is also protected from potential competitors moving closer.

   At $20, she would split the customers with Wife's Place. When both charge the same price, customers go to the closer of the two restaurants. In this case, Mom's would get 50 customers. At $40, she gets no customers (because all would prefer to go to Wife's). To get all 100 customers, she would have to give meals away for free (so that, at this point, $P = $0). Fitting these points into a demand equation, we have

$$P = \$40 - 0.4 \times Q$$

The MR equation is

$$MR = \$40 - 0.8 \times Q$$

Letting $MC = MR$, we have $8 = 40 - 0.8Q$. Solving for Q, we get 40 customers. Using the price equation (not the MR equation!), $P = $24.

   This question raises another issue. Why do restaurants advertise cooking "just like mom's" but none advertise cooking "just like wife's" when most moms are also someone's wife?

10. Use the marginal revenue equation:

$$MR = P\left(1 - \frac{1}{\eta}\right)$$

and recall that to maximize profits, $MR = MC$ in both markets. In market A, it should charge $84. In market B, it should charge $56. Note that the higher the price elasticity of demand, the lower the price it should charge.

---

[5]Disneyland once charged admission and sold tickets. The best rides required the most expensive E ticket, from which the phrase "as good as an E-ticket" comes from. Now, Disneyland just charges admission and rides are free.

11. Because $MR < MC$, it should contract if it stays in business. However, at its current level of output, its price is not covering its average variable cost. If it were a competitive firm, we could definitely say it should shut down. But since it's a monopoly, the price will go up as it reduces Q (as will its AVC). It is quite possible that, as Q falls, P will rise above its AVC and make a profit at its optimal level of Q. Without more information, it is impossible to say whether it should shut down or just contract.

12. Maximizing profits per unit is not the same as maximizing total profits. If a firm does maximize its profits per unit, it will be earning less than the maximum total profits. We have

Average profits = Total profit / Q = Profits per unit
Marginal profits = Addition to total profits due to another Q = $MR - MC$

At the maximum total profits, Marginal profits = 0 while, with hope, Average profits > 0.

Using the average/marginal rule, because the marginal is below the average, average profits (or profits per unit) will decline. If the firm stops where average profits are at a maximum, such that Marginal profits = Average profits > 0, then it is stopping short of getting the maximum total profits it can!

Here is a simple example:

Q	Total Profits ($)	Marginal Profits ($)	Average Profits ($)
1	10	10	10
2	15	5	7.50
3	18	3	6
4	18	0	4.40

Using the maximum profit per unit rule, the firm will settle for a profit of $10 (at $Q = 1$). If it goes to where marginal profits equal zero ($Q = 4$), it earns the most it can, $18! Believe me, $18 is better than $10.

13. a. $5 a box.
    b. $5 for the first box and $1 for the second. This could be sold two boxes for $6, or one box for $6, the second one free.

14. The group with the higher price elasticity of demand pays the lower price; those with the more inelastic demand, the higher price.
    Pair A: Kids will pay less because their lower income makes them more price sensitive and their demand more elastic.
    Pair B: Tourists usually pay less because they can shift their travel time around and go different places on different airlines. On the other hand, business persons usually must fly on certain days and, most often, on short notice. This makes their demand more inelastic. Airlines charge less to tourists by offering tickets for a lower price when they are ordered in advance.
    Pair C: All pay the same for the meal. However, because the markup on drinks is so much higher than that on food, we say that drinkers pay more (that is, the price of their drinks exceeds its marginal cost by a much higher amount). Their demand for wine with their meal is more inelastic.

15. a. It will produce four units, where the $MR = MC = 4$ and $P = \$7$.
    b. If it acted competitively (treating P as its marginal revenue), it would have produced $Q = 6$. This is the social optimal level. By not producing units 5 and 6, the loss in net benefit equals $1.50 for unit 5 ($1.50 = P - MC = \$6 - \$4.50$) and $0 for unit 6. This totals to $1.50.

   c. A price ceiling of $5 would change all the numbers in the price column to be $5 and cause *MR* to also equal $5: It would then produce six units.
16. His $MC = \$0$. His *MR* is $\$1{,}000 - 200Q$ so $Q = 5$. If he paints a sixth painting per month, he will pay for it in the form of lower total dollar sales per month. So Art draws the line at five paintings.
17. a. True for monopoly and for competitive firm.
   b. False for monopoly (for which $P > MR$) and true for competitive firm.
   c. True for monopoly and uncertain for competitive firm.
   d. True for monopoly and false for competition.
   e. False for monopoly (only by chance will be at minimum *ATC*) and true for competition.
   f. False for monopoly (no supply curve) and true for competition.
   g. True for both.

Chapter Eleven

Between Competition and Monopoly

INTRODUCTION

It has been said that all business owners wish for monopoly in the markets they sell their output in and wish for competition in the markets they buy their inputs in. More monopoly means the sellers get together to keep the price above cost and refuse to undercut each other's prices in order to get more business. More competition means that sellers will undercut their competitors' price until the price is bid down to cost. Economists have devised several models to describe the forces behind these cases.

A STORY

When I was a new and naive teacher, I announced the following grading policy for my tests. The highest score on the test would get a 100. If several got the same highest score, they would all get 100. Other scores would get proportionally lower grades. My tests, at that time, were all multiple choice. Imagine my surprise when I gave the test and all students on all the questions circled the letter B! Because all their answers were the same, they all got the same score, and since this score was also the highest score, they all got 100! Obviously, the students had gotten together and agreed to put down the answer B on all questions. They were acting like a monopoly.

Obviously, I had to introduce an element of competition. To do this, I had to find some way to make it pay for an individual student to cheat on the students' agreement. *Cheating* in this case meant putting down the correct answers! Under my original policy, no one could do better by cheating so none cheated. So how could I make it worthwhile for some to undercut the others? I added the following to my policy, "If one student scores 20 points above all the other students, I'll give that student an A for the course. Furthermore, I will keep the grade a secret by mailing back grades." On the next test, more than half the class broke away from the "only B" mold, and those who didn't got very low grades (because I made sure not one correct answer was B!). None got 20 points above the rest of the students, but many tried. Why did my plan work? Because it now paid one student to cheat by being honest, assuming the others put down all B answers. Competition caused many students to try this. They undercut the monopoly price but, as befits the perfect competition model, no one earned any profits.

Points to note:

On the second test, all students would have been better off (or no worse off) if they had acted as a monopoly.

The incentive to cheat on the agreement caused some students to cheat, which is equivalent to competitive firms bidding the price down to cost.

The smaller the class and the more the students knew each other, the more likely the monopoly agreement would have held.

If I had openly announced the grades, the persons putting down the correct answers could be identified and punished, making it more likely that the monopoly agreement would have held.

HOW THIS CHAPTER IS ORGANIZED

This chapter goes from the most competitive industrial structure to the most monopolistic. Remember the two forces in the preceding story: the force of competition (where competitors have the incentive to undercut the price until it is bid down to cost) and the force of collusion (where firms get together and act as a monopoly). In this chapter, as we go from model to model, the force of competition dwindles and the force of collusion becomes stronger and stronger. The models all fall between perfect competition and monopoly. They are

Perfect Competition
Perfectly Contestable Markets
Monopolistic Competition
Oligopoly
Cartel
Monopoly

PERFECTLY CONTESTABLE MARKETS

In a perfectly contestable market:

1. There may be a few or even one firm, and
2. There are no barriers to entry and no start-up costs.

As a result, any new firm can immediately produce and market the good at the same cost as the existing firms.

In this case, if the existing firms raise their price above cost, new firms immediately enter and bid the price back to cost. The price equals the minimum *ATC*. The result is the same as with perfect competition, only we don't need a large number of firms to achieve it.

This model illustrates how low start-up costs and low barriers to entry make it more likely that the competitive result of no profits will result. Consider, as an example, the market for submarine sandwiches. This industry has very low start-up costs (one can buy the necessary equipment used for less than $2,000). Advertising consists of a sign on the door. There is little brand loyalty. As a result, most owners of these types of restaurants work long hours and earn little. Prices reflect cost, and most owners are happy to earn back their opportunity cost.

MONOPOLISTIC COMPETITION

An industry characterized by monopolistic competition has

1. Many firms and
2. No long-run barriers to entry, but
3. Firms sell a similar but not identical product.

As a result of the last criterion, each firm faces a downward sloping demand curve (because there is no perfect substitute for their product). That is, $P > MR$. As a result of the first two criterion, entry into the industry causes economic profits in the long run to be bid to zero. Thus, in the long run, $P = ATC$.

The consequences of monopolistic competition follow.

Consequence 1: Firms practice product differentiation, seeking to make their product seem different and better to its customers. Often, they do this by advertising their differences or by designing their product so it appears different. Examples include toothpaste, headache remedies, and underwear.

Consequence 2: In the short run, the firm acts just like a monopoly. Because no one produces a product identical to theirs, each firm can raise its price without losing all its customers. That is, the demand curve slopes downward. They produce where $MR = MC$. Figure 11.1 shows the representative firm earning a profit in the short run (note that $P > ATC$ at Q^* where $MR = MC$).

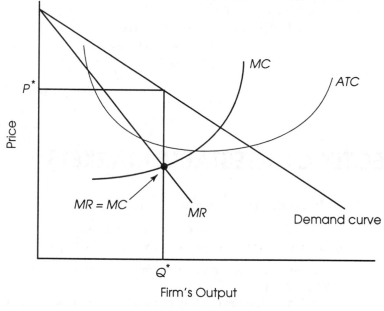

Figure 11.1

Consequence 3: Like perfect competition, $P = ATC$ in the long run. Unlike perfect competition, $P > $ minimum ATC.

In Figure 11.1, each firm is earning a profit. As a result, new firms enter the industry. The new rivals cause each firm to lose some customers such that the demand curve (and MR curve) move down and to the left. Entry continues until economic profits are bid to zero. However, the demand curve still slopes down. So the tangency of the demand curve and the long-run ATC curve occurs where the ATC is also sloping down. Figure 11.2 shows the results.

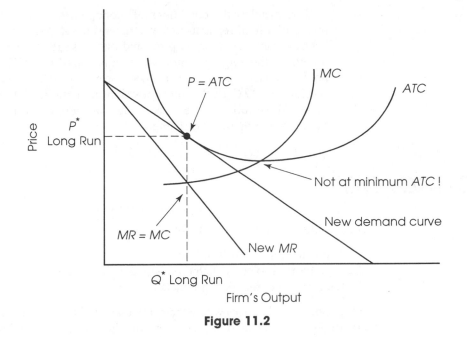

Figure 11.2

Points to note:

New firms entering the industry force the demand curve to move left until this result occurs.

Q occurs where $MR = MC$.

Because $P = ATC$, no new firms will now enter this industry.

The ATC at Q^* is higher than the minimum ATC (where $ATC = MC$).

$P >$ Minimum ATC.

Consequence 4: All firms have excess capacity because each firm's output falls short of the Q where it can produce at the minimum ATC. Because $P >$ Minimum ATC, each firm seeks ways to shift its demand curve out as each added unit of output adds to its profits. Special promotions, coupons, advertising, giveaways, and frequent price wars are all events that may occur in markets with monopolistic competition. They would not occur with perfect competition.

Thought Question

Space Station Alpha XI, as you well know, is a long round tube that measures 10 miles around. Crew members are located at equal intervals along the long service corridor that circles the station. Food replicators can be located at equal intervals. All food replicators have exactly the same costs, can serve exactly the same food, and the eating lounges all have the same dull blue-green decor. The only factor differentiating the food replicators are how close each is to crew members and the price of a meal. Crew members eat at the food replicator whose price plus travel cost is lowest. Thus, crew members are willing to pay up to their travel cost more for the meal that's close by. If owners of food replicators can freely locate where they want and there are no long-run barriers to entry, what will determine where replicators will locate and how many there will be? Will food be produced at the least cost?

This matches the conditions of monopolistic competition. Each owner of a food replicator faces a downward-sloping demand curve because each can raise its price and only lose its most distant customers. In the long run, entry will continue until $P = ATC$. Food will not be produced at the least cost because each restaurant has $P = ATC$ > Minimum ATC. Each replicator will be underutilized. In this sense, there will be too many replicators, just as there might be too many brands of toothpaste and shampoo.

OLIGOPOLY

In an industry characterized by oligopoly,

1. There are only a few firms, and
2. High barriers to entry such that there is no long-run entry into the industry, and
3. Each produces identical products.

Oligopoly usually arises where there are large up-front costs to setting up a firm and marketing its product such that existing firms have large economies of scale. As a result, the larger firms can use a price war to drive new firms out of the industry.

Condition 3 in the preceding list is not essential. It makes the analysis simpler and does match some industries (such as aluminum and steel).

Oligopoly firms are like monopoly firms in two ways. First, because there are only a few firms, each faces a downward-sloping demand curve like a monopoly. Second, with barriers of entry keeping new firms out, they can earn profits in the long run just as a monopoly can.

But an oligopoly differs from a monopoly in one crucial way: Each firm's demand depends upon the price the other firms set. There is a mutual interdependence because the actions of one firm affect the others. If one cuts its price, the demand curves of the other firms shift in. Similarly, if one firm raises its price, the demand curves facing the other firms shift up.

Examples of oligopolies are the automobile, cigarette, and breakfast cereal industries.

COLLUSION AND COMPETITION IN OLIGOPOLIES

Because each firm's actions affect the other firms, the outcome is uncertain. If firms collude, they will be best off acting like a monopoly, maximizing profits for the whole industry as if they were one firm. On the other hand, if they are bitterly competitive, it is quite possible that the industry will set the perfectly competitive price of $P = MC = ATC$.

To show this indeterminacy, we draw two demand curves for each firm. The first demand curve shows the demand curve facing each firm when all firms act together, all charging the same price. This reflects the results of collusion. The collusion could be explicit (for example, the price being set by the CEOs at a secret meeting) or implicit (each firm learning over time that it is best not to undercut the price of the others). The second demand curve shows what happens when the firm acts alone, raising or lowering its price, with none of the other firms changing their prices. This demand curve shows the benefits to a single firm of acting competitively. Figure 11.3 shows these curves, where the firm (and the industry) initially sets a price of $20 (Why $20? Because of the indeterminacy of the price, we have to start somewhere.)

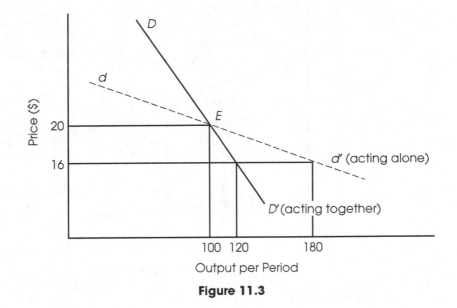

Figure 11.3

Points to note:

At $P = \$20$, all firms sell 100 units of output. If there are four firms, industry output is 400.

DD' shows the demand curve when all firms act together, setting the same price.

dd' shows the demand curve when a single firm sets its own price while the others still charge a price of $20.

If all firms charge $16, each firm sells 120 units. If there are four firms, industry output is 480. Each firm has an equal share.

If a single firm sets a price of $16 while the others still charge $20, it can sell 180 units of output. Although the 180 figure is made up, it must be larger than 120 because the single firm, being the only one with the lower price, will capture a larger share of the market than the other firms. The others now will sell less than 100 units (some of their business being taken away by the firm with the lower price).

If a firm cuts its price from $20 to $16, it will sell 180 units if the others don't cut their price and 120 units if they do. Its sales depend upon what the others do!

OLIGOPOLY: THE KINKED DEMAND CURVE MODEL

As we've seen, the results in oligopoly are indeterminant. If firms vigorously compete, the competitive price ($P = ATC$) could emerge. If they collude, the monopoly price could emerge ($MC = MR$ for the industry).

One simple model of oligopoly is the kinked demand curve model. In this model, we assume that (1) when a firm raises its price, it acts alone because the other firms refrain from going along (so the firm is on demand curve dd'), but (2) when the firm cuts its price, the other firms match its price cut in order to maintain their market share (so the firm is on demand curve DD'). In both cases, the other firms seek to increase or maintain their market share. The resulting demand curve is kinked, as shown in Figure 11.4.

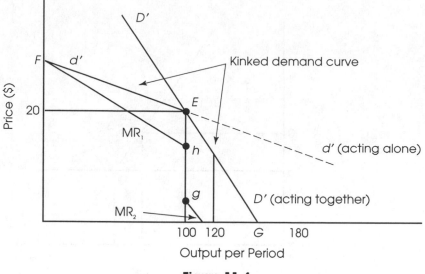

Figure 11.4

Points to note:

The kinked demand curve is *FEG*.

Along segment *FE*, the firm acts alone. The other firms keep their price at $20 while this firm raises it price above $20. Many of its customers leave it and their business goes to the other firms (who still charge $20), whose market share goes up.

Along segment *EG*, all firms act together. The other firms cut their prices to match that of the firm shown. If they didn't, they would lose business to the firm cutting its price.

MR_1 is the marginal revenue curve associated with demand curve *dd'* (acting alone). MR_2 is the demand curve associated with demand curve *DD'* (acting together).

If the marginal-cost curve falls between these two curves (between *h* and *g*), the firm will keep its price at $20 (at the kink).

Output will be determined where $MR = MC$. But note that the kinked demand curve has a marginal revenue curve with a long vertical section (between *h* and *g*). *MC* can fall anywhere between *h* and *g* and the firm will keep its price at $20! It will also keep output at 100. Large changes in marginal cost will not affect output or price.

The kinked demand-curve model predicts that prices will be slow to change in oligopolic models. This is called *price rigidity*. The prediction of price rigidity has proven to be wrong. Prices go up and down in oligopolic industry just as much as they do in other industries.

OLIGOPOLY: THE DOMINANT FIRM (PRICE LEADERSHIP) MODEL

When does an elephant eat? When he wants to! This old riddle gives the essence of the dominant-firm model of oligopoly. In this model, one dominant firm sets the price for the whole industry. As a result, it is called a *price leader*.

In the dominant-firm model,

1. There is one dominant firm,
2. The rest of the firms who compete for the rest of the market are small, and

3. There is limited entry into the industry, so the dominant firm can maintain profits in the long run without worrying about too many small firms taking away its business.

Usually, the smaller firms are assumed to have higher costs than the dominant firm and, being small, act just like perfectly competitive firms (producing where $P = MC$).

The results are that the dominant firm acts like a monopoly, knowing the smaller firms will follow its price. If they don't, it engages in a price-cutting war that punishes them severely. Its willingness to suffer losses (which in the short run may seem irrational) is a credible threat, which results in higher profits in the long run. Other firms learn that it is best to follow its lead in setting higher prices.

Thought Question

Microhard, Inc. dominates the software market. It has a constant marginal cost of \$10 per unit output. Ten other firms compete in its market, each having the following marginal costs:

Q	1	2	3	4	5
MC	\$10	\$11	\$12	\$13	\$14

The market demand curve for software is

Price	\$14	\$13	\$12	\$11	\$10	\$9
Q^D	50	55	60	65	70	75

Derive the demand curve facing Microhard, Inc.

Table 11.1 shows how we derive the demand curve facing Microhard. At each price, first find out what each of its 10 competitors will supply at that price (using the $P = MC$ rule for competitive firms). For example, at $P = \$12$, each of the 10 firms will supply three units. Next, add up this supply to get the combined supply of the small firms. At $P = \$12$, this equals 30 units ($= 3 \times 10$). Finally, subtract this from the market demand at this price to get what Microhard can sell. At $P = \$13$, the market demand is 60, so Microhard faces a demand of 30 units (60 minus the 30 units the other firms sell). The increase in total revenue gained by lowering its price from \$14 to \$13 is \$195. As Microhard's output goes up by 15 units, the MR per unit is \$195 divided by 15 or \$13.

TABLE 11.1

DERIVATION OF RESIDUAL DEMAND CURVE FACING DOMINANT FIRM MICROHARD INC.

Price (\$)	Market Demand	Supply of 10 Small Firms	Residual Demand for Microhard	Total Revenue for Microhard (\$)	Marginal Revenue for Microhard (\$ per unit Q)	Marginal Cost for Microhard (\$ per unit Q)
14	50	50	0	0	—	10
13	55	40	15	195	195/15 = \$13	10
12	60	30	30	360	165/15 = \$11	10
11	65	20	45	495	135/15 = \$9	10
10	70	10	60	600	105/15 = \$7	10
9	80	0	80	720	120/20 = \$6	10

What price should it set? Assume that the firm can only set the price in dollar increments (for example, it can charge $7 but not $7.50). What is its Q?

It will charge $12, because at a lower price, its $MR < MC$.

Here are some conclusions about dominant-firm oligopolies.

Result 1: The more elastic the supply of other firms, the more elastic the demand curve facing the dominant firm. This will tend to reduce the price it sets. In the preceding example, if the supply curve of other firms were perfectly elastic at $11, the dominant firm would lower the price to $11.

Result 2: The smaller the dominant firm's share of the market, the more elastic is the demand curve facing it. This also results in a smaller price.

The dominant-firm model fits the data for many industries much better than does the kinked model. Because all firms are better off in the long run following the lead of the dominant firm, this is not a surprising result.

CARTELS

A cartel has an explicit agreement among firms, sometimes backed up with a legally enforceable contract, that allows it to centrally set prices and allocate output and profits among its members. Even though cartels are illegal in the United States, they are legal in many parts of the world.

Cartels are like oligopolies. There are few firms with limited entry. But because the price is centrally determined and enforced, all firms act alike. The results will be that the cartel acts just like a monopoly. It sets its price at the monopoly level, where the industry's $MR = MC$.

That would be the end of the story (Cartel = Monopoly) if cartels didn't have one problem that monopolies do not have. This problem is the cartel-cheating problem: Each member has an incentive to cheat by undercutting the cartel's price. At the monopoly price, $P > ATC$. So each firm can increase its individual profits if it can get new business, even if it's at a slightly lower price. So each firm seeks out new business by secretly offering to cut its price. They can't do this openly or they'll be punished by the cartel. Instead, they'll try to find some hidden way. For example, they might sell their output at the cartel's price but offer the buyer a rebate by declaring a certain percent of what they bought defective, even though it was perfectly good. Another way of lowering the effective price is to offer higher quality and more service. This form of nonprice competition also takes the form of advertising.

Cartel cheating reduces the profits of all firms. Often, buyers will play one firm against another. Eventually, the pressure becomes so great and the cheating so widespread that the cartel collapses. To avoid this, some cartels in Germany have a central office that does all the selling for the industry, sets the standards for the industry, and enforces the rules.

Another cartel problem is how to allocate the profits among firms. Do the bigger firms get a bigger share of the profits? Or do all get an equal share? If bigger firms get a bigger share, then all firms have an incentive to become bigger! This results in excess capacity. When this occurs and, in addition, the industry demand falls (perhaps because the economy is in a recession), the cartel often breaks apart, and a price-cutting war erupts.

Thought Question

Old Man Martin is willing to pay up to $120 a day to have his yard tended to. There are three gardeners in town who are capable of doing the job. Each would be willing to accept as little as $10 a day. They get together and form the Rip Off Old Man Martin Cartel. It sets the price at $120 and each of the three takes $40. Each works one out of every three days. How and why does each have an incentive to cheat on the cartel agreement?

If any of them can work more than one out of three days and get paid $120 for that day's work, which only cost them $10, they will be better off. One of them might work harder, hoping Old Man Martin will notice and hire him more often. Another might offer Old Man Martin a kickback by bringing him a meal from home. The third could buy more expensive tools and double his shop size and claim, as a result, that he deserves a bigger share of the profits. These are all examples of the ways firms try to cheat on the cartel agreement.

GAME THEORY

The theory of games is a framework for analyzing oligopoly or any other situation where the behavior of people affects one another. Let's examine a two-firm game where each firm has to choose to maintain the current (monopoly) price or cut it. Because it is the monopoly price, both firms together are best off when both charge the monopoly price. Similarly, they both are worse off if both cut their price. However, to make the game a game, it must be that if one cuts the price and the other maintains the monopoly price, the price cutter must be better off than with their share of the monopoly profit.

A payoff matrix shows the gains and losses to each player for each of his or her choices and for each rival's choice. Suppose that two airlines, Alice's Airline and Bob's Airline, serve Littletown Airport. Alice and Bob each have to decide individually to charge a high fare or a low fare. The following matrix shows their profits depending upon how they choose. For the moment, assume they only get to choose once; after that, they are stuck with their choice forever.

		Bob's Airline Choices ($)	
		High Fare	**Low Fare**
Alice's	High Fare	Alice: 200	Alice: 20
Airline		Bob: 200	Bob: 350
Choices ($)	Low Fare	Alice: 350	Alice: 50
		Bob: 20	Bob: 50

Points to note:

Each cell shows the payoffs from the strategy to Alice and Bob. For example, when Alice charges a high fare and Bob charges a low fare, Bob gets $350 in profits while Alice gets only $20 (because Bob gets most of the business).

The total combined profit is highest when both charge high fares.

The total combined profit is lowest when both charge the low fare.
When one charges the low fare and the other the high fare, the low-fare airline gets more than it did charging the high fare. But their combined profit is lower.

If Bob and Alice could collude and draw up a contract between them, they would both set high fares. But suppose they can't collude? Suppose instead, that in the morning, they each drop their decision into a box and that decision becomes final. What will each do? Bob's thinking might go like this: "If Alice charges a high fare, I'm best off if I charge a low fare. If Alice charges a low fare, I'm best off if I charge a low fare. Hence, I'm best off in either case by charging a low fare." Thus, Bob, being rational and sensible, charges a low fare. However, Alice, also being rational and sensible, does the same thing and sets the low fare. The result? Both choose the worse strategy! What is best for each is worst for both! Note, however that this is the competitive equilibrium result.

This outcome is referred to as the prisoner's dilemma, a name derived from the original example of this problem (which we present later). Each player uses what is referred to as the *maximin strategy*. In this strategy, each player decides what is the worst that could happen (the *min* in maximin) and then chooses the best of these (that is, they *max* over their *mins*). This result explains why tobacco companies spend heavily on advertising to the detriment of industrial profits. Thus, when TV cigarette advertising was outlawed, the profits and stock prices of tobacco companies went up!

Note that, in our example, both players have the same best strategy (low price) no matter what the other chooses. When this occurs, the best strategy is called a *dominant strategy*. When both players have a dominant strategy, the result is an example of a Nash equilibrium (named after economist John Nash). A Nash equilibrium occurs for players A and B when, given their choices, player A (given B's choice) can do no better, and, similarly, B (given A's choice) can do no better. If one strategy appears to dominate in an industry over time, it most likely reflects a Nash equilibrium because none of the parties think they can do better by changing.

Thought Questions

The following illustrates the prisoner's dilemma. Two persons, Alice and Bob, commit a crime. The DA pulls them in and puts them in separate rooms. She says to each, "If you both confess, you'll each get 20 years in jail. If you both stay silent, I won't have enough evidence and you'll both go free. But if one of you confesses, I give you only 1 year in jail while the other will get 25 years in jail." In this problem, both staying silent is the collusion solution (or, as it is called in the game theory, the *cooperative solution* as it maximizes the two players' joint welfare). But because Alice and Bob are in separate rooms and cannot cooperate, how will each decide?

Alice will say to herself, "If Bob confesses, I'm better off confessing also. If Bob stays silent, then I'm better off confessing. Hmmm, this is easy. I'll confess." Switch the names Alice and Bob and you'll see that Bob confesses also. Result: Both get hard time for 20 years!

Go back to the story at the beginning of this chapter and show the two payoff matrixes for students cooperating on the test (all putting down the answer B) or noncooperative behavior (putting down what they think are the right answers). Assume there are only two students who, coincidentally, also have the names Alice and Bob. Assume that when they put down what they think is the right answer, they get a 75 (if they had read this book, it would have been a 95!). If one puts down all Bs and the other student puts down the right answers, the all B test will get a score of 25 (as one quarter of the right answers are B).

Initially, before I modified the rules, the payoff matrix was as follows:

		Bob's Choices	
		All Bs	Right Answers
Alice's Choices	All Bs	Alice: 100 Bob: 100	Alice: 25 Bob: 75
	Right Answer	Alice: 75 Bob: 25	Alice: 75 Bob: 75

In this case, Alice says, "If Bob puts down all Bs, I'm best off also putting down all Bs. If Bob puts down the right answers, I'm best off putting down the right answers. In this case, there is no dominant strategy. But since we're both better off putting down all Bs, I pick B." If Bob says the same thing, both Alice and Bob will put down all Bs.

After my change in the rules, the new payoff matrix is as follows:

		Bob's Choices	
		All Bs	Right Answers
Alice's Choices	All Bs	Alice: 100 Bob: 100	Alice: 25 Bob: A for course
	Right Answer	Alice: A for course Bob: 25	Alice: 75 Bob: 75

Now, Alice will say, "If Bob puts down all Bs, I'm better off putting down the right answers. If Bob puts down the right answers, I'm better off putting down the right answers. So I'll put down the right answers!" Bob says the same thing. Both adopt the maximin strategy and get a 75. Of course, this is a sneaky trick on the teacher's part, promising a reward (the A for the course if one student gets 20 points above all the others) when the teacher knows that students will act in a way that none get the reward. I don't know about you, but I would never buy a book from such a sneaky teacher!

GAME THEORY IN LIFE

In many of our interactions with other persons, cooperative behavior in general generates the highest total output. However, often one person, by being noncooperative, can do still better, but at the expense of others. This leads to everyone acting noncooperatively, with the result that all are worse off.

For example, a physician tries to make an out-of-court settlement with a patient who is suing him. Some agreement will be better for both as compared to a lengthy and costly trial. But if the physician makes a reasonable offer, the patient can use it in court to get even more. The result is that both will go to court and be jointly worse off.

Here's another example: An airline and its pilot union are negotiating a new labor contract. If neither compromises, a crippling strike occurs. If only one compromises, it loses heavily while the other gains a lot. But if both compromise, the two jointly are best off. Unfortunately, the strike is the likely outcome. One solution is to have what's called *final offer arbitration*. Both the union and the firm make an offer, and the arbitrator picks which is better. If one asks too much, the arbitrator is more likely to reject that offer. The empirical result is that such a procedure results in fewer strikes.

Finally, a worker and a boss do best if both act honestly. The honest boss would reward the honest worker according to what the worker produces. However, the boss might be better off being dishonest, promising the worker a share of the profits if the worker is honest but then not giving the worker anything (using some invented excuse). On the other hand, the worker may be in a position to steal from the company without getting caught. The result of game theory suggests that the boss and the worker will be dishonest (the boss not giving the worker any share of the profit and the worker stealing from the firm). This result is to the detriment of both because it will eventually result in lower profits and lower wages.

However, if a game is played again and again over time, a different optimal strategy emerges called tit-for-tat. If one is playing a game with the same person again and again, it is generally best to act honestly (cooperatively) until the other person cheats on you. Then, in the next game, you cheat on her (this is the tit-for-tat). Then, in the next game, you return to being honest and continue with this strategy. Over time, both persons will find it best to act honestly.

CRIB NOTES

More competition: *P* close to *MC*.

More collusion: *P* close to monopoly *P*.

Perfectly contestable markets: No barriers to entry, few firms. Result: $P = ATC$ or firms enter.

Monopolistic competition: Many firms producing close but not perfect substitutes, no long-run barriers to entry. Result: Short run: Like monopoly. Long-run: Entry until $P = ATC$. But $P > MC$ and $ATC >$ Minimum ATC. Excess capacity. Other results: Advertising, periodic price wars.

Oligopoly: Few firms, barriers to entry. Each firm's actions have large impact on other firms. Result is uncertain. If cooperative, monopoly. If competitive, competitive result.

Kinked demand curve oligopoly: If one firm raises *P*, others keep old *P* and firm loses business. If lower *P*, price war. Result: Same *P* for wide range of *MC*.

Dominant-firm oligopoly: One big firm, many small competitors.

Small competitors follow big firm P. Big firm sets P knowing this.

Cartel: Few firms, barriers to entry, firms collude to set price. P set at monopoly P. Each firm has incentive to cheat at $P > ATC$.

Game theory: Analyzes situations where firms or individuals interact while attempting to achieve their own goals.

Maximin strategy: Given what opponent does, do what is best for you. Collusion is best for both. Cheating by one best for that one only. Cheating by both makes all worse off. Maximin result: All cheat. Leads to prisoner's dilemma where all worse off.

Tit-for-tat: If game played repeatedly, collude until other cheats, then cheat for one turn. Return to collusion until other cheats again.

Review Questions

---

1. Which type of markets do the following situations best reflect (perfect competition, contestable markets, monopolistic competition, oligopoly, cartel, monopoly)?
   a. There are many clothing stores in a town, each selling its own distinctive designs.
   b. There is one fruit stand in town. It is easy to set one up across the street.
   c. There are three makers of a specialized drill press that requires a substantial investment in research and development and in worker training to produce.
   d. A milk board buys all the milk from all the dairies in a state, tells each dairy how much to produce, and is the only seller of milk in that state.
   e. One major firm dominates the cereal industry, but many small firms actively compete.
   f. Only one company produces a cure for baldness.

2. Pizza Pizza is one of many pizza stores in Collegetown. Pizza Pizza has a special recipe that has created a loyal following of customers who believe its pizza is best. Its marginal cost for pizzas is $5 at its profit-maximizing level of output. Show that its price will exceed $5.

3. In question 2, Pizza Pizza has an average cost of $5 at the optimal level of output. Suppose this occurs at its minimum ATC of producing pizza. It and every other pizza store has the same situation.
   a. Is Pizza Pizza making a profit?
   b. If there are no barriers to entry to this industry, what will happen to the number of firms in the long run? What will happen to profits? What will happen to the price? What will happen to ATC? Will the price equal or exceed $5?

4. What type of market (from competition to monopoly) will likely feature these types of ads?
   a. An ad saying that buying diamonds will bring you love.
   b. An ad for Jerry's Jewelry Store, suggesting that Jerry's highly trained gemologists do a better job than any one else and never mistake glass for diamonds.
   c. An ad for a grocery store featuring its low, low prices.

5. Use the following market-demand curve to answer the following questions:

TABLE 11.2

Quantity Demanded	1	2	3	4	5	6	7	8
Demand Price ($)	20	18	16	14	12	10	8	6

a. What price and quantity would a monopoly have if it has a constant average and marginal cost of $8 a unit?

b. What price and quantity would a competitive industry have if each firm has a constant average and marginal cost of $8?

c. What price and quantity would one firm have if the market is contestable and anyone can enter? All have a constant average and marginal cost of $8.

d. If there are two firms, both with constant average and marginal cost of $8, what price and quantity will they agree on if they collude successively?

e. Given that the price in part d has been set, why would it pay one of the firms to cut its price?

f. If both cut prices, what price and quantity will emerge?

6. Acme, Inc. produces widgets in a oligopolic industry. It has the kinked demand curve show in Table 11.3.

TABLE 11.3

Quantity Demanded	1	2	3	4	5	6	7
Demand Price ($)	20	19	18	17	14	9	5
Marginal Revenue							

a. Where does the kink occur?

b. Fill in the *MR* column.

c. If $MC = \$10$, what price and output will it have?

d. What if $MC = \$8$? 6?

e. How much would MC have to fall before it lowered the price?

7. In a really quaint town, 500 tourists a day are willing to pay $22 for a quaint town tee-shirt. Because the tourists buy a tee-shirt from the first tee-shirt shop they come upon and are too busy to shop around, it doesn't pay a tee-shirt shop to lower the price below $22. A tee-shirt shop has a daily fixed cost of $1,000 and each quaint town tee-shirt costs $2 to make. How many tee-shirt shops will there be in quaint town in the long run? How is this excess capacity? Assume each tee-shirt shop sells equal numbers of shirts, all sharing the market equally.

8. Alice and Bob go to a restaurant and agree ahead of time to split the bill. As a result, the cost to Bob of ordering the $10 flaming dessert is only $5 (Alice picking up the other half). Similarly, the cost to Alice of ordering it is only $5. Each values the dessert at $6. If they got together and cooperatively talked about it, neither would order the dessert. But this is America and, let's face it, we Americans are just too polite! So Alice and Bob face the following payoff matrix. For example, when Alice does not order dessert but Bob does, Alice is worse off by $5 (her share of Bill's cost) and Bill is better off by a net $1 ($6 worth of dessert minus $5 in cost).

		Bob's Choices ($)	
		No Dessert	**Order Dessert**
Alice's Choices ($)	No Dessert	Alice: 0 Bob: 0	Alice: –5 Bob: +1
	Order Dessert	Alice: +1 Bob: –5	Alice: –1 Bob: –1

If both use the maximin strategy, who'll order dessert and why?

9. Two companies, Alice's Widget Works and Bob's Widget Works, are the only two firms in an oligopoly. Over time, each has learned to not undercut the price of the other. However, each can choose to advertise as much as it wants. If neither advertises, their joint profit is greatest. If both advertise heavily, neither makes a profit. But if one advertises and the other does not, the firm that advertises makes much more.
   a. Using game theory and the following payoff matrix, what is the likely outcome if this game is played once?
   b. What if it's repeated over time?

		Bob Choices ($)	
		No Advertising	**Heavy Advertising**
Alice's Choices ($)	No Advertising	Alice: 100 Bob: 100	Alice: -25 Bob: 150
	Heavy Advertising	Alice: 150 Bob: –25	Alice: 0 Bob: 0

10. In a small fishing village, there are 10 fishermen. Each can catch 50 fish a day, but if they all do this, the stock of fish in their local lake will be depleted within 10 years. Only if each catches 20 fish a day will the stock of fish be able to reproduce enough to ensure a steady catch for all into the future. All would be better off when each catches 20 fish a day. However, any one of them would be better off by cheating on the agreement and catching extra fish. But if all do this, they are all worse off. How will the following factors affect the likelihood that the fishermen will cooperate and not cheat?
   Factor A: All 10 fishermen are good friends.
   Factor B: There are 20, not 10, fishermen.
   Factor C: It is easy to cheat without getting caught.
   Factor D: One of the fishermen is a loner and also the kick-box champion of Southern France.

11. A dairy cartel buys milk from producers and resells it at a monopoly price to consumers. It then shares its profits among producers according to their herd sizes. If a milk producer produces more milk than it sells to the dairy cartel, it must dump the milk. It is illegal for any producer to sell milk by itself. If there are no limits on herd size, what will happen in this cartel in the long run?

12. Why will a decline in the demand for milk, if prolonged, cause the cartel to break up and a price war to break out?

Answers

1. a. Monopolistic competition
   b. Contestable market
   c. Oligopoly
   d. Cartel
   e. Oligopoly (dominant-firm model)
   f. Monopoly

2. Pizza Pizza faces a downward-sloping demand curve. As a result, its price exceeds its marginal revenue. It produces where $MR = MC = \$5$ so the price must exceed $5 as $P > MR = \$5$.

3. a. Because $P > \$5$ and $ATC = \$5$, Pizza Pizza is making a profit.
   b. Other firms will enter the industry. They will enter until profits equal zero. In the long run, $P = ATC$. The price of pizza will fall. However, the greater number of firms cause each firm's output to fall. As the firms' output falls below the level where the minimum ATC was achieved, ATC will go up (as each firm moves to the left along the rising left side of the U-shaped ATC curve). So $ATC > \$5$. Thus, $P = ATC > \$5$.

4. a. Monopoly. Usually, only a monopoly would advertise for a general product without mentioning a brand name because it gets all the business for that product.
   b. Monopolistic competition or an oligopoly (where each firm has a differentiated product). The purpose of this ad is to generate a loyal customer base so that the firm can maintain a higher price.
   c. An ad featuring mainly price reflects competition, especially if this type of ad is common. It could reflect an occasional price war in a market with monopolistic competition or oligopoly.

5. a. A monopoly sets its output where market $MR = MC$. This occurs at $Q = 4$ (because the increase in total revenue from $Q = 3$ to $Q = 4$ is $8). The price will be $14.
   b. Firms will enter until the price is bid down to $8 and $Q = 7$.
   c. Even if there is only one firm, it knows that if it raises its price above $8, new entrants will take away its business. So it sets $P = \$8$ and produces seven units.
   d. They will agree on the monopoly price and output because this gives them the biggest joint profit. Total profits equal $24, which they'll probably split so each gets $12.
   e. If one firm can price discriminate and cut its price to $12 to get one more customer, it will add $4 to its profits (= $12 – $8) for a total profit of $16. If it sets it price to $12 and gets all the market's output (because the other firm keeps it price at $14), it will make a profit of $20. In either case, this is better than the $12 it got when splitting the monopoly profit.
   f. Price cutting leads to the competitive solution of $P = \$8$ and $Q = 7$.

6. a. It occurs at $P = \$17$. Below that price, other firms cut their price along with this firm, and it takes correspondingly higher price cuts to get another unit of output.
   c. $Q = 4$ and $P = \$17$ (using marginal analysis, increase Q as long as $MR > MC$).
   d. $Q = 4$ and $P = \$17$.
   e. It would have to fall to $2 before the firm cut the price from $17. Then, even if it fell to zero, the firm would never lower the price below $14. See Table 11.4.

TABLE 11.4

Quantity Demanded	1	2	3	4	5	6	7
Demand Price ($)	20	19	18	17	14	10	6
Marginal Revenue	20	18	16	12	2	−10	−18

7. This problem illustrates how monopolistic competition generates excess capacity. The number of tee-shirt shops increases until none makes a profit. Because each shirt sells for $22 and has a variable cost of $2, the average fixed cost per shirt must be $20 if each store is not to make a profit. Because total fixed cost (per day) is $1,000, an *AFC* of $20 means each store sells 50 shirts a day. There are 500 tee-shirts sold a day divided among all the stores, each of which is selling 50 shirts when they break even; therefore, there will be 10 tee-shirt shops (500/50 = 10) in the long run. There is excess capacity because one tee-shirt shop could have sold all 500 shirts at a lower average cost (of $4).

8. Both will order dessert and, on net, be worse off. Alice will say, "If Bob does not order dessert, then I'm better off ordering dessert. And if Bob does order dessert, then I'm also better off ordering dessert. So I'll order dessert." Bob, following the same logic, will also order dessert. This problem illustrates why large groups who split the bill tend to order more than when each pays his own tab. It also illustrates why some restaurants don't split the tab.

9. a. Both will choose to advertise heavily. Alice will say, "If Bob doesn't advertise, I'm best off advertising heavily. If Bob advertises heavily, I'm better off advertising heavily. So I'll advertise heavily." Bob will also follow this logic.

   b. Using a tit-for-tat strategy, both over time will learn to not advertise.

10. Factor A: More likely to cooperate.

    Factor B: Less likely to cooperate (the more likely each person is to say, "Someone else is cheating and so I might as well cheat too").

    Factor C: Less likely to cooperate.

    Factor D: Less likely to cooperate.

11. Each producer will increase its herd to get a greater share of the profits. But when all do this, no one's share goes up. Instead, all will be stuck with excess capacity. Entry and excess capacity will grow until profits are bid to zero.

12. If producers are breaking even and demand then falls, they'll be making losses. If losses are great enough, it may appear to some that they'd be better off breaking off from the cartel rather than going bankrupt. The result will be a price war, and, most likely, even greater bankruptcy.

Chapter Twelve

Antitrust and Regulation of Markets

DREAM ON

I had a dream last night. I dreamed the people of America had found a new cause. All across America, they took to the streets shouting the words I find dear. Angry mobs stormed Washington, holding placards with the same words. What were these words that stirred the souls of men? "Economic efficiency! We want economic efficiency!" Then I woke up. Economic efficiency just doesn't have the ring to it that "freedom, justice, and equality" does. Few lives have been lost in its cause. Yet nations have crumbled and their wealth has been squandered because they acted inefficiently.

ECONOMIC EFFICIENCY

An economy that is efficient is getting the most value from its resources. Marginal analysis allows us to see how competition can lead to the efficient result. Suppose an economy has the marginal benefit (*MB*) and the marginal cost (*MC*) of baby shoes shown in Table 12.1. How many pairs of baby shoes should the economy produce to maximize the net benefit to society?

TABLE 12.1

Marginal Benefit (*MB*) and Marginal Cost (*MC*) of Baby Shoes							
Quantity	1	2	3	4	5	6	7
MB ($)	14	12	10	8	6	4	2
MC ($)	2	3	4	5	6	7	8

The first pair is valued at $14 and costs $2 in resources to produce. It adds $12 to the net benefit of the economy. The second pair adds another $9 ($12 – $3); the third, $6; the fourth, $3. On the fifth pair, $MB = MC$. The last pair adds nothing to net: This is the optimal number of baby shoes. All five pair together have a net benefit to society of $30 (= $12 + $9 + $6 + $3 + $0). This would be the social loss if all five pair were lost in a hotel fire.

If the baby shoe industry is competitive, then the socially optimal number of baby shoes will be produced. The marginal benefit of baby shoes is reflected in the demand curve for baby shoes. The marginal cost of baby shoes is reflected in the competitive supply curve for baby shoes. Because demand equals supply in competitive markets, the optimal number of baby shoes will be produced (the Q where $P^D = P^S$ and social MB = social MC).

This example can be used to show two of the main objections to using economic efficiency as the sole criterion for evaluating social welfare. The first objection is that it ignores the poor (as well as the issue of inequality). For example, someone might say, "What about the shoeless babies of poor parents who cannot afford the luxury of baby shoes! The demand curve only shows what people can afford, not what they need. The government should help the poor by subsidizing the production of baby shoes." An answer to this is that instead of having numerous programs to subsidize this and that good, very little of each actually helping the poor, it is far more efficient to directly give the poor money and let them decide what they really need.[1] This leads to the second objection of using economic efficiency. Recall that economic efficiency uses what people are willing to pay to evaluate benefits and costs. The second objection is that people may not know their true needs. In this case, someone could argue, "Yes, it may be more efficient to give money to the poor, but what if they spend it on their own consumption and ignore the plight of their own children? Society must represent the needs of the children who can't speak for themselves." Similarly, when valuing the cost and benefits of improving the environment, it is argued that the government must represent future generations, which are not reflected in current prices. The validity of these statements depends upon the validity of the proposition that those running our government are wiser and more farseeing than the general populace.

Allocative efficiency occurs when all mutually advantageous trades take place. Allocative efficiency is achieved when any additional reallocations of goods will make someone worse off. However, if there is one trade that has not taken place and that would make someone better off and no one worse off, then allocative efficiency has not been achieved. Allocative efficiency is also called *Pareto efficiency*. Competition is allocatively efficient because for the marginal good produced, $P = MC$. Producing more (where $P^D < MC$) would make someone worse off because it costs more than it is worth. Producing less (where $P^D > MC$) would make someone worse off because he can't get what he was willing to pay for.

CONSUMER AND PRODUCER SURPLUS

The total net benefit of producing any particular good is divided between the good's consumers and the good's producers. The net benefit going to consumers is called the *consumer surplus*: It is the difference between the value consumers put on the good and the price they actually pay. The net benefit going to producers is called the *producer surplus*: It is the difference between the price they receive and the marginal cost of the good. Table 12.2 shows how these surpluses would be calculated from the example in Table 12-1. The competitive price was $6.

---

[1]One concept that is useful here is *target efficiency*. If the target is to help the poor, target efficiency measures how much of the many programs that claim to help the poor actually do.

TABLE 12.2

Calculating Consumer and Producer Surpluses

Quantity	1	2	3	4	5
MB ($)	14	12	10	8	6
Price ($)	6	6	6	6	6
MC ($)	2	3	4	5	6
Consumer surplus attributable to each unit of the good ($)	8	6	4	2	0
Producer surplus attributable to each unit of the good ($)	4	3	2	1	0

Total consumer surplus (for $Q = 5$) is $20
Total producer surplus (for $Q = 5$) is $10
Total net benefit (for $Q = 5$) is $30

Points to note:

Net benefit = Consumer surplus + Producer surplus.

The consumer surplus for each unit is its demand price (*MB*) minus its price. The third unit, for example, is valued by consumers at $10 but costs $6, so it adds $4 to the net benefit of consumers.

The producer surplus for each unit is its price minus its supply price (*MC*).

The third unit sells for $6 and costs $4: It adds $2 to the net benefit of producers.

Figure 12.1 shows how consumer and producer surpluses are calculated from demand and supply graphs. Consumer surplus is the area between the demand curve and the price. Producer surplus is the area between the supply curve and the price. The sum of these areas is the good's net benefit to society. In Figure 12.1, the good sells for $12 and 40 units are competitively produced.

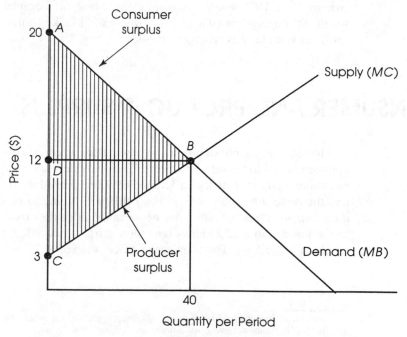

Figure 12.1

Points to note:

The consumer surplus equals area of triangle ABD.
The producer surplus equals area of triangle DBC.
Area of a triangle = ½ × base × height.
Consumer surplus = $160 = ½ × 40 × $8.
Producer surplus = $180 = ½ × 40 × $9.
Total net benefit = Area ABC = $340 = ½ × 40 × $17.

THE SOCIAL LOSS FROM MONOPOLY

Because $P > MC$ for monopolies, they stop short of producing all the units of the good that are worth more to consumers than they cost the producer. The economy would be better off if monopoly produced more. Suppose in Table 12.3 the market is controlled by a monopoly. Note that the "MB to consumers" is the good's demand price.

TABLE 12.3

Monopoly Output							
Quantity	1	2	3	4	5	6	7
MB to consumers ($)	14	12	10	8	6	4	2
MR to monopoly ($)	14	10	6	2	-2	-6	-10
MC ($)	2	3	4	5	6	7	8

The monopoly will produce as long as $MR \geq MC$. In this case, it will produce only three units at a price of $10. This falls short of the socially optimal level of five units. Because units 4 and 5 are not produced, society is worse off by the net benefit attributable to these units not being produced. The lost net benefit equals $3 for the fourth unit $(P - MC)$ and $0 for the fifth, or a total loss of $3. Thus, the social loss from monopoly equals $3, the total lost net benefit.

Why not include the sixth unit? First, it would not be produced by competitive firms, so its net benefit is not lost. Second, its net benefit is negative, because it costs $3 more in resources than it is worth to consumers.

A monopoly is not allocatively efficient because $P > MC$. In Table 12.3, the fourth unit is worth $8 to consumers and costs the monopoly only $5 to produce. A trade, at say $P = $7, would make the monopoly and consumer better off. But the trade doesn't take place because the monopoly would have to lower the price on all its units, and this makes it not worth it to the monopoly (assuming it cannot price discriminate).

A monopoly causes a social loss because it produces too little, not because it charges too much. Be careful! Don't think this loss occurs because it is making big profits. It occurs only because $P > MC$. As a counterexample, if the monopoly were a perfect price discriminator, charging a different price for each unit equaling the price on the demand curve for each unit, it would make the largest possible profit and yet cause no social loss because it would produce where $P^D = MC$.

Figure 12.2 shows the social loss due to monopoly. The social loss is the area of triangle ABC. This area measures the lost net benefit from the goods whose $P^D > MC$ and which the monopoly does not produce. This social loss is also called a dead-weight loss as no one gets the potential net benefit from these goods.

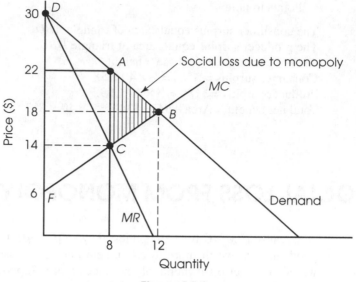

Figure 12.2

Points to note:

A competitive industry would have produced 12 units of good at $P = \$18$.

A monopoly produces 8 units, with $MR = MC = \$14$. The price is $22.

Unless stated otherwise, we assume the monopoly can only charge one price and cannot price discriminate.

The social loss equals the lost net benefit attributable from unit 8 to unit 12.

The social loss equals $16 ($= \frac{1}{2} \times 4 \times \$8$), the area of triangle ABC.

If the monopoly were a perfect price discriminator, it would produce 12 units. There would be no social loss. Its profits would be $144 ($= \frac{1}{2} \times 12 \times \$24$).

The net benefit under competition is $144 ($= \frac{1}{2} \times 12 \times \$24$), the area of the triangle DBF. This is society's maximum net benefit.

If the monopoly is a perfect price discriminator, its profits equal society's net benefit, so a perfect discriminator produces the socially optimal amount and makes the highest profit obtainable.

The net benefit under monopoly is area $DACF$, or $128.

The difference between $144 (net benefit of competition) and $128 (net benefit from monopoly) is $16, the social loss from the monopoly.

REGULATING MONOPOLIES WITH PRICE CEILINGS

A correctly placed price ceiling can cause a monopoly to increase its output while at the same time lower its price. It does this by making the effective demand curve the monopoly sees flat and horizontal just like the demand curve facing a perfectly competitive firm. Over the range the price ceiling is effective, the monopoly can produce more, and its price doesn't fall. As a result, its MR = Price ceiling. Figure 12.3 illus-

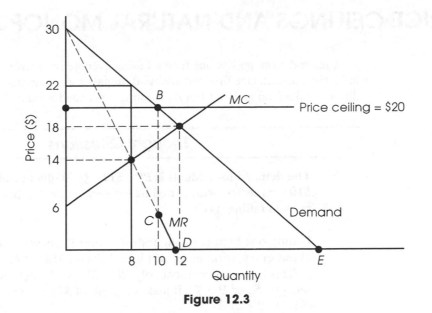

Figure 12.3

trates this result. A price ceiling of $20 increases output from eight to ten units and lowers the price from $22 to $20.

Points to note:

The price ceiling is $20; the monopoly can charge less, but not more.
The new demand curve seen by the monopoly is *ABE*.
The price ceiling is effective from *A* to *B*, that is, up to 10 units of output. Beyond $Q = 10$, the monopoly could only sell more by lowering the price below $20.
The new *MR* curve is *ABCD*. *AB* is the new *MR* curve holding over the range the price ceiling is effective. In this range, $MR = P = \$20$. *CD* is the old *MR* curve that is still effective. *CD* can be ignored.
With no price ceiling, the monopoly produces eight units of output and sells them for $22 each.
With the $20 price ceiling, $P = MR = \$20 = MC$ at $Q = 10$.
Setting the price ceiling where the demand curve crosses the *MC* curve ($P^D = MC$) yields the highest possible output. If the price ceiling equals $18, $Q = \$12$.
A price ceiling below $18 will reduce output below 12.
A price ceiling of $14 will cause $Q = 8$, the monopoly output.
A price ceiling below $14 will reduce output below the monopoly output.
A price ceiling above $22 would be ineffective and have no impact on the monopoly's output.

The key to determining the effects of a price ceiling is:

1. If the price ceiling is below what the monopoly would charge anyway, then output will be where price ceiling line hits *MC* or demand curve, whichever is *first*.
2. If the price ceiling is above the monopoly price, it is ineffective. The price will equal the monopoly price.

If regulators know the marginal cost of the monopoly, they should set the price ceiling equal to the *MC* where $P^D = MC$. This is called *marginal cost pricing*.

191

PRICE CEILINGS AND NATURAL MONOPOLIES

A natural monopoly is one facing falling average costs over the whole range of the industry's output. One firm can always dominate such an industry. Because these conditions make monopoly a natural outcome, it is called a *natural monopoly*.

Thought Questions

The demand for widgets is $P^D = \$12 - Q$. Widget production costs $10 for the first widget and $2 for each extra. (Notice that this results in falling *ATC*).

If only one firm is in the industry and it doesn't have to worry about entry, what price will it set? (Note: $MR = \$12 - 2Q$).

This firm is a pure monopoly. With $MR = 12 - 2Q$ and $MC = \$2$, it sets $Q = 5$ and P = $7. It makes a profit of $17 (= TR - TC = \$35 - (\$10 + \$2 \times 4)$.

What price could the one firm charge to make sure another doesn't enter? (Assume the two firms share the market and charge a price that covers their *ATC*.)

If the firms actually share the market, we have Table 12.4. A price of $4 will cover the cost when each firm produces two units. If the monopoly charges a price of $4, or less, a second firm would have no incentive to enter. Even though this is less that the $7 a pure monopoly would charge, it ensures the current firm of unchallenged profits in the future.

TABLE 12.4

Total Q	Each Firm's Q	TC for Each Firm ($)	ATC for Each Firm ($)	Market Price ($)
2	1	10	10	10
4	2	12	6	8
6	3	14	4.67	6
8	4	16	4	4

As we saw previously, the major government solution to monopolies is to impose a price ceiling. However, for natural monopolies, a price ceiling equal to the natural monopoly's marginal cost ($P = MC$) will cause it to go out of business (because $ATC > P$).

There are two main solutions to this dilemma.

1. One solution is to have the regulatory agency set the price equal to *MC*. This requires that the government subsidize the monopoly to cover its losses.
2. A second solution is to let the monopoly charge its average cost. This results in the output being less than its socially optimal level, but it gets rid of the need to subsidize the monopoly.

A natural monopoly has a cost of $16 for the first unit it produces and $4 for each added unit. The demand curve for its output is $P^D = \$12 - Q$.

Suppose we try solution 1. Let the ceiling price be set at the monopoly's marginal cost. How much loss will the monopoly sustain if it produced where $P^D = MC$? What subsidy would be necessary to keep it in business?

For the natural monopoly, we have Table 12.5. If the price ceiling is set at the marginal cost of $4, the monopoly would produce at $Q = 8$. But at $4 a unit, it's making a loss: It will go out of business unless it gets a subsidy! Its loss is $1.50 a unit ($P - ATC = -\$1.50$) or a total loss of $12. To produce eight units at $P = \$4$, the monopoly would have to receive a subsidy of $12. Why not give this monopoly a subsidy of $1.50 a unit? Because if it got this amount, it would produce more than eight units. This would not be socially optimal because the social marginal benefit of the added units (P^D) is less than their marginal cost.

TABLE 12.5

Total Q	TC ($)	ATC ($)	Market Price ($)
1	16	16	11
2	20	10	10
3	24	8	9
4	28	7	8
5	32	6.40	7
6	36	6	6
7	40	5.71	5
8	44	5.50	4

Now try solution 2. Here the monopoly is allowed to charge its average cost (*ATC*). What is the appropriate price ceiling for this monopoly? What will Q be? What is the socially optimal level of Q?

If the price ceiling P is set at ATC, the regulatory agency would set $P = \$6$, and the monopoly would produce six units. It would cover its cost and would not want to produce more (because the MR of the seventh unit would be $-\$2$). No subsidy is necessary, but the monopoly is not producing at the socially optimal level of output, which is eight units.

Another solution is to let the monopoly practice price discrimination[2]. For example, in the preceding question, the regulatory agency could allow the monopoly to charge $6 for the first six units and $4 for all subsequent units. This would cover its cost, and the monopoly would produce where $P = MC$ at $Q = 8$.

Most electrical utilities practice price discrimination. Typically, they are allowed to charge home users a higher rate than industrial users. Industrial users get the lower rate because they have the more elastic demand for electricity (because they can more easily move).

Figure 12.4 shows the graphical analysis of a natural monopoly.

---

[2]This solution need not work if the added profits still don't cover the monopoly's fixed costs.

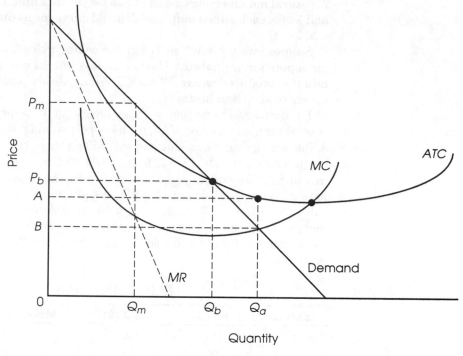

Figure 12.4

Points to note:

The unregulated monopoly will produce Q_m units and set its price at P_m.

Regulations setting the price ceiling at ATC will set P at P_b and the monopoly will produce Q_b units.

Regulations setting the price ceiling at MC will set $P = MC$ at Q_a. The monopoly must receive a subsidy equal to $(A - B)$ times Q_a, which is its loss if has to produce at Q_a.

WHOM DO REGULATORS REALLY REPRESENT? THE CAPTURE HYPOTHESIS

The possibility of increasing a monopoly's output with a price ceiling is one of the central reasons for direct public regulations of monopolies. But just because it is theoretically possible for regulators to set a price ceiling and increase a monopoly's output, it does not mean that it will.

The capture hypothesis predicts that the government regulatory agency will eventually be captured by the industry it runs. When captured, the agency will then serve the industry's interest at the expense of the public's interest. The logic behind this prediction is that the industry has the greatest direct interest in getting the agency to rule in its favor. Thus, the industry is willing to spend a great deal of money to get the favor of politicians and regulators. Also, because regulators are often drawn from the industry and often return to the industry later, it is often in the regulators' interest to serve the industry well.

When an agency is captured, it becomes a tool for imposing higher costs on customers and creating greater monopoly, not less. Let's look at each of these in turn.

1. Higher costs. For example, most government regulatory agencies set their rates so that the regulated industry earns a certain return on their investment. This is the way most utilities are regulated. The use of such cost plus price setting encourages the industry to act inefficiently since the public will pick up the tab for mistakes and cost overruns. For example, when many electrical utilities made unprofitable investments in nuclear power, the government agency controlling them often allowed them to pass these losses on to customers in the form of higher rates. In the private sector, the public is not forced to pay for business's mistakes.

2. Greater monopoly. Government regulators often create monopoly and act to keep competition out. For example, in the past, they have kept electrical utilities from competing with one another. Where companies do compete, prices drop dramatically. Towns served by more than one cable TV company pay about half the rate of the town where the friendly local cable company has a government-granted monopoly. Similarly, between 1940 and 1970, the Interstate Commerce Commission reduced the number of licensed trucking companies, giving each company greater monopoly power. When these monopolistic regulations were gotten rid of, trucking rates dropped dramatically. Similarly, competition among airlines was once prohibited by the government. When the airline industry was deregulated by the Airline Deregulation Act of 1978, airfares fell by 30%, and the rate of airline accidents fell (because with competition, airlines had to care about safety more).

ANTITRUST: BREAKING MONOPOLIES UP

Antitrust laws have the goal of promoting competition and preventing monopoly. They attempt to do this in two ways. First, they have been used to break monopolies into smaller firms. Second, they have outlawed cartels and prohibited business practices aimed at creating a monopoly.

The main antitrust laws follow:

1. Sherman Antitrust Act (1890): The first major antitrust law, which sought to prohibit combinations, trusts, and conspiracies to restrict interstate or international trade. It was aimed at the Standard Oil Company, which had near-monopoly control of the market for refined oil and the various trusts in such industries as lead, sugar, and whiskey that sought to control their output and prices.

2. The Clayton Act (1914): Broadened the government's antitrust power by outlawing specific business practices including:
   - Price discrimination if not justified by cost differences and if the effect is to lessen competition substantially or create a monopoly. For example, it made illegal Standard Oil's making a contract with railroads shipping their oil to charge more to other oil companies.
   - Tying contracts that force other goods to be bought from the same firm and to prevent using a competitor's product, when the purpose is to reduce competition.
   - Interlocking directorates where one person would be on the board of directors of several firms in the same industry.
   - Corporate stock acquisition with the goal of reducing competition.

3. Federal Trade Commission Act (1914): Established a commission to prevent unfair competition. *Unfair* wasn't defined, but the FTC has acted to prevent deceptive ads as well as enforce the various antitrust laws.
4. Robinson-Patman Act (1936): Designed to protect smaller sellers from unfair competition from bigger firms. This act prohibited special price discounts to larger firms unless justified by lower costs. In effect, this law actually promoted the monopolies of small-town merchants and was used for many years to prevent merchants from offering merchandise at a price less than manufacturer's suggested retail price.
5. Cellar-Kafauver Antimerger Act (1950): Outlawed mergers that might reduce rivalry or create a monopoly.

One of the problems in enforcing antitrust laws is that it is difficult to distinguish between (1) a firm that dominates a market because it has a superior product and better price (both of which are legal) and (2) a firm that dominates a market because it has conspired to eliminate competition. Sometimes it is clear that a practice is monopolistic, such as an explicit price-fixing agreement between competitors. But most of the time it is not. For example, suppose a large firm undercuts the price of its smaller rivals. Is that competitive? Or is its goal to eliminate the competition and raise its price later?

To help with this problem, the following two legal criteria are often used.

1. The rule of reason holds that acts that are beyond normal business practices that unduly restrain competition (such as excluding rivals) can be used to infer the intent to monopolize. Size and share of market are not, under the rule of reason, necessarily illegal. An unreasonable restraint of trade must be shown. However, explicit intent need not be proven. The rule of reason was abandoned by the courts in the 1940s when it ruled that Alcoa was in violation of the law because it was too big, in spite of the lack of any evidence that it had tried to restrain trade.
2. Courts also take into account how competitive a firm is in its relevant market. The relevant market is not only the market for the firm's goods, but also includes the market for close substitutes to the firm's goods. For example, DuPont had a monopoly on cellophane (such as Saran Wrap), but it successfully argued that it was a relatively small firm in the relevant market of wrapping products, which included aluminum wrap. It showed that cellophane had a high cross-elasticity of demand with other packaging materials.

ARE ALL MONOPOLIES BAD?

Suppose I invented the cure for cancer and sold it for $100. My cure would soon monopolize the cancer drug market: I would have a monopoly. But such a monopoly would be beneficial because it makes people better off, lowers costs, and expands productivity. For this reason, our government grants monopolies (called patents and copyrights) to scientific and artistic works.

On the other hand, suppose I buy up all existing cancer cures and double their price. In such a case, my monopoly is making other people worse off, and output is being reduced.

So not all monopolies are bad (nor are all monopolies good). In some cases, the public demands monopoly. They buy brand name goods, they go to movies featuring such well-known monopolists as Arnold Schwarzenegger, and they go to the exclusive restaurants changing the highest prices. Such monopolies exist because people do not have the time or skills to learn about all the possible alternatives. It is far cheaper to go with the best known good.

THE DRAWBACKS OF ANTITRUST LAWS

Antitrust law is not supposed to break up good monopolies due to a cost advantage or superior product. In theory, it is only aimed at bad monopolies. But the history of antitrust laws suggests that this is not always the case. For example, Alcoa, the developer of the market for aluminum, was broken up because it was a superior marketer that met customers' demands before any competitor could! Another criticism of antitrust law is that it is unnecessary. History has shown that attempts to control an industry have usually failed due to competition and rivalry (the decline of OPEC is an example). Diamonds may be forever, but monopoly is not, unless it is a diamond monopoly. DeBeers has had a monopoly on diamonds for more than 70 years. Competition is setting in, but I would settle for 70 years of monopoly profit!

CRIB NOTES

Social net benefit of good: Distance between P^D and P^S (or demand $P - MC$) summed over Q produced.

Social cost of monopoly: Lost NB due to less Q. Not due to higher P!

Price ceiling between monopoly P and MC will increase monopoly profit. Best price ceiling (biggest Q and net benefit) where demand curve crosses MC.

Natural monopoly: Falling ATC and MC, so $ATC > MC$.

If regulators set $P = MC$ for natural monopoly, must subsidize it as $ATC > P$.

If regulators set $P = ATC$ for natural monopoly, no subsidy but not at optimal Q.

Price discrimination sometimes allows optimal Q.

Capture hypothesis: Asserts regulators will act to help industry, not public.

Review Questions

Note: In this section and on almost any test you'll get, assume the monopoly is a single-price monopoly, only able to charge one price for all the units it sells. Only if the question so states should you assume that a monopoly can price discriminate, that is, charge different prices for different units.

1. A monopoly has a constant $MC = ATC$ of $10. It faces the following demand curve: $P^D = \$50 - Q$.
   a. What price will it charge? What quantity will it produce?
   b. What is the social optimal output?

    c. What is the social loss associated with this monopoly? (Hint: It is usually best to draw the graph in this type of problem.)

    d. What price ceiling will yield the highest output?

    e. What price ceiling would put the monopoly out of business?

2. Why does a competitive firm take the demand price as its *MR*? This question illustrates the answer. A monopoly produces 20 units and sells them for a price of $30. If 21 units were sold in its market, it would have to lower its price to $29. Assume the monopoly is currently producing 20 units.

    a. What is the monopoly's *MR* for the 21st unit?

    b. What if a new firm enters and adds one more unit to the monopoly's 20 (from the previous problem). What is the new firm's *MR* for the 21st unit?

    c. Why does the price, and not the monopoly's *MR*, reflect the social marginal benefit of the good?

    d. What does this imply about the demand curve?

3. a. Is Demi Moore a monopoly because she was paid $20 million for a recent movie?

    b. Suppose Demi Moore made $20 million in economic profits. Assume she could have made two more Moore movies in the same year whose price exceeded their economic cost by $10 million. (Note: Economic cost includes only the opportunity cost of Demi Moore's time and not her share of the profits.) What is Demi Moore's social cost?

4. Use this table to answer the following questions.

Quantity	1	2	3	4	5	6
Demand Price ($)	28	24	20	16	12	8
Supply Price ($)	8	12	14	16	18	20

    a. If you wanted to maximize society's net benefit from this good, what level of output would you select? What is the largest net benefit?

    b. How does this compare to the competitive results?

    c. What is the consumers' surplus? The producers' surplus? Their sum?

    d. How many units would a monopoly produce?

    e. What is the social net benefit of this production (from part d)? What is the social loss?

    f. What is the optimal price ceiling to impose upon the monopoly?

    g. What range of price ceilings will increase output above the level in answer d?

5. Fred has a monopoly on Fred's Spring Water, which flows freely at the rate of 2 gallons an hour from a spring in his backyard. If he bottles and sells one bottle an hour, he can sell them for $10 a bottle. If he bottles and sells two bottles an hour, he can sell them for $5 a bottle. To keep the problem simple, assume that these are his only two choices and that antitrust law prohibits him from practicing price discrimination. It costs him $2 for each bottle he sells (*MC* = $2).

    a. Of the two choices, which will he choose?

    b. Why is the choice not allocatively efficient?

    c. What is the social loss from his monopoly?

    d. What would the social loss be if he could practice perfect price discrimination? What is the consumer surplus in this case?

6. "All firms produce unique products. Therefore all firms are monopolies." Does uniqueness imply monopoly?

7. One of the horror stories about monopolies goes like this: "Once upon a time, a big firm entered a competitive market and cut its price below costs. This drove the small firms out of business. The big firm then charged a monopoly price." Assume all firms have the same unit cost (i.e., the big firm is not a natural monopoly with a cost advantage).
   a. What does this story assume about barriers to entry?
   b. Why is this assumption questionable given the number of small competing firms?
   c. Read the answer to this question to find a cheaper way to establish a monopoly (ignoring the existence of antitrust law).

8. Watt's Electrical Utility has a fixed cost per customer of $1,000 a year (the annualized cost of building its facilities) and a marginal cost of electricity of $10 a kilowatt. Each customer's demand for electricity is $P^D = \$40 - 0.1Q$, where Q is kilowatts per year.
   a. If you are a government regulator and wanted to impose marginal cost pricing, what type of rate structure would you impose (include an annual connect charge to cover the fixed cost plus a per watt charge). Will customers be willing to pay this and what amount of electricity will they use? A connect charge is a charge just to have electricity brought into your home.
   b. If you were a dishonest government regulator and Watt's promised you 10% of the profit, what rate structure would you let them charge? Answers for two rate structures: (i) a connect charge plus a per watt charge and (ii) a single price per watt charge and no connect fee.

9. At one time, advocates of nuclear power argued that nuclear power plants, once built, would produce electricity for free ("customers will be able to use as much as they want"). Suppose this were the case. It costs $1,000 per customer in annualized cost to build the plant and the MC of electricity is then zero. Marginal cost pricing would let customers, after paying a connect charge, pay nothing more. Each customer's demand for electricity is $P^D = \$30 - 0.2Q$.
   a. What is Q under marginal cost pricing?
   b. (This question is very hard.) What would average cost pricing charge? What is Q?
   c. What is the social cost of using average cost pricing instead of marginal cost pricing?

10. Acme, Inc. has a monopoly on the production of a highly sought-after road runner kit. It currently is producing the monopoly output and charging the monopoly price. Then Mr. Acme Sr. decides to become a good monopoly. He still produces the same output but charges a price reflecting his marginal cost, such that he makes no profits. Does becoming a good monopoly change the social loss caused by Acme?

11. Next, in the saga of Acme, Inc. Mr. Acme Sr. is kicked out by the board of directors, led by the evil Mr. Acme Jr. Jr. Acme makes Acme into a perfect price discriminator. As a perfect discriminator, Acme, Inc. charges the highest price possible for each and every unit. Each added unit sells for its demand price, but the price on the previous units are not cut! In this way, the evil Mr. Acme Jr. sucks the maximum profit possible from consumers. In doing so, he increases output to

the point where the demand price for the last unit equals its marginal cost. Does becoming evil change the social loss caused by Acme?

Answers

1. a. $P = \$30$ and $Q = 20$.
   b. MB $(P^D) = MC$ at the socially optimal Q. As $MC = \$10$, $P^D = MC = \$10$. Solving for Q, that makes $P^D = \$10$, $Q = 40$. This is the level of output a competitive industry would produce.
   c. Units 20 through 40 are not produced. The net benefit associated with this area (ABC in the following figure) is $\frac{1}{2} \times$ base $\times$ height or $\frac{1}{2} \times \$20 \times 20 = \$200$.

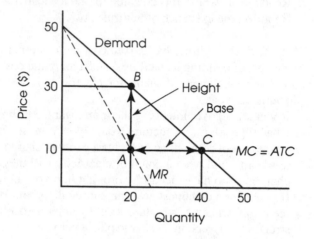

   d. A price ceiling of $10 will cause the monopoly to produce 40 units.
   e. A price ceiling of $9.99 will cause the monopoly to go out of business. This example shows the risk of imposing a price ceiling because most firms have constant returns to scale and a constant ATC curve as shown.
2. a. For the monopoly, the new unit sells for $29 but, to sell it, it must cut the price on its previous 20 units by $1. So the MR of the 21st unit is $9 (its price of $29 minus the cost of the resulting price cut on the previous units).
   b. The new firm produces only one unit, the 21st unit. The market price of that unit is $29. That's the new firm's MR also. $MR = \$29$ for the new firm because (1) it is only producing one unit, and so (2) it doesn't have to cut the price on any previous units it was producing. On the other hand, the monopoly loses $20 on its 20 units of output when the new firm lowers the market price by $1 (from $30 at $Q = 20$ to $29 at $Q = 21$). But the new firm doesn't care about the monopoly; it only cares about its own revenues!
   c. The market price reflects the most that demanders will pay for a unit: They value the 21st unit at $29. They won't pay more and they would be happy to pay less. Thus, the demand price reflects the marginal benefit of the good to consumers. The monopoly's MR is the marginal benefit of the good to the producer. The problem with monopoly is that it values an added unit of output at less than consumers do. So it produces too little.
   d. The demand curve is society's marginal benefit curve. However, there are exceptions we'll discuss in the next chapter.
3. a. No. Demi Moore is a monopoly because she doesn't produce the socially optimal level of movies. She refrains from making too many movies because it would reduce the salary she can command (due to overexposure). From an economic point of view, she has been underexposed.

    b. The lost net benefit is the $10 million in foregone net social benefits because this reflects the difference between the marginal benefit and costs of the two movies not produced. As this problem shows, sometimes less is Moore.

4. a. Social $MB = P^D$, social $MC = P^S$. Using marginal analysis, one should increase Q as long as $MB > MC$. Stop at $P^D = P^S$ at $Q = 4$. This maximizes net benefits, which equals $38 ($20 from unit 1 plus $12 from unit 2 plus $6 from unit 3 and $0 from unit 4).

    b. The competitive results will be the same. That's why competition is socially optimal. The price will be $16 and $Q = 4$.

    c. The consumer surplus equals $24, the sum of $P^D - P$ or $12 for unit 1 ($28 − $16) plus $8 for unit 2 plus $4 for unit 3 plus $0 for unit 4. The producers' surplus is $14, the sum of $P - P^S$ or $8 for unit 1 plus $4 for unit 2 plus $2 for unit 3 plus $0 for unit 4. The sum of the consumers' and producers' surplus equals the total social net benefit of $38.

    d. A monopoly would produce 2 units: (It increases Q as long as $MR > MC$; this is true for units 1 and 2. For unit 3, $MC > MR$: Its MC is $14 while its $MR = $12. The monopoly would lose $2 in profits from producing the 3rd unit.)

    e. The social net benefit from $Q = 2$ is $32, the sum of $P^D - P^S$ or $20 for unit 1 plus $12 for unit 2. The social loss is from units 3 and 4 not being produced: This equals $6.

    f. A price ceiling set at the competitive price of $16 (where $P^D = P^S$) will cause the monopoly to produce $Q = 4$ and maximize social net benefits.

    g. A price ceiling between $20 and $14 will cause the monopoly to produce three or more units. If it's more than $20, it's ineffective, as demanders will not buy the good. If it's below $14, the monopoly is better off not producing the third unit.

5. a. The marginal benefit to Fred of the first bottle an hour is $10. The marginal benefit of the second bottle is $0 (because his total revenue is still $10). His marginal cost is $2 a bottle. He'll choose to bottle only one bottle an hour.

    b. It is possible to arrange a trade between Fred and some consumers of the second bottle and some price between $5 and $2 that will leave both better off, assuming he still gets $10 for the first bottle an hour. Thus, Fred is not allocatively efficient.

    c. The social loss is $3 an hour, the difference between the market price of the second bottle ($5) and its marginal cost ($2).

    d. If he could charge $10 for the first bottle and $5 for the second, two bottles will be produced, and there will be no social loss. Note in this case all of the social net benefit ($11 an hour) goes to Fred in the form of being a producer's surplus. The consumer surplus is $0 in this extreme case of perfect price discrimination.

6. The concept of *relevant market* suggests that firms producing competing goods that are close substitutes in the consumer's eyes are not monopolies.

7. a. The story assumes a high barrier to entry, or the big firm would find after it raised its price that new competitors would enter its market and force the price back to its competitive level. If barriers to entry were low, it could cut its price to gain market share, but the threat of competition would keep its price down.

    b. The existence of many small competing firms suggests that barriers to entry are low, or there would only be a few oligopolic firms.

    c. Driving other firms out of business by price cutting is very expensive. It is cheaper to buy the other firms. One can buy these firms with borrowed funds, using the bought firm's assets as collateral. When all firms are bought, and assuming there is a high barrier to entry, one can then charge a monopoly price and raise the joint value of the assets of all firms and pay off the loan. This procedure has no net cost! This is in fact what many of the trusts did (except they usually issued the trust's stock to the firms they bought).

8. a. The annual connect charge would be $1,000 and the per watt charge would be its marginal cost of $10. Consumers would buy 300 kilowatts at $10 per unit. This has a consumer surplus of $4,500 ($= \frac{1}{2} \times \$30 \times 300$). Because this exceeds the hook-up charge of $1,000, customers would be willing to pay it.

   b. (i) To get the most dollars possible in profits, you would let Watt's charge a $4,500 connect charge and charge a $10 per kilowatt. This gives the company a $3,500 per customer profit ($4,500 less the $1,000 in fixed cost and no added profit on per watt charge as it equals the MC).

   (ii) If it can't charge a connect fee, a profit-maximizing single price for electricity would be the monopoly price of $25 a kilowatt. This gives the monopoly a profit of $1,250 (equal to $15 per kilowatt profit times 150 kilowatts demanded at $25 minus the $1,000 in annual fixed costs per customer).

9. a. $Q = 150$. Set $P^D = MC = \$0$ and solve for Q.

   b. Under average cost pricing, $P^S = \$1,000/Q$. Letting $PD = PS$, we have

$$\$30 - 0.2Q = 1,000/Q$$

Multiply both sides by Q:

$$30Q - 0.2Q^2 = 1,000$$

Rewrite as $0.2Q^2 - 30Q + 1,000 = 0$ and use the binomial theorem[A] to solve for Q. $Q = 50$ or 100. As a regulator wanting to get the most benefit to consumers, you would select the bigger: $Q = 100$. $P = \$10$.

   c. The social loss is from units between 100 and 150 not being produced. As the $MC = 0$, this equals $250 ($= \frac{1}{2} \times \$10 \times 50$). Draw diagram to verify this.

10. No. The social loss is exactly the same. The social loss comes from the net benefit lost from the reduced output of the monopoly. The only thing Mr. Acme has done is reduced the monopoly's profit and increased the consumer's profit (known to you as the consumer's surplus).

11. Yes. Acme now produces the socially optimal level of output. Society's net benefits are maximized. Also, because Acme's profits in this case equal society's net benefit, Acme's profit are the highest possible!

[A]Note: If $aX^2 + bX + c = 0$ then $X = \dfrac{-b \pm \sqrt{b^2 - 4ac}}{2a}$

Chapter Thirteen

Public Choice and Externalities

INTRODUCTION

In free and competitive markets, people will produce the socially optimal level of output for all goods in the most efficient manner. This is true, provided there is (1) no fraud or misinformation and (2) no externalities. The presence of misinformation and externalities leads to market failure—from a social point of view, the market produces too many or too few goods. One role of government is to outlaw fraud, provide information, and eliminate externalities.

We'll focus on externalities in this chapter. An externality occurs whenever a good's full social costs and benefits are not completely borne by those producing and consuming them. There are two types of externalities.

1. Negative externalities result when an activity imposes uncompensated costs on people. In this case, the social cost of a good (the cost borne by everyone) exceeds its private cost (the cost borne by those producing the good). The classic case is the factory that pollutes a nearby stream and destroys the farms and fisheries downstream from the factory.
2. Positive externalities result when an activity creates benefits for people who don't have to pay for the benefits. In this case, the social benefit of the good (the benefit everyone gets) exceeds its private benefit (the benefit to those paying for it). The classic case of this is the apple farmer who benefits from the nearby beekeepers because more bees result in more apples. The beekeeper may not get all the benefits of raising bees.

ONE MAIN CAUSE OF EXTERNALITIES: THE LACK OF PROPERTY RIGHTS

Next time you are out, stop by a public phone. Look at its condition. Smell it. Then compare it to your own phone. Which is in better shape? Most likely your own phone. It's your phone and so you take care of it. People care about what they own.

The same holds true for all resources. To put it in economic terms, ownership internalizes cost and benefits and leads to a resource being optimally used. But the ownership must be complete. If someone damages my property, I should have the right to sue them. That is, they must own the damage they do to others.

Conversely, the lack of property rights leads to externalities. This in turn leads to the failure to use resources optimally. Suppose that tomorrow a law makes all cars public property. By law, all cars must be parked on the street with their keys in the ignition. Every one has the right to drive any car of their choosing. Now, ask yourself this question: How many weeks will it take before 95% of all cars are not running and need repairs?

Why will the cars soon break down and not be fixed? The answer is that the absence of ownership makes repairing a car a positive externality. It benefits everyone who might drive the car in the future. If you repair a car, you won't get all its benefits. So you have no incentive to keep the cars in good running condition, and all cars are overused. As a result, getting rid of property rights in cars makes car repair a public good no one wants to pay for.

In just the same way, no one owns the fish in the sea. Thus, no one has any incentive to keep the fish "in good running condition." Instead, people have overfished (overused) the seas, and many fish are in danger of extinction. If fish were like privately owned cars, they would be taken care of. Similarly, because no one owns public forests, they tend to be poorly taken care of, especially when compared to private forests run by lumber companies.

The absence of property rights results in what is called *the tragedy of the commons*. In medieval England, farmers could graze their sheep and cattle in the commons, which was grazing land open to all. As a result, the commons was overgrazed and destroyed. Even though the social benefit of keeping the commons in good shape was high, the private benefit to any individual farmer was small. Because of the absence of private property rights in the commons, keeping it up was a positive externality. The result was the tragedy of starving farmers.

ANOTHER CAUSE OF EXTERNALITIES: TRANSACTION COSTS

A market failure occurs when people impose externalities upon others without bearing their full costs or benefits. The Coase theorem (named for its founder, Ronald Coase) states that if (1) there is private property and (2) no transaction costs, then there will be no market failures. What's key to this is that it doesn't matter who owns what property! The outcome will always be the same, and it will result in the socially optimal production of goods.

Consider the following example. The Apex Widget Company dumps its foul wretched waste into a stream. Downstream, these foul wretched wastes wash over on the crops of Downstream Farms (this is the extent of the damage). The pollutants cost Downstream $20,000 a year in lost crops. It would costs only $12,000 a year for Apex to clean up its waste and leave the stream clean. From a social point of view, Apex should pay the $12,000 because it saves $20,000.

There are two sets of possible property rights that could exist. Under the first set, Apex does not have the right to pollute the stream unless Downstream Farms gives permission (that is, Downstream Farms effectively owns the stream). Under the second set of property rights, Apex owns the stream and has the right to dump its wretched waste whenever it wants.

What the Coase theorem says is that in both cases (Apex or Downstream owning the stream), the result will be the same and that this result will be the socially optimal outcome (in this case, of no pollution)!

First, assume Downstream owns the stream. It can tell Apex "Pay $20,000 if you want to pollute!" Apex will say "No. It's cheaper for us to pay $12,000 to get rid of the pollution." So the pollutants get cleaned up.

Second, assume Apex owns the stream. Downstream can tell Apex, "I'll pay you $20,000 to not pollute the stream." Apex says, "Yes. You pay us $20,000 and we'll spend $12,000 to clean it up and we'll make $8,000 in profits." In this case, also, the stream gets cleaned up.

To be sure you get the point of this example, suppose it still costs $12,000 to clean up the pollution but that instead the pollution only results in $8,000 a year in damage. In this case, the socially optimal choice is to allow the pollution: The damage it does is less than it costs to clean it up. Work through both the preceding cases and show that is what will occur in both cases. In particular, show that when Downstream owns the stream, it will choose to have the stream polluted.

In both of these cases, it is the absence of transaction costs that allows the socially optimal bargain to take place. Assume the cost to those downstream of the pollution is still $20,000 and it costs Apex $12,000 to clean it up. But now suppose one million people live downstream. It is still socially optimal to Apex to stop pollution. However, when Apex has the right to pollute, all one million persons have to get together to bargain with Apex to get it to stop pollution. Most likely, transaction costs will prove too high for this to occur! Thus, Apex will continue polluting.

Therefore, even with property rights, when transaction costs are too high, externalities can occur. This is particularly true if the externality affects many people and if it is hard to identify who is affected. One solution is a class-action suit.

Thought Question

Felicity likes peace and quiet and is willing to pay $100 a day to have peace and quiet. Next door, Simon likes to play his stereo at full blast and is willing to pay $80 a day to listen to his stereo. Show that if Felicity has the right to peace and quiet, the result will be peace and quiet. Show that if Simon has the right to play his stereo at full blast, the result will be peace and quiet. Assume that there are no transaction costs.

In both cases, Felicity will have her silence. If she has the right to peace, Simon will offer her $80 to play his stereo but Felicity will turn him down because she values silence at $100. If Simon has the right to play his stereo, he will accept a bribe somewhere between $80 and $100 from Felicity to turn it off. In both cases, the outcome is socially optimal.

ONE SOLUTION: TAXES AND SUBSIDY

In many cases, property rights may be difficult to establish (such as to the fishes in the sea) and transaction costs too high (such as for pollution). Taxes on negative externalities and subsidies for positive externalities are one solution, assuming they are correctly placed.

Tax on Negative Externalities

Figure 13.1 shows the demand and supply of a good whose production involves polluting the air. Because pollution imposes costs on the general public, the social marginal cost of the pollution (*SMC*) exceeds the private marginal cost (*PMC*) of making the good by the good's external marginal cost (*EMC*) of $4. The private marginal cost is the marginal cost to the producers of the good. The social cost is the cost to everyone, including the public and the producer. In this case, the pollution from each added unit costs the public $4. So we have

$$SMC = PMC + EMC \text{ and } SMC > PMC \text{ when } EMC > 0$$

We assume there are no positive externalities in this diagram so the demand curve reflects both the social marginal benefit (*SMB*) and the private marginal benefit (*PMB*) from making the good (*SMB* = *PMB*).

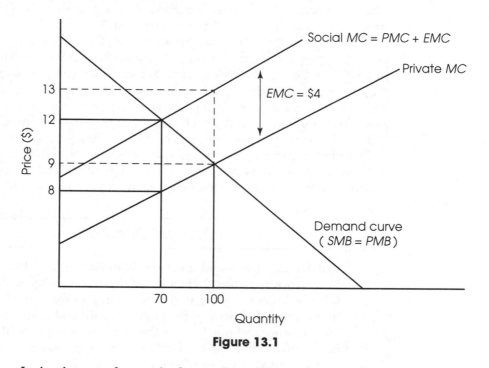

Figure 13.1

In the absence of a tax, the free market will produce 100 units of the good and sell them for $9 (where *PMC* = *PMB*). But because *SMC* = *PMC* + *EMC*, the socially optimal level of production is only 70 units (where *SMC* = *MB*). At 100 units, the goods cost society $13, which is $4 more than they are worth to consumers.

An optimal tax would equal $4, the good's external marginal cost (Tax = *EMC*). This makes the *SMC* curve in effect the industry's *PMC* curve and leads it to produce only 70 units and sell for a price of $12.

One complaint about taxes is that they raise cost. But in this case taxes actually lower costs. The social cost of the good at 100 units is $13 ($9 price plus $4 pollution cost). The social cost at 70 units is only $12, one dollar less!

Subsidy for Positive Externalities

Figure 13.2 shows the demand and supply of a good whose production involves a positive externality. This is because the good reduces bad breath. Because the good creates benefits for more than just its buyers, its social marginal benefits (*SMB*) exceed its private marginal benefits (*PMB*) by its external marginal benefit (*EMB*) of $4 (that is, the public benefits by $4 per unit more than does the private buyer). So we have

$$SMB = PMB + EMB \text{ and } SMB > PMB \text{ and } EMB > 0$$

We assume there are no negative externalities in this diagram so the supply curve reflects both the private and social marginal cost of making the good (*PMC = SMC*).

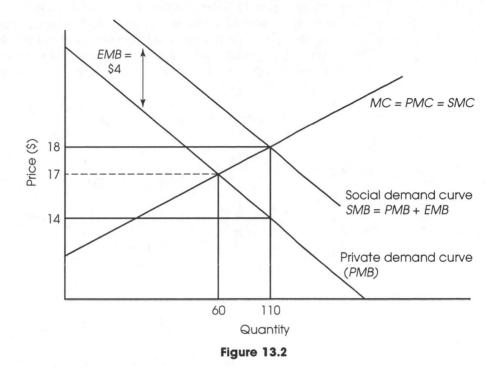

Figure 13.2

In the absence of a tax, the free market will produce 60 units of the good and sell them for $17 (where *PMC = PMB*). But because *SMB > PMB*, the socially optimal level of production is 110 units (where *SMB = MC*). At 60 units, the good is worth $4 more that it costs.

The socially optimal subsidy is $4 per unit, equal to the good's external marginal benefit (Subsidy = *EMB*). This causes suppliers to produce 110 units and sell them for $14. The suppliers' marginal cost is $18 minus the $4 per unit subsidy.

POLLUTION AND REGULATIONS

Government regulation of pollution illustrates some of the principles we've been talking about. Pollution is a negative externality. Because of transaction costs, it is too difficult for people to, by themselves, bargain with firms for the optimal level of pollution.

Two solutions have emerged: (1) taxing pollution and (2) limiting the amount of pollution.

1. One solution has been to tax polluters. Emission charges[1] are common in Europe. Water polluters have to pay a waste disposal tax. There is also an emission charge

---

[1]Emissions are not in themselves pollutants, but they often contain pollutants.

on gasoline. Figure 13.3 illustrates this case. It shows the average miles driven per person and the private and social cost of driving when the public drives the miles shown. The social cost includes the private cost plus the cost of pollution emitted by cars. In the absence of any taxes, the average person drives 30 miles a day at a private cost of 10 cents a mile. But the social cost is 22 cents a mile because at 30 miles, the added mile causes the car to emit pollution costing the public 12 cents. Figure 13.3 shows pollution costs rising as more miles are driven. This reflects the scientific finding that pollution has rising marginal costs. An emission tax equal to the difference between the social and private marginal cost will result in the optimal level of driving. People will drive on average 20 miles a day, paying 13 cents per mile. The emission charge will be 5 cents a mile.

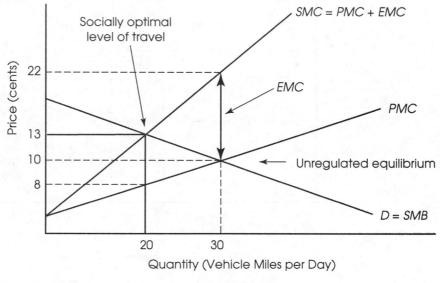

Figure 13.3

Points to note:

The tax lowers the social cost of travel.

The authorities have to know all the costs and how they change to properly impose the correct emission charge.

The social loss from not imposing a tax is $1.20 a day, equal to the area of the triangle on the right-hand side of the optimal level. Area = ½ × 12 cents × 10.

To reduce pollution to a lower level than shown is not socially optimal.

2. The second solution is limiting the amount of pollution. In place of a tax, the government can regulate and limit the amount of pollution allowed. In Figure 13.3, for example, if could permit people to only drive 20 miles a day. Many environmental regulations have taken this form.

   One drawback of simply imposing the same limits on all persons is that this fails to take into account individual differences. In the preceding example of driving, some people have a greater demand for driving than others. Similarly, some people drive cleaner cars than others. A law that restricted them all to driving 20 miles a day would be very costly for many of the drivers. In addition, no one would have any incentive to have a cleaner car!

   Because of this drawback, some pollution regulations allow firms to trade permits to pollute. First, the regulating agency decides how much pollution it wants to allow in a given area. Next, it issues pollution rights to the firms in the area.

Each firm gets the right to emit a certain level of pollutants. Finally, the agency allows firms to trade the permits with each other. (In the car example, this would be like allowing drivers who want to drive long distances to buy miles from others.) All firms can buy and sell permits. When permits can be bought and sold, the result is that pollution will be cleaned up in the most cost-efficient manner possible.

Thought Questions

Firm A and Firm B both emit three units of pollutants. The government mandates that each firm only emit one unit. Firm A has a marginal abatement cost (the cost of getting rid of one unit of pollutant[2]) of $50 a unit. Firm B has a marginal abatement cost of $1,000 a unit.

What is the cost of pollution clean up when both are allowed to pollute only one unit and this right is not tradable?

Firm A's cost would be $100. Firm B's cost would be $2,000. The total cost of getting rid of four units of pollution would be $2,100.

Suppose, instead, that each has a permit to emit one unit of pollution and these permits were tradable? What would happen and what would the cost be?

Firm B would be willing to pay up to $1,000 for the right to pollute one more unit (because that is what it would save in clean-up costs) and Firm A would be willing to sell a unit for $50 or more (because that is what it would cost Firm A to clean up another unit). So, for some price between $50 and $1,000, Firm B will buy Firm A's right to pollute one unit. A will now clean up three units for a total cost of $150, and B will clean up one unit for $1,000. The total clean-up cost will be $1,150, which is far cheaper than in the previous answer. This is because the high-clean-up-cost firms will be willing to buy the permits from the low-clean-up-cost firms. Trade results in pollution being cleaned up by the firms with the lowest clean-up costs!

In Sweet High Valley, there are only two polluting firms, Firm A and Firm B. The marginal abatement costs (*MAC*) are shown in the Table 13.1. Thus, if Firm A were allowed two units of pollutants, it would cost it $1,050 to clean up units 3 through 7 ($400 + $300 + $200 + $100 + $50). We assume unit 8 for Firm A has an *MAC* of zero. Notice that the more units cleaned up (as you move from right to left!), the marginal cost of cleaning up pollutants (*MAC*) rises.

TABLE 13.1

Units of Pollution	1	2	3	4	5	6	7
MAC of Firm A ($)	600	500	400	300	200	100	50
MAC of Firm B ($)	250	190	120	70	30	10	0

---

[2]The marginal abatement cost could include the cost of reducing output (which would be the foregone profits) rather than cleaning up the pollutant produced, if cutting back on output is cheaper.

If the regulatory agency allows each firm to have three units of pollutants (so that each has to clean up four units of pollutants), what is the total cost of cleaning up?

Both firms have to clean up four units of pollutants. They start on the right-hand side of Table 13.1. Firm A's cost is $650. Firm B's cost is $110. The total cost is $760.

How would you determine the cheapest way to clean up a total of six units of pollution in Sweet High Valley? How does this compare to the previous answer?

You would clean up the cheapest unit first. Going in this order, you would clean up the seventh unit at Firm B (B7), then its sixth unit (B6), and so on, until, in effect, you've crossed out the eight lowest numbers in Table 13.1. The order will be B7, B6, B5, A7, B4, A6, B3, B2. So, it is cheapest to clean up eight units by having Firm A clean up two units and Firm B clean up six units. A's cost will be $150, and B's cost will be $420. The total cost will be $570, which is cheaper than having both clean up four units each (which would cost $760).

If the regulatory agency issues each firm a tradable permit to emit three units of pollutants, what trades will take place? What is the resulting total cost of cleaning up? How does this compare to your previous answer?

Firm A is willing to buy two of B's permits (and B is willing to sell them). The first permit saves Firm A $300 and costs Firm B only $120 (in added clean-up costs). The second saves Firm A $200 and costs Firm B only $190. A third would save Firm A $100 and cost Firm B $190: Firm B would not sell it. This is exactly the same solution as in the previous answer: Firm A cleans up two units and B cleans up six. Once again, trading causes the clean up to be done in the most cost efficient manner.

Economists typically favor taxes over regulations because taxes allow for individual differences in demand. As long as everyone is paying the full cost of what they are doing, social welfare will be optimized. Regulations that set the same standards for everyone are not optimal for everyone. For example, pollution control equipment raises the price of a car by $2,000. This might be too little in Los Angeles and way too much in Montana. One drawback of taxes, as compared to regulations, is that the government has more of an incentive to increase them until they are too high.

THE OPTIMAL LEVEL OF POLLUTION

What level of pollution should a regulatory agency allow? Pollution is costly. How costly is subject to controversy. But let's pretend we are all-knowing and have precise figures on pollution's cost. Similarly, it is costly to get rid of pollution. Let us also suppose that we know these costs. How then do we decide what is the correct level of pollution? There are two costs society faces:

Total cost = Total pollution cost + Total pollution abatement cost

The socially optimal level of pollution minimizes the sum of these two costs. We can use marginal analysis to assist us. Let Q be the quantity of pollution allowed. The marginal cost of increasing Q by one unit is the bad that occurs: Total pollution costs go up. Los Angeles gets smoggier. More fish die from acid rain. More people have a higher risk of getting sick. The marginal benefit of increasing Q by one unit is the reduction in pollution abatement costs. Q should be increased as long as $MB \geq MC$. At the optimal Q, $MB = MC$. Figure 13.4 shows the results. It assumes the marginal benefits of more pollution is declining. You can see this better when you realize that pollution is getting smaller as you move left in Figure 13.4. Because the cheapest ways to reduce pollution will be used first, the subsequent units of pollution will cost more to clean up. Similarly, the marginal cost of pollution is shown to be increasing. This means the higher the level of pollution, the more costly a given addition is in terms of the damage it does.

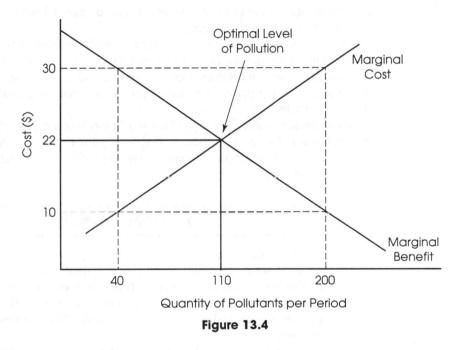

Figure 13.4

Points to note:

At $Q = 40$, there is too little pollution. Its MB of $30 (the cost saving from not getting rid of it) exceeds its benefit of $10.

At $Q = 200$, there is too much pollution. Its MB of $10 (that's how much would have to be spent to get rid of the 200th unit) is less than its MC of $30.

The optimal level of pollution is 110 units per period. Its MB equals its MC.

Some people might argue that the concept of an optimal level of pollution is wrong. Surely, they would say, the only acceptable level of pollution is no pollution. Let us ask ourselves exactly was this means. It means that no matter what the cost of getting rid of all pollution is, it would be worth it! But is this true? Right now, anyone can get rid of pollution by moving to Antarctica, which is relatively pollution-free. Most are not willing to pay this high a price to get rid of pollution. So we can conclude that at some price, they would rather have pollution. One could also wear a gas mask to get rid of pollution; once again most people are not willing to bear this high a cost to get rid of pollution. The cost to our economy of environmental legislation has not been cheap. One EPA study puts the costs of complying since 1970 at $1.4 trillion (in 1990 dollars) or about 2.1% of gross domestic product (GDP) per year (about $1,800 per family of four).

PUBLIC GOODS: A TYPE OF EXTERNALITY

A pure public good is a good many people can consume without diminishing the amount consumed by others. Music at a concert is an example. My hearing the music does not diminish what you hear. This is unlike most goods, such as apple pie at a picnic. The amount of apple pie I eat diminishes how much others can enjoy. Apple pies are thus a private good.

The marginal benefit from another unit of a public good is the sum of its marginal benefit of all persons consuming it. If we could observe each person's demand curve for the public good, then we could calculate the total demand for the public good by adding the demand curves vertically (and not horizontally as for other goods). Thus, if 20 persons are willing to pay $10 to hear a second hour of a public concert, the demand price for its second hour is $200.

Public goods become a positive externality when the cost of excluding people from consuming it becomes too high. This is not a problem at a concert because tickets can be sold at the gate. But it does become a problem for a good like the military defense of our nation. If our nation is protected for me, it is hard to exclude you from getting the same benefit.

When exclusion costs are high, there is a free-rider problem. A free rider enjoys the benefits of a public good without having to pay for it. When enough people become free riders, the good might not even be supplied. Then, everyone, including the free riders, is worse off.

Thought Question

Suppose the upkeep of our highways was paid for by voluntary contributions, collected by highway patrol officers standing by the highway with little tin cups. If the contributions go to keeping roads well-maintained and if everyone is worse off if we have poorly maintained roads, then why would there be free riders on the road?

One person's contribution isn't going to make a perceptible difference. So why give? If everyone thought like this and didn't give, there still wouldn't be much benefit to giving. There would be a lot of people free-riding over potholes.

A solution to providing public goods is to collect taxes.

PUBLIC CHOICE

Public choice theory analyzes how decisions are made by the public sector. For many years, economists have implicitly assumed that governments will act to maximize the well-being of society.[3] Whenever a market failure was identified, they proposed that government should correct it. But over time this naïve view has changed.

---

[3]According to Kenneth Arrow's famous impossibility theorem, it is impossible to sum a population's preferences into a social preference function. This makes statements like "maximizing the social welfare," and "policy X is the best for society" meaningless.

While economists have always assumed that firms and households act in their own self-interest, only in recent years have economists begun to assume that government bureaucrats and politicians are also motivated by self-interest. Given that they do act selfishly, the next step is to ask why governments act the way they do.

One can think of public sector officials (politicians, government regulators, civil servants) as being part of a firm. Just like owners of a private firm, they (1) are often motivated by their own self-interest; (2) face trade-offs due to scarcity; (3) have to make choices. Similar to businesses, political parties compete for the votes of the public.

But the public sector differs in significant ways from the private sector. Typically,

1. The goods provided by the public sector are furnished free.
2. They are paid for by taxes, which individuals have to pay even if they don't like the mix of goods and services offered by the public sector.
3. The choice of public goods and services is determined largely by voting.

In the private sector, consumers day in and day out vote for the goods they want. If a firm produces a good no one wants, it goes out of business. In contrast, people vote in elections once every few years and vote between two candidates, each offering a vague package deal of goods and services. Only one package will win and be offered. Even if most people don't want a particular good (say, subsidies to hog farmers), this good still may be in the overall package deal offered by the political party they vote for. In the private sector, if less than half the public wants blue shirts, blue shirts will be provided. In the public sector, if less than half the public want a given candidate, they get nothing.

Can majority voting be depended upon to reveal the preferences of the majority of voters? Interestingly, the answer may be "No." The voting paradox states that how a majority will vote on a set of issues depends upon on the order in which the issues are presented. They may vote for A over B and vote for B over C. Yet, they may then vote for C over A! As you know from math, $A > B$ and $B > C$ implies $A > C$. But this is not true in voting! What may be the worse deal could come out a winner, depending on the order things are voted on. Whoever controls the sequencing of issues has great control over what issues will win or lose. That's one reason why political parties and political leaders play an important role.

VOTING MODELS

The following models seek to explain what determines how public choices are made.

Model 1: The Median Voter Model

The median voter model predicts that when two politicians are running for office, they will position themselves near the opinion of the median voter. The median voter is the voter at the 50th percentile on a given issue. In this model, if a politician strays too far from the median, they'll get run over!

For example, suppose there are 101 voters and the only issue in the campaign is the percent of national income that should be collected in taxes. We line voters up so that those who want the lowest taxes come first. Suppose the first person thinks 0% of income should be taxed, the second wants 1%, the third 2%, and so on, all the way to the

101th voter who wants 100% of income collected in taxes (they work for the government). The median voter wants 50% of income taxed (this example comes from Sweden). Fifty persons want less (0%, 1%, . . . 49%), 50 want more (51%, 52%, . . . 100%). It can be shown that if one candidate takes the median votes position (a 50% tax rate) and the other takes a different position, the median voter candidate will always win. Suppose the other person advocates a 40% tax rate. The median voter candidate will win the vote at a minimum of those who want 50% or more. This gives them the election (51 votes at a minimum out of 101). They may even pick up some of those who want a tax rate of 41% to 49%. The same is true if the other candidate advocates a higher tax rate than the median, say a 51% rate. Now the median voter candidate again wins with 51 votes (this being the sum of the 0% voter, through the 50% voter, all of whom prefer the 50% tax rate over the 51% tax rate). The only position where both candidates have an equal chance of winning is when both take the position of the median voter.

Model 2: Logrolling

The median voter model does not explain the phenomena of special interest politics. Why are special interest groups successful at getting passed favorable legislation that most of the population opposes? The answer is logrolling, the practice of trading votes between special interests to pass legislation giving something to each group. For example, textile mill owners in South Carolina may want a tariff against cheap textile imports. The wheat farmers in Ohio may want more farm subsidies. These two groups get together and agree to vote for each other's bills. With this type of vote trading, the log of special interest bills gets pushed through Congress like a bunch of logs rolling down Capitol Hill.

Single-issue politics is a type of logrolling. Suppose I could convince 20% of the population that every town square should have a 50-foot gold statue of James T. Kirk, captain of the starship *Enterprise*. Further, suppose I convinced them to vote based upon this single issue alone. They would vote for any candidate promising to build these statues, no matter what other issues the candidate stood for. Most likely, we would eventually get these statues built, despite the fact that 80% of the population thought James T. Kirk was overweight, the statue way too expensive, and really wanted Spock anyway.

The following game illustrates the drawbacks of logrolling. Ten voters (the public) sit in a circle. There is one person in the middle who gets to play the government. The government promises six of the players $3 if they vote for a tax of $2 on each person. Because the six players net one dollar with this bill, they'll vote for it. But the public on net is worse off. They pay $20 to the government and get $18 back. Bill after bill like this could pass, affecting different players at different times, until it is quite possible that they all are worse off. Yet, each player will continue to vote for the bills favorable to them because, in fact, they are in a prisoner's dilemma.

Model 3: Rational Voter Ignorance

The model of rational voter ignorance states that it is irrational to make fully informed votes. The likely benefits of voting are small because few elections have ever been decided by one vote. Balanced against this are the considerable costs of being well informed. Therefore, this model concludes that a rational person will not vote, much less become a fully informed voter.

What the rational voter ignorance model implies is that special interests, who do have an incentive to pass legislation that benefits themselves, may well prevail over the interests of the majority of voters. Special interests have both the incentives and the means to influence votes and politicians to get what they want passed. On the other hand, the general population, who must pay for the special interest legislation in higher taxes and higher prices, does not have the incentive to oppose this legislation.

This general observation leads to a basic principle in politics: It pays to be small. While on general issues it's better to have a majority on your side, when it comes to special interest legislation, it is better that there are only a few persons who benefit. For example, if a bill gives $200,000 per person to 1,000 people, it has a good chance of passing. But if it gives $200,000 per person to one million persons, it has almost no chance of passing because its costs would be huge and all too obvious to the majority of voters. Thus, small groups have a better chance of passing legislation under the screen of voter ignorance. This leads me to predict that as the fraction of retired persons gets larger, Social Security benefits will be drastically cut. My reasoning is that at some point, the costs of Social Security on workers will become too high for the majority of people (who'll be working) to ignore. One study suggests that if the Social Security and Medicare programs continue as they now are, as the baby boomers retire, the tax rate will have to be 70% to pay for it. Workers then will vote to cut it, most likely on the day I retire!

Rational voter ignorance can also lead to ideological voting. Ideology lowers the cost to voters of knowing how the politician is likely to vote. Successful ideologies are likely to be simple and easily communicated.

Model 4: The Tiebout Hypothesis

Although not strictly a model of public choice, this model can be used to predict how in a mobile world governments may be lead to change. Imagine a world in which anyone could move and live anywhere at no cost. Suppose, to make this example clearer, that the only governments were city states, such as those that existed in ancient Greece. Each city would compete with the others to attract customers. The city with the best set of taxes and city services would make the most profit for the governing classes. Competition would lead all cities to offer the optimal packages of services at the lowest cost. Otherwise, its citizens would go elsewhere. This result is called the Tiebout hypothesis. Notice that it does not predict that no government services will be provided; instead, it predicts that government services will be optimally provided where marginal benefit equals marginal cost.

What this model suggests is that decisions should be put at the lowest level of government possible, consistent with there being no externalities. Schooling, for example, should be determined at the city level and not the state or federal level. Studies have shown that local school boards are more responsive to public demands and are more efficient than are state-controlled school systems. As another example, pollution that affects a whole region should be controlled at the regional level; having it determined at the city level creates externalities.

To some extent, the movement of multinational firms between nations and the bidding between states for companies to relocate in them reflect some of the workings of the Tiebout hypothesis. Such movement forces governments to act more favorably toward those who are mobile. I have yet to hear an ad for a state that says, "Move your company to our state and pay big taxes and get lousy service."

CRIB NOTES

Externality: Full cost not borne by suppliers (negative externality) or full benefit not borne by buyer (positive externality).

Solutions: (1) property rights plus low transaction costs (Coase theorem says it does not matter then who has property rights just that someone does).

(2) Negative externality: $EMC > 0$, free market Q at $PMC = SMB$ and $SMC > SMB$. Solution: Tax = EMC.

(3) Positive externality: $EMB > 0$, free market Q at $PMB = SMC$ and $SMB > SMC$. Solution: Subsidy = EMB.

(4) Limit pollution. Tradable permits minimize abatement costs.

(5) Optimal pollution minimizes sum of total pollution cost plus total abatement cost. Q^* where marginal pollution cost = marginal abatement cost.

Public good: Benefit to one person does not reduce benefit to others. If exclusion costs high, get free rider problem.

Public choice theory: Politicians and government officials maximize their interests, which need not be public interest.

Voting paradox: Rational voters presented with pairs of choices may give irrational response (choice $A >$ choice B, $B > C$, and $C > A$).

Logrolling: Special interests trade votes to get majority.

Rational voter ignorance: MB of voting is so small that rational will not vote.

Review Questions

---

1. For each of the following, identify whether it is a positive or negative externality, what sort of market failure (too much or too little) will result, and if a subsidy or tax correctly set could remedy the resulting market failure.
   a. Well-maintained yards increase the value of the whole neighborhood.
   b. Playing loud music after midnight wakes up the whole neighborhood.
   c. Feeding the poor keeps them off the neighborhood streets, which makes everyone feel better.
   d. Burning leaves and trash pollutes the air.
   e. Policing the streets keeps the neighborhood safe.

2. There are 1,000 workers in the company you work for, all covered by the company health care plan. The plan works like this. Everyone can get as much health care as they want for free. At the end of the year, the company adds up all the costs, divides it evenly among all workers, and deducts it from their salaries. Show that in this case, getting health care will be a negative externality and people will get too much.

3. Use the following table to answer these questions:

Quantity	1	2	3	4	5	6	7
SMB ($)	20	18	16	14	12	10	8
SMC ($)	4	6	8	10	12	14	16

SMB is the social marginal benefit of the good, and *SMC* is the marginal social cost.

a. If there are no externalities, how many units of the good will a competitive market produce? How many should be produced if the goal is to maximize the social net benefit from the good?

b. Suppose the product is breath mints and that the buyers only get half the total benefit from the good. How many will be produced? How many should be produced? What tax or subsidy would make the amount produced equal what should be produced?

c. Suppose the product is pigs. Because, in this example, pigs stink so much, the neighbors of the pig farms bear half the cost of raising the pigs. The pig farmers bear the other half. How many pigs will be raised? How many should be raised? What tax or subsidy will correct the market failure?

4. This problem illustrates the tragedy of the commons. A money machine one day goes haywire. Every second, it spits out another dollar. The dollars begin to pile up. But once someone comes forward to pick up a dollar, the sensor in the money machine turns it off and it stops spitting out dollars. There are ten people watching this happen. The longer they wait, the more there is. Assume that after an hour the money machine stops and that, in the meantime, no one else comes by.

a. What policy is best for the ten persons taken together as a group?

b. What policy is best for each individual?

c. How does this illustrate the tragedy of the commons? How would property rights help?

d. How does it illustrate why the ocean is overfished?

5. Suppose an added ton of sulfur dioxide in the air has an external marginal cost of $40 in urban areas and $20 in rural areas. Also assume that if firms had to pay these external marginal costs, they would, as a group, only emit half of what they currently do. You work for the government and have to choose from the following rules. Which is most efficient and why?

Rule 1: Each firm must cut its sulfur dioxide emissions in half.

Rule 2: All firms must pay a tax of $30 per ton of sulfur dioxide emitted into the air.

Rule 3: Urban firms must pay $40 a ton tax on sulfur dioxide emission while rural firms must pay $20 a ton.

6. Why is knowledge a public good? What does this imply about the production of knowledge in free markets? What are some of the ways governments seek to remedy this?

7. This problem illustrates Coase theorem. A bass farmer and a sewage plant share a lake. The sewage plant can dump its waste into the lake, or for $200 a ton, it can ship it to a toxic waste dump. The bass farmer's profits depend upon how much the sewage plant dumps into the lake.

Sewage Dumped into Lake (tons per week)	0	1	2	3	4	5	6
Weekly Profits of Bass Farm ($)	2,000	1,950	1,850	1,700	1,500	1,250	950

a. If the same person owned both firms, how much dumping would she allow?

b. If there are different owners and the bass farm owns the dumping rights, how much dumping would it allow? (Assume no transaction costs.)

    c. If there are different owners and the sewage firm owns the dumping rights, how much dumping would it allow? (Assume no transaction costs.)

    d. What is the outcome if no one owns the lake? How might the government help?

8. Cows emit BOFLAT (bovine flatulence). Suppose it is proven that BOFLAT is a major factor in causing global warming. Because it is difficult to retrofit cows with pollution control equipment, the government can limit the amount of beef sold or impose a tax on beef equal to the marginal external cost of the cow's BOFLAT. Why is the BOFLAT tax better?

9. The following example illustrates the voting paradox. Dobbs, Effron, and Francis sit on the city council. There are three proposals to help revitalize the downtown area. They plan to compare two of the projects, select the one getting the most votes, and then compare the winner with the third project and vote again. Their individual rankings of these projects (1 being the one they want most; 3 being the least) are as follows:

	PROJECT A	PROJECT B	PROJECT C
Dobbs	1	2	3
Effron	2	3	1
Francis	3	1	2

    a. If Project A is compared to B, which will win?

    b. If Project B is compared to C, which will win?

    c. If Project A is compared to C, which will win?

    d. How does this illustrate the paradox of voting?

    e. How would you arrange the two votes to get A to win?

    f. How would you arrange the two votes to get B to win?

    g. How would you arrange the two votes to get C to win?

10. Why, in most presidential elections, do Republican candidates sound more conservative during the primaries than they do in the presidential election, and why do Democrats sound more liberal in primaries?

Answers

1. (a, c, and e) Positive externality. Too little will occur. Subsidy.
(b and d) Negative externality. Too much will occur. Tax.
Note that in this case, a neighborhood covenant could internalize many of these externalities. Most covenants do not impose taxes or grant subsidies. Instead, most use regulations to limit or prohibit certain activities. Why are limits and regulations better than taxes in this case? The reason is that taxes gives the homeowners' organization too much of an incentive to raise taxes too high and to tax activities that are not really externalities.

2. The program makes the cost of the system an externality to each buyer of health care. To illustrate, suppose there is an operation that costs $2,000 and is worth $20. Would a worker want the operation? Its marginal benefit to the worker is $20 and its cost is only $2, the worker's share of the $2,000 cost that is borne by all 1,000 workers. The $1,998 is a negative externality the worker has imposed upon all the other workers. If all workers got this operation, it would cost each $2,000 in lost salary. They would be $1,980 worse off (because each pays $2,000 in health care insurance for an operation worth $20). From the social point of view, too much of this good is demanded. Yet, everyone has an incentive to have the operation!

3. a. If there are no externalities, $PMB = SMB$ and $PMC = SMC$, so the competitive market will produce five units of the good, where the market price will be $12. This will maximize the social net benefit from producing the good, which equals $40 (summing $SMB - SMC$ from one through five units).

   b. In this case, $PMB = \frac{1}{2} SMB$ while $PMC = SMC$. Thus, the buyer is only willing to pay $10 for the first unit. Only three units will be produced, and they will sell for a price of $8. But if the value of those who benefit from breath mints are included, five units should have been produced. This market failure can be corrected by a $6 per unit subsidy on breath mints. Five units will then be produced, with the buyer paying $6 but the seller getting $12 for each unit.

   c. In this case, $PMC = \frac{1}{2} SMC$ while $PMB = SMB$. Thus, the seller only pays $2 to produce the first unit. Seven units will be produced at a price of $8. But given the total cost of hog farming, including the neighbor's costs, only five units should be produced. This market failure can be cured by a tax of $6 per unit on sellers. The market price will be $12, with the buyer paying $12 and the seller paying $6 per unit in direct costs and $6 per unit in taxes.

4. a. The best policy is to wait an hour until the machine runs out of dollars. The whole group will get the most it can. In this case, $3,600 or $360 per person.

   b. The best policy for the individual is to grab the money and run. They should do this even before $360 falls out. Why? Because otherwise, it is highly likely that someone else in the group of ten will grab the money and run! It's better to get a few dollars than nothing.

   c. The commons were overgrazed because no one owned the benefits of keeping them from being overused. Similarly, the stack of money is not allowed to grow because no one owns the benefits of allowing it to grow. Incidentally, in cases of money freely falling out of money machines, the law clearly states that the money belongs to the nearest economist!

   d. Oceans are overfished because no individual privately owns the benefits of waiting to let the stock of fish grow.

5. Rule 3 is most efficient. In all areas, it causes firms to fully pay the external marginal cost (EMC) their pollution imposes on others (so that $SMC = PMC + $ tax). In contrast, rule 2 will result in too much pollution in urban areas (tax $< EMC$, $SMC > PMC + $ tax) and too little in rural areas (tax $> EMC$, so that $SMC < PMC + $ tax on the margin). Rule 1 does not allow the reallocation of cleaning costs to the firms with the lowest cost of cleaning up. Most likely, it will result in too much pollution in urban areas and too little in rural areas.

6. Knowledge is a public good because one person's consumption of it does not decrease another person's consumption of the same knowledge. As a result, free markets tend to underproduce knowledge. An example of the external benefits of knowledge is that countries just developing a private enterprise system tend to grow faster than countries with a well-developed capitalistic system. This is in part because the former can get for free all the information that it took other countries billions of dollars to create. One solution for some types of knowledge is to make it private property for a limited number of years with patents and copyrights. Many firms do this by keeping their processes secret. But basic knowledge (such as understanding the origin of the universe or the structure of DNA) can't be patented. Thus, many governments subsidize scientific research.

7. a. Going right on the table, as long as the lost profits from an added ton dumped is less than $200, the owner will dump it. The first ton costs $50 in lost fishery profits, which is cheaper than the $200 to ship it out. The second ton costs $100 in lost fishery profits. Instead of paying $200 to ship it out, it's cheaper to dump it. The owner will dump 4 tons (she's actually indifferent as what to do with the

fourth ton, but we'll assume she dumps it). She'll ship the fifth ton because it costs $250 in lost profit. She'll lose less if she ships it.

b. The sewage firm is willing to pay the fishery up to $200 for the right to dump each ton. At that price, the fishery will sell the sewage plant the right to dump 4 tons a week.

c. The fishery is willing to pay the sewage firm up to its lost profits to not dump a ton into the lake. The sewage firm will want $200 a ton to not dump. At this price, the fishery can pay the sewage plant to not dump all but 4 tons of sewage a week into the lake. When there are no transaction costs, the answer is always the same, no matter who owns the right to dump into the lake. But, as the next answer indicates, someone has to own the right to dump!

d. If no one owns the lake, the preceding agreements could be made and a third firm could come along and dump its sewage into the lake. This would make the agreement useless. The result is that too much sewage will be dumped into the lake. The government could correct the situation by declaring one of the firms owner of the lake or by taxing all sewage that is dumped (the tax equaling the lost profit to the fishery).

8. If meat eaters are willing to pay the full cost of beef, then from an economic point of view, they should be allowed to buy and eat beef (as $SMB \geq SMC$). It would only be by accident that a regulation would limit beef to this amount. It is far more likely that the regulations will allow too much or too little beef to be sold.

9. a. A will win (with two votes from Dobbs and Effron).

b. B will win (with two votes from Dobbs and Effron).

c. C will win (with two votes from Effron and Francis).

d. A is preferred to B, B is preferred to C, yet C is preferred to A! How can A be better than B and B better than C, yet C comes out on top of A?

e. First vote: B versus C. B wins. Second vote: A versus B. A wins.

f. First vote: A versus C. C wins. Second vote: C versus B. B wins.

g. First vote: A versus B. A wins. Second vote: A versus C. C wins.

10. In the primary, the median voter in the Republican party is more conservative and the median voter in the Democrat party is more liberal. But in the main election, the median voter is more in the center, which is where the candidates will also tend to be.

Chapter Fourteen

Government and Taxes

INTRODUCTION

Federal taxes in 1995 equaled $5,000 for every man, woman, and child in the United States. State and city taxes add another $2,500 in taxes for every man, woman, and child. In addition, the private sector's cost of meeting government regulation, which is a form of taxation, equaled about $1,000 for every man, woman, and child. So I ask you, citizens, *is* this annoying child really paying its fair share?

We are going to analyze first the effects of taxes and then, later, the effects of government spending.

THE REAL BURDEN OF GOVERNMENT

Even if you never paid a dollar in taxes in your life, you most likely have paid for taxes in some way. That's because many taxes are passed on to consumers in the form of higher prices and on to workers in the form of lower wages. Even if you know exactly what you paid in taxes last year, down to the last penny, that isn't what you actually paid! Taxes affect the economy in so many ways it is hard to really know who bears the burden of paying taxes. It is quite possible, for example, that the corporate income tax is paid for by workers in the form of lower wages.

What is the cost of government to the economy? Later, we'll look at some of its benefits. But right now, we want to add up all of its costs. The cost of government is the opportunity cost of the resources its actions take away from the private sector. This includes (1) the dollar cost of the government goods and services (such as defense, police protection, and the justice system), (2) the deadweight loss due to taxes, and (3) the misallocation of resources due to regulations. Let's examine each of these in turn.

Cost 1: Dollar Cost of Government Goods and Services

Total government spending on public goods and services was 28% of gross domestic product (GDP) in 1990, up from 23% in 1960. This included the spending at the federal, state, and local level. It includes spending for which the government purchases a good or service, including police services, highways, education, and military defense.

It excludes Social Security because Social Security represents what is called a *transfer payment,* which is any payment not in exchange for a good or service. Welfare payments are also transfer payments and are not counted as part of the government's goods and services.

To repeat the key point of this section, the government's main burden is the goods and services it takes from the private sector and reallocates to the public sector's use. It does not matter how this is financed. The government could borrow money to pay for it or it could use taxes to pay for it. So let's be really clear on this: One should not use taxes to measure the government's burden!

Cost 2: The Deadweight Burden of Taxes

Even though tax dollars are not added to the cost of government, the deadweight burden caused by collecting the taxes is an added cost of government. Taxes form a wedge between the demand price and the supply price of a good. The bigger the wedge, the less of the good is produced. The reduced output results in a deadweight loss. Figure 14.1 illustrates how this loss is measured.

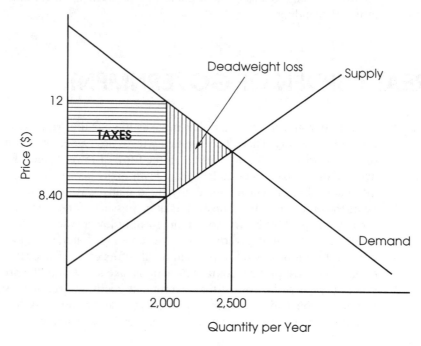

Figure 14.1

Points to note:

The tax rate is 30% of the price of the good. Thirty percent of $12 is $3.60. Twelve dollars minus $3.60 is $8.40.

Total tax dollars collected is $7,200 (= $3.60 × 2,000).

The tax causes output to fall by 500 units. The net benefit loss from these 500 units not being produced is the deadweight burden of the tax.

The deadweight loss is the area of the triangle. Here, it's $900 (= ½ × 500 × $3.60).

The burden of government due to this tax is $900. The $7,200 of tax dollars collected is already counted as a burden in the public goods and services they bought.

A main burden of taxes is that it causes people to work less. Using Figure 14.1, assume the quantity referred to is the hours worked per year and the demand schedule is the demand by employers for work hours. An income tax of 30% would cause the results shown in Figure 14.1: The worker will work fewer hours and there will be a deadweight loss for the reduced hours of work. One note: The decrease in the hours of work caused by taxes is smaller than that shown.

Studies put the deadweight loss from collecting one added dollar of taxes at about 34 cents[1] Obviously, this is the sort of issue that excites a lot of controversy, but the figure is likely to be in this range. What this means is that for every dollar collected in taxes, another 34 cents is lost in the form of foregone net benefits from less output produced and fewer hours worked.

Cost 3: The Cost of Regulations

The government imposes many regulations on businesses. Although these regulations may produce benefits, they also incur costs. One estimate of the burden of regulations is between $4,000 and $5,000 a year per household. That's about 13% of the average annual household income. For example, it has been estimated that FDA regulations cost $359 million per approved drug. The public ultimately pays for this added cost. That's why drugs in the United States are twice as expensive as they are in the rest of the world.

WHAT ABOUT TRANSFER PAYMENTS?

Transfer payments, as stated previously, are money given to people and not in exchange for goods or services. The transfer in transfer payments means the money is transferred from the taxpayers to whomever gets the money. The main types of transfer payments are Social Security and welfare. The main welfare programs are AFDC (Aid to Families with Dependent Children) and food stamps.

These are not counted as part of the burden of government on the economy because, even though taxpayers are worse off, the beneficiaries are better off by the same amount. On net, the impact of transfer payments on the private sector is zero.

THE ECONOMICS OF GIFTS

A few days ago, I saw a friend of mine give a dollar to a beggar holding a sign saying, "Need Money For Food." Being rather brash, I walked up to my friend and said, "Would you have given that beggar a bottle of liquor?" My friend said, "no." "Well," I replied, "that's what you just did." Even if the beggar said he needed money for food, even if he took that dollar bill to the deli and bought food, what matters is how that dollar changed his spending. My guess is that he'll spend the same on food, with or without that dollar. But I also guess that his consumption of alcohol will go up by nearly a dollar.

This is the key insight to the economics of gifts. Recall that economics focuses on changes in human behavior. So when economists study the effects of gifts, they look at how the gift changes the person's behavior. What we often find is that the change need not have anything to do with what constitutes the gift.

---

[1]This is deadweight loss at the margin. The average deadweight loss per dollar collected is smaller.

Thought Questions

Bill earns and spends $400 a week. He spends $100 a week on food and $300 on other items. The government then gives Bill $100 a week in food stamps that can only be spent on food. After this, Bill spends $110 on food and $390 on other items. What impact did the food stamps have on Bill's behavior?

The $100 in food stamps caused Bill to consume $10 more in food. What happened to the other $90? It got spent on other items! But how can this be, you might say, when the food stamps can only be spent on food? The answer is that Bill stopped spending $90 of his own money on food and kept spending the other $10 he earned on food. To this $10 he added the $100 of food stamps to buy $110 of food. Then he takes the $90 he had been spending on food to buy other things.

Farmers favor food stamps because they believe they increase the demand for food. Is this true?

Yes, food stamps do increase the demand for food but, and this is important, not dollar for dollar! A million dollars of food stamps might increase the demand for grocery store products by $300,000 and, of this, farmers would be lucky to see $50,000. Getting rid of food stamps would not have that much of an impact on farmers. What's more, the people from whom the taxes were collected to pay for food stamps are going to reduce their food consumption by some small amount. The net effect of food stamps on farmers' output is likely to be small.

The U.S. government gives the country of Smallia $100 million to build a dam. Had the U.S. government not given the money, the dictator of Smallia would have built the dam anyway but would not have built a $100 million presidential palace. What did the U.S. government really give the country of Smallia?

The U.S. government in effect gave Smallia a $100 million presidential palace. And, just think, we thought we gave a dam!

MARGINAL AND AVERAGE TAX RATES

A key distinction is between marginal and average tax rates. The marginal tax rate is the tax rate one pays on the last (marginal) dollar one earns. In contrast, the average tax rate is the average tax one pays on all the dollars one earns.

Thought Question

In Smallia, citizens pay no tax on the first $10,000 they earn, they pay a 10% tax on every dollar earned between $10,001 and $20,000, and a tax of 20% on every dollar earned above $20,000. What is the marginal and average tax rate for the follow taxpayers? Refer to Table 14.1.

A. Earns $5,000
B. Earns $15,000
C. Earns $25,000
D. Earns $200,000

TABLE 14.1

Taxpayer	Taxes Paid ($)	Marginal Tax Rate	Average Tax Rate
A	0	0%	0%
B	500	10%	3.33%
C	2,000	20%	8%
D	37,000	20%	18.5%

For example, taxpayer D pays $0 on the first $10,000 he makes. Added to this, he pays $1,000 on the next $10,000 he makes. And added to this is $36,000 on the next $180,000 he makes. This sums to $37,000 in total taxes paid.

In a *progressive tax system,* the marginal and average tax rates go up with income. The marginal/average rule states that as the marginal tax rate goes up, the average rate follows but at a slower rate. Thus, the average rate < marginal rate. This can be seen in Table 14.1.

In a *regressive tax system,* the marginal and average tax rates go down with income. The marginal/average rule states that as the marginal rate goes down, the average rate follows, so that the average rate > marginal rate.

Thought Questions

In Smallia, citizens pay a 20% tax on the first $10,000 they earn, they pay 10% tax on every dollar earned between $10,001 and $20,000, and no taxes on every dollar earned above $20,000. What is the marginal and average tax rates for the following taxpayers? Refer to Table 14.2
A. Earns $5,000
B. Earns $15,000
C. Earns $25,000
D. Earns $200,000

TABLE 14.2

Taxpayer	Taxes Paid ($)	Marginal Tax Rate	Average Tax Rate
A	1,000	20%	20%
B	2,500	10%	16.7%
C	3,000	0%	12%
D	3,000	0%	1.5%

Do the rich pay less in taxes with a regressive tax system?
Not necessarily. In the preceding example, the rich do not pay less in taxes. Change the example slightly (making the tax rate 1% for income above $20,000), and the rich would pay more. However, the rich pay a lower average and marginal tax rate.

In a *proportional or flat tax system,* everyone pays the same marginal and average tax rate. Thus, the average tax rate = marginal tax rate. Most flat tax proposals before Congress are slightly progressive. Their marginal tax rate is 0% up to some income level and a fixed rate after that. In such schemes, the average tax rate is less than the marginal tax rate but quickly approaches it as income goes up. For example, under one plan, single taxpayers pay nothing until they earn $13,100 and then 20% on every added dollar in earnings. A person earning $13,100 has a marginal and average tax rate of 0%. A person earning $20,000 more, or $33,100, pays $4,000 in taxes. A person earning $40,000 more, or $53,100, pays $8,000. A person earning $80,000 more, or $93,100, pays $16,000 in taxes. The marginal rate is 20% in all cases. The average tax rate is 12.1%, 15.1%, and 17.2%

TAXES AND TAX REVENUES

Higher taxes do not necessarily mean that more taxes will be collected. This proposition is illustrated in Figure 14.2 by the Laffer curve, named after the economist Arthur Laffer, who first constructed the curve. On the horizontal axis is the tax rate on income and on the vertical axis is the tax revenue, the total dollars in taxes collected per year. We know that if the tax rate is zero, no tax dollars will be collected. We also suspect that if the tax rate is 100%, no tax dollars will be collected. Why is that? At a tax rate of 100% the government is taking away everything you earn, so why work at all? If no one works, then no taxes are collected. So we have two points on the graph: no taxes collected at tax rates of 0% (point A) and 100% (point C). As the tax rate goes up from 0%, the government starts to collect more tax dollars (going from point A to point B). But at some tax rate, and this need not be halfway, raising the tax rate causes people to cut back so much on working (and other taxable activities) that the tax dollars collected begin to fall. This is shown on the segment from B to C. At tax rate T, the most tax dollars (D) are collected.

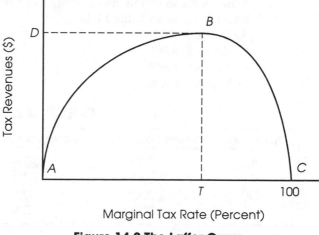

Figure 14.2 The Laffer Curve

Notice that it is the *marginal tax rate* that is on the horizontal axis. Recalling the lessons of marginal analysis, you should realize that it is the tax rate on the margin that matters. Suppose you paid a tax rate of 0% on the first $20,000 you earned and paid a tax rate of 100% on every dollar you earned above $20,000. If you are like most persons, you would never earn more than $20,000 because the marginal tax rate is 100%. Your average tax rate is 0% but your marginal tax rate is 100%. It is the marginal tax rate that matters!

Empirically, tax revenues probably peak around a marginal tax rate of 40%. Most of the decrease in taxes after that point comes from tax evasion rather than people working less (which they do, but not by much). For example, in the 1980s, the federal tax rate on the very rich fell from 70% to 28%, the actual percent of income paid in taxes by those making over $1,000,000 a year rose by 4%. The main reason was that the economy was coming out of a recession. But there is also evidence that more taxes were paid because the lower rate caused the rich to evade taxes less.

MAJOR DISTORTIONS IN OUR CURRENT TAX SYSTEM

By taxing some activities and not others, our current tax system redirects resources away from their most efficient use. Some of the major distortions caused by our current tax codes follow.

1. The use of historical cost for depreciation—Businesses can deduct from their income a certain percent of the cost of their plant and equipment. When this deduction accurately reflects the cost of wear and tear on plant and equipment, there is no problem. However, when there is inflation, the cost of wear and tear (reflected by the price of eventually replacing the plant and equipment) goes up. But because businesses have to use the original historical cost, their deduction is smaller than it should be. The result is that their reported taxable income is unrealistically high because they are deducting too little. Consequently, they pay more in taxes. The effective tax rate on capital in 1973 when inflation reached 16% was near 91%. This had a devastating impact on investments and seriously harmed the economy. One study suggests that every 10% increase in prices causes a reduction in after-tax profits and investments so much that economic growth in slowed by 1%.
2. Treating inflation gains as capital gains—Suppose I buy $10,000 worth of Acme Ink, Inc., and it grows to $20,000 in 20 years. This sounds like I did pretty well! But suppose that inflation was 3.6% over these years. If it was, then the $20,000 has about the same purchasing power as the $10,000 did. So, in effect, I've not made a penny. Yet the $10,000 gain in the value of stock is taxed as if it were a real gain! Suppose I pay $3,000 in taxes. Now I'm worse off for having made the investment. I would have done better consuming the money. The same is true for taxes on the gain in the value of investments. Because one can't deduct the change in the purchasing power of the investment, it is likely that the investment will be overtaxed.
3. Mortgage interest deduction—Homeowners are allowed to deduct from their income the interest they pay on the mortgages on their homes. On the other hand, homeowners do not have to report the income they earn on their homes, including the implicit rent it produces (that is, the value of the services it generates) or its change in value. That's a good deal! You get to deduct your costs but not count your income! As a result, too much of our nation's capital has been channeled away from more productive investments into homes.
4. Not taxing interest paid on municipal and state bonds—Because the interest earned on municipal and state bonds is free from federal taxation, they pay a

lower rate of interest than do equivalent corporate bonds. The result is that cities and municipalities don't have to earn as much interest on their investments as do private corporations. Thus, a private investment paying 7% might be passed over because after taxes it only pays 4%. The money will be invested instead in a tax-free investment paying 5%. The result is the nation's capital is being redirected toward lower paying investments, making it less productive.

SOME ALTERNATIVES TO THE INCOME TAX

Currently, most taxes are collected by an income tax. Some of the proposed taxes to replace or partially replace our current income tax follow.

1. A *consumption tax* is a tax on spending, not earning. The part of income that a person saves would not be taxed. An example of a consumption tax is the sales tax. The advantage of a consumption tax is that it does not penalize savings and investments. As a consequence, total savings increase. The main drawback of a consumption tax is that a rich person might not pay very much in taxes if she invests most of her income. A response is that the rich person is indirectly paying a tax because she is consuming less. Furthermore, the money invested may be more beneficial to the public than if the same amount were spent by the government.

2. A *flat tax* taxes all income at the same percentage rate. By eliminating most tax deductions, the current income tax could be replaced with a flat tax of around 19% to 23%. Most flat tax proposals would reduce tax evasion by making all income equally taxable. For example, firms currently have an incentive to give workers relatively too many fringe benefits (such as health care and life insurance) because they are an untaxed form of compensation. One advantage of a flat tax comes from the theory of public choice. If all persons have to pay the same tax rate, then all have the same incentives to vote for higher or lower taxes. On the other hand, with an income tax and its many deductions, it is possible for politicians to play one group off another and raise taxes in slow increments. When the income tax was first introduced, it was promised that only the rich would ever pay an income tax. As a result, the income tax had the support of the general public who were more than glad to let others pay for their government. That's not the way it turned out.

3. *User taxes and fees* apply when the beneficiaries of government goods and services can be identified and taxed. For example, a gasoline tax is a type of user tax that pays for the road systems people drive on. Similarly, many areas charge for garbage service.

4. A *value-added tax* (*VAT*) is paid by each business on their value added. The value added equals the difference between revenues and inputs the business buys from other firms. For example, if Acme buys $4,000 of raw materials from another company and hires workers for $8,000 to process it into widgets, which it sells for $20,000, its value added is $16,000. Thus, value added equals the profits and money it paid for any inputs as long as it didn't buy the inputs from other firms. Because the price of any good reflects the sum of the value added to it by all the firms making it, a VAT is equivalent to a sales tax on all goods. The main advantage of a VAT over a sales tax is that it is harder to evade. With a VAT, each firm reports to the government the inputs it bought. These inputs are other firms' sales.

Thus, most of the sales in an economy end up being reported to the government with a VAT.

A VAT can be like a flat tax, such that, in effect, everyone pays the same percent of their income in taxes. Alternatively, it can be made to fall more on the rich by being higher on the goods the rich buy.

TAX INCIDENCE: WHO REALLY PAYS THE TAXES

The rich do pay more taxes in the United States. In 1989, the bottom 20% of households paid 4.6% of their income in taxes, the next 20% paid 8.9%, and on up to the top 20%, who paid 19.6% of their income in taxes. Because the rich earn more, this means that the top 20% paid 54% of federal income taxes in 1990.

Who really bears the taxes? Economics tells us that taxes fall on the inelastic. Those who can't shift their income to lower-taxed activities, those who can't move their economic activity to other lower-taxed countries or to the underground economy, and those who can't hire accountants to find tax deductions are inelastic and will tend to bear taxes. Now, I can't be certain about this, but doesn't this sound like the typical middle-class taxpayer? The rich probably do pay more, but I suspect they bear fewer taxes than they pay.

Thought Question

In Smallia, the only tax is a 50% tax on profits. Smallia's private sector borrows heavily in international credit markets at a world interest rate of 8%. Assume that its private sector is highly competitive. Such business profits only reflect the return on the capital invested in the business. Furthermore, assume that its goods are sold in competitive world markets. Who bears the 50% tax? What would happen to net after-tax profits if the 50% tax on profits were abolished?

Workers bear the tax in the form of lower wages. Businesses can't raise their price to pay the tax because that would make them not competitive in the world markets. Thus, if they don't lower wages, they won't be able to earn 16% in before-tax profits to pay the 50% tax plus pay an 8% return to their foreign investors. So workers have to lower their wages to get work. The profit tax really falls on the inelastic factor of production—workers. If the tax were abolished, investment opportunities would expand, and the new investment would bid up the wages of workers. In equilibrium, at the new higher level of investment, businesses would earn 8% and pay this to their foreign investors. That is, the corporate income tax leaves corporate after-tax profits unchanged! Notice how close this problem comes to describing the world we live in.

TAXES AND EQUITY

There are many ideas of what makes a tax system fair. These ideas often conflict. The main ones are listed here.

1. The *benefits principle* says people should pay taxes in proportion to the benefits they receive from government. The rationale for this is that it is wrong to steal. Thus, it isn't right that, except for helping the poor, one group benefits at the cost of another. Thus, the benefit principle concludes that those who benefit from a government program should pay for it.
2. The *ability to pay principle* is that those who earn more should pay more because they can afford to. The philosophical basis for this principle was best enunciated by Willie Sutton, a famous bank robber, who, when asked why he robbed banks, replied, "because that's where the money is."
3. *Horizontal equity* says that equals should pay equal taxes. If you earn $20,000, no matter how, and I earn $20,000, then we both should pay the same taxes.
4. *Vertical equity* says that unequals should pay unequal taxes. If you earn $20,000 and I earn $40,000, then I should pay more taxes than you. This is consistent with progressive taxes, proportional taxes, and even, in some cases, regressive taxes. All it says is that people who earn more should pay more.

GOVERNMENT SPENDING

The basic contributions of economists to the principle of government spending is that, aside from helping the poor, its marginal benefits should exceed or equal its marginal costs. Most governments do not use this principle. One study found that government agencies tend to understate the cost of their projects by 50%. Few attempt to measure the benefits of their programs, especially as an ongoing process with constant feedback.

Governments like to emphasize how many jobs their programs create. Yet, this ignores how many jobs were destroyed by taxes necessary to pay for the government's programs. There is a case in serious recessions for government programs to create jobs. But because programs never go away, in good times or bad, it is better if the programs are also efficient.

The emphasis on jobs created is actually perverse. Wouldn't it be better if by magic all the mail in America could be delivered by just one postal worker named Fred? All the other postal workers would be in other jobs, producing other goods, so that we would get the mail delivered and all these other goods too. The fewer the people and the fewer the resources it takes to produce a given government service, the more our economy can produce with its limited resources and, as a result, the more per capita income will be!

CRIB NOTES

Burden of government: Foregone cost of government spending. Includes (1) cost of government purchases of goods and services (includes government employment), (2) deadweight cost of taxes, and (3) cost of regulations imposed upon private sector. Does not include transfer payments (payment not in exchange for services or goods, such as welfare and Social Security).

Economics of gifts and payment-in-kind (such as food stamps):
  (1) Value of gift to recipient $\leq$ Dollar cost of gift.
  (2) Impact on consumption: Amount of good given $\geq$ Amount person increases consumption of good.
Marginal tax rate: Percent of last dollar earned paid in taxes.
Average tax rate: Percent of total taxes/total income.
Progressive tax system: Marginal and average tax rate increase as income increases

Marginal $\geq$ Average tax rate.

Proportional tax system: Marginal and average tax rate same as income increases

Marginal $=$ Average tax rate

Regressive tax system: Marginal and average tax rate decrease as income increases (taxes paid may go up with income)

Marginal $<$ Average tax rate.

Laffer curve: Tax revenues go up and then down as tax rate increases. Two points on curve:

Tax revenues $=$ 0 when tax rate equal 0% or 100%.

Consumption tax: Tax consumption spending, not income. Savings are deductible.
Flat tax: All income taxed at same rate. No deductions in most flat tax programs.
VAT: Value-added tax: Each firm pays tax on its value added.
  Value added $=$ revenue $-$ Purchases from other firms
  Final value of goods $=$ Sum of value added
Tax equity principles:
  Benefit principle: Tax levels reflect benefits people getting.
  Ability to pay: Tax levels reflect money people make.
  Horizontal equity: Persons earning same income should pay same tax.
  Vertical equity: Person earning more should pay more taxes (need not be higher % in taxes, just more taxes).

Review Questions

1. In the nation of Motorania, taxpayer A earns $40,000 and pays $4,000 in taxes while taxpayer B earns $80,000 and pays $6,000 in taxes. Is the tax system of Motorania progressive, proportional (flat), or regressive?

2. The government in Motorania spends nothing on goods and services. It does give $20 million to retired citizens. Its collects $20 million in taxes to pay for this, and these taxes cause $4 million in deadweight cost. What is the cost of the government on the economy in Motorania?

3. The government in Motorania buys $20 million in goods and services, collects $15 million in taxes, and borrows the remaining $5 million. Its taxes produce no deadweight costs. What is the cost of government in Motorania?'

4. What is the deadweight cost of the tax shown in the following figure?

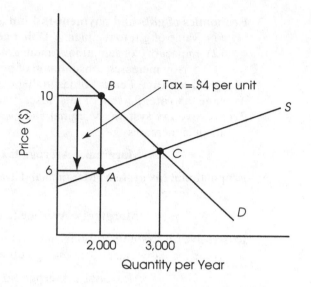

5. People on Social Security lose 50 cents in Social Security benefits for every dollar they earn. (This only applies to those under age 70 and only after a certain level of income has been reached.) What is the implicit tax rate due to this feature of Social Security? What are its likely effects on the work hours of retirees?

6. Which of the following are government purchases of goods and services and which are government transfer payments?
   a. The Apollo Space mission.
   b. Subsidy to agriculture and industry.
   c. Social Security.
   d. Salary received by federal employee.
   e. Unemployment benefits paid to a laid-off worker.

7. "The local city council gave $500 worth of clothing to all the poor families in town. Therefore, these families will have $500 more in clothing than before." Is this correct?

8. The following table shows a demand and supply curve for wheat. Use it to answer these questions.

Quantity	1	2	3	4	5	6	7	8
Demand Price ($)	16	14	12	10	8	6	4	2
Supply Price ($)	4	6	8	10	12	14	16	18

   a. How much wheat will be bought and at what price?
   b. If the government imposes a $4 per unit tax, how much will it collect? How does that compare with a $8 tax, a $12 tax, and a $16 tax? What does this illustrate?
   c. What is the deadweight loss associated with each tax?
   d. If the government subsidizes wheat with a $12 per unit subsidy, what is the deadweight loss of the subsidy? Is the subsidy itself a cost to the economy?

9. If the government gives $1,000 of food stamps to a poor family, will the family now have $1,000 more food than before?

10. Suppose you want Fred, the mailcarrier, to eat twice as much food as he currently consumes. Assume that Fred will spend $10 on food for every $100 increase in his income. Fred's income is currently $10,000 a year and, true to form, he spends $1,000 a year on food. How many food stamps, good only for food, would you have to give Fred to increase his food consumption to $2,000 worth of food
    a. if food stamps can be bought and sold, dollar for dollar; and
    b. if it is impossible to resell food stamps?

11. John makes $20,000 a year in his job, on which he pays 10% in income tax or $2,000 in taxes. Mary owns stock in Acme, Inc. Her share of Acme's profit is $20,000. These profits are taxed at a corporate tax rate of 10% or $2,000. Then the $18,000 is paid out to her in dividends, upon which she pays another 10% in income tax, or $1,800. So Mary pays $3,800 in taxes on the $20,000 in income she earned. In effect, her income has been taxed twice.
    a. Is the corporate income tax horizontally equitable?
    b. Is it vertically equitable? (Assume her share of Acme's profit is $15,000.)

12. If corporate bonds pay a 10% interest rate, what rate does a tax-free municipal bond have to pay when the marginal income tax rate is 30%? If a municipal bond pays 5%, what rate must a corporate bond pay to be competitive with it when the marginal tax rate is 30%?

13. This question compares a 10% sales tax with a 10% VAT tax. Firm A grows seeds from scratch and sells them for $10. Firm B buys these seeds and grows wheat, which it sells for $30. Firm C grinds this wheat into flour, which it sells for $36 to a baker. Firm D bakes the bread and sells it to its customers for $50.
    a. A sales tax applies only to the final good in this chain, the bread being sold to the customer. How much will the sales tax be? What will the baker gain by not reporting the sale?
    b. A VAT tax applies to the value added of each firm. What will each firm pay in taxes? What does this sum up to? What will the baker gain by not reporting the sale?

14. This question illustrates how inflation increases the effective tax rate on corporate profits because depreciation and replacement costs are not indexed. Acme, Inc., buys a big chunk of ice for $1,000 once each five years. Over the next 5 years, it lets buyers come in and chip away one fifth of the ice chunk. It charges the buyers a total of $300 a year to do this. Its true profits are True profit = $300 − Replacement cost of ice chipped off. It pays a 30% tax on its reported profit = $300 − $200, where $200 is one fifth of its historical cost of buying the ice chunk.
    a. If ice chunk costs hold steady, how does its true and reported profits compare? What is the effective tax rate on true profits?
    b. If ice chunk costs go up, such that by the fifth year, the cost of buying a new ice chunk is $1,250, what is Acme's true profit? Reported profit? The effective tax rate on true profits? (Assume sales remain at $300.)

Answers

1. It is regressive. Taxpayer A pays 10% of his income in taxes. Taxpayer B earns more and pays less in percent terms. Taxpayer B pays 7.5 % of his income in taxes.
2. Only the $4 million in deadweight cost. The $20 million is a transfer payment. Those paying it are $20 million worse off, but this is offset by the fact that those

getting it are $20 million better off. Nobody benefits from the $4 million in dead-weight cost.

3. It is $20 million in goods and services that otherwise would have gone to the private sector. The fact that part of this was paid for with borrowed money doesn't matter. Twenty million dollars' worth of goods and services have been redirected from the private to the public sector.

4. Two thousand dollars. The deadweight cost is the lost net benefit resulting from 1,000 fewer units being produced (from 3,000 to 2,000). This is measured by the distance between the demand curve (*MB*) and the supply curve (*MC*) summed over the 1,000 units. This equals the triangle *ABC*. Its areas equals ½ × base × height or ½ × 1,000 × $4.

5. The implicit tax rate is 50%. If a retired person earns $1,000 more, his Social Security payments go down $500. As a result, his income only goes up $500. That is the same increase that would occur if his income were taxed at the 50% rate. The result is that retirees work fewer hours than otherwise. Many work up to the point where the earnings penalty kicks in.

6. a. and d. Government purchases of goods and service.
   b, c, and e. Transfer payments.

7. No. Most likely, the families cut back on their own expenditures for clothing, so that the net addition in clothing was less than $500, and perhaps, considerably less.

8. a. $P = \$10$ and $Q = 4$ (where demand equals supply)

   b.

Tax	Q	Tax Revenue
$4	3	$12
$8	2	$16
$12	1	$12
$16	0	$0

   This illustrates the Laffer curve. As the tax goes up, tax revenues first rise and then fall.

   c.

Tax	Q Not Produced	Deadweight Loss
$4	fourth unit	$0
$8	third, fourth units	$4
$12	second–fourth units	$12
$16	first–fourth units	$24

   d. $Q = 7$ as $P^D = \$4$ while $MC = \$16$. The deadweight loss is the excess of *MC* (measured by the original P^S) over marginal benefit (measured by *PD*) for units 5, 6, and 7. This adds up to $24 ($4 for the fifth unit plus $8 for the sixth and $12 for the seventh). The subsidy (which totals $12 × 7 units or $84) is a transfer payment from taxpayers to suppliers and so is not a deadweight cost. This explanation will be adequate to answer this question on a test. There are two additional costs not usually mentioned in textbooks, and you are not normally expected to include these on a test. First, there is a deadweight loss incurred to collect the $84 to pay the taxes. Second, wheat farmers may have spent resources in getting the government to give them the subsidy. The cost of this rent-seeking activity is also a deadweight cost to the economy. It could add up to as much as the $84 in subsidies!

9. No. The family will take the money it was spending on food (up to $1,000), use the food stamps to buy the same amount of food, and then spend the freed-up money on whatever they want. Some of what they want may be food, but not $1,000 more food. Food consumption will go up far less than $1,000.

10. The goal is to get Fred to consume $2,000 worth of food.
    a. If he can resell the food stamps you give him, then you would have to give him

$10,000 worth of food stamps! He will then have, after selling his food stamps for cash, an income of $20,000 and will spend 10% of that ($2,000) on food.

    b. If he can't resell the food stamps, then Fred is stuck using them for food. You have to give Fred $2,000 worth of food stamps to get him to consume $2,000 worth of food. Why not just $1,000? Because if you give Fred $1,000 of food stamps, he'll stop spending his own money on food and use the food stamps to buy food, and use the money he's saved to buy what he wants, which most likely is not food. You have to add another $1,000 of food stamps, bringing the total of $2,000 of food stamps, to force him to eat $2,000 worth of food.

        This problem illustrates why the government makes it illegal to resell food stamps. If they were easy to resell, food stamps would only increase the food consumption of the poor by a small amount.

11. a. The double taxation of corporate profits (first by the corporate income tax and then by the personal income tax) is not horizontally equitable. Both Mary and John made the same income, but Mary paid more in taxes.

    b. It is not horizontally equitable. If Mary earns less (only $15,000), she still pays more ($2,850)!

12. The municipal bond only has to pay a 7% interest rate. That makes it equal to the corporate bond, which also pays 7% after tax. Let mi = municipal interest rate (in % terms), i = market (taxed) interest rate (in % terms), and t = marginal tax rate (in decimal terms), then when the two rates are competitive:

$$mi = i\,(1 - t), \text{ or } i = mi/(1 - t).$$

So if $mi = 6\%$, then the competitive i equals $6\%/(1 - 0.3)$ or 8.57%.

13. a. Ten percent of $50 is $5 in taxes. The baker would gain the $5 in taxes if she didn't report the sale.

    b. Firm A pays $1 because its value added is $10.
       Firm B pays $2 because its value added is $20 ($30 – $10).
       Firm C pays $0.60 because its value added is $6 ($36 – $30).
       Firm D pays $1.40 because its value added is $14 ($50 – $36).

        The VAT taxes add up to $5 because the value added adds up to $50. That is, the price of the final good equals the sum of the values added. The baker would gain $1.40 if she didn't report the sale. That's a lot less than when there is a sales tax.

        Notice that firm B has the incentive to report A's sale of $10. If B failed to do this, its reported value added would be $10 higher and its tax would be $1 higher. Similarly, C has an incentive to report B's sales and D has an incentive to report C's sales. Only D is in the position of not reporting a sale and not getting caught. Thus, at most, only $14 of the $50 value added has a chance of going unreported and untaxed.

14. a. Its true and reported profits are the same because the replacement cost of the ice chipped off is still $200. It pays $30 in taxes (which is 30% of its reported profit of $100). Its effect tax rate is also 30% because $30 is 30% of its true profit of $100.

    b. Its true profit is now $300 – $250 = $50. But its reported profit is still $100 and so it must pay a $30 tax. The effective tax rate is now higher. It's 60% because $30 is 60% of the true profits of $50.

Chapter Fifteen

The Derived Demand for Inputs

INTRODUCTION

Recently, a major star received $20 million to be in a movie. Many persons complained about the extravagance of this salary. Yet, few asked why the studios were willing to pay $20 million. The answer is that the studios expected that by hiring this star, the attendance at this movie would go up enough that it was worth the $20 million! If the star didn't get it, the movie studio heads would have gotten it.

The star's salary is derived from the extra dollars the public is willing to pay for his added presence in a movie. In the same way, the value of any input is derived from the dollars consumers are willing to pay for what the input adds to output. For example, if hiring another worker adds three widgets an hour to output and widgets sell for $4, then a widget worker adds $12 per hour. The $12 becomes the value of the worker to the employer and, through competition, becomes reflected in his wage. All workers, from movie stars to economists, from brain surgeons to janitors, tend to get paid by the value of what they add.

This is why we call the demand for inputs the *derived demand for inputs*. The input's demand is derived from consumers.

MONOPOLY AND COMPETITION

There are two extremes in every market: perfect competition (many firms) and pure monopoly (one firm).

There are two types of markets: markets for outputs and markets for inputs. The markets for outputs can be competitive or monopolistic. The markets for inputs can also be competitive or monopolistic. A firm that has a monopoly in its output market (the market it sells its output in) is a monopoly. A firm that has a monopoly in its input market (the market its hires its inputs in) is called a *monopsony*. Monopsony does not mean "I have only one Sony." It is Latin for only one buyer, just as monopoly means only one seller.

A firm that is a monopoly in its output market can also be perfectly competitive in the market it hires its inputs in. For example, the only grocery store in a town may be a monopoly, but it also may compete with other employers for its clerks. Similarly, a firm that is a monopsony in the market it buys its inputs in may also be perfectly competitive in the market it sells its output in. For example, the only employer in a small town may be a monopsony, but it is perfectly competitive in its output market, which may well be a highly competitive international market. So we have four possible combinations as shown in the following table.

		Output Markets	
		Competitive	Monopoly
Input	Competitive	Perfect Competition	Monopoly
Markets	Monopoly	Monopsony	Monopoly, Monopsony

What distinguishes a monopoly from a competitive firm is that the monopoly must lower its price to sell more. As a result, its marginal revenue from selling another unit is less than that unit's price ($MR < P$) because it equals that unit's price minus the loss in revenue for the price cut on previous output. For a competitive firm, $MR = P$ because it can sell all its output at the market price. What distinguishes a monopsony from a competitive hiring firm is that the monopsony has to raise its wage to hire more workers (or the price of the input it hires). As the result, the marginal cost of hiring another factor (called marginal factor cost, MFC) is greater than the wage ($MFC > W$) because it equals the wage plus the added cost of the wage increase for the previous workers hired. For a competitive firm, $MFC = W$ because it can hire all its workers at the market wage.

For example, a monopoly can sell 10 units of output at $8 and 11 units at $7.50. What is the marginal revenue of selling the 11th unit of output? $2.50. This equals $7.50 for the 11th unit less the 50 cents per unit loss (due to price cut) times the 10 units whose price was cut (= $7.50 − 0.50 × 10).

A monopsony can hire 10 workers at $7.50 or 11 workers at $8.00. What is the marginal factor cost of hiring the 11th worker? $12.50. This equals $7.50 for hiring the 11th worker plus the added 50 cents in wages for the first 10 workers hired (= $7.50 + $0.50 × 10).

COMPETITIVE MARKET FOR INPUTS

We will start with the simplest case. The firm is perfectly competitive in its output market and is perfectly competitive in its input market. Because this is the main case used in textbooks, we will consider all its ramifications before turning to the other cases at the end of this chapter. So until we say otherwise, all the following sections are about competitive input and output markets.

Instead of talking about inputs, we will make our example more concrete by talking about workers. Each input is a worker who works a fixed number of hours per period. To keep things simple, we will pretend that workers are exactly like machines. Like a particular machine, all workers are assumed to be exactly alike and all are interchangeable. Just as machines don't tire, don't strike, and don't have bad Mondays, our workers don't tire, don't strike, and are eager beavers when that alarm clock rings on Monday morning!

To the firm, the market for labor (or for any input) looks like the curve in Figure 15.1. The firm can hire all the workers it needs at the same wage. Marginal factor cost is the cost of hiring another unit of an input. In this case, the *marginal factor cost* of another worker unit is the wage. When we say *wage,* we are including the actual wage plus any other worker related costs such as the costs of fringe benefits and workplace amenities. If worker input is measured by hours, then the wage is the hourly wage; if worker input is measured by a standard worker year, then the wage is the annual wage.

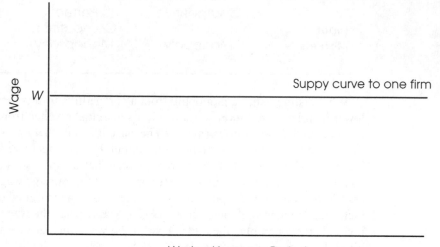

Figure 15.1

How many workers should the firm hire? Let L stand for the number of workers (L stands for labor). Each worker costs W, the wage. The firm wants to maximize its profits:

Profits = Total revenue – Total cost

or

Profits = $P \times Q - W \times L$ – Cost of other inputs.

Using marginal analysis, we look at the good and bad effects of increasing L by one unit.

Step 1: We first measure the good things that occur when the firm adds one more worker (L) to its labor force:

Marginal benefit of one more worker = $P \times MP$

where MP is the worker's marginal product. MP is the increase in output (Q) due to hiring one more worker. P is the price. So if $MP = 4$ and $P = 5$, the worker adds four units to the firm's output, and the firm can then turn around and sell those four units for a total of \$20. The marginal benefit of this worker to the firm is \$20.

Step 2: Next, we measure the marginal factor cost of hiring a worker (one more unit of L):

Marginal factor cost of one more worker = W

where W is the appropriate wage.

Step 3: Increase L as long as $MB \geq MC$ as

Change in profit due to one more worker = $P \times MP - W$

Step 4: Stop at (or never go beyond) where

$W = P \times MP$ at the L that maximizes profits.

Up to this L, hiring more workers increases the firm's profit as $MB > MC$. Beyond this L, $MC > MB$, so the firm will find its profits falling.

Thought Questions

Use Table 15.1 to answer the following questions.

TABLE 15.1

Labor Units	1	2	3	4	5	6	7
Marginal Product	9	8	7	6	5	4	3

If the wage is $20 and the price of output is $4, how many workers will the firm hire? What if the wage is $20.50? $19.50?

The firm hires five workers. The first worker brings in $36 in revenue (= $4 × 9) and costs $20: This adds $16 to the firm's profits. The second worker adds $32 to revenues and $20 to costs and so adds $12 to profits. (Recall that *revenues* refers to total sales and not profits!) The fifth worker adds $20 to revenue and $20 to costs and so it makes no difference if the firm hires the fifth worker or not. We call such a tie by saying the firm covers its costs and so hires the fifth worker. If the fifth worker costs $20.50, the firm's profit would be reduced by $0.50 and so the firm would hire only four workers in this case. If the fifth worker costs $19.50, the worker adds $0.50 to profits and the firm will hire the fifth worker. But they won't hire the sixth worker in this case because the sixth worker only brings in $16.00—not enough to cover the $19.50 wages!

If the wage is $12 and the price of output is $3, how many workers will the firm hire? If $W = \$24$ and $P = \$6$? If $W = \$48$ and $P = \$12$? Why is the answer the same in all cases?

The answer in all cases is six workers, whose *MP* is 4. The answer is the same in all cases because the wage (W) is the same ratio to price (P) in each case. Rewriting the marginal hiring condition, the firm will hire the worker when $W/P \geq MP$. For example, if we double W and P, the ratio of W/P is unchanged, and the firm will still employ the same number of workers. In all cases, $W/P = 4$.

If the firm hires four workers, what is its total output? What is the highest wage it would pay to hire four workers?

Because *MP* is the addition to output, it follows that Q = Sum of *MP*. Here, at $L = 4$, $Q = 30$. The highest wage it would pay is $P \times MP$ of worker 4 ($P \times 6$).

The wage is $20, the price is $4, and the firm hires workers 1 through 5. If the first worker quits, how much will output and its revenues fall?

Because the firm can shuffle workers around, the *MP* lost is the smallest. Output will fall by five units, and revenue will fall by $20.

Figure 15.2 shows the hiring decision graphically. The marginal hiring rule is

hire if $P \times MP > W$

or, rewriting,

hire if *MP* > *W/P*

For example, if $MP = 10$ and $P = \$2$, then W/P equals 5. This is the minimum MP the worker needs to produce to cover his wage. If $MP = 4$, for example, the worker will only bring in $8, which is insufficient to cover his wage of $10. If $MP = 6$, he brings in $12, which does cover his W and so he will be hired.

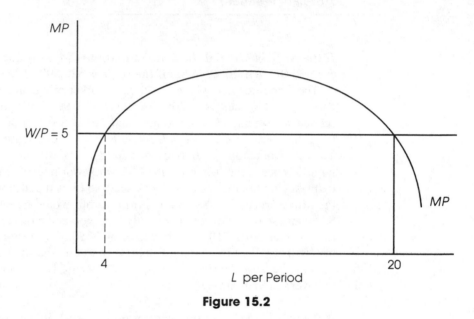

Figure 15.2

Points to note:

W/P equals 5 and the firm hires 20 workers.
At $L = 20$, $W/P = MP$.
At $L = 4$, $W/P = MP$, but the firm will never hire here. That's because up to $L = 4$, the firm has been losing money as $MP < W/P$ or $P \times MP < W$.
The firm will only hire where MP is declining, coming down from above the W/P line. If MP is rising, it pays to continue to hire more workers.
Note also what this solution holds for any wage that is five times the price. It holds for $W = \$5$ and $P = \$1$, it holds for $W = \$10$ and $P = \$2$, and it holds for $W = \$1,000$ and $P = \$200$!

There is one problem with Figure 15.2. It shows that the firm loses money on workers 1 through 4. To hire 20 workers, it must be able to make up for these early losses on workers 5 through 20. How can we tell if it pays for the firm to hire any workers? The answer is the firm will make money if workers on average cover their wages. This occurs if $P \times AP \geq W$, where AP is the average product of workers ($AP = Q/L$). We thus have two conditions for hiring.
Condition for hiring another worker:
Marginal hiring condition: $P \times MP \geq MP \geq W$.
Average hiring condition: $P \times AP \geq W$ or $AP \geq W/P$.
Figure 15.3 shows both of these conditions.

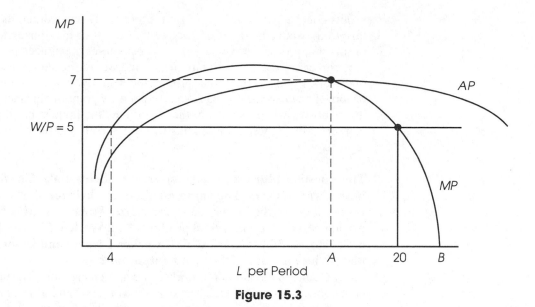

Figure 15.3

Points to note:

The firm hires 20 workers where $MP = W/P$. Beyond $L = 20$, the marginal hiring condition does not hold.

At $L = 20$, $AP > W/P$ so the average hiring condition is met.

If W/P exceeds 7, the average hiring condition is not met, and no workers will be hired.

If $W/P = 7$, the firm will hire A workers. This is the minimum number of workers the firm would ever hire.

If the wage is zero, the firm hires B workers. This is the maximum number of workers the firm would ever hire.

This firm's hiring zone is between $L = A$ and $L = B$. In this zone, both MP and AP are declining.

The firm will never knowingly hire fewer than A workers. Fewer than A workers may be profitable, but being in the hiring zone is more profitable still.

The firm hires in the hiring zone (between where employment has the maximum average product to where the marginal product sinks to zero). A key point to note is that in this zone, the average product of workers is falling. A great true-false question goes like this: "Firms maximize the productivity of workers." The answer is false. Worker productivity is another term for the average product per worker (AP). Only at the start of the hiring zone is average product at its highest. As the firm is likely to hire more than this, the firm does not maximize average productivity!

Thought Questions

The first worker hired adds 20 units to output. The second worker adds two units. A third adds none. The price of output is $10. The wage is $5. How many workers will the firm hire if it wants the highest productivity per worker? How many if it wants the highest profits (assume the only costs are wage costs)?

It will hire one worker to maximize average product (which equals 20 in this case). If it hires two workers, the average product falls to 11. But if it wants the highest profits, it will hire two workers. Total profits equal \$210 (= \$220 − \$10). If it hired only one worker, its total profits would be only \$195. Note that the firm maximizes total profits, not profits per worker! Hiring one worker maximizes profits per worker but the firm will hire the second worker because the second worker adds to their total profits. Incidentally, you can quickly become known as the company smarty-pants by pointing this fact out to the bosses when they claim they want the "the highest profit per worker." My suggestion: Keep this fact to yourself and the economics tests you take.

This question addresses a common error students make. The firm hires three workers. They have numbers on their tee-shirts corresponding to the order they are hired. Worker 1 (the first worker hired) has a marginal product of 10. Worker 2 has an *MP* of 8. Worker 3 has an *MP* of 6. If worker 1 leaves and is not replaced, how much will the firm's output fall?

By 6 units. By assumption, workers are interchangeable. The tasks being done by worker 1 are taken over by workers 2 and 3. The tasks being done by worker 3 are no longer performed, so output falls by 6. The moral of this story is that workers are not valued by what they are doing. They are valued by what the marginal worker does.[1]

SHORT-RUN DEMAND FOR INPUTS

In the short run, the number of firms is fixed. The demand for labor (or whatever input we're talking about) is the horizontal sum of each firm's demand. The height of this demand curve reflects the marginal benefit of labor, which equals price times *MP*. The only trick in adding up all the firm demand curves is that as employment goes up, two things happen. First, as L goes up, the *MP* falls. Second, as L goes up, output goes up, and so the price (P) falls as industry supply (Q) goes up. To correctly draw the industry's demand curve, you have to be careful to pick the right P at each employment.

Thought Question

There are 100 firms in an industry. For each firm, the 10th worker has a marginal product of 5 and the 11th worker has a marginal product of 4. When all firms hire 10 workers, industry output is 2,000 units, which sells for a price of \$10. If all firms hired an 11th worker, industry output would be 2,400, and the demand price for output would fall to \$9. What is the industry's demand price for the 1,000 workers? For 1,100 workers?

Fifty dollars for 1,000 workers and \$36 for 1,100 workers. For 1,000 workers, each firm is hiring 10 workers whose *MP* is 5 and P is \$10 so the demand price for the 10th worker by each firm is \$50. At a wage of \$50, each firm will hire 10 workers and this adds up to

---

[1] Some compensation schemes set wages by the importance of the job the worker does. These schemes ignore that a worker is worth the value of what the marginal worker does, not what the actual worker does. As such, they needlessly raise the compensation costs of firms.

1,000 workers hired. For 1,100 workers, each firm employs 11 workers. The 11th workers' MP is 4 and the price is then $9, so the marginal benefit of the 11th worker is $36. At a wage of $36, the firm will hire 11 workers and the industry demand, summed over the 100 firms, will be 1,100.

Figure 15.4 shows the demand curves for labor when we take account of the price change (this is the industry demand curve) and the demand curve when we don't.

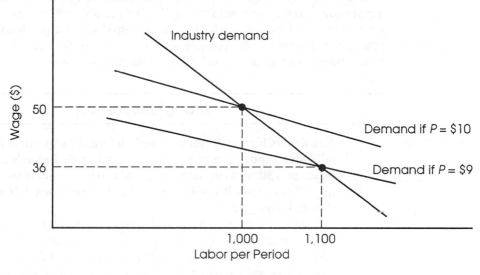

Figure 15.4

Points to note:
At $L = 1,000$, $P = \$10$ and $MP = 5$.
At $L = 1,100$, $P = \$9$ and $MP = 4$.
On the Price = $10 demand curve, $P \times MP = \$40$ at $L = 1,100$.
On the Price = $9 demand curve, $P \times MP = \$45$ at $L = 1,000$.
The industry demand curve is steeper than the price constant demand curves because in addition to MP falling as L goes up, the price is also falling as Q goes up.

LONG-RUN DEMAND FOR INPUTS

In the long run, competition forces firms to use the most cost-efficient combination of inputs. It will hire each input until its wage equals P times its MP (here, wage stands in for the price of whatever input we are talking about) or

$$\textbf{Wage} = \textbf{price} \times \textbf{\textit{MP}}$$

Suppose there are only two inputs, labor hours (L) and capital hours (K). The price of a labor hour is W (the hourly wage) and the hourly price of capital is R (which is the hourly cost to the firm of renting capital to itself). We should then have

$$W = P \times MP_L$$
$$R = P \times MP_K$$

243

where MP_L is the marginal product of labor and MP_K is the marginal product of capital. Solving out P, we have

$$\frac{MP_L}{W} = \frac{MP_K}{R}$$

What does equality say? On the left is the marginal product of labor per dollar. On the right is the marginal product of capital per dollar. The equality says to hire all inputs such that the last dollar spent on each yields the same increase in output. This is the *law of equiproportional benefits* as applied to inputs.

If this equality does not hold, the firm can get more output at the same cost by shifting spending to the input with the higher MP per dollar. Note that this equality only holds where the firm is minimizing the cost of producing output. It does not hold at any other point. Do not use this equality to solve for MP or W or R unless you are told the firm is being efficient or, equivalently, minimizing its costs.

Thought Question

The firm is hiring 10 workers and 20 units of capital. It faces the following input prices: $W = \$20$ and $R = \$40$. Labor's marginal product is 30, and capital's marginal product is 80. Is the firm being efficient (can it produce more at the same cost)? If not, how should it change?

I suggest setting up these problems in the format shown in Table 15.2. Reading the bottom column, it shows that capital offers a higher marginal product per dollar (2) than does labor (1.5). The firm can raise output without increasing its cost. Here's how. It can (a) buy one dollar less of labor (which will reduce output by 1.5 units) and then (b) buy one dollar more of capital (which will increase output by 2 units) such that (c) at the same total cost it gets on net 0.5 units more output![2]

Rewriting the equiproportional equation (equal MP per $), we have

$$\frac{W}{R} = \frac{MP_L}{MP_K}$$

This states that when the firm is efficiently producing output at its least cost, the ratio of input prices should equal the ratio of marginal products. So if labor costs twice as much as capital, labor should have twice the marginal productivity.

TABLE 15.2

Input	Labor	Capital
MP	30	80
Price of Input ($)	20	40
MP/Price of Input	1.5	2

In the long run, the demand for any input is described by the following formula:

$$L^D = Q^D \times \textbf{Labor per unit output}$$

---

[2]This is an approximation and assumes inputs are divisible and that output is proportionately affected by inputs over a small range of change in the inputs.

where L^D is the units of labor demanded by employers, Q^D is the units of output demanded, and labor per unit output is the number of workers the firm will hire to produce one unit of output when the firm is producing output at the least possible cost. The firm is employing labor efficiently when the law of equiproportional benefits holds.

The impact of any event on labor demand can be broken into the following effects.

1. The scale effect. This is the effect of the event on Q^D. The term *scale* comes from the *scale of production*. As an example, a higher price of capital will raise the price of a good produced. This in turn will reduce the quantity of Q demanded by consumers. The scale effect of this event will be to reduce the units of labor demanded in this industry in the long run.
2. The substitution effect. This is the effect of the event on labor per unit output. As an example, an increase in the price of capital will cause the firm to substitute labor for capital, raising the labor used per unit output. The substitution effect of this event will be to increase the units of labor demanded per unit Q.

As can be seen, an increase in the price of capital may increase or decrease labor demand, depending upon which effect is stronger. Empirically, in almost all cases, the scale effect dominates. A higher price of capital will on net reduce the labor demanded in a given industry.

What will happen if in a given industry wages and all input prices go up 10%? Scale effect: The price of output (which reflects costs in the long run) will go up 10%, and this will reduce the output demanded (Q^D). This is called a pure scale effect. Substitution effect: This will leave the labor per unit output unchanged as the ratio of W/R is unchanged (see the law of equiproportional benefits). Net effect: Labor demand will fall, as L goes down with Q.

What if, in a single industry, wages go up to 10%? Scale effect: The higher wage will increase costs. This in turn will increase the supply price. The price will go up and output demanded will fall[3]. Substitution effect: The firm will now find

$$\frac{MP_L}{W} < \frac{MP_K}{R}$$

Capital now has a higher MP per dollar, so the firm will substitute capital for labor! L/Q will fall. Net effect: A wage increase will cause labor demand to fall in the long run for two reasons: the scale effect (due to higher price) and the substitution effect (due to a higher ratio of wages to the price of other inputs).

Thought Questions

Use the following information for the widget industry to answer these questions.

Initially, $Q = 1,200$. For every dollar increase in the price of output, demand falls by 20 units.

If $W/R = 1$, widget firms use 3 units of labor and 2 units of capital to produce 1 widget.

If $W/R = 2$, the firms use 1.5 unit of labor and 4 units of capital to produce 1 widget.

Initially, $W = \$10$ and $R = \$10$.

---

[3]The increase in unit cost and price will be less than 10% because the price of other inputs is not changing in this example.

How many units of labor will be initially employed in the widget industry? What is the price of widgets (assume competition bids the price down to costs)?

3,600. Use $L = Q^D \times$ Labor per unit output. Because $W/R = 1$, the labor per unit output is 3 units. So $L = 1,200 \times 3 = 3,600$. The price of widgets equals its unit cost, which equals the cost of the inputs used to produce it: $50 (= \$10 \times 3 + \$10 \times 2)$.

If the wage goes up to $20, how many units of labor will now be employed?

1,200. Because $W/R = 2$, labor per unit output is 1.5. The price of output is now $70 (= \$20 \times 1.5 + \$10 \times 4)$. Because the price has gone up by $20, Q is reduced by 400 to 800. So $L = 800 \times 1.5 = 1,200$. Notice that if a firm did not change its mix of labor and capital, keeping it at 3 L and 2 K, its unit cost would be $80. Such firms would be driven from business.

If the wage and the price of capital both go to $20 a unit, what will employment now be?

600. Because $W/R = 1$, labor per unit output is 3. The price of output is $100 (when all input prices double, unit cost also doubles). Because the price has gone up (from the initial case) by $50, demand falls by 1,000 units from 1,200 to 200. So $L = 200 \times 3 = 600$. In this case, there is a scale effect but no substitution effect (because W/R is unchanged).

FACTORS SHIFTING THE DERIVED DEMAND CURVE FOR LABOR

Holding wages constant, with factors will increase or decrease the demand for labor, (thus shifting the curve right (increase) or left (decrease)? Table 15.3 shows the main factors. An increase in the output demanded increases the labor demanded.

TABLE 15.3

Factor	Shift in Factor	Shift in Derived Demand Curve
Output Demanded	Increase	Increase (shift to right)
	Decrease	Decrease (shift to left)
Price of	Increase	Decrease
Complementary Input	Decrease	Increase
Price of Substitute Input	Increase	Uncertain (increase if substitution effect bigger than scale effect)
	Decrease	Uncertain (decrease if substitution effect bigger than scale effect)
Change in Productivity for One Firm	Increase	Increase
	Decrease	Decrease
Change in Productivity for All Firms	Increase	Increase (if demand is elastic)
		Decrease (if demand is inelastic)

Complementary inputs are inputs used closely together, such that if the price of one goes up, the price of the pair goes up, causing the firm to demand less of both. Similarly, if the price of one goes down, the price of the pair goes down, and the firm demands more of both. The scale effect makes these effects even stronger. Examples of complementary inputs are trucks and their drivers along with chefs and ovens. Highly skilled workers and capital are complements. When high energy prices and high interest rates in the late 1970s made capital more expensive, the demand for highly skilled workers fell, as did their wages.

Substitute inputs are inputs that can be substituted for one another. Suppose that robots are substitutes for workers. When the price of robots goes up, the firm substitutes workers for robots (up to some point). This is the substitution effect. But the higher price for robots, since some will still be used, raises the price of output. This reduces the output demanded. This is the scale effect. Q is down, but labor per unit of output is up: The net effect is uncertain. Empirically, the scale effect usually is stronger.

If worker productivity (MP and AP) shifts up for one firm, its demand for labor goes up (because its demand curve reflects $P \times MP$). Note that when we say MP shifts up, we are holding L constant. An increase in productivity means the MP is higher for each and every L than it was before.

If worker productivity (MP and AP) shifts up for all firms in the industry, industry output must go up. This means the price will fall. What will the net effect on $P \times MP$ be? If demand is elastic, the lower price increases the industry's total revenue. In turn, this increases the amount spent on labor, raising labor demand. If demand is inelastic, the lower price reduces the industry's total revenue, decreasing what's being spent on labor and reducing labor demand. Empirically, the impact of greater productivity is to increase employment. This reflects the fact that for most industries, the demand for their output is price elasticity. A main exception is farming because the demand for food is inelastic. The growth of farm productivity has resulted in a decreased demand for farmers.

FACTORS AFFECTING THE ELASTICITY OF DERIVED DEMAND FOR INPUTS

$$
\frac{\text{Elasticity of}}{\text{input demand}} = \frac{\underline{\text{Percent change in quantity of input demanded}}}{\text{Percent change in input's price}}
$$

Both changes are stated in positive terms (this may differ from some textbooks, but this follows standard economics conventions). If wages go up 10% and labor demanded falls by 5%, the elasticity of labor demand is 0.5. If the elasticity of labor demand equals 1.5, a 10% increase in the wage reduces labor demanded by 15%.

When labor demand is elastic (greater than 1.0), an increase in the wage reduces total wages ($W \times L$). When labor demand is inelastic, an increase in the wage increases total wages ($W \times L$). It is not surprising that unions tend to be in industries where the demand for labor is inelastic.

Labor demand (or the demand for any input) is more elastic (the demand for labor curve is flatter) when:

1. *MP* falls less as the input increases. This makes the demand for labor curve (reflecting $P \times MP$) fall less. An input's MP tends to fall less when there are a large number of inputs it can substitute for.

2. The demand for output is more elastic. The more elastic output demand is, the less price falls when more output is sold. Thus, the labor demand curve (reflecting $P \times MP$) falls less.
3. It is easier to substitute other inputs for labor. For example, if workers and robots are close substitutes, then workers can be easily replaced by robots. Thus, a higher wage will reduce quantity of labor demanded dramatically. On the other hand, a lower wage will cause the firm to replace robots with workers. This makes the demand for labor more elastic.
4. The input's initial share of total cost is big. The bigger labor's share of cost is, the more the price will go up when the wage goes up. As an approximation:

**Percent change in price = Input's initial share of cost
× Percent change in input's price**

where the share is stated as a decimal (and not as a percent!).

For example, if labor's share is 25% and the wage goes up 10%, the price will go up approximately 2.5% (= 0.25 × 10%). If labor's share is bigger, say 75%, the same 10% wage increase will increase the price by 7.5% or three times as much. So when its share is bigger, the price goes up more and demand for output will fall by more. This makes labor demand more elastic. An exception occurs when there are close substitutes for labor (or whatever input we are talking about). But in general this rule holds. In fact, one of the main predictors of whether an industry will be unionized is labor's share of cost. The smaller labor's share of cost is, the more likely demand for labor is inelastic and the more likely the industry will be unionized.
5. The supply elasticity of other inputs is greater. Suppose aluminum and steel are close substitutes in the making of car engines. An increase in the price of steel will reduce the demand for steel as an input into making engines. But by how much? If aluminum is in elastic supply such that the auto industry can get more at the same or only slightly higher price, the demand for steel will fall a lot as aluminum is substituted for it. This makes the demand for steel by the auto industry more elastic. On the other hand, if aluminum is in inelastic supply (for example, if aluminum plants are currently running at capacity), then to substitute aluminum for steel means dramatically higher aluminum prices. Thus, the more inelastic the supply of aluminum is, the less of it will be substituted for steel when steel prices go up. In turn, this makes steel demand by the auto industry less elastic.
6. The industry has a longer period of time (the long run) to adjust to the higher price. The more time, the easier it is to make the changes necessary to adjust to using different inputs in different ratios.

MONOPOLY AND THE DEMAND FOR LABOR

Up to now, we've assumed that both input and output markets are competitive. If a firm is a monopoly in the market it sells its output in and a competitor in the market it buys its inputs in, then the only change we need to make is to replace price with marginal revenue in the marginal benefit of labor formula:

Marginal benefit to monopoly of labor = $MR \times MP$

Because $P > MR$, the monopoly's demand curve for labor will be vertically below a competitive firm's demand curve (whose demand curve reflects $P \times MP$). Also, the monopoly's demand curve for labor will likely be steeper as MR falls faster than price as

Q goes up. The result is that a monopoly will demand less labor. This makes sense because a monopoly also produces less.

The results derived previously for competitive firms also hold for monopolies: just replace P with MR.

Figure 15.5 compares the two cases:

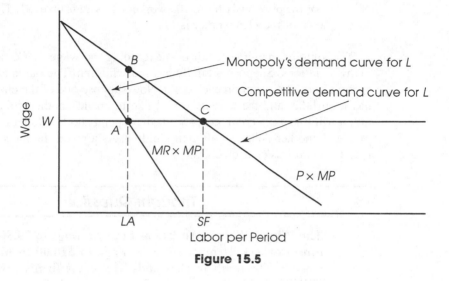

Figure 15.5

Points to note:

A monopoly will hire *LA* workers at wage *W.*

A competitive firm will hire *SF* workers at wage *W.*

The monopoly demand curve is steeper because *MR* falls faster than *P.*

The monopoly hires too few workers from a social point of view because the marginal benefit of workers to consumers ($P \times MP$) is, at the margin, above the social marginal cost of workers (W). The social loss (or deadweight cost) is area *ABC.*

Going from *LA* to *SF* makes society better off. At least, that's what people who moved from LA to SF tell me.

MONOPSONY

A monopsony is a sole buyer in an input market. They have such market power that when they hire more of the input, the input's price goes up. A key assumption we make is that the monopsony pays the same wage to all workers. For example, if it hires one worker for $5 but has to pay $6 to hire a second worker, we assume both workers get $6. As a result of this equal wage assumption, the marginal cost of an input to a monopsony exceeds its price. The basic equation is

Marginal factor cost of input = Price of input + Δ Price × Old amount of input

Thought Question

A firm currently hires 100 workers for $10 an hour. To hire another worker, it must raise the wage for all its workers to $10.01. What is the marginal cost of the 101th worker?

$11. The worker's wage is $10. Added to that is the one cent extra for the previously hired 100 workers: this adds up to $1. The marginal cost of the 11th worker is $11.

The logic of marginal factor cost exceeding the wage ($MFC > W$) can be seen in many situations. Suppose a family has four children. The parents, to be fair, agree to spend an equal amount on each child. Now suppose one of the children, little Roscoe, has a birthday and the parents would like to spend another dollar on Roscoe. How much will that extra dollar cost? $4! If they spend another dollar on Roscoe, they have to spend another dollar on all their children. As a result, families with more children tend to spend less on each child.

Thought Question

The Wiggly Widget Works has to pay a wage of $9.50 to attract nine workers. It must raise its wage to $10.00 to hire a tenth worker. The tenth worker adds $12 to the firm's revenue. Will WWW hire the tenth worker?

No. The marginal factor cost of hiring the tenth worker is $14.50, which equals the tenth worker's wage plus the $4.50 needed to raise the nine workers' wages to $10.00. The firm will not hire the worker. Not employing this worker represents a social loss of $2 because consumers value this worker's output as $12 and the worker's time cost is $10.

Figure 15.6 shows how the labor cost of a monopsony exceeds the wage.

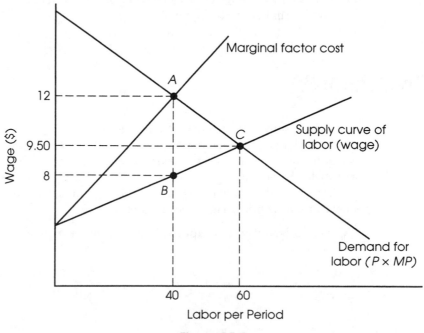

Figure 15.6

Points to note:

The monopsony hires 40 workers, going to point A where $MFC = P \times MP$ at $12.
MFC is the marginal factor cost.

The monopsony pays a wage of $8, this being at point B on the supply curve of labor.
The marginal factor cost ($12) exceeds the wage ($8).

If the monopsony acted competitively (treating the wage as its MFC), it would hire 60 workers at a wage of $9.50.

The social loss due to monopsony is area ABC, which equals $40 ($= \frac{1}{2} \times 20 \times \$4$, where $20 = 60 - 40$ and $4 = \$12 - \$8$).

One of the very standard test questions is to show the students Figure 15.6 and ask what wage will be paid. More often than not, they answer the wage at point A (in this case, $12). But no firm would pay more than $8 to hire 40 workers! The wage will always be on the supply curve of labor.

Thought Question

A firm faces the following supply curve of labor:

Labor	1	2	3	4	5	6	7	8
Wage	$5	$6	$7	$8	$9	$10	$10	$11

How many workers will it hire if all workers have a marginal product of 8 and the price of output is $2?

First, add the marginal factor cost column:

Labor	1	2	3	4	5	6	7	8
Wage	$5	$6	$7	$8	$9	$10	$11	$12
MFC	$5	$7	$9	$11	$13	$15	$17	$19

Points to Note:

The first labor's wage and MFC are the same (ask yourself why).

When the supply curve goes up in equal increments (here, by $1), the MFC goes up by twice as much (here, by $2).

The MFC can be derived by calculating the change in total wage costs at each level of employment. For example, at three workers, total wage costs are $21. At four workers, it's $32. The difference is $11, the MFC of the fourth worker.

The firm will hire six workers. Each worker's marginal benefit to the firm is $16 ($= P \times MP$). Up through six workers, each adds more to revenues ($16) than they cost ($MFC$) so the firm hires them. But the seventh and higher workers add more to cost than they do to revenues: The firm will not hire them.

MONOPSONY AND THE MINIMUM WAGE

If a firm is a monopsony, a carefully chosen minimum wage (between W and $P \times MP$ at the current L) can increase employment. How can it do this? Because the minimum wage makes the supply curve of labor that's seen by the monopsony look perfectly flat. This takes the Δ Wage term out of the MFC equation, making

$$MFC = \text{Minimum wage}$$

In Figure 15.6, a minimum wage set between $8 and $12 will increase employment. To determine how many workers will be employed, draw a horizontal line from the wage on the vertical axis and go to the first curve it hits (either the demand or supply curve). Ignore the *MFC* curve! For example, a minimum wage of $9.50 will cause the firm to hire 60 workers. In fact, this is the most workers a minimum wage can cause the firm to hire because the wage is set where the demand and supply curve cross. Any higher or lower wage will move employment below 60.

This logic also applies to a union. A union dealing with a monopsony can cause the monopsony to increase employment. But if the union (or minimum wage) is set too high, employment will be decreased. For example, in Figure 15.3, a wage of $14 will cause the firm to reduce employment below 40 workers.

Thought Questions

All workers have a $P \times MP$ of $20. The supply curve of labor facing a monopsony follows:

Labor	1	2	3	4	5	6	7	8
Wage	$10	$12	$14	$16	$18	$20	$22	$24

How many workers will the monopsony hire? What wage will it pay?

Adding an *MFC* column, we have

Labor	1	2	3	4	5	6	7	8
Wage	$10	$12	$14	$16	$18	$20	$22	$24
MFC	$10	$14	$18	$22	$26	$30	$34	$38

The firm will hire as long as $P \times MP \geq MFC$. It will hire three workers.

How many workers will it employ if the government imposes a minimum wage of $18? Of $24?

A minimum wage of $18 will cause the firm to hire five workers. A minimum wage of $18 causes the *MFC* of workers 1 through 5 to be $18. But worker 6, whose wage of $20 exceeds $18, has an *MFC* of $30. Similarly, workers 7 and 8 have their original *MFC*. A minimum wage of $24 will cause the firm to not hire any workers, as no worker brings in more than $20.

What minimum wage will maximize employment?

A minimum wage of $20 will cause the firm to hire six workers. Any higher minimum wage will reduce employment to zero because all workers have an $MB = P \times MP$ of $20.

THE FOURTH CASE: MONOPOLY AND MONOPSONY

This is the mother of all firms. In its output market, it sets the price. In its input market, it sets the wage. It has:

MB of added worker $= MR \times MP$ where $MR = P + \Delta P \times$ Prior Q
MC of added worker (MFC) = Wage $+ \Delta$Wage $\times$ Prior L

Figure 15.7 illustrates this and the previous three cases.

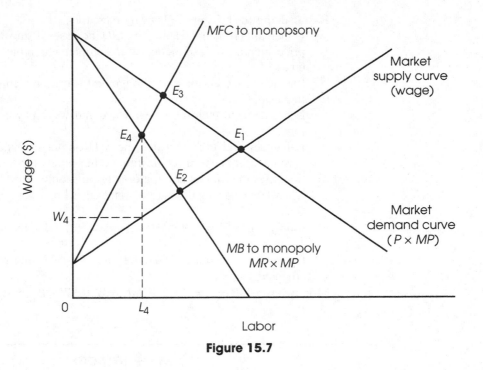

Figure 15.7

Points to note:

The monopoly plus monopsony firm goes to point E_4, hires L_4 workers at wage W_4.

If firms are competitive in both markets, the market will be at point E_1, where the market demand and supply curves cross.

If the firm is a monopoly but is competitive in the input market, it will be at point E_2.

If the firm is competitive in the output market but a monopsony in the input market, it will be at point E_3. Note that the wage it pays is on the supply curve, not the MFC curve.

Competition in both markets maximizes employment.

Competition in both markets maximizes wages.

CRIB NOTES

Monopoly: Single seller.

Monopsony: Single buyer.

Competitive firm: MB of $L = P \times MP$. $MFC = W$.

ΔProfit due to 1 more $L = P \times MP - W$.

Marginal hiring rule: Hire if $P \times MP \geq W$. Average hiring rule: $L > 0$ only if $P \times AP \geq W$ at optimal L.

Optimal L at $W = P \times MP$ or $W/P = MP$.

Short-run demand: Sum of firm demand, taking into account change in P.

Long-run demand for $L = Q^D \times$ Labor per unit Q.

Change in $Q =$ Scale effect.

Change in L per unit $Q =$ Substitution effect.

Law of equiproportional benefits: Firm is minimizing costs in long run if

$$\frac{MP_L}{W} = \frac{MP_K}{R}$$

Labor demand shifts up if Q or L/Q increases.

Q increases if demand shifts up. L/Q increases if substitute input price increases, L/Q increases if complement input price decreases.

Labor demand elastic (> 1): Wage and wage payments ($W \times L$) move opposite.

Labor demand inelastic (< 1): Wage and wage payments move together.

Labor demand more elastic when (1) output demand is more elastic, (2) it is easier to substitute other inputs for L in production, (3) other inputs are in more elastic supply, and (4) usually, when labor has small share of total cost. Point 4 is not always true.

Monopoly: MB of $L = MR \times MP =$ increase in TR due to one more L. $MC = W$.

Optimal L at $W = MR \times MP$. Because $P > MR$, hire less L than competitive firm.

Monopsony: MB of $L = P \times MP$. $MC = W + \Delta W \times L_{old} > W$.

Review Questions

1. Why do barbers in rural Brazil earn less than barbers in Brooklyn when both have the same marginal product?

2. What is the benefit of hiring one more worker?

3. Why does labor cost more to a monopsony?

4. Why does a competitive firm stop hiring workers?

5. Continuing question 4, what additional reason does a monopoly have to stop hiring workers? And what about a monopsony?

6. Fill in the following table. The firm is competitive in both input and output markets. The price of output is $10 and the wage is $50. How many workers will the firm hire?

Labor	Output	MP	Total Revenue ($)	Total Costs ($)	Profits ($)	Marginal Benefit of Worker ($)	Original Cost of Worker ($)
0	0	na	0	25	−25	na	
1	8						
2	15						
3	21						
4	26						
5	30						

7. Using the figures from the table in question 6, how many workers will the firm hire if the wage is $49? $51? $80? $70? $60? $40? Assume the firm can only hire a discrete number of workers.

8. If the wage doubles to $100 and the price doubles to $20, how will this change the answer to question 6? (Note that when we and most tests say the price doubles to $20, we mean the market demand curve has shifted up such that the firm can sell all the output it wants at $20. We do not mean the firm tries to sell its output at $20 when other firms are charging $10; in this latter case, it couldn't sell any output and would be out of business.)

9. At $L = 20$, Wobbly Widget Works, a competitive firm, the average worker produces 8 units and the 20th worker has a marginal worker product of 10 units. The marginal product is declining. The demand price for each unit is $10, and the wage is $90. Should the firm hire the 20th worker?

10. What is the hiring zone for this competitive firm?

L	1	2	3	4	5	6	7	8	9	10
Q	2	5	11	16	20	23	25	26	26	25
MP	2	3	6	5	4	3	2	1	0	−1
AP	2	2.5	3	4	4	3.83	3.57	3.25	2.9	2.5

11. The big boss boasts, "Our workers are producing the highest output per worker possible. We are the most efficient firm in the industry!" If you didn't care about your career, how would you shoot the big boss down?

12. There are 100 firms in the Wrangly Widget industry. For each firm, the first worker hired has a marginal product of 5, the next worker has a marginal product of 4, the third worker's MP is 3, and so on (worker 4's $MP = 2$ and worker 5's $MP = 1$). The demand function is

$$P^D = \$19 - 0.01 \times Q$$

Derive the demand curve for labor in this industry.

13. Suppose the industry in question 12 is taken over by a monopoly. Redo the table, replacing P with MR.

14. How will the following events shift the demand curve for labor in the Wispy Widget industry? Indicate the direction of the scale effect and the substitution effect.
    Event A: The price of electricity goes up. Electricity is a complement to labor in making wispy widgets.
    Event B: The price of electricity goes up. Electricity is a substitute to labor in making wispy widgets.
    Event C: The demand for widgets goes down.
    Event D: Productivity goes up, increasing MP and AP of widgets. Demand for widgets is elastic.
    Event E: The wage goes up.

15. A firm uses two inputs, labor and capital. An hour of labor has a marginal product of 26 while an hour of using capital has a marginal product of 10. Labor's hourly wage is $20. Capital's hourly cost is $10. Is the firm minimizing its costs? If not, should it reduce both labor and capital, reduce labor and increase capital, or increase labor and reduce capital?

16. A firm can hire 100 workers at a wage of $100 a week. It can hire 101 workers at a wage of $101 a week. What is the marginal factor cost of hiring the 101st worker?

17. A monopsony sells all its output at a price of $2. It faces the following table:

Labor	1	2	3	4	5	6	7	8
MP	10	9	8	7	6	5	4	3
W	1	2	3	4	5	6	7	8

   a. How many workers will it hire? What wage will it pay?
   b. If a minimum wage of $10 is imposed, how many workers will it hire?
   c. What minimum wage will maximize total employment?

18. A school system has a policy of paying all teachers the same salary, regardless of the fields in which they teach. One out of five teachers it employs is a science teacher. Assume that if the school system pays a wage that's below the average wage in a field, it will have to settle for lower quality teachers. Suppose there is an increase in demand for scientists, such that their market wages go up. The school system investigates whether it should raise the wages of its science teachers in order to remain competitive or whether it should settle for a lower quality of science teacher. If the cost of attracting the quality of science teachers it wants is an increase in their salary of $6,000 a year, then what is the *MFC* of getting better science teachers?

19. How will the following events affect the wage elasticity of labor demand in the U.S. textile industry?
   Event A: Textile firms set up numerous plants, allowing them, if need be, to shift employment from domestic workers to foreign workers.
   Event B: The supply elasticity of other inputs increases as the plants and farms supplying other inputs increase their capacity.
   Event C: A change toward more capital-intensive technologies results in labor having a smaller share in total costs.
   Event D: Due to foreign competition, the demand for domestic textiles becomes more elastic.
   Event E: Textile plants move to more rural areas, where the supply of managers is more inelastic.

Answers

1. Wages reflect $P \times MP$. Even though MP may be the same, the P for a haircut is lower in rural Brazil. That is, consumers in rural Brazil, having a lower average income, place a lower value on haircuts. As a result, the derived demand for haircuts is lower in rural Brazil.
2. The amount they add to total revenue. If the firm is competitive, this equals $P \times MP$. If the firm is a monopoly, this equals $MR \times MP$.
3. The wage is the same to a monopsony as it is to a competitive employer. But the cost of hiring another worker is higher to a monopsony because it is facing a rising supply curve of labor. If it hires another worker, it has to pay that worker his wage plus raise the wage for all its other workers. It is the equal wage for all workers assumption plus the rising supply curve that makes a monopsony's $MFC > W$.
4. Because the MP declines. As long as $P \times MP \geq W$, the competitive firm keeps hiring workers. Because P and W stay the same as the firm expands, the only thing that can change in this equation is the marginal product. As the firm hires more workers, MP falls. At some point, it falls so low, that for an added worker, $P \times MP < W$. This worker and any other added workers are not hired. If MP did not decline, the firm would be willing to hire all the workers in the universe.

5. In addition to declining *MP*, the monopoly also faces a declining *P* and *MR*! Because it values workers at *MR* × *MP*, it doesn't hire when an added worker has *MR* × *MP* < *W*. A monopsony, in contrast, faces a rising wage. It doesn't add a worker when *P* × *MP* < *MFC*.

6.

Labor	Output	MP	Total Revenue ($)	Total Costs ($)	Profits ($)	Marginal Benefit of Worker ($)	Original Cost of Worker ($)
0	0	na	0	25	−25	na	50
1	8	8	80	75	5	80	50
2	15	7	150	125	25	70	50
3	21	6	210	175	35	60	50
4	26	5	260	225	35	50	50
5	30	4	300	275	25	40	50

Points to note:

The change in *TR* equals the marginal benefit of the worker.
The marginal benefit of the worker equals *P* × *MP* (in this competitive case!).
The marginal cost of each added worker is the wage.
The change in profits equals *MB* − *MC* of each added worker.

The firm will hire four workers, maximizing profits at $35. It could also hire three workers and get the same profit. We call the time at *L* = 4 because the workers' marginal benefit ($50) covers their marginal cost ($50).

7. The firm hires as long as *P* × *MP* ≥ *W*.
   At *W* = $49, *L* = 4.
   At *W* = $51, *L* = 3.
   At *W* = $80, *L* = 1.
   At *W* = $70, *L* = 2.
   At *W* = $60, *L* = 3.
   At *W* = $40, *L* = 5.
   Notice how the marginal benefit column is the firm's demand curve for labor.

8. The firm will still hire four workers. Nothing changes in terms of output or employment. That's because the marginal hiring condition is *MP* ≥ *W/P*. Doubling *W* and *P* leaves *W/P* unchanged, thus leaving the number of workers whose marginal product meets this condition unchanged.

9. No. Even though the worker meets the marginal hiring condition (*P* × *MP* ≥ *W*), she fails to meet the average hiring condition. The average worker is producing $80 worth of goods but costs the firm $90. Because the marginal product is diminishing, the firm's maximum *AP* will be below 10 units. The firm should hire no workers! It is not even covering its wage costs.

10. From five workers (where *AP* = *MP* and *MP* is declining) to nine workers (where *MP* = 0). This firm would pay at most a wage that is four times its price and hire five workers. Any higher wage and it would be better off shutting down. If the wage is zero, it will hire nine workers.

11. You would point out that the goal is to maximize profits, not productivity. If the firm is maximizing profits, it should be in the zone where marginal and average product are falling. Thus, it should not be where average product is highest. Going on, as you pull out a chart, you give this example.

Labor	1	2	3	4
Output	4	10	12	12
AP	4	5	4	3
MP	4	6	2	0

If $W = \$4$ and $P = \$10$, the firm will maximize profits by hiring three workers. Profits will equal $108. If it maximized average product, it would hire two workers. Its profits would be less, only $92.

12. The demand for labor reflects marginal benefit to the firm ($P \times MP$). So we assume all firms hire the same number of workers and calculate P and MP.

Labor	MP	q-firm	Q-Industry	Price ($)	$P \times MP$ Industry ($)
100	5	5	500	14	60
200	4	9	900	10	40
300	3	12	1,200	7	21
400	2	14	1,400	5	10
500	1	15	1,500	4	4

Points to note:

When each firm employs 1 worker, the industry employs 100 workers. Hence, the first column.

Q-Industry equals q-firms $\times$ 100, where 100 is the number of firms. Recall that we assume all firms act alike.

The price comes from substituting Q-Industry into the demand (P^D) equation. For example, when Q equals 1,200, $P^D = \$19 - 0.01 \times 1,200 = \$7$.

The industry's demand curve for labor is the last column, $P \times MP$. At a wage of $60, the industry will employ 100 workers. At a wage of $40, the industry will employ 200 workers. At a wage of $21, 300 workers will be employed.

This question shows that industry demand for labor falls because of diminishing marginal product and a falling price needed to sell the larger output.

13. Go back to the monopoly chapter. Recall that the marginal revenue starts at the same place as the price but falls twice as fast (this is true only for straight-line demand curves). So we have $MR = \$19 - 0.02 \times Q$. The new table follows:

Labor	MP	q-firm	Q-Industry	MR ($)	$MR \times MP$ Industry ($)
100	5	5	500	9	45
200	4	9	900	1	4
300	3	12	1,200	-5	-15
400	2	14	1,400	-9	-18
500	1	15	1,500	-11	-11

The last column shows points on the monopoly's demand curve for labor.

14. Event A: The demand for labor will go down (shift left). The scale effect is negative (the price of labor goes up and Q demanded goes down). The substitution effect is also negative (the rise in the price of a complement reduces the amount of labor per unit output).

Event B: The demand for labor may go up or down. The scale effect is negative (P goes up and Q demanded falls), but the substitution effect is positive (the rise in the price of a substitution increases the labor per unit output).

Event C: The demand for labor goes down (shifts left). The scale effect is negative (the Q demanded falls). There is no substitution effect (this event does not change the ratio of the wage to the other input prices).

Event D: The demand for labor goes up (shifts right). The scale effect is positive (greater productivity lowers the price of supplying widgets, which in turn increases the Q sold). On the other hand, an increase in productivity means Q/L is now higher. Turning Q/L upside down, this means the amount of labor per unit output (L/Q) is going down.[4] The net effect of these two events is positive when the demand for output is elastic. If demand were inelastic, the net effect would be negative.

Event E: This event does not shift the demand for labor curve. Instead, the demand for labor curve shows the impact of a change in the wage on employment! A higher wage has a negative scale effect (it increases the price and reduces the Q consumers buy) and a negative substitution effect (the firm substitutes other inputs for labor).

15. Set up the table like we did in this chapter:

Input	Labor	Capital
MP	26	10
Price of Input ($)	20	10
MP/Price of Input	1.3	1

The firm is not minimizing its cost because it is not getting the same MP per dollar from both labor and capital. Because labor has the higher MP per dollar, it should employ more labor and less capital. For example, $1 taken from L and spent on K will increase Q by a net of 0.3 unit while leaving the total cost unchanged. The answer "hires less labor and capital" is wrong because if the firm is fully utilizing all inputs, when it hires fewer of all inputs, it can't produce its current output at any cost! If it gets rid of one input, it must hire more of another to continue to produce the current output.

16. $201. This equals its wage of $101 plus the $100 needed to raise the other 100 workers' wages by $1. An alternative method of deriving the results is to simply calculate the total wage cost in each case ($101 × 101 versus $100 × 100) and calculate the increase. In this case, we have $201 = $10,201 − $10,000.

17. Adding the MB and the MFC of labor to the monopoly to this table, we have the following table:

Labor	1	2	3	4	5	6	7	8
MP	10	9	8	7	6	5	4	3
W ($)	1	2	3	4	5	6	7	8
MB = P × MP ($)	20	18	16	14	12	10	8	6
MFC ($)	1	3	5	7	9	11	13	15

a. $L = 5$. The monopsony will hire as long as $MB \geq MFC$. At $L = 5$, $W = \$5$.

b. $L = 6$. Replace the MFC column with $10.

c. $W = \$8$ or $W = \$7$ will maximize employment at $L = 7$. Any higher or lower minimum wage will reduce employment below seven workers.

18. $30,000 per better science teacher. $6,000 more for each science teacher plus $24,000 for the $6,000 raise given to each of the four other nonscience teachers.

---

[4]This is not a substitution effect, because an increase in productivity means the firm is getting more output for its existing inputs. Thus, it needs fewer of all inputs to produce a given amount of output. No input is being substituted for another. So we'll call this a productivity effect.

This problem illustrates why a policy of equal pay penalizes hiring better people in selected positions. It also shows why the public school system is set up to get the lowest quality of teachers in the fields where demand is highest.

19. Event A: More elastic. U.S. textile labor now has a close substitution in production: foreign textile labor.

   Event B: More elastic.

   Event C: Less elastic (in most cases).

   Event D: More elastic.

   Event E: More inelastic.

Chapter Sixteen

Labor Markets

INTRODUCTION

The price of a can of beans is pretty much the same around the nation. Similarly, the price of a high-quality wrench is pretty much the same no matter where you go. Yet, the price of labor varies widely, even in local markets. Of course, wages vary by skill level. But even after accounting for differences in skills, wages still differ dramatically. Why is this so? Why does labor's price, of all inputs, vary so much? That is the key question in this chapter.

A MODEL WHERE WAGES ARE THE SAME

In economics as well as in math, a key method of thinking about a problem is to create a set of assumptions that results in the problem not existing. Why do this? Because we then know that the cause of the problem must come from one or more of the assumptions being wrong. This allows us to focus our attention on the likely causes of the problem.

The problem we have is, Why do wages differ even for workers of similar skills and talents? So let us now create a model where all equally skilled workers get the same wage! Assumptions:

1. All workers are equally skilled.
2. All jobs are exactly alike in nonwage amenities, having the same fringe benefits, working conditions, distance to work, and so on.
3. There is competition among workers and among employers.
4. Employers want to maximize profits.
5. Workers can change jobs quickly and at no cost; similarly, employers can change workers quickly and at no cost.
6. Workers are well informed at to what jobs pay.

Result: All jobs will pay the same wage. This wage will be the market wage where the demand for labor equals the supply of labor.

Proof: If a firm pays below the market wage, all its workers will quit, and it will go out of business.

If a firm pays above the market wage, it will have a surplus of applicants, so it can lower its wage and still have workers until the wage reaches the market level.

Therefore, all firms will pay the same wage.

This result is called the law of one price: In competitive markets, one price tends to emerge for a given type of good or input. Figure 16.1 illustrates this result.

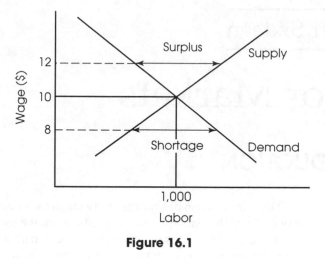

Figure 16.1

Points to note:

The market-clearing wage is $10, and 1,000 workers are employed.

If the market or one firm pays a higher wage (for example, $12), there is a surplus of workers over jobs. The resulting competition between workers will bid the wage back to $10.

If the market (or one firm) pays too little (for example, $8), there is a shortage of workers relative to jobs. The resulting competition among employers bids the wage back up to $10.

An individual firm can tell if it is paying too little if its quit rate is too high and its application rate is too low.

An individual firm can tell if it is paying too much if its quit rate is too low and its application rate is too high.

MODIFYING THE MODEL TO EXPLAIN WHY WAGES DIFFER

Now we will modify each assumption and see how its modification may make wages differ. Note that as we modify each assumption, we assume the others still hold.

Modified Assumption 1: Workers differ in skills. Doctors make more than street sweepers because consumers value more the skills of doctors.

Modified Assumption 2: Jobs differ in nonwage amenities. Competition will cause the differences in money wages to just be offset by the differences in nonwage amenities. This result is called the theory of *compensating differentials*. Each job pays a full wage such that

Full wage = Money wage + Nonmoney wage

where the nonmoney wage is the dollar value workers place on fringe benefits, working conditions, job safety, commuting time, and other job-related amenities. In the model of compensating differentials, the result is that all jobs pay the same full wage, and so

Differences in money wages = – Differences in nonmoney wages

Thought Question

Job A and Job B are exactly alike except that Job A has a health care plan worth $5 an hour to workers and Job B has a health care plan worth $2 an hour to workers. If differences in wages reflect a compensating differential and Job A pays a money wage of $10 an hour, what does Job B pay? Which job will workers prefer?

Job B pays $13. It must pay $3 more in money wages to make up for $3 less in health care benefits. Workers are indifferent between these two jobs because both pay the same full wage ($15).

Modified Assumption 3: Workers or employers collude. Worker collusion in the form of unions is common. Union workers earn about 10% more than nonunion workers of the same skill. Employer collusion is less common. One example is that colleges collude to pay their student athletes a wage of zero. In this case, a student athlete might earn nothing while a similarly skilled professional athlete could earn millions.

Modified Assumption 4: Employers discriminate among workers (and don't maximize profits by hiring only the cheapest). Discrimination results in certain groups earning more. Because this is an important problem, we'll discuss discrimination in more detail later in the chapter.

Modified Assumption 5: Frictions prevent wage equality. Moving costs, retraining costs, and many other costs reduce the mobility of workers between jobs. This slows and sometimes prevent wages from converging. Studies of income differences between states shows that incomes do converge over time, but at a very slow pace of about 2% a year.

Modified Assumption 6: Workers are poorly informed about better jobs. The main way workers learn about available jobs is from other workers. Those workers out of the loop are likely to end up with lower wages because they don't hear about the good jobs. This applies more to lower-wage jobs because firms with high-wage jobs usually can afford to widely advertise their openings. Search theory models how workers find out about jobs and seek out openings. The result is that wages will vary more when the cost of searching for jobs is higher.

MODELS OF SKILL DIFFERENCES

One of the main sources of wage differences is differences in skills. Two of the main models of skills are described next.

Model 1: Human Capital

Human capital is a set of skills that a worker acquires through school and on the job. Because acquiring these skills is costly, workers will only learn these skills if they pay more. Thus, the human capital model predicts that in the long run the wage differential for different school levels will reflect their costs. Like all capital, learning a skill has an up-front cost. This up-front cost includes direct costs, which are out-of-pocket expenses such as tuition and books, plus indirect costs, which are mainly the foregone wages one could have earned had one not attended school (or the foregone value of leisure time if that is what was given up to attend school).

Like all capital, skills pay off over many years. In the case of human capital, this payoff is in the form of higher wages (or if the employer is making the investment in training, in the form of higher productivity). Education thus can be evaluated in terms of its yield on percent rate of return. Over the years, the rate of return to education is on the order of 7%, after subtracting out the effects of inflation. Compared to other investments, that's a good rate of return. (Currently, the rate of return to college is much higher.)

Thought Question

Sharon decides to get a one-year MBA. The tuition costs and other direct costs add up to $18,000. Had she instead gone to work directly from college, she would have earned $22,000. If she gets the MBA, her earnings will be $4,000 a year higher than what she would have earned from the college degree. What is the rate of return on the MBA? Use the approximation (good if she works more than 20 years) of

$$\text{Rate of return (\%)} = \frac{\text{Increase in earnings due to added education} \times 100}{\text{Total cost of added education}}$$

Ten percent. The increase in earnings is $4,000. The total cost of education is the direct cost plus the indirect cost of foregone earnings, or $40,000 (= $18,000 + $22,000). So the rate of return is 10% (= [$4,000 / $40,000] × 100).

Model 2: Noncompeting Groups

A noncompeting group is a set of workers with skills that can't be duplicated (at least in the short run). As a result, an increase in demand can leave them with a higher wage than similar workers. For example, when oil prices went up, the salaries of oil geologists skyrocketed into the hundreds of thousands. For a few years, these geologists were a noncompeting group. At that time, they were few in number and it took years to become a skilled oil geologist. As a result, they had it very good.

Sometimes the noncompeting group is a group of people with natural skills or traits possessed by no other people. It is estimated, for example, that beautiful people earn about 15% more per year in sales and other people-oriented careers.

EFFICIENCY WAGE MODELS

In efficiency wage models, higher wages cause workers to become more productive. One of the earlier models focused on poor countries where the higher wage allowed workers to buy food and thus become stronger and more productive workers. Later models pointed out that a higher wage might pay for itself by reducing turnover costs (turnover costs are the costs associated with replacing the workers who quit or who are fired). Still another model, the shirking model, argued that paying workers a higher wage than they could get elsewhere gave them an incentive to want to keep their current job. Such workers would be more motivated to not shirk on the job because the fear and cost of getting fired is greater. The firm saves money in this case by not having to supervise workers as much. One study showed that workers in large plants are paid 10% more than they are in smaller plants. It may be that monitoring is harder in larger plants and the 10% premium keeps workers in line.

DISCRIMINATION

Discrimination occurs when two workers who are equally productive are paid different wages (or offered different opportunities for working and advancement).

The key question to ask is, Why would an employer discriminate? That is, why would an employer hire the higher-wage worker at all? Suppose there are only two types of workers, those with red hair and those with brown hair. Otherwise, they are identical and equally productive. If we observe red-haired workers being paid $3 more per hour, then it follows that employers could have saved $3 an hour by hiring only brown-haired workers. So why would employers pay more for red-haired workers? The economic answer must be that someone dislikes brown-haired workers.[1]

The economic consequences of discrimination depend upon who is discriminating. Let's examine each case assuming brown-haired workers are discriminated against.

Who Discriminates: Customers

Brown-haired workers will earn less in jobs that directly deal with customers. To get customers to accept working with them, they have to, in effect, pay the customers by offering to work for less than the equally efficient red-haired workers. On the other hand, in jobs where the customers can't tell who is producing the good—which is for most retail products—discrimination by customers couldn't exist.

Evidence: Better-looking people earn about 15% more than ugly people in occupations where they directly deal with people, such as real estate agents, layers, stockbrokers, and other service-type jobs. They have less of an advantage in other jobs.

Who Discriminates: Employers

Impact 1: Brown-haired workers will earn less in all jobs. To get employers to hire them, they have to accept a lower wage. For example, suppose all employers dislike working with brown-haired workers by $1 an hour per brown-haired worker. If red-haired workers earn $10 an hour, brown-haired workers would have to accept a wage of $9 an hour. Note that if brown-haired workers have a wage of $8.50, all employers would hire brown-haired workers! They are being more than compensated for their distaste! Let $D = \$$ dislike for brown-haired workers (per hour). D is called the discrimination coefficient. It reflects by how much employers dislike the group being discriminated against. What employers care about is not the wage of the worker, but the net wage, after accounting for their dislikes:

Net wage of brown-haired worker to employer
= Brown-haired worker's wage + D

In equilibrium, all workers will be paid with the same net wage to employers (so that all can get jobs) so we'll have

Brown-haired worker's wage = Red-haired worker's wage − D

---

[1]Equivalently, they may like red-haired workers. In terms of discrimination, it does not matter whether someone likes X or dislikes non-Xs. The effect is the same. We'll treat the dislike version.

Thought Question

An employer's *D* for brown-haired workers is $4. That is how much they dislike having them around. If red-haired workers earn $20 an hour, then what wage will entice this employer to hire the brown-haired workers?

$16. At $16, the employer is indifferent between hiring the red-haired worker at $20 or the brown-haired worker at $16. That's because both then have a net of $20. If brown-haired workers earn a wage below $16, this employer will prefer to hire all brown-haired workers because they are then cheaper!

Evidence: After accounting for the main factors affecting a worker's productivity (such as job experience and schooling), women and blacks earn less than white males. These results may reflect our inability to account for all the factors affecting productivity. But this persistence across data sets and time suggests otherwise. One study of people having sex change operations found that men who became women earned less while women who became men earned more than before.

Impact 2: As a group that's discriminated against gets larger, their pay will get lower. Employers are likely to differ in the degree they discriminate. In terms of our model, the *D* differs from employer to employer. Unbiased employers have a *D* of zero. Those who are very biased have a big *D*. Brown-haired workers seek out employers with the smallest *D* because they will get higher wages with these employers. But if more brown-haired workers enter the work force, they will have to take a still lower wage to get the more discriminating employers to hire them.

Thought Question

There are five employers, each with one job. Red-haired workers are paid a wage of $10 an hour. The discrimination coefficient, *D*, for these employers are

Employer	M	N	O	P	Q
D	$1	$2	$4	$4.50	$6

If there is one brown-haired worker, what will her wage be? If there are two? Three? In each case, who will they work for?

The following shows the highest wage each employer is willing to pay brown-haired workers:

Employer	M	N	O	P	Q
D	$1	$2	$4	$4.50	$6
Highest Wage	$9	$8	$6	$5.50	$4

If there is only one brown-haired worker, she will work for employer M and get a wage of $9. If there are two, the wage of brown-haired workers will sink to $8. This lower wage is necessary to get employer N to hire the second brown-haired worker. Note that in this case, employer M will also pay $8! While they did pay up to $9, when there are two brown-haired workers, they can lower the wage to $8. When there are three brown-haired workers, the wage will be $6, and they will work for employers M, N, and O.

Impact 3: Discrimination should be eliminated in the long run in competitive industries. If some employers don't discriminate, as seems likely, they will have lower costs because, in this case, they are not hiring the high-priced red-haired workers. Their lower costs will allow them to underprice the discriminating employers and, in the long run, drive them from business.

Evidence: Even though the degree of discrimination against blacks has fallen (even before the antidiscrimination laws were passed), discrimination still persists. This suggests that employers are not the source of discrimination. We've also seen that customers can't be guilty for most jobs (because they can't tell who made the good). So who is left?

Comment: Most texts only consider discrimination by employers. The next case is presented in the interest of discovering the source of discrimination.

Who Discriminates: Employees

Case 1: Employees are substitutes.

Impact: Workers will get the same wage but work in separate workplaces. To see why, suppose red-haired workers dislike brown-haired workers. Any employer mixing red-haired workers with brown-haired workers will have to pay more to the red-haired employees, thereby raising their cost. Thus, it is cheaper to separate the two groups.

Case 2: Employees are complements.

Impact: Brown-haired workers could earn less, and competition would not cause discrimination to be eliminated. To illustrate this case, suppose managers are complements to workers (each is needed in a certain ratio to produce output). Suppose all managerial jobs are filled with red-haired workers. In addition, assume that red-haired workers dislike supervising brown-haired workers (or alternatively, they prefer supervising their "own kind," red-haired workers). If an employer hires brown-haired workers, they must pay their managers more. Thus, if brown-haired workers are to get jobs, they must work for less. On net, their lowered pay must compensate the employer for the higher pay of the supervisors. Conversely, an employer hiring red-haired workers is willing to pay them more because they can then pay their managers less. Because all employers (those with red-haired workers and those with brown-haired workers) all have the same cost, competition will not get rid of discrimination.

Evidence: This model is consistent with discrimination existing in the long run and being unaffected by competition. Some studies show that managerial pay is higher when managers work with a predominantly black workforce.

Differences in pay may accurately reflect the worker's productivity and yet be the result of other types of discrimination discussed previously. One model of this is the case of the self-fulfilling prophecy. Suppose that it is commonly believed that red-haired children are more clever (even if this is not true). As a result, they are given more math and science courses. Furthermore, the red-haired children themselves believe they are better and so drive themselves harder. The result is that they become more clever and productive and earn higher wages. Then, the discrimination becomes reinforcing because red-haired workers are, in fact, more clever.

UNIONS

Unions are institutions that have the right to set the wage (as well as other working conditions) for all workers employed by the firms they have organized. No worker has the right to underbid the wage the union sets. Historically, union wages have been about 10% higher than nonunion wages.

A union faces the industry's demand for labor curve. The higher the wage it wants, the fewer the jobs its members will have. Figure 16.2 shows this case. The nonunion wage in this industry would have been $10, where the demand curve meets the supply curve. But the union can set the wage higher. A wage of $12 an hour, for example, results in $2 more in wages but, in this case, 3,000 fewer jobs. In this example, a 20% wage increase results in 6% fewer jobs. This fits a wage elasticity of labor demand of 0.3, which is the average elasticity we observe.

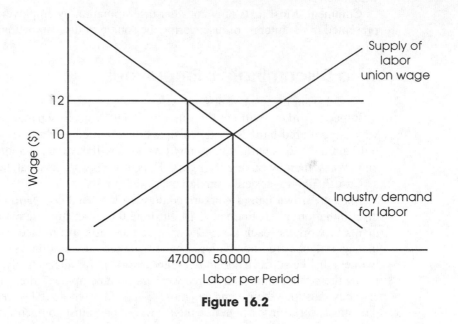

Figure 16.2

FACTORS FAVORING UNIONS

In general, unions tend to be in industries where the demand for labor is inelastic. When labor demand is more inelastic, a higher wage results in fewer jobs being lost. The job loss will be smaller, the smaller the wage elasticity of labor demand is. In the previous chapter, we reviewed the elements that make the wage elasticity of labor demand smaller (or more inelastic): a smaller cost share for labor, a lower price elasticity of output demand, and a reduced ease of substituting other inputs for union labor. Of these factors, cost share is most important: Unions are almost always in capital-intensive industries where labor's share of cost (measured before the wage is increased) is small.

Competition from nonunion firms can also result in union job losses. As a consequence, unions tend to survive best in industries with high barriers to entry for new firms. This prevents new (nonunion) firms from entering and bidding down the wage. An example of this is the longshoreman's union: After they unionized all the docks on the few bays where ships can easily unload, no new firms could enter! The lowest-wage longshoremen now earn $77,000 a year. An example going the other way is the deregulation of the airlines: Competition has weakened the hold of the pilot's unions. As a result, pilot wages have fallen.

IMPACT OF UNIONS ON NONUNION WORKERS' WAGES

Unions have two main effects on nonunion wages.

The Spill-Over Effect

The spill-over effect occurs when unions, by decreasing employment in the union jobs, cause the disemployed workers to seek jobs in the nonunion sector, with the result that nonunion wages are lower. In Figure 16.2, 3,000 union workers lost their jobs. They will spill over into the nonunion sector and seek jobs there. This added supply reduces the nonunion wage.

The Wage Threat Effect

The wage threat effect occurs when nonunion firms raise wages to avoid being unionized. This generally occurs for nonunion plants and firms in highly unionized industries that are most threatened by unionization. For example, the Saturn plant in General Motors is nonunion but pays union wages.

Which effect predominates? If the wage threat effect predominated, such that all wages, union and nonunion, were increased, then we would witness massive unemployment! This has occurred in Europe, which has experienced high union wage increases and high unemployment in recent years. But in the United States, this pattern has not been observed. We can conclude that the spill-over effect predominates for the nation. Most likely, the threat effect predominates only in highly unionized industries and areas.

UNIONS AND MONOPSONISTIC EMPLOYERS

When employers are monopsonies, a union can increase employment at the same time it increases the wage. We saw this is true for minimum wage. The following problem illustrates this case.

Thought Questions

The marginal benefit (marginal revenue product) of each worker for the Acme Widget Company is $20 for the first worker, $19 for the second, $18 for the third, and so forth (decreasing $1 for each added worker). If one worker is employed, it pays a wage of $2. If two workers are employed, it pays a wage of $4 to both; when it employs three workers, the wage rises to $6 per worker. As it employs each successive worker, the wage continues to rise by $2.

Table 16.1 shows the marginal benefit (marginal revenue product, *MRP*) and marginal cost (marginal factor cost, *MFC*) of hiring a worker.

TABLE 16.1

Labor	1	2	3	4	5	6	7	8
MB of L: MRP ($)	20	18	16	14	12	10	8	6
Supply Wage ($)	2	4	6	8	10	12	14	16
MC of L: MFC ($)	2	6	10	14	18	22	26	30

How many workers will a monopsony hire?

The firm will hire four workers, where $MB = MC$ of labor. It will pay a wage of $8. (Be sure you understand why the wage is below the MC of labor!)

Suppose Acme is unionized. What union wage would maximize employment?

The union can increase the wage and increase employment as long as its wage is between (or equals) the MRP and the supply wage. A union wage of $12 is the highest wage it can pay to get the highest possible level of employment of five workers. A wage of $12.01 would reduce employment to four workers. A wage below $10.00 will cause only four workers to want to work.

What is the highest wage that the union can demand without reducing employment below the initial level in the first question?

At the level of employment in the first question of four workers, the MRP is $14. This is the highest wage the union can demand without reducing employment to three workers.

Now let us answer the same questions for Figure 16.3

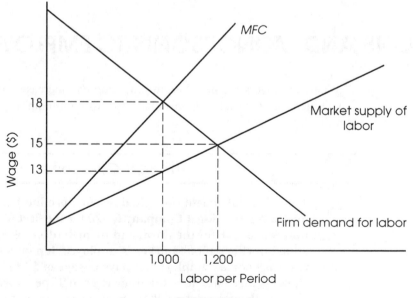

Figure 16.3

In the absence of a union, the wage will be $13, and employment will be 1,000 workers. Also, at 1,000 workers, the $MRP = MFC = $18.

The union can maximize employment at $15 and $L = 1,200$ workers. At a higher wage, the higher wage moves along the demand curve of labor curve and moves employment below 1,200 workers. At a lower wage, the higher wage moves along the market supply curve of labor, reducing labor supply (and employment) below 1,200 workers.

At $L = 1,000$ (the level in the first question), the union can demand a wage of $18. The wage of $18 becomes the new marginal cost of labor for the firm, and it will hire 1,000 workers. A higher wage will reduce employment below 1,000 workers. So watch out! It is false to say on a true-false question, "A union facing a monopsony will cause employment to go up." I, of course, would never stoop to try to trick you with such a petty question, but your teacher might.

THE SUPPLY OF LABOR

So far, we have focused on why wages differ from worker to worker. Now we turn to another topic: the supply of the hours of work by individuals. In this section, when we speak of the wage, we are referring to the market hourly wage being paid to all workers. This is an important point. If only one firm raises its hourly wage above that being paid by other firms, then it can always demand that its workers work more hours. On the other hand, if all firms raise their wages, they may find that they are forced to reduce their workers' hours of work (otherwise, their workers will quit). In this case, we say that labor supply may be backward-bending, going down when the market wage goes up.

In the past 100 years, real wages have increased dramatically. As a result, male workers have worked fewer hours per week. In 1900, the average work week was 55 hours; today it is around 40 hours. Even though the work week has not shrunk appreciably since 1950, the weeks worked has continued to shrink. In contrast to this pattern for males, women have responded to higher wages by working longer hours per week, per year, and per lifetime.

Why these divergent results? To answer this question, we need to ask the question of what determines how many hours a person wants to work. Economists of course do the opposite. We ask, What determines the number of hours a person does not want to work? We call, for antiquated reasons, nonwork hours *leisure*. Leisure time is just non-work time. Leisure time can be spent resting, or it can be spent working hard at scrubbing floors, cooking dinner, and cleaning clothes. Since in a given day, work hours + leisure hours = 24 hours, an hour more of leisure means one hour less of work!

The demand for leisure is determined the same way as the demand for any other good. Its price is the wage the worker earns. The worker buys one more hour of leisure by working one less hour. Thus, if a worker earns $12 an hour, then buying another hour of leisure has a price of $12 in foregone wages. When the price of any good goes up, recall that this has a substitution effect (as a result of the higher relative price of the good) and an income effect (as a result of the change in the worker's income). What is different about the demand for leisure is that an increase in its price (that is, an increase in the worker's wage) increases income! Just as an increase in the price of orange juice can cause an orange grove owner to buy more orange juice, so it is that an increase in the wage can cause a worker (who owns time) to buy more leisure and work less!

A change in the wage has two effects.

Effect 1: Income effect—Leisure is a normal good. Thus, when income goes up, workers demand more leisure and work fewer hours. The income effect of a higher wage is to decrease work hours; the income effect of a lowered wage is to increase work hours. Sometimes, people get more income without an increase in the wage. For example, they win a lottery or inherit money. This is a pure income effect, and they respond by working fewer hours.

Effect 2: Substitution effect—An increase in the price of any good makes that good more expensive. The substitution effect says that, holding income constant, a higher price reduces the demand for the good. Here, the good is leisure and its price is the wage. The substitution effect of a higher wage is to reduce the leisure demanded and so increase work hours; the substitution effect of a lowered wage is to increase leisure and reduce work hours.

Table 16.2 summarizes these effects. In all cases, the net effect is uncertain. Empirically, people working only a few hours have only a small income effect (because the increase in income is small) and so the higher wage tends to cause them to work more hours. Married males have an income effect that dominates the substitution effect: Higher wages cause them to work fewer hours. Married females are the opposite. For them, the substitution effect dominates so that higher wages cause them to work more hours. For single persons, the two effects appear to be about equal. They work about the same number of hours regardless of the wage.

TABLE 16.2

	Wage Change	Income Effect	Substitution Effect
Impact on	Wage Up	Up	Down
Leisure Demanded	Wage Down	Down	Up
Impact on Work Hours	Wage Up	Down	Up
	Wage Down	Up	Down

These results are summarized in the backward-bending supply curve of labor. At low wages, the substitution effect dominates (from *A* to *B* in Figure 16.4) so that as the

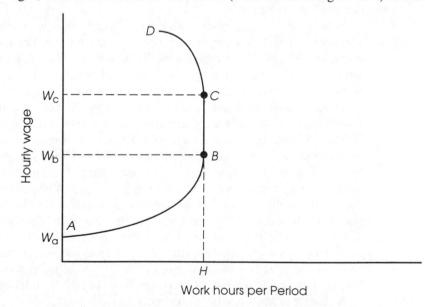

Figure 16.4 The Backward Bending Labor Supply Curve

market wage goes up, hours of work go up. Over some range, both effects are balanced, so that as the market wage goes up, hours of work stay the same (from B to C). Finally, at higher wages, the income effect dominates so that a higher wage results in a fewer hours of work (from C to D). Note that a higher wage will never cause someone to not work! Why? Because if you aren't working, there can't be any increase in income from a higher wage and so there can't be any income effect! Theoretically, it is possible that a higher wage could cause someone to cut hours so much they earn less annually. However, this has rarely been observed.

Points to note:

The worker will not work at a wage below W_a.
Between wage W_a and wage W_b, the substitution effect dominates the income effect.
   A higher wage increases work hours and a lower wage decreases work hours.
Above wage W_c, along segment CD, the income effect dominates the substitution effect. A higher wage decreases work hours and a lower wage increases work hours.
The backward bend occurs along segment CD.
Between B and C, the wage has no effect on the hours of work.
The most this worker will work is H hours.

Thought Question

How will the following events affect Alfred's work hours (assuming he can change them freely)?

Event 1: Alfred gets a higher wage and his income effect dominates.
   Event 1: He will work fewer hours.

Event 2: Alfred gets a lower wage and his income effect dominates.
   Event 2: He will work more hours.

Event 3: Alfred gets a higher wage and his substitution effect dominates.
   Event 3: He will work more hours.

Event 4: Alfred gets a lower wage and his substitution effect dominates.
   Event 4: He will work fewer hours.

Event 5: Alfred wins $20,000 a year for life.
   Event 5: He will work fewer hours (this event evokes a pure income effect).

Event 6: Alfred is working 2,000 hours a year and earns $10 an hour. Then his boss gives him a raise to $11 an hour. However, at the same time, his property taxes go up by $2,000 a year. Note that if he continues to work 2,000 hours, his net after-tax income will be unchanged but his hourly wage will be higher.
   Event 6: He will work more hours. At 2,000 hours, there is no income effect, yet there is a substitution effect. The substitution effect will cause him to work more hours. Whenever you see a crazy example like this (with a change in wage offset by some other change so on net income is unchanged), focus on the substitution effect!

CRIB NOTES

Compensating differential: $\Delta W = - \Delta NW$ where Δ refers to difference between jobs in same market. Competition results in all jobs paying the same full wage. NW = nonmonetary wages

Other causes of wage differences: Skill differences, discrimination, frictions (such as cost of changing jobs), poor information (due, in part, to high search costs).

Discrimination: D = dollar dislike for disliked group.
By employer: Hire disliked group only if Wage of disliked group $\leq$ Wage of others $- D$. Low D employers hire dislikes first: marginal D goes up as more dislikes. Discriminating employers have higher wage costs and higher cost. In long run, competition should get rid of discriminating employers.
By customer: Leads to lower wage in jobs where customer sees worker.
By substitute workers: Leads to separate work places but equal wages.
By complementary workers (like managers): Leads to lower wages that competition does not get rid of.

Efficiency wage models: Higher wage causes higher MP (or lower other costs).

Unions: More inelastic the demand for labor, fewer jobs lost when W rises.
If unionize monopsony, if union wage between nonunion W and $P \times MP$, can raise employment and wage.
Effect on nonunion firms:
Spill-over effect: Displaced union workers depress nonunion wages.
Threat effect: Nonunion firms raise wages to prevent unionization.

Labor supply: Higher wage has
1. Income effect: More income, more leisure wanted, less work hours
2. Substitution effect: Higher wage makes price of leisure higher, want less leisure and more work, so work more.
Net effect uncertain.

Backward-bending supply curve: Hours worked first go up and then down as hourly wage goes up.
Forward bend (wage up, hours up): Substitution effect stronger.
Backward bend (wage up, hours down): Income effect stronger.

Review Questions

---

1. An employer notices that his application rate is lower than that of his competitors while his quit rate is higher. What is the likely cause?

2. If all workers have the same dislike of working in dangerous jobs, then in equilibrium, which jobs will they prefer? Safe jobs or dangerous jobs?

3. Why do employers provide fringe benefits to workers?

4. The government requires all employers to supply restrooms for workers. Suppose this law was rescinded. What incentives does an employer then have to supply workers with restrooms?

5. An employer comes upon his workers and finds them sleeping. "Why," he demands, "aren't you working?" They reply, "Because we didn't hear you coming!" What model of wage differences does this joke reflect?

6. If customers don't want to buy stock from females, then in which of these jobs are women most likely to earn less?
   Job A: Buying and selling stocks on the trading floor of the New York Stock Exchange.
   Job B: Buying stocks for the mutual funds of a large corporation.
   Job C: Stockbroker at a local office that deals with the public.

7. If Irish persons like to work with other Irish persons, how is this likely to affect wages and the workplace? Assume workers are substitutes such that Irish workers can do jobs non-Irish persons can do.

8. Acme has a health care plan workers prefer by $2 an hour but a supervisor would be willing to pay $3 an hour to get rid of. Backme is close to town, which workers value at $4 an hour. If both jobs pay the same full wage, how do their money wages compare?

9. Can a union raise wages and employment at the same time?

10. True or False? A union facing a monopsony will cause employment to go up.

11. Sarah can invest her money and earn a 10% rate of return. Alternatively, she can invest her money in getting an MBA. The MBA has a direct cost of $25,000. She takes the MBA at night, so she doesn't forego any earnings. But she does forego $35,000 in leisure time taking courses and studying. If she were making $40,000 a year, what must her new post-MBA earnings be to justify getting the MBA?

12. Why does college enrollment go up in recessions?

13. The Foxfire Plant employs 1,000 workers for 250 days a year. Its current plant and all its workers live in town. The daily travel cost per mile for each worker, including the cost of travel time, is $1. The plant's lease is about to be renewed. The annual rent on the plant is $800,000. But another plant located 2 miles from town can be rented for $600,000 a year. Assuming there are no costs to moving from plant to plant, should Foxfire stay where it is or move? Assume it wants to keep its worker's full wage at its current level.

14. In the efficiency wage model, how will the following events change the wage Acme is paying?
   Event A: A new law prohibiting locker searches makes it harder for Acme to monitor its workers.
   Event B: High unemployment rates make it harder for workers to find another job.
   Event C: Acme shifts from batch to assembly line production, making the cost of shirking higher to Acme.
   Event D: Computer monitoring makes it cheap to monitor workers, right down to the amount of time they take to get a bathroom break.

15. Draw a demand and supply graph for one worker's work hours, where the wage is the marginal benefit of working and the marginal cost of working is the foregone value of leisure time. Show a graph for each of these cases.
    Case A: The worker wants to, and does, work 8 hours at $10 an hour.
    Case B: The worker decides not to work at all at a wage of $10 an hour.
    Case C: The worker works 8 hours at $10 an hour and 2 more hours in a second job at $8 an hour.

16. How are the following events likely to affect Martha's hours of work, assuming she is free to adjust her hours at her current wage?
    Event A: Her wage goes up and the income effect dominates.
    Event B: The company begins paying for all her child care costs while maintaining her hourly wage at its current rate.
    Event C: The tax codes are changed so that her current after-tax wage goes up but, due to the reduction in tax deductions, Martha will still earn the same after-tax income if she continues to work her previous hours of work.
    Event D: Martha wins $50,000 a year for life in a lottery.

17. Why do most college professors earn more than janitors?

18. Why do English college professors tend to earn less than business college professors?

19. Professional accountants are pushing to make the requirement to become a certified accountant five years of college, instead of four years. In the long run, how will this effect the wages of accountants? Will new accountants be better off?

20. How will the following events affect the level of union wages that a union demands? Assume that unions demand a higher wage, the more inelastic the demand for labor is.
    Event A: The demand for output becomes more inelastic.
    Event B: Competition from foreign firms makes the demand for unionized firms output more elastic.
    Event C: A change in technology makes labor's share in cost larger.
    Event D: A change in technology makes it easier for the firm to find substitutes for union labor, including replacing them with foreign labor.

21.   Use the following table to answer these questions.

Workers	1	2	3	4	5	6	7	8
Wage ($)	200	250	300	350	400	450	500	550
MRP ($)	800	750	700	650	600	550	500	450

a. If the firms in this industry are competitive in the input market, how many workers will be hired? At what wage?
b. If this is one firm and it is a monopsony, how many workers will it hire and at what wage?
c. If this monopsony is unionized, what is the most workers the union can get this firm to hire? What wage will it then be demanding?
d. What is the highest wage the union can demand and still have employment at the level in question b?

Answers

1. The full wage he pays workers is below the market wage. He needs to raise his money wage or to improve his nonmoney wage. This could include paying better fringe benefits, improving working conditions, and treating workers better.

2. They will prefer both equally. This is due to compensating differentials in pay. The dangerous job will have to pay more in money wages to make up for its lower non-money wages. On net, both jobs will pay the same full wages. So while workers prefer the nonmoney wages of the safe job, they are indifferent between the full wages in both jobs because they are the same. Don't confuse nonwage preferences with full wage preferences!

3. An employer will prefer to give a worker a fringe benefit when the fringe benefit costs the employer less than what the worker is willing to pay (in reduced wages) to get the fringe benefit. For example, suppose the worker is willing to give up $100 in wages to get more health care and it costs the firm only $80 to supply it. The employer can lower the worker's money wage by $100, supply the added health care, and save $20. The worker's full wage will be unchanged but the employer's per worker cost will be lower.

4. The cheap answer has something to do with smell and other stuff I won't mention. The economic answer is the same as in question 3. Workers are willing to pay for the fringe benefit of having a restroom. To see this, suppose an employer didn't supply a restroom. Most likely, the wage they would have to pay would be very, very high. It's cheaper to supply the restroom because its cost is more than offset by the lowered wages the employer can then pay.

5. The efficiency wage model. If the firm pays the workers sufficiently more than they get elsewhere then they will not shirk on the job. They don't shirk because if they do, they fear getting caught and fired. The workers in the joke obviously are not being paid enough.

6. Job C. In both jobs A and B, customers have no idea who is doing the trading for them, so they can't discriminate.

7. This is a form of discrimination. This will lead to separate workplaces. Some will employ Irish persons. Others will employ non-Irish persons. Wages will be the same.

8. Backme will pay $5 less in money wages. Acme has a nonmoney wage of −$1 ($NW_A = \$2 + [-\$3]$). Backme has a nonmoney wage (NW_B) of $4 so

$$NW_B - NW_A = \$5$$

Thus, $W_B - W_A = -(NW_B - NW_A) = -\$5$, where W_A and W_B are the respective money wages.

9. If the union has organized competitive firms, then the answer is no. The firms will be on their demand curves for labor, so that a higher wage will cause them to cut back employment. If the union has organized a monopsony firm, then the answer is yes. It is possible for it to raise the wage and employment at the same time. That's because it makes the supply of labor curve seen by the firm horizontal and this, over some range, makes the monopsony's MFC lower.

10. False. A union facing a monopsony can cause employment to go up. But if it sets the wage too high, it will cause employment to fall.

11. The total cost of the MBA is $60,000. To earn a 10% return, it must increase earnings by $6,000. So her new earnings must average $46,000 a year at a minimum to justify the investment.

12. Because the indirect cost of a college education (the foregone wages) is lower, so college is cheaper. As a result, more people go to college then.

13. Moving to the new plant saves $200,000 in rent costs. But Foxfire will have to raise its money wage to keep workers' full wage the same. Traveling to the new plant will cost each worker $500 a year, so Foxfire will have to raise each worker's wage by $500. Adding this up across all 1,000 workers, the added wage cost will be $500,000. It is better off staying in town. Some firms ignore this and don't change wages when moving farther away from workers. The result is a lower full wage, a higher turnover rate, and a harder time attracting new workers. The costs of these often add up to more than what a higher wage would have cost.

14. Event A: Will raise the wage. Lower monitoring means the probability of getting caught is less. This gives workers a greater incentive to shirk. Acme has to offset this by paying a still higher wage.

    Event B: Will lower the wage. The event reduces the incentive for workers to shirk. So Acme can lower its wage a bit.

    Event C: Will increase the wage. The benefit to Acme of preventing shirking is now higher, so it will have to raise the wage to make sure it is less likely to occur.

    Event D: Will lower the wage. Increased ease of monitoring makes it more likely a shirking worker will be caught, so workers have less incentive to shirk. Acme can thus lower its wage. This event has occurred in many workplaces where workers type or telephone. Computers allow continuous monitoring.

15. The demand curve is the marginal benefit of working curve, or the wage curve. The supply curve is the marginal cost of working curve, which is rising. It rises because the more hours one works, the fewer hours of leisure one has and so the cost of giving up yet another hour of leisure is higher.

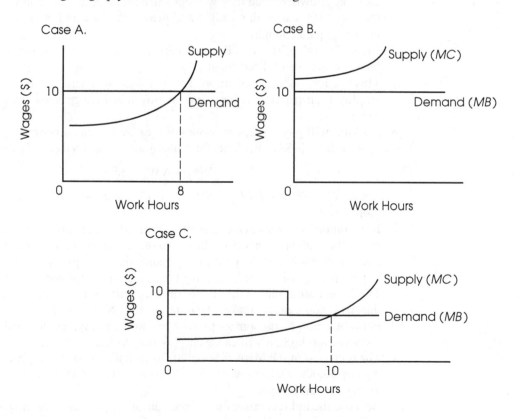

16. Event A: She will work fewer hours.
    Event B: She will work fewer hours (this event has a pure income effect because she has the same wage but more disposable income).
    Event C: She will work more hours. At her previous hours of work, this event leaves income unchanged but her hourly wage is higher so there is a substitution effect and no income effect (at her previous hours). The substitution effect will cause her to work more hours than before.
    Event D: She will work fewer hours. This event has a pure income effect.
17. The theory of human capital tells us that people will not invest in learning more unless it pays. Becoming a college professor is very costly in time and money. Becoming a janitor is fairly cheap. Thus, college professors must earn more or there would be no college professors.
18. The nonmoney wages of being an English professor appeal to many, many people. As a result, there is an ample supply of people who are willing to become college professors at a low money wage. On the other hand, the number of persons who put a high nonmonetary value on teaching business is rather small. So they want their full wage paid more in a higher money wage. Also, they have a higher opportunity cost in that they could have worked in business instead. On the other hand, an English professor has fewer alternative opportunities. Perhaps he would otherwise have become a janitor.
19. The human capital model predicts that a higher cost of education (as a result of the fifth year) will eventually lead to a higher wage for accountants. The higher wage will compensate them for the higher cost. New accountants will not be better off because their higher future wage is offset by their higher educational costs. Only older accountants, who already are certified, will benefit.
20. Event A: Union wage will likely go up as labor demand is more inelastic.
    Event B: Union wage will likely go down as labor demand is more elastic (or less inelastic).
    Event C: Union wage will likely go down, as a higher labor share usually makes labor demand more elastic.
    Event D: Union wage will likely go down, as the demand for union labor has become more elastic.
21. a. Demand equals supply at seven workers and a wage of $500.
    b. Add an *MFC* row (calculate the increase in total wage as the monopsony hires each added worker).

Workers	1	2	3	4	5	6	7	8
Wage ($)	200	250	300	350	400	450	500	550
MRP ($)	800	750	700	650	600	550	500	450
MFC ($)	200	300	400	500	600	700	800	900

The monopsony will hire as long as $MRP \geq MFC$. It will hire five workers and pay a wage of $400. Yes, the wage is below the *MFC*!
    c. A union can demand a wage of $500 (where the market demand equals the market supply of labor) and maximize employment at seven workers. Any higher wage will reduce labor demand; any lower wage will reduce labor supply.
    d. If the union wants five workers employed, it can demand a wage up to $600, the *MRP* of the fifth worker. Any higher wage and the firm will cut employment back to four workers.

Chapter Seventeen

Interest, Rents, and Profits

OLD LABELS AND NEW MEANINGS

In economics as it once was taught, there were four inputs and four types of income. Labor earned wages, capital earned interest, land earned rent, and entrepreneurs earned profits. Today, we recognize that all inputs earn all four types of income. For example, workers investing in their education are creating human capital and some of their increased earnings will be, in effect, an interest return on this investment. Also, workers are acting as entrepreneurs when they get an education because they are betting that the career they study will be in demand. If they bet correctly, they'll make a profit. If not, they'll make a loss. Finally, should a worker turn out to have a unique skill, he'll be able to earn a "rent" on the skill. Thus, labor earns all four incomes.

So let's redefine these terms.

Wages are the payments reflecting the worker's opportunity cost of time.

Economic rent is the payment to any input that is in perfectly inelastic supply. The test of whether a payment is a rent is this: Would a still higher payment increase the supply of the input? If not, it is rent. We add the term *economic* to the term *rent* to distinguish it from the rent paid on an apartment.

Interest is the price paid for the use of funds over a period of time. These funds may be used to invest in physical capital (such as plant and machinery) or in human capital (such as more education). Capital has up-front costs that later produce a stream of income over time. The part of these incomes that pay back for the sacrifice involved in supplying the up-front costs is interest income.

Economic profits are the excess of total revenues over costs (including the opportunity cost of the owner's time and investment). Total revenues reflect the value of the resources in their current use. Costs reflect the opportunity cost of using the resources elsewhere. The difference is profits. Profits are made when a person finds a better way to use resources than their previous use. Profits thus emerge from doing something different and better in a way that consumers prefer.

Now let us examine each of these types of income separately (except for wages, which we've already covered). Remember though that most inputs earn several of these types of income.

INTEREST

Interest is the price paid for the use of funds over time. If you lend me $1,000 today and I pay you back $1,100 next year, you've earned $100 in interest (we're using real dollars here so that the impact of inflation has been taken out).

To compare different investments, we express the annual income from these investments as a percent of the initial up-front investment. This is the *rate of return* the investment pays, which is also called the investment's *yield*. In the simplest case, if I invest $1,000 in a worm farm and it pays $100 a year, year after year, forever, its rate of return or yield is 10%. In this simple case (only!),

$$\text{Rate of return} = \frac{\text{Annual income}}{\text{Initial investment}} \times 100$$

Other formulas are used when the investment lasts less than forever.

A firm should invest in a project when

Project's rate of return ≥ Interest rate

where the interest rate is the rate it can borrow at (or, the rate it can earn if it invests the money elsewhere when this rate is higher than the rate it can borrow at). Also, in this simple case, the firm's annual profit from the investment equals

Profit = Investment × (Rate of return − Interest rate)

Thought Question

Assume the following investments last forever. Assume the firm can borrow money at an interest rate of 10%. Should it make the following investments? Why or why not?
Investment A: Costs $5,000 and pays $600 a year forever.
Investment B: Costs $20,000 and pays $1,800 a year forever.

The firm should invest in investment A. Here's why. This investment has a rate of return of 12%, which is greater than the 10% interest rate the firm borrows at. That means the firm nets 2%. To be specific, it makes $600 a year. It costs $500 a year in interest, which is the 10% interest rate it takes to borrow the $5,000, so it nets $100 a year free and clear. That's 2% of $5,000, where 2% = 12% − 10%.

The firm should not invest in investment B. Its rate of return falls short of the interest rate so it is a bad investment. Here's why. It makes $1,800 a year. But the firm must pay $2,000 a year in interest to pay for the $20,000 it borrowed to make the investment so it loses $200 a year. $200 is 1% of $20,000.

HOW INTEREST RATES ARE DETERMINED

What determines interest rates? The simple answer is demand and supply. So let's go through the what and the who of supply and demand.

What is demanded and supplied? The answer is loanable funds, the money used to finance investments and other uses for loans (like the government's debt and consumer loans).

Who supplies loanable funds? The answer is savers. Savers forego current consumption, take the saved funds, lend them to others, and get paid back later. In effect, they give up $X in consumption today in exchange for $Y of consumption in the future. Because savers prefer a dollar today over a dollar tomorrow, to get them to give up a $X today requires that $Y be greater than $X! That is, savers want to be paid interest!

A wrong answer is banks. Banks are middlemen between savers and lenders. Savers are the ones who really lend money. Banks borrow the money from savers and then lend it to other borrowers such as businesses and consumers. Without savers, banks would have nothing to lend.

The supply of loanable funds goes up with the interest rate. That's because the more savers can earn by saving, the more they save.

Who demands loanable funds? The answer is mainly businesses. Consumers and governments also borrow money. But it's easiest to focus on businesses. Think of each business as having a menu. At the top of the menu are those delicious projects that have the highest rates of return. As they go down the menu, each successive project has a lower and lower rate of return. The demand curve for loanable funds is the sum of all these menus. At an interest rate of 10%, for example, businesses borrow to fund all those projects on the top of menu that pay 10% or better. If interest rates fall to 9%, they will still invest in all these "10% or better" projects but add all the other projects paying between 9% and 10%. So as the interest rate falls, the loanable funds borrowed (or demanded) go up. Thus, the demand for loanable funds goes up with lower interest rates.

Figure 17.1 shows the market for loanable funds. The market rate of interest will be 10%, where demand equals supply. One hundred fifty dollars will be saved and lent by the suppliers of loanable funds, and $150 will be borrowed and invested by the demanders of loanable funds. (Obviously, the $150 is being used to keep the example simple. If you want more realism, feel free to add all the zeros you want to these numbers.)

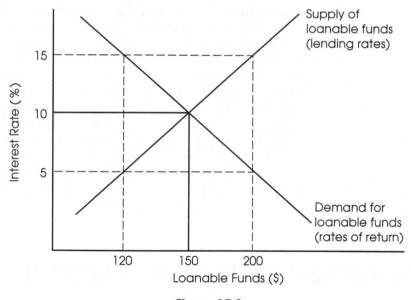

Figure 17.1

At an interest rate of 15%, there is a surplus of funds. Suppliers (savers) are willing to lend $200 but demanders (borrowers) are only willing to borrow $120. Only $120 will be lent and borrowed at 15%. The surplus of $80 of loanable funds (= $200 − $120) will drive the interest rate down. At an interest rate of 5%, there is a shortage of funds. While demanders want to borrow $200, savers are only willing to lend $120. The shortage of $80 of loanable funds will drive interest rates up. At 10%, the market is in equilibrium.

What if there is a price ceiling on interest rates? Suppose the market is in equilibrium at 10% interest rate, as shown in Figure 17.1. Then the government imposes a 5%

ceiling on interest rates. The government claims this will make more funds available. But will it? The answer is no. At 5%, only $120 will be lent. Total lending will fall by $30 (down from $150). Because there is a shortage of funds, lenders can pick and choose who to lend to. Only the safest lenders will get funds. Poorer persons, small businesses, economists, and consumers are likely to find their applications for loans stamped "application denied."

What will increase the demand for loanable funds? That is, what will cause the demand curve to shift up and to the right? The answer is any event that increases the rates of return on business projects. Some examples are lower tax rates on capital, growing demand for the business's output, falling prices for capital equipment and other inputs, and technological innovations that reduce the project's cost and raise its output. Also, as the business section of the paper would put it, "growing optimism by investors" will increase the demand for loanable funds.

An increase in the demand for loanable funds will increase interest rates and the funds borrowed. A decrease will lower interest rates and reduce the funds borrowed.

What will increase the supply of loanable funds? That is, what events will cause the supply curve of loanable funds to shift right and vertically down? The answer is anything that causes savers to want to save more. For example, an increased desire to save for the future, an increase in the life span, and a sudden increase in income that is not expected to last. The latter is called a transitory increase in income. People that get a transitory increase in income typically spread out its consumption over several years and so initially save a large share of the increase when they get it. Also, savings tend toward a fairly constant fraction of national income. Thus, an increase in national income will increase the supply of savings.

Most changes in the supply of loanable funds come from foreign savers. Foreigners tend to supply more loanable funds to the United States when the United States pays higher interest rates than they can make in their own country. For example, suppose a recession in Europe occurs while the U.S. economy is doing fine. The poorer investment prospects in Europe will likely increase the supply of loanable funds to the U.S. economy.

An increase in the supply of loanable funds will lower interest rates and increase the amount of funds borrowed and lent. A decrease in the supply of loanable funds will raise interest rates and reduce the funds borrowed and lent.

THE MARKET RATE OF INTEREST

The market interest rate can be broken into these parts:

**Market interest rate = Pure (real) rate of interest +
Expected rate of inflation + Risk premium for interest rate change +
Risk premium for default risk**

In addition, on smaller loans (such as on credit cards), a premium for the administrative costs of making the loan becomes a significant factor. Let's look at each of these in turn.

Pure (Real) Rate of Interest

The pure or real rate of interest is what savers demand as compensation for waiting to consume. This is the rate savers would have to be paid on a totally safe investment when there is no inflation or risk to worry about. The "real" term means that the effect of inflation has been taken out so that we are comparing real dollars of equal purchasing power. For example, if savers are indifferent between $1,000 in real goods today and $1,100 in real goods in a year, then the real interest rate is 10%. This reflects the degree savers discount future dollars by.

Expected Rate of Inflation

Inflation makes future dollars worth less. The expected rate of inflation is what savers demand as added compensation for getting dollars that are worth less. Suppose savers are indifferent between $1,000 in real goods today and $1,100 in real goods in a year. Suppose also that they expect prices to go up 5% (that is, an inflation rate of 5%). This means that they want 5% more in actual dollars in a year or $1,155 (= $1,100 × 1.05). The interest rate is then 15.5% ($155/$1,000 × 100). This is, as an approximation, the real rate of interest (10%) plus the expected rate of inflation (5%). If r is the real interest rate and p is the expected inflation rate, then the interest rate on a totally safe investment would be

$$i = r + p + (r \times p)$$

where i, r, and p are all expressed as decimals. So we have an interest rate of 15.5% [$0.155 = 0.10 + 0.05 + (0.10 \times 0.05)$]. Because the $r \times p$ term is usually small, it is ignored. So we say the interest rate equals the real rate of interest plus a premium for the expected rate of inflation, or $i = r + p$.

Risk Premium for Interest Rate Change

Most bonds pay an amount of interest that was set when the bond was initially issued. For example, suppose the government borrows $1,000 for 30 years and pays 8% on the $1,000. We say the $1,000 is the face value of the bond (because this number will be printed on the face of the bond). Similarly, the 8% is the coupon rate of the bond. This bond has, when issued, a maturity of 30 years. This bond pays $80 a year (= 8% of $1,000) for 30 years and then pays back its face value of $1,000. So on its first day of issue, a bond is usually worth its face value, and on the day of its retirement, it's worth its face value. But what about in between? The value of the bond can go up or down as the market interest rate goes down and up. This makes the bond risky and savers, not liking risk, want a little extra compensation for this risk. Normally, the farther the bond is from its retirement date, the more the bond can vary in price and the higher is the risk premium. For example, a 3-month government bond has very little risk. On the other hand, a newly issued 30-year bond can have its price buffeted around a lot by changes in the interest rate. Thus, it is the riskier investment.

The result is what's called a *normal yield curve*. The yield curve plots the interest rate on the vertical axis and the years remaining on the bond (which is called its *maturity*) on the horizontal axis. A normal yield curve is positively sloped such that the interest rate goes up with longer maturities (or waiting times until the bond is retired). This positive slope reflects the fact that longer maturity bonds must pay more to compensate savers for their greater interest rate risk.

Risk Premium for Default Risk

Although the U.S. government is not likely to go bankrupt, this is not true for other borrowers. In the past, many corporations, states, and cities have gone bankrupt and stopped paying interest on the bonds they had issued. This is called a *default*, and it is an ever-present risk. Savers thus demand a premium for this added risk. Several rating agencies, including Moody's and Standard and Poor, rate bonds by their default risk. The higher the risk, the higher the interest rate.

Thought Question

How would the following events affect the interest rate Acme Widget Works has to pay on its upcoming offering of 10-year bonds?

Event A: The Federal Reserve Board (the government agency that controls the U.S. money supply, and indirectly, the rate of inflation), in a sudden change in policy, announces that "We love inflation! Yes, we want lots and lots of inflation!"
Interest rates will go up because of a higher expected rate of inflation.

Event B: Standard and Poor, impressed by Acme's large holdings of cash, raise the credit rating on Acme.
Its interest rate will be lower because of a lower premium for default risk.

Event C: Savers, after watching lots of ads on TV, want to spend more now. As a result, they dislike waiting to consume (that is, they discount the future more).
Event C: Interest rates will be higher because of a higher real rate of interest.

Event D: Savers suddenly become convinced that interest rates are becoming more volatile, expecting them to go up and down more in the future.
Event D: Interest rates will go up because of a higher risk premium for interest rate changes.

PRESENT VALUE

The *present value* of $X in N years is its value today. It is today's demand price for future dollars. For example, if you would pay up to $800 today to get $1,000 in a year, we say the present value of the $1,000 is $800. Note that you pay the $800 by saving and lending it!

Present value and future value (the $X in N years) are linked by the interest rate. This is what interest rates do. That's their job. So please employ them. In particular, we define interest rates so that the present value of $1 in one year is $1/(1 + i)$, where i is the interest rate expressed as a decimal. So if the interest rate is 10%, the demand price for $1 one year from now is $0.9091 [= $1/(1.10)]. Dividing by $1 + i$ effectively discounts the future value into its lowered present value. The higher the interest rate, the more future dollars are discounted. If you are willing to pay at most $800 today for $1,000 in one year, what is the interest rate you are discounting the future $1,000 by?

Set up the equation:

$$\text{Present value} = \frac{\text{Future value in one year}}{1 + i} \quad \text{or} \quad \$800 = \frac{\$1,000}{1 + i}$$

and solve for i. You should get $i = 0.25$ or, expressed in percent terms, 25%.

What about $X in 2 years? It gets discounted twice, once for each year. So we have

$$\text{Present value} = \text{Future value in 2 years} \times \frac{1}{1 + i} \times \frac{1}{1 + i}$$

$$= \frac{\text{Future value in 2 years}}{(1 + i)^2}$$

If $i = 10\%$, this says that to get \$1,210 in 2 years, at an interest rate of 10% ($i = 0.10$), you would pay (lend) at most \$1,000 today [\$1,000 = \$1,210/(1.10)^2 = \$1210/(1.21)].

In general, for $X in N years, you'll discount it over and over again for N times so that

$$\text{Present value of } \$X \text{ in } N \text{ years} = \frac{\$X}{(1 + i)^N}$$

Now here is the blue-light special. Suppose you are promised $X next year, another $X the year after that, and $X a year for every year into the infinite future. How much is the present value of all these $X? It is X/i! This is a very simple formula! Don't confuse it with the one-year formula! This is a forever formula. Thus, at an interest rate of 10%, a yearly payment of \$100, year after year, century after century, one millennium after another, forever is worth \$1,000. To see why, suppose you can invest at 10%. And suppose you put \$1,000 in the bank. In a year, it grows to \$1,100. You take out the \$100 and reinvest the \$1,000 for another year at 10%. Next year you take out \$100 and reinvest the \$1,000 again. If you keep doing this, you can get \$100 a year, year after year, forever. So \$100 a year forever is worth \$1,000 and no more. Why, blue-light shoppers, pay more?

Thought Questions

Mary has several projects she must choose between. All cost $1,800, and only one can be chosen. Because they all cost the same, the best project is the one having the future income with the highest present value. What is the present value of the following streams of income? Use an interest rate of 10%. Which should she choose?

Stream A: $1,100 in 1 year plus $1,210 in 2 years. (Hint: Just add up the present values. Here, add the present value of $1,100 to the present value of $1,210.)

Stream B: $4,668.74 in 10 years.

Stream C: $250 a year, year after year, forever.

Stream A: Has a present value of \$2,000 (= \$1,100/1.10 + \$1,210/1.10^2 where 1.10^2 = 1.21)

Stream B: Has a present value of \$1,800 (= \$4,668.74/1.10^{10} where 1.10^{10} = 2.59374).

Stream C: Has a present value of \$2,500 (= \$250/0.10).

She should choose the project with stream C. Note that if the project costs more than $2,500, she should not invest in any of these!

Professor Smart has a highly valued case of wine. She can sell it today for $10,000. If she waits one year, she can sell it for $10,700. Which should she prefer? Her interest rate is 10%.

The present value of selling it today is, obviously, $10,000. The present value of $10,700 in one year is $9,727.27 (= $10,700/1.10). She should sell it today. Another way of looking at this problem is to ask what she would have in a year if she sells today and invests the money at 10%? She would have $11,000, which is more than she would get by waiting to sell it, and so selling now is better for her.

Repeat this problem, using a 5% interest rate.

The present value of selling it today is $10,000. The present value of $10,700, using 5% is $10,190.48 [= $10,700/1.05]. She should wait a year to sell it. Another way of looking at this problem is to ask what she would have in a year if she sells today and invests the money at 5% She would have $10,500, which is less than she would get by waiting to sell it, and so she is better off waiting.

PRESENT VALUE: ANOTHER VIEW

Present value is the value today of dollars paid in the future, but there is another way to look at present value. Present value is the amount of money that would have to be set aside today to meet the future payments if one invests at the current interest rate. For example, if I'm obliged to pay $50 a year, year after year, forever, how much do I have to set aside today? The answer is the present value of $50 per year forever. At an interest rate of 10%, this would be $500, since when I invest the $500 at 10%, it will earn $50 a year. On the other hand, if the market interest rate is 5%, I would have to set aside $1,000, since, at 5% I would have to invest the $1,000 to earn $50 a year. Note that the higher the interest rate, the lower the present value is. That is, the higher the interest rate, the less one needs to set aside to meet future obligations.

Thought Question

Mary just inherited a million dollars. She wants to set aside enough to have an income of $50,000 a year for the next 20 years. The rest she wants to consume. At current market interest rate of 10%, the present value of $50,000 a year for 20 years is $425,678. How much does she want to set aside? What will happen if the interest rate falls?

$425,678 can be invested today at 10% and pay out $50,000 a year for 20 years (after 20 years, no money will be left). So Mary can save $425,678 and consume the rest. If interest rates fall, she will have to set aside more! That's because at a *lower* interest rate, the present value of $50,000 for 20 years is *higher.* For example, at an 8% interest rate, she would have to set aside $490,907. If the market rate falls to 5% she would have to set aside $623,111.

MAKING INVESTMENT DECISIONS WITH PRESENT VALUE

Investments have up-front costs, such as the building of a plant. Then, over time, they generate income. The key rule in making an investment decision is this: The investment should be made when

Present value of future incomes ≥ Up-front costs

where the present value is calculated by using the appropriate interest rate. For a firm, the appropriate interest rate is the higher of (1) the interest rate it must pay on borrowing new funds and (2) the best rate of return it could earn on alternative investments.

The profit from an investment is called its present value:

Net present value = Present value of future income – Up-front costs

For example, suppose I can build a plant that costs $10 million and whose future stream of income has a present value of $13 million. And suppose everyone, including bankers and other investors, agree with these numbers. It would be possible for me to borrow $10 million to build the plant, turn around and sell it for $13 million, and pocket the $3 million difference. If you've ever wondered how financiers make millions and even billions, this is how.

Another investment rule: If you want to choose among several projects, choose the one with the highest net present value.

Thought Questions

A machine cost $4,000. It lasts 2 years and has no scrap value (that is, it has no value when scrapped or gotten rid of after 2 years). In each year, it produces $2,400 in income. Should the firm invest in the machine if its interest rate is 10%?

Yes. The present value of year 1's $2,400 is $2,181.82 (= $2,400/1.10). The present value of year 2's $2,400, is $1,983.47 (= $2,400/1.10^2 and $1.10^2 = 1.21$). The sum of these is $4,165.29. So the net present value of this machine is $165.29. It should be invested in!

Answer the preceding question, assuming the firm can only borrow at a 20% interest rate.

No. The present value of year 1's $2,400 is $2,000 (= $2,400/1.20). The present value of year 2's $2,400 is $1,666.67 (= $2,400/1.20^2 and $1.20^2 = 1.44$). The sum of these is $3,666.67. So the net present value of this machine is a negative $333.33 (– $333.33 = $3,666.67 – $4,000.00). It should not be invested in!

In other cases, one faces a choice among several costly alternatives. In this case, the rule is this: Choose the alternative whose costs have the lowest present value. This keeps costs at a minimum.

Thought Question

Bob has to choose between (1) buying a car today for $20,000 and selling it for $14,520 at the end of 2 years or (2) leasing the car for 2 years, paying $5,000 today and $5,000 in one year. In both cases, he has to pay all maintenance costs. Which is the better choice if his interest rate is 10%?

Calculate the present value of the cost in both cases. Choice 1 has a cost today of $20,000, but this is offset by $14,520 in 2 years. So we have to deduct the present value of $14,520 from the cost of buying the car today. The present value of choice 1 is $8,000 (= $20,000 − $14,520/1.10² and 1.10² = 1.21). Choice 2 has a cost of $5,000 today, whose present value is $5,000. The present value of year 1's $5,000 is $4,545.45 (= $5,000/1.10). The present value of choice 2's cost is the sum of these, or $9,545.45. Choice 1 is cheaper: Bob should buy and not lease.

ECONOMIC RENTS

Economic rent is any payment that does not affect the supply of the input. Saying this definition another way, economic rent is a payment to an input that is in perfectly inelastic supply. Alternatively, rent is the excess of a good's actual price over the good's supply price.

In Figure 17.2, this input earns a rent when its price goes above $200. In this case, each unit earns an annual rent of $80 and total rents equal $1,600 (= $80 × 20).

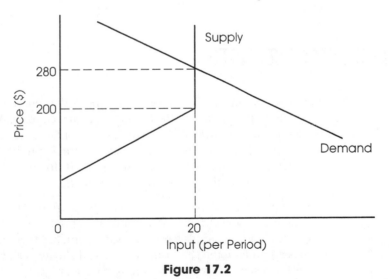

Figure 17.2

Points to note:

The rent of $80 is the difference between the price ($280) and the marginal cost of producing the input ($200).

Any input that earns more than it costs to produce another unit is earning a rent.

In the range that an input earns rents (from $200 up in Figure 17.2), the following propositions are true:

1. A tax on economic rents does not affect its supply. For example, a tax of $50 a unit will not reduce its supply. However, after the tax exceeds $80, the supply will fall.
2. A price ceiling on economic rent will not reduce its supply. On the other hand, a price ceiling will create a shortage and will likely lead to the input being misallocated from a social point of view. In Figure 17.2, a price ceiling of $210 will only affect the input's economic rent and the supply will remain at 20 units. But there will be a shortage of this input because, at $210, demand exceeds supply. Suppose the units of this good are then rationed randomly among demanders. This means that some of the units will likely go to those who value it less than $280, its original price. This reduces the value of the uses this input is being put to. For example, suppose a unit goes to a demander who values the input at $215. In the absence of price controls, this unit would have gone to someone valuing it at $280 or more. Say they valued it at $400. The social loss for this unit alone is $185 (= $400 − $215).

Even though economic rent does not affect supply, it performs the important economic function of allocating inputs to their most valued uses.

Who earns rent? Any input whose price exceeds the supply price, which is the marginal cost of supplying another unit of the input. For example, if the technology of building a particular printing press is well known and has no patents on it, then competition will likely bid the price of this printing press down to its cost, and it will earn no rents. On the other hand, if the firm producing the press has specific know-how and patents on some of the machine's technology, then no one can reproduce the machine. In this case, it is possible (but not guaranteed) for this firm to earn rents on the machine, selling it for a price exceeding its cost. Also, a piece of land that is unique because of its location (say, being on Wall Street or on a beach) can earn an economic rent if people are willing to pay for its uniqueness.

ECONOMIC PROFITS

Economic profits equal total revenues minus the total cost of all other input payments (including payment for the owner's time and capital). As you can see, economic profits are residual payments. It is similar to economic rent in that it is the excess of price over cost. But unlike economic rents, economic profits can be bid away by competition in the long run. (Most texts don't add this distinction.)

Economic profits arise from three main activities:

1. Innovation: Economic profits arise from finding better ways to allocate resources. As you'll recall, in the long run, prices in a competitive industry equal costs. If someone finds a cheaper way to produce the same good, she'll be able to make a profit in the short run. Similarly, if she finds a new and more valued good for the resources to produce, she'll make a profit.
2. Risk-bearing: Because of uncertainty about the future, many people have to in effect place a bet by committing resources to one of many possible outcomes. Only a few will win. To get people to make these bets, it is necessary that the winnings of the winners far exceed their cost; otherwise, no one would make the bet.
3. Limiting supply below its competitive level: This is how monopolies make their profit. In this case, the profits come at the cost of society.

Thought Question

Each of four drug companies has committed $50 million in research to find a cure for the dreaded widget disease. Each has an equal chance of finding the cure. Only one will. What profits will the curve have to pay at a minimum for each of these companies to be willing to invest the $50 million?

The present value of the profits will have to equal at least $200 million. Each firm has one-quarter chance of getting the prize of $200 million, whose expected value is ¼ times $200 million. Thus, profits have to, in this case, at least cover the costs of those seeking them (assuming they have correctly calculated the odds of winning). The winning drug company will appear to be making obscene profits, but in fact these profits mostly reflect the costs of others.

There are two sources for a nation's wealth: (1) Producing more of what an economy already has with its current technology and (2) producing old goods in new ways and producing new goods, innovation. In command economies, prices are determined by government commands rather than by markets. Command economies that outlaw profits can do (1) but do not do (2) well at all. One picture said it all. When Poland went to the price system, a picture appeared in the paper showing a Polish-made car thrown away in a dumpster. Poland, under a nonmarket command-type socialistic economy, had produced a lot of the 1940-era cars. But when compared to cars being produced by market economies, they were worthless!

CRIB NOTES

Interest rates: Payment for foregoing consumption and lending money.

Simple case: Rate of return (%) = [X/I] × 100, where

X = annual payment, made yearly, year after year, forever.

I = up-front investment cost.

Rule: Invest if rate of return ≥ borrowing rate.

Present value of $X paid yearly forever = X / i, where i is decimal.

Present value of $X paid once in N years at interest rate i = $X/(1 + i)^N$.

Rule: Invest if Present value of all returns ≥ Up-front costs.

Demand for loanable funds: Schedule of interest and how much businesses (and others) will borrow. Shifts up if business projects more profitable.

Supply of loanable funds: Schedule of interest rates and how much savers will lend. Shifts up if people willing to save more at given interest rate.

Rent: Payment to resource in fixed supply. Also amount payment exceeds supply price. Results: Tax on rent doesn't affect supply. Rent control does not affect supply but leads to misallocation.

Profit: Excess of payment over economic cost. Profits can result from using resources in better way, which benefits society, and risk-taking. They can also come from reducing output below its competitive level, which harms society.

Review Questions

---

1. John invested time and money in a college education specializing in chemical engineering. Had he not gone to college, he would have earned $20,000 a year. Had he invested the same time and money elsewhere, he would have earned an annual income of $10,000 a year. It turns out that chemical engineers are in hot demand, so he earns $35,000 a year. What part of his earnings are wages (for the opportunity cost of his time had he not gone to college), what part is interest, and what part is economic profit?

2. In what sense is it true that interest rates reflect the impatience of savers?

3. In what sense is it true that interest rates reflect the productivity of capital?

4. On the remote and isolated island of Remota, there is only one good, Crusonium. Crusonium grows at a 5% rate. Any proportion of it can be cut down and used for food, clothing, and shelter. So the people of Remota face a choice: consume Crusonium now or have 5% more Crusonium next year. What will the market interest rate be in Remota?

5. Suppose people saved 10% of their income, regardless of the interest rate. Show the demand and supply of loanable funds. What will happen to investment when the productivity of capital goes up?

6. How will the following events affect the demand curve for loanable funds (D), the supply curve of loanable funds (S), the interest rate (i), and investment (I)? Use +, −, or 0 to indicate increase, decrease, or no change.
   Event A: Savers become more future oriented and increase their savings.
   Event B: Business firms become more pessimistic about the future.
   Event C: The corporate tax rate is reduced.
   Event D: Due to an advertising campaign for a beer that says, "Do it now!" savers put a higher value on current consumption and a lower value on future consumption.

7. Why do corporate bonds pay a higher rate of interest than an equivalent U.S. government bond? ("Equivalent" here means they are issued at the same time and have the same maturity.)

8. You can buy U.S. Treasury bills that pay $1,000 in one year. They pay no explicit interest. Instead, they sell for a discount that reflects the rate of interest. If the market interest rate is 10%, what will a 1-year Treasury bill sell for?

9. A *perpetuity* is a bond that pays a fixed interest payment forever. Suppose you can buy a perpetuity that pays a constant $50 a year, year after year, forever. If the interest rate is 10%, what will the price of such a perpetuity be?

10. Florida announces that it has a $20 million pot in its lottery. The wining ticket will pay $1 million a year for 20 years.
    a. Is the winning ticket worth $20 million?
    b. Does Florida have to set aside $20 million to pay off the prize winnings?
    c. It can be shown that at an interest rate of 8%, one dollar paid every year for 20 years has a present value of $9.82. Answer questions a and b with specific numbers.

11. You own an auto dealership. You can spend $200,000 today to increase your inventory of cars. This increased inventory would increase your profits by $230,000 at the end of the year. You have to pay 10% to borrow these funds. Should you make this investment?

12. Bill buys a home in 1990 for $100,000. Over the next 10 years, he rents it out. His rents cover his yearly direct cost of renting the home. At the end of the 10 years, he sells the home for $200,000. Did he make a good deal? Assume the interest rate is 10% and note that $1.10^{10} = 2.5937425$.

13. Which of the following reflects an example of someone collecting an economic rent? Person A who loves his job so much he would work for free. Yet, he gets paid $100,000 a year. Person B is a landlord who collects $1,200 a month for a rental apartment. This covers the cost of renting, including the time and interest cost. Person C is a farmer, who, because of her special talent, earns $50,000 a year when other farmers, on the same land, would have earned only $30,000.

14. There are 50 firms in an economy. All firms are exactly alike. Each has one new project that has a return of 15%, another project paying 14%, another paying 13%, and so forth (each added project paying 1% less than before). Each project has an upfront cost of $1,000. Describe the demand for loanable funds curve.

15. An artist paints one painting a year, which he can sell for $800,000. If he didn't paint, he would earn $50,000 a year elsewhere.
    a. How much economic rent is he earning?
    b. If price controls mandate that all paintings must sell for $100,000 or less, how many paintings will he supply?
    c. What is the social loss of the price control if the painting is sold to someone valuing it at $300,000?

16. A storm devastates a local community, leaving it without electricity. The price of ice triples. Explain the role of profits in getting the ice to this community.

17. A builder discovers an ingenious way of using silly putty to cut the cost of building homes in half. Who will benefit from this and how? Give your answer for both the short and long run.

Answers

1. $20,000 is the wages this worker could have earned otherwise and reflects the opportunity cost of not going to college. Another $10,000 is the interest return on his investment. The last $5,000 is economic profit. (Note: It could also be economic rent if his seniority and other barriers to entry prevent it from being bid away).
2. Savers are impatient because they prefer having a dollar today rather than a dollar in the future. This is true even if there is no inflation. So to get them to give up a dollar today, they have to be paid more than a dollar in the future. The more is the interest rate they earn. The more impatient savers are, the higher interest rates will be. On the other hand, if savers were not impatient, they would lend money out at a zero interest rate!
3. Capital produces a rate of return. The demand for loanable funds reflects the rate of return on marginal capital investments. The more productive capital is, the higher interest rates will be. On the other hand, if capital weren't productive, busi-

nesses would not be willing to borrow funds at all, and the interest rate would be zero.[1]

4. The interest rate will be 5%. That's because the rate of return on all investments (not consuming Crusonium) will be 5%. The demand for loanable funds (which in this case is Crusonium) will be perfectly elastic at 5%, being a horizontal line at 5%. The figure illustrates the odd case, where I^* is the amount that will be invested.[2]

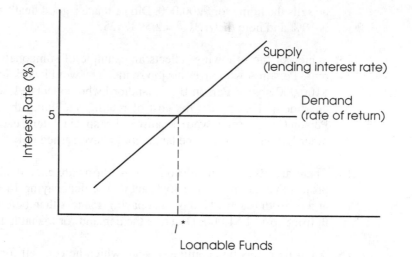

5. In contrast to question 4, the supply of funds will be perfectly inelastic. An increase in the productivity of capital will increase the demand for loanable funds (shown by shift from D to D'). This will raise the rate of interest (from 6% to 9% in the diagram), but in this case, investment will be unaffected.

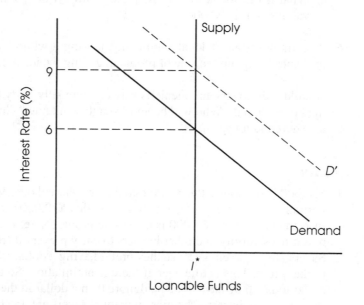

[1]There is no need to worry on this score. Straightening out all railroad tracks would produce a rate of return of about 1% (in fuel savings from not having to make the turns). Filling in the Gulf of Mexico is another winning investment, also paying back 1%. Other nifty but low-paying investments include blowing up the moon (to get rid of tides) and building a canal to bring Arctic waters down to the equator (to even out the weather).

[2]Recall that investment is the net addition to the current capital stock. So I^* is the addition to the island's stock of growing Crusonium.

6. Event A: $D\,0, S+, i-, I+$
   Event B: $D-, S\,0, i-, I-$
   Event C: $D+, S\,0, i+, I+$
   Event D: $D\,0, S-, i+, I-$

7. There is a higher probability that a corporation will default on its interest payments so a corporate bond must pay a higher interest rate. This higher rate reflects the premium for default risk. Both government and corporate bonds must pay the real (pure) rate of interest plus a premium for interest rate risk and for expected inflation. As an approximation for longer-term bonds, if there is an $x\%$ chance that bond will default in a given year, the risk premium will equal $x\%$. So if a government bond pays 8% and there is a 1% chance a corporation will default in a given year, the corporate bond will pay about 9% a year.

8. It will sell today for the present value of $1,000 in one year. So it will sell for $909.09 (= $1,000/1.10) when the interest rate is 10%.

9. $500 (= 50 / 0.10). Note that this dividing by i formula is used when the interest is paid year in and year out. Dividing by $1 + i$ is for when the interest is paid only once and that once is in one year.

10. a. Because future dollars are worth less than current dollars, the present value of the prize is worth less than the sum of its payments. It will be worth less than $20 million.

    b. Because Florida can invest now and earn interest, it doesn't need to set aside the full $20 million to make future payments. It can set aside considerably less.

    c. (a) At 8%, the $1 million a year has a present value of only $9.82 million to the winner instead of $20 million. (b) Florida can set aside the present value, $9.82 million, and pay out of this $1 million a year. As you can see, the "$20 million" is hype: It overstates the value and the cost of the prize! The equation for finding the present value of $X paid for N years at an interest rate of i (expressed as a decimal number) is

$$PV = \frac{1}{i} \cdot \left[1 - \frac{1}{(1 + i)^N} \right]$$

11. Yes. The present value of $230,000 in one year at an interest rate of 10% is $209,091 (= $230,000/1.10). This is worth more than the up-front cost of $200,000.

12. It is a bad deal. Bill invested $100,000 in 1990 (which is today in the present value problems as it is at the beginning of the investment). He gets paid back $200,000 in 10 years. The present value of $200,000 in 10 years is $77,108.62. That's worth less than $100,000. Bill is better off with the $100,000 today than with $200,000 in 10 years.

13. Person A earns a rent of $100,000. Even if his wage fell to $0, he would still work in this firm. Person B earns no rent. Person C, the farmer, earns $20,000 in rent, which is a rent on her special talent, which is in limited supply. The $30,000 reflects the return on time and capital investments.

14. The following table shows the demand for investment curve:

Market Interest Rate	Demand for Loanable Funds ($)
15%	50,000
14%	100,000
13%	150,000
12%	200,000
11%	250,000
every lower % increases demand for loanable funds by $50,000	

At 15%, each firm invests in only the first project (which they break even on). This adds up to $50,000. At a market rate of 14%, each firm invests in the first and second project. So each borrows and invests $2,000, adding up to $100,000. At 13%, each borrows and invests in three projects, adding up to $150,000.

15. a. $750,000
    b. One.
    c. At least $500,000. The person buying the painting valued it at least at $800,000. Instead, it goes to someone valuing it at $300,000. So at least $500,000 in value is being lost due to the price ceiling.

16. The higher price of ice means ice is now more valued in this community than elsewhere. Now it becomes profitable to bring more ice to this community rather than sell it elsewhere. So the role of profits is to attract the supply of ice that this community needs. Without the profits, there would be a shortage of ice and those without ice will be worse off.

17. In the short run, the builder will obviously benefit because he can continue to sell homes for their current price but build them for a much lower cost. Not so obvious though is that consumers will also benefit. The builder cuts cost by using fewer resources (say, nails and lumber). These resources now are in less demand so their prices fall. They then are used elsewhere, at a lower price, and the price of the goods using them will now be cheaper. So even if home prices do not fall, other prices will. In the long run, competition will bid the price of homes down to their new lower costs. Now, home buyers will make a profit in the form of a higher consumer surplus!

Chapter Eighteen

Poverty, Equality, and Economic Growth

INTRODUCTION

What causes poverty? The absence of income! This seemingly stupid answer is actually on the mark. Only in the most unusual of cases does someone sneak around and cause people to become poor. Instead, people are poor because they lack the resources, education, and opportunity to become productive and earn a higher income.

What causes inequality of income? Differences in income! Once again, a seemingly stupid answer. But inequality occurs because people differ in the ability to earn income. These differences arise because of differences in innate ability, differences in learned skills, and, yes, differences in resources, education, and opportunity to earn a higher income.

It is important to note that poverty and inequality are not the same thing! People often say, "I don't like inequality," when what they really mean is that they don't like seeing people living in poverty. For example, there is a glaring inequality between Bill Gates and Donald Trump, because Bill Gates earns at least ten times what the Donald earns. This really upsets me! How often have I cried myself to sleep, asking myself how our society can blindly stand aside and allow this glaring inequality in incomes to continue?

Economic growth supplies the resources and the opportunities for people to earn a higher income. Whether in fact this opportunity will be made available to them is another issue. But without the wealth created by economic growth, we can guarantee that poverty will be widespread.

POVERTY

Someone is officially poor in the United States if his income falls below the official poverty income threshold. This threshold is a measure of a minimum subsistence income, which is calculated as being three times the annual cost of a diet that is considered to be minimally acceptable. Why three times? Because studies of poor persons show they spend about one third of their income on food and diet. If a person's cash income, including government cash assistance, falls below the threshold, then the person is classified as being poor. In 1990, a family of four with a cash income of $13,359 or less was classified as living in poverty. Since 1960, the number of people classified as poor has dropped from 40 million (22.2% of the population) to about 33 million in 1990 (13.5% of the population). If the cash value of Medicare, food stamps, and subsidized housing had been added to cash income, only 25 million or 10 percent would have been classified as being poor in 1990.

PROGRAMS TO HELP THE POOR

There are two ways to help the poor.

1. One way is to increase the poor's productive abilities so that they can earn higher wages. Empirically, this way has not proven to be very effective when applied to adults. In most studies, adults who are poor and who get aid in the form of education and job training get only small increases in wages. These increases are so small that they would have been better off being directly paid the money spent on their education. On the other hand, money spent on improving the education of poor children, particularly programs aimed at very young children, appears to be effective.
2. Another way to help the poor is to give them cash or in-kind benefits. The two main programs giving the poor cash are AFDC and SSI. Aid to Families with Dependent Children (AFDC) gives money to single-parent families (usually headed by females) that have dependent children and whose earnings are low. AFDC cash assistance varies from state to state because states pay about half the cost. Also, the cash received by a person goes down as the person earns more. Supplemental Security Income (SSI) benefits the aged, blind, and disabled. Several programs supply in-kind benefits (in-kind means in the form of goods rather than cash), including Medicaid, food stamps, and housing assistance.

GOALS OF WELFARE PROGRAMS

The following are three goals that most people would like a welfare program to meet:

1. Make the poor better off.
2. Give the poor an incentive to work.
3. Reduce the cost of the program.

It is usually impossible to change our welfare programs without making one of these goals worse. Let's see why.

Most welfare programs, taken together, consist of two parts. First, there is a basic benefit one gets if one doesn't work. Second, there is some formula for reducing benefits as one earns more. As an example, in 1990, an average welfare recipient who didn't work received $5,000 in cash from the government plus another $4,000 in in-kind benefits, for a total income of $9,000. This is the basic benefit one gets if one doesn't work. Next, let's look at how our welfare system reduces its benefits as one earns more. A poor person in 1990 who earned $10,000 received $1,000 in benefits plus $1,700 in in-kind benefits. After subtracting taxes of about $700, she had an income of $12,000. Thus, the person who went out and worked enough to earn $10,000 only increased her spending income on net by $2,000! The effect of reducing benefits is equivalent to taxing the earnings of the working poor. In this case, the equivalent tax rate is 80%. This reduces the incentive to work!

What can be done? We'll focus on the two parts of every welfare program: the basic benefits and the reduction in benefits as one earns more. First, suppose we reform welfare by reducing basic benefits. This will reduce the cost of welfare and will also increase the incentive for people to work (as they get less when not working). This advances goals 2 and 3. But it also makes the poor worse off, thus defeating goal 1.

Second, suppose we instead reform welfare by reducing the rate at which welfare benefits fall as one earns more (but keep basic benefits the same). This will encourage people to work and will make the poor better off. This advances goals 1 and 2. On the other hand, this change would raise the cost of the program, defeating goal 3. To see why it will likely increase the cost of welfare, imagine that there were no reduction in welfare benefits at all. Then everyone, from the poorest person to billionaires, would be getting the same welfare benefits! This would make welfare very, very costly.

There are other changes that promise some remedy. One proposal is to replace the welfare system with a wage subsidy for the poor. Those capable of work would get no benefits unless they worked. Employers hiring them would get a per hour subsidy, which they would be required to give to these poor persons in the form of a higher wage. This program would slightly raise costs and would give an incentive for people to work. It can be structured so that most of the poor are no worse off.

INEQUALITY

Income inequality is usually measured by comparing income of families. A *family* is, according to the statisticians, two or more persons related by birth, adoption, or marriage and residing together. One way to measure income inequality is to compare percent shares of total annual money income with percent share of population. To do this, line up families from the poorest on the left to the richest on the far right. Put each group into a percentile of the population. For example, in a population of 1,000 families, the ten poorest families would be in the lowest 1%, the next ten would be in the 2% slot, and so forth. Next, as you move from left to right, add up the total income of all the families so far and express this as a percent of total national income. This will go from 0% to 100% as you go from right to left. The result is called a *Lorenz curve,* which plots the percentage of national income enjoyed by each percentage of families ranked according to their income. Figure 18.1 shows a Lorenz curve.

Points to note:

If there is no income inequality, the Lorenz curve would be the straight line from 0 to C. For example, at point *a,* 30% of the families would earn 30% of national income. At point *b,* 80% of the families would earn 80% of national income.
The curved line shows an example of a Lorenz curve when income is unequal. At point *A,* 30% of the poorest families earn only 10% of national income. At point *B,* 80% of the lower-income families earn 50% of national income.
At point *B,* going the other way, the top 20% of the families earn the other 50% of the national income. At point *A,* the top 70% of the families earn 90% of the national income.
Between points *A* and *B* are 50% of the families (80% − 30%). This group earns 40% of national income (50% − 10%).
The greater the area between the diagonal line (from 0 to point *C*) and the Lorenz curve, the greater the inequality.

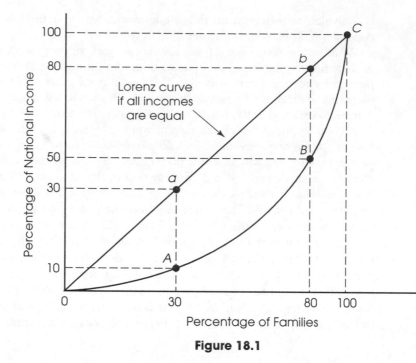

Figure 18.1

Over the century, income inequality has been relatively stable. It has changed, but not dramatically. During the Great Depression, income inequality became greater, while after World War II up through 1970, it became smaller. Since 1970, it has increased, until today it is about where it was in 1940. Similar forces are also operating worldwide. However, Europe did not experience the same increase in inequality as the United States did because of their large welfare program, strong unions, and higher minimum wages. Instead, what did happen in Europe was an increase in unemployment, with the result that younger persons and women had fewer job opportunities.

Income inequality is, in part, caused by differences in abilities among people, differences in initial opportunities, and differences in luck. But beyond these obvious explanations, there are other reasons for inequality. Two of the main reasons are:

1. Difference in investment in human capital—Education and the acquisition of skills cost time and money. Therefore, those people who invest in acquiring skills will demand and get a higher income that compensates them for their costs.
2. Year-to-year fluctuations in income—Suppose there are only two types of jobs, both paying the same average income. Half the jobs are stable, paying $20,000 a year. Half the jobs are unstable, paying $30,000 in one year and $10,000 in the other. In any given year, 25% of the workforce will earn $10,000, 50% will earn $20,000, and another 25% will earn $30,000. The distribution of income will look very unequal, yet everyone is earning the same average income!

GROWTH OF INCOME INEQUALITY

In the United States, income inequality has been growing since the early 1970s. What's more, most industrial nations started to experience similar forces. A possible explanation follows. A new technology was introduced in this period, the computer. Whenever a new technology is introduced, initially it is only the better educated and those more capable of handling change that can take advantage of it. Thus, these persons earn more while those lacking these adaptive skills earn less. Income inequality increases. Over time, the techniques of the new technology become standardized and made simple. Division of labor then allows the less skilled to utilize them. At this point, income inequality shrinks (as it did in the 1950s and 1960s). Evidence that the growth in income inequality is due to new technology is that (1) the income inequality has been growing within occupations, suggesting the cause is not a change in demand between occupations or due to a change in industrial structure; and (2) the widening gap between college and high school graduate's income has occurred.

ECONOMIC GROWTH

Economic growth is usually measured as the growth in per capita real income.

There is a very simple concept here that is essential for you to grasp. It is this. A nation's output per person equals the nation's income per person. Each individual may not get what they produce, but taken together, the sum of incomes equals the sum of what is produced.[1] As a result, the only way to raise income per person is to increase output per person.

Economic growth is a measure of how much income per person, and thus, output per person, has gone up in a given year. The rule of 72 tells us how important economic growth is. The rule of 72 says that if something grows at 7.2% a year, it will double in 10 years. If it grows at $X\%$, it will double in $7.2/X$ times 10 years. If economic growth per capita grew at 7.2%, income would double every 10 years (as it has in South Korea and Hong Kong). If it grew at 3.6% (half of 7.2%), it would double every 20 years. If it grew at 1.8%, it would double every 40 years. Therefore, if an economy can increase its economic growth rate from 1.8% (about what it is now in the United States) to 3.6%, then in 40 years, per capita income will go up four times instead of doubling. That is, going from 1.8% to 3.6% will produce twice the level of per capita income in 40 years. If the United States had done this starting in 1960, we would be twice as rich. Instead of an average family income of $35,000, the average family would be earning $70,000.

What will increase the output per person and thus increase economic growth?

1. Increased capital per person—The more capital per worker, the higher the marginal product and the more produced. Capital is created by savings, so it is not surprising that those countries that save more tend to be those that grow more. China, for example, saves 40% of its income and has been growing more than 10% a year.

    There was a great experiment proving the importance of capita per person. It was called the Black Plague. The Black Plague occurred in the 1300s and wiped out one third to two thirds the population. But it left the capital stock and technology unchanged. As a result, the capita per person about doubled. As a result, per capita income also grew dramatically. Those that survived did well.

2. Increased education—The importance of education (and knowledge) was illustrated by another economic experiment, called World War II. After the war, Germany's physical capital was destroyed but its human capital remained intact. It had been bombed back to a very primitive state. Yet, within 10 years, it was one of the leading industrial nations. This was because its population was well-educated and highly skilled.

---

[1]Except for borrowing from (or lending to) foreign nations. For the United States, this is relatively small in percent terms.

Better-educated people are quicker to adopt new technologies and are better able to manage in the face of change. Thus, education and new technologies are synergetic: both reinforce one another as they increase output and incomes.

3. Better technology (technological progress)—Technological progress occurs when the same resources produce more than before. This results from better techniques, better management, and better ways of doing things. Although more physical capital and more human capita per person result in more inputs per person, technological progress results is more output per input.

The invention of electricity illustrates the impact of a new technology. Its impact on growth was slow. Initially, various technologies for creating and transporting electricity competed with each other. Only over time did the necessary small inventions and products come forth that allow us to fully utilize electricity as we do today. Only the occasional power outage reminds us how important it is. Overall, it took about 40 years for factories and households to fully capture the productive benefits of electricity.

4. Starting out behind—Being behind has its advantages. A country that starts out today to grow does not have to reinvent electricity nor spend billions creating useful computers. Instead, they can send their students to U.S. universities and have them return with the knowledge they need to become productive. The diffusion of technology by imitation is a lot cheaper than inventing it in the first place. The result is that economic growth rates are higher in poorer countries but they slow as these countries approach the levels of other countries. That is, both economic growth rates and income levels, over time, tend to converge. Poor countries, such as Japan after the war, grew faster as they imitated the technologies of the more advanced countries. But as they approached the leading edge of technology, their growth rates slowed down as they too had to invest in new technologies. Similarly, in the United States, the poorer states (such as those in the South) have been growing faster as they slowly converge with the richer states.

5. Good governments—Statistically, the larger the government, the slower the rate of growth. Does this mean that all the government does slows economic growth? The answer is no. A good government that secures property rights, allows patents that reward innovations, builds highways and other infrastructures, and educates its public will promote economic growth. But much of what governments do decreases economic growth. This is done by taxing citizens and spending the money on projects whose costs far exceed their benefits. This is waste and it acts as a drag on an economy. For example, when canals were introduced into the United States in the 1800s, they were successful and made the governments and regions that invested in them better off. Unfortunately, for governments, success often breeds failures. Almost every city and state set off on a canal building spree, whether the canals were needed or not. It turned out they were not needed because railroads proved to be more efficient.

ACCOUNTING FOR GROWTH (ADVANCED SECTION)

Growth accounting is a method of accounting for the sources of economic growth. Let us see how it would be used with a simple model. Suppose a nation's total output (Q) is greater the more labor it has (L), and the more capital it has (K). In addition, how much Q it gets from a given amount of L and K is determined by its technology[2]. If output is produced with constant returns to scale, then, given its technology, an equal percentage increase in L and K should increase Q by the same amount. More generally,

$$\% \Delta Q = \textbf{Labor share} * \% \Delta L + \textbf{Capital share} * \% \Delta K + \textbf{TFP}$$

where labor share is labor's share of national income and capital share is capital's share of national income (because there are only two inputs, these shares add up to one), and $\% \Delta L$ is the percent growth in labor inputs (measured by the total hours worked). *TFP* stands for total factor productivity. It is the increase in output growth not accounted for by input growth. Sometimes this is incorrectly referred to as *technological progress*. It does include the effects of technological progress, but it also includes the effects of having better-educated workers, having better ways of managing workers and resources, having better ways of marketing goods, and taking advantage of economies of scale.

Productivity is the real output per worker hour. It equals Q/L, or real gross domestic product divided by total labor hours. To keep things simple, we'll refer to Q/L as output per worker, because this corresponds to income per worker.

To see what determines productivity, the preceding equation can be rewritten as

$$\% \Delta Q/L = \textbf{Capital share} * \% \Delta K/L + \textbf{TFP}$$

This says that the growth in output per worker hour equals capital's share of output (which is one third) plus the growth rate per worker due to the growth in total factor productivity.

From 1960 to 1973, capital per worker (K/L) grew a total of 25%. Output per worker (Q/L) grew 25% over this period. Since one third of 25% is 8.3%, this means that *TFP* equals what's left unexplained, or 16.7% (= 25% − 8.3%). In this period, the change in total factor productivity, or technological progress, was responsible for most of the economic growth.

From 1973 to 1983, K/L increased 16% and Q/L increased 4.8%. This means that in this period, *TFP* was −0.5% (4.8% − ⅓ × 16%). Did our economy regress in this period? The answer is no. Technological progress did continue, but several events hurt the output per person. First, there was the dramatic rise in energy prices, which had the effect of rendering much of our capital obsolete. Second, there was a set of very costly environmental regulations that diverted investment away from increasing productivity toward cleaning the air. This reduced the effective K. While clean air does add to our utility, its value is not counted as part of our output. So not measuring the value of clean air hurt Q/L because the reported Q was below the actual Q (which includes the value of clean air). Third, our economy shifts away from manufacturing toward the service sector. Unfortunately, the way we measure the output of the service sector tends to understates its growth rate. As a result, the measured Q/L was likely smaller than the actual Q/L. Since then, the economy has returned to its usual path.

CRIB NOTES

Poverty: Income < poverty income threshold level (= 3 × subsistence diet cost).

Welfare programs: Basic benefits (if do not work) plus rate at which benefits reduced as earn more. Reducing basic benefits results in more people working and lower program costs, but it makes the

---

[2]It also depends how efficiently it uses its resources.

poor worse off. Reducing the rate at which benefits are reduced results in more people working and makes poor better off, but it increases program costs.

Inequality: Shown by Lorenz curve. More bowed-in to southeast, more unequal.

Economic growth in per capita income: Growth in per capita output. To increase Q/L, increase K per L, increase human capital per L, increase technological progress (more output per input).

Review Questions

1. In calculating the poverty rate, the U.S. government measures income by adding up money income from all sources, including money income from government transfers, such as Social Security, unemployment compensation, and welfare cash payments.

   a. Another way to calculate income is to use only money income from private sources (for example, wage income). How would the poverty rate using this measure of income compare to the government's measure? What would the poverty rate using this figure reflect?

   b. Still another way to measure income is to take the government's measure of income and add it to the cash equivalent of in-kind government programs (such as food stamps, Medicare, rent subsidies, and school lunch programs). How would the poverty rate using this measure of income compare to the government's rate? What would the poverty rate using this figure reflect?

2. There are two countries, A and B. In country A, each citizen is poor once every 5 years on average. This happens randomly (imagine each person annually drawing a number from one to five and the people drawing a 1 get to be poor that year). In country B, 1 out of 5 persons are poor and they stay poor for their whole life (similarly, the not poor never become poor).

   a. What is the poverty rate in each country?

   b. In which would you say is poverty a worse state to be in?

3. Which of the three goals listed in the text for welfare programs would be advanced or harmed by the following changes in the welfare program?

   Change A: Basic benefits are reduced to $100 a year.

   Change B: A negative income tax is implemented. It would pay people the current basic benefit if they didn't work and reduce their benefits by 15 cents for every dollar they earn. (This is called a *negative* income tax because poor people get money from the government. This is the *negative* or *opposite* of what most of us do, which is pay money to the government.)

4. From the following table, draw a Lorenz curve.

Fifth of Families	Lowest Fifth	Second Fifth	Third Fifth	Fourth Fifth	Top Fifth
Percentage Share of Total Money Income (U.S., 1990)	3.9	9.6	16	24.1	46.4

5. Assume that all education increases earnings by 10% of its cost. For example, people spending $30,000 on education will earn, on average, $3,000 more per year than they would have otherwise. Next, assume that the cost of education is purely the foregone cost of what one could have earned had one worked instead of attending school. Assume high school graduates earn $20,000 a year. Calculate what those with 1 year of college will earn. Next, calculate what people with 2 years of college will earn (be careful to note the new opportunity cost of the second year). Do this for 8 years (which approximates how long it takes to get a doctorate).
   a. What does this say about the earnings of those with more education?
   b. If the rate of return on other investments is 10% and if this were the actual income by educational level, then does this show income equality or income inequality?

6. How would the following events likely affect income inequality?
   Event A: An increase in profit-sharing plans, such that worker's average income is the same but year-to-year income goes up and down more.
   Event B: The tax structure is made more progressive, taxing the rich at a higher tax rate than before.
   Event C: Increased welfare benefits to each child in poor families.
   Event D: A higher minimum wage plus an increase in the basic welfare benefits for those not working.

7. How will the following events affect per capita income? (Hint: Ask if it raises total output per person.)
   Event A: A nuclear war is fought with neutron bombs that destroy people, not capital.
   Event B: Scientists discover a pill that eliminates sleep. As a result, everyone works 3 hours more a day than before.
   Event C: Unions raise wages. Assume total union employment remains unchanged.
   Event D: The income tax is made more dramatically progressive, such that all persons earning more than $50,000 a year are taxed at 95% tax rate.
   Event E: A new fertilizer quadruples farm productivity, such that the same inputs produce four times the food. However, the total amount of food produced remains unchanged because people have all the food they want.

8. A welfare program has the following schedule for payments:
      $400 per month in basic benefits if you don't work.
      $150 per month can be earned without any loses of benefits.
      Above earnings of $150 per month, the recipient loss 80 cents in welfare benefits for every dollar earned.
   a. At what level of earnings will this person no longer get any welfare benefits?
   b. Calculate the implicit tax for persons earning slightly less than this amount.
   c. What is the tax on someone earning more? Ignore the effects of any income and social security taxes.

9. Marvin spends only $100 a year on medical care. Then he qualified for Medicaid, which pays for all his medical expenses. He then demands medical care that costs $1,000 a year.
   a. Are Marvin's Medicare costs of $1,000 worth $1,000 to Marvin?
   b. Draw Marvin's demand and supply curve for medical treatment, assuming a supply price of $100 per treatment. What is the gain to Marvin of receiving Medicaid? (Assume his demand curve is a straight but downward-sloping line).

10. True or false: Without technological progress, there would be no economic growth (in per capita terms).

11. Between 1983 and 1994, K/L grew 10.3% and Q/L grew 13.6%. Using the growth equation, what was the percent technological change (TFP) in this period?

12. The following graph shows two production functions. A production function relates K/L to Q/L, given current technology. As a result of diminishing marginal product, the output per worker (Q/L) increases at a decreasing rate with the capital per worker (K/L). PF_0 is production function in year 0. PF_1 is the production function in year 1. In year 0, the nation is at point A. In year 1, the nation is at point C.
    a. What letters show the increase in per worker output?
    b. Some of this growth in per worker output is due to greater savings and investment, resulting in more capital per worker. What letters show this growth?
    c. Some of this growth in per worker output is due to technological progress. What letters show this growth?

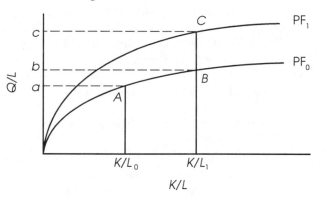

Answers

1. a. Because this measure of income does not add in government welfare, more people will have incomes that fall below the official poverty line. So the poverty rate will be higher when this figure is used. In 1991, the government's poverty rate was 14.2 percent while the poverty rate using only private income was higher at 21.8 percent. This is what the poverty rate would be if all government assistance stopped (assuming poor people didn't start working more as a result).

    b. Because this measure makes income higher, fewer people will have incomes that fall below the poverty line. So the poverty rate using this measure of income would be smaller than the government's rate. In 1991, while the government's rate was 14.2%, the poverty rate using this broader measure of income was 11.4%. This measure reflects the true welfare of people, when including the value of all the benefits they get. However, to say this, we must assume that the value to the poor of the in-kind benefits equals their cost. As we saw with the economics of gifts, that is probably not the case. The poor would probably rather have had the cash, so the value of in-kind benefits is less than their cost.

2. a. Both countries have a 20% poverty rate. In both A and B, in a given year, 20 out of 100 citizens will be classified as being poor.

    b. It would be worse to be poor in country B. In country A, poverty is short-lived and equally shared. In the United States, somewhere between 20 and 50% of those classified as being poor in any given year are persistently poor (that is, they'll remain poor for 8 or more years).

3. Change A: This will meet the goal of reducing the cost of the welfare program and the goal of encouraging more people to work. It will harm the goal of making the poor better off, because those who can't find work will be worse off.

   Change B: Because this program will result in the poor losing fewer benefits as they work more, this will meet the goal of making the poor better off and the goal of giving more of them an incentive to work. On the other hand, it will likely cost more, hurting the goal of containing the cost of the welfare program.

4. The relevant plot points are

Y-Axis	0%	3.9%	13.5%	29.5%	53.6%	100%
X-Axis	0%	20%	40%	60%	80%	100%

   where the y-axis is the vertical axis, reflecting total percentage of income, and the x-axis is the horizontal axis, reflecting the percentage of families.

5. a. Earnings grow in a compounded fashion with education. In this case, earnings with N years of education equal 1.1^N times \$20,000. A person with one added year of education earns \$22,000. If that person goes another year, he will add \$2,200 to his earnings (10% of \$22,000), or make \$24,200. A person with 8 years of education will earn \$42,872. This is more than twice what a high school graduate would have earned.

   b. This would appear to show inequality. Yet if the rate of return on other investments is 10%, then all the persons would have the same present value of income. That is, they would all be earning equal incomes after the foregone costs of education were accounted for. Thus, it would show perfect income equality!

6. Event A: This will increase income inequality because, even though all get the same on average, some will get more while others will get less.

   Event B: This will decrease income inequality.

   Event C: This will decrease income inequality. However, it may be that in the long run, this could cause mothers on welfare to have more children and this, in turn, could increase income inequality.

   Event D: This will decrease income inequality. The poor who keep their jobs will get more and those who lose their jobs (from the higher minimum wage) will also get more.

7. Event A: This will increase the capital per remaining person, increasing per capita income.

   Event B: This will increase per capita income.

   Event C: If union employment is unchanged, this will have no effect on per capita income, as total output will remain unchanged as does employment. What will happen is that higher union wages will cause a transfer of income from business owners (in the form of reduced profits) and nonunion workers (in the form of higher prices for union-made goods) to union workers. If union employment falls, but total employment stays unchanged, then the unemployed union workers will now be working in the nonunion sector. Because they will be less productive there (otherwise, they would have taken the nonunion job), this will lower total output. In this case, output (income) per person will fall.

   Event D: This will reduce the work and entrepreneurial efforts of rich people and thus reduce per capita output (and thus income) per person.

   Event E: This will increase per capita income. Given that food production is the same but only one fourth of the resources as before are needed, the other three fourths of farm resources are now available to produce other goods. This will raise total output.

8. a. $650. Ask yourself how much you have to earn to lose $400 in benefits. Let X be this number. You'll lose 80% of X in benefits. Thus, we have at the break-even point of losing $400, $0.80X = 400$. Solving for X, we have $X = \$400/0.80$ or $X = \$500$. That is, 80% of $500 is $400. Then add this to the $150 (the amount you are not taxed on). So if you earn $500 on top of $150, or $650 a month, you'll lose all benefits.

   b. The implicit tax rate is 80% for those earning between $150 and $650. For every dollar earned, they lose 80 cents in benefits, so they net only 20 cents in added income.

   c. The tax rate for those above $650 is 0%.

9. a. Medicaid must be worth less to Marvin than it costs. If the extra $900 were worth $900 (or more) to Marvin, he would have gotten it before on his own. Because he didn't, it must be that he preferred the $900 cash to the $900 added medical care.

   b. We know two points on Marvin's demand curve: one treatment at a price of $100 and ten treatments at a price to Marvin of $0. So we have the following graph:

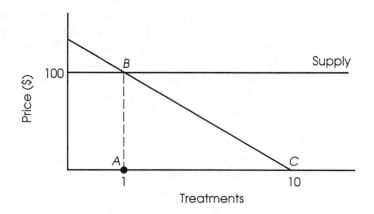

The value of the first treatment is $100 (as that is what Marvin gains by having Medicare paying for it). The value of the next nine treatments to Marvin is the area under his demand curve from 1 to 10. This is the area of triangle ABC, which is ½ × 100 × 9, or $450. So the total value to Marvin of $1,000 of Medicare is $550.

10. False. There are two ways to increase the output per person. One is technological progress (making more with what you have), and the other is increasing the capital and other inputs per person (increasing what you have). The second way is always possible and adds to growth. However, adding capital per person requires savings. If capital has a diminishing marginal product, then at some point, it will not pay to save and people will want to maintain the same capital per person year after year. At this point, without technological progress, there will be no growth in output per person.

11. It was 10.2% (= 13.6 − ⅓ × 10.3).

12. a. Output per worker grows from a to c (as the economy moves from A to C).

   b. The growth in output per worker due to increased capital per worker (growing from K/L_0 to K/L_1) is from a to b, as the economy moves along the same production function (PF_0).

   c. The growth in output per worker due to technological progress is from b to c, as the economy moves to a higher production function PF_1.

Chapter Nineteen

International Trade

TRADE

We are all foreign traders. We import (buy) goods and services from others and we export (sell) goods and services (like work) to others. This is not just an analogy. International trade, domestic trade, your buying and selling: all are the same economic act. And it is a fundamental discovery of economics that people trade to become better off and that trade makes people better off.

Let's be very about clear this point. As a result of free and voluntary trading, both sides of the trade are better off. One side does not benefit at the expense of the other. If that were true, the trade would not take place. Trade is mutually beneficial.

Let's take this logic another step. You trade because it makes you better off. Conversely, any household that did not trade with others and instead tried to make everything for itself would suffer a dramatic decrease in its welfare. In just the same way, any nation that tried to make everything itself and not trade with other nations would also suffer a decrease in its welfare.

People who oppose free trade are called protectionists. Why do protectionists oppose trade between nations when trade between persons and all trade within a nation makes everyone better off? Because although international trade makes most people better off, it does make some people worse off. But, on the whole, its benefits far exceeds its costs.

MEET THE HOMESTEADS

To analyze international trade, we will first analyze a simple case: the foreign trade of a single household. The Homestead household is proud and hard-working. Pa Homestead keeps a sharp eye on the Homestead's imports and exports. He records the family doings every day in a big ledger. Each page reflects that day's activities. He divides each page in two columns, the left column being imports and the right column being exports. Under imports, he writes all the goods and services the Homesteads buy from the outside world. Under exports, he writes all the goods and services the Homesteads sell to the outside world.

For one Monday, he has written the following:

Imports	Exports
Ma $50 of groceries	Ma $45 selling sewing at fair
Pa $10 of tobacco	

Notice that for this Monday, the Homesteads have run a trade deficit of $15 because their imports of $60 exceed their exports of $45. Do they panic? No, because they meet this difference out of their savings account. Could this go on forever? No, because at some point their savings will be run down.

On Tuesday, he writes:

Imports	Exports
Little Junior $20 of toys	Pa $100 selling labor to factory

On this day, they had a trade surplus of $80, because they had exports of $100 exceeding their imports of $20. Do they celebrate? No, because this is normal. Could this go on forever? Yes. But the Homesteads are not stupid. Some money sitting in the bank is nice as a cushion, but too much is a waste, especially when it could better used being spent on capital (such as farm equipment) or even consumption.

One day, Big Junior, who has been working in Washington, D.C., for the Foreign Trade Commission, comes home and examines these books. "Pa," he announces, "we need to have a trade surplus. Don't you know that these imports are killing us!" Pa, concerned, asks, "What can we do?" Junior carefully analyzes the books and comes up with the following suggestion. Ma, instead of importing groceries, shall make them herself. "This," announces Big Junior, "will provide her with employment and help our trade balance."

But Ma, having read economics books, says, "Big J, your head is full of mush! It takes me 10 hours a week selling exports (by selling my sewing to foreigners) to buy the groceries and it would take me 40 hours a week to make my own groceries. I would have to plow the fields, pick the crops, and turn them into food. Your idea would make me worse off by 30 hours! Quite frankly, I don't know why you're so concerned about the trade surplus when you should be concerned about whether our family is getting the best use of our time and resources, not to mention my back!"

Big Junior is not finished. He turns to Little Junior. "Little," he announces, "I'm going to make you help our trade surplus. For every dollar you spend on toys, you have to pay me another dollar. We'll call this a 100 percent tariff. Of course, you could buy my old toys and not pay that high tariff. But that's good because it keeps the trade within the family. And I promise to spend the money you give me with the family! This will make all of us better off." Little Junior, who has read economics books on his mother's knee replies, "Big J, your head is full of mush. I'm worse off because I'm not getting all the toys I want! Paying a higher price is a bad deal for me. Yes, it may make you better off, but at my expense. And because our family doesn't get as many good toys as it would without your silly tariff, our family as a whole will be worse off!"

Thus, poor Big Junior had to return to Washington, D.C., to sell his ideas.

TARIFFS AND THE ART OF THE BAD DEAL

You know what a good deal is. You get more than you give away. In foreign trade terms, a good deal is when the value of your imports (what you get) exceeds the value of your exports (what you give away).

People like Big Junior try to peddle tariffs and trade restrictions by trying to focus your attention away from making a good deal. Here are some typical distractions they often use.

Foreign Trade Is Costing Us Jobs

Here, the false focus is on jobs. To show why this focus is wrong, imagine what would happen if our nation bought imports from a foreign nation that just sat on our money and never used that money to buy exports from us? That is a very good deal. We get the imports at no cost! But won't these cheap imports cost us jobs? The answer is no. The people who would have made the imports can now do something else. Our nation will then have the imports for free plus all the added goods these persons produce.

The United States actually does import goods from a foreigner that has never yet bought any exports from us! This foreigner is the sun. It gives us light and heat. By doing so, it puts hundred of thousands of electricity workers out of jobs! Yet, we've seemed to manage rather well, and these workers are working elsewhere producing other goods and making us all better off.

Thought Question

True or false: If all Americans had to shut their blinds and keep their lights on during the day, this would provide jobs for American electrical workers and would make America better off!

False. Being forced to pay for light in the daytime would create more electrical worker jobs. But these jobs would come from other sectors of the economy, where their work is more highly valued! Focus not on jobs (which will always be somewhere). Focus on the good deal. Buying sunlight for free is a very good deal. Our nation would be worse off if forced to not take advantage of it.

Foreign Nations Restrict Our Exports So We Should Restrict Their Imports to Us

Here, the false focus is on fairness. It is true that many nations put restrictions on their citizens that keep them from buying goods from the United States.[1] The issue is, however, whether imposing a tariff on the goods from these nations makes our citizens better off. The answer is no. Trade occurs because it is mutually beneficial. Our citizens get goods from the foreigners because they would rather have the goods than the dollars they pay. And what do the foreigners do with the dollars? They can sit and stare at them. That would make our nation better off because we would get their goods for the price of printing a piece of paper. But, alas, they don't do this. They use the dollars to buy our goods. So trade does take place, even if it is restricted! Of course, if the foreign nations removed their restrictions, they and the United States would be even better off. Imposing a tariff moves us the other way, making us worse off, because it denies our citizens from making all the good deals they can!

Thought Question

The governor of Florida knows that Florida is, at its highest point, only 300 feet above sea level. He discovers one day that most of Tennessee is several thousand feet above sea level. Therefore, goods going from Florida to Tennessee must travel uphill, which raises their cost. Goods going from Tennessee to Florida go downhill, which lowers their cost. The Florida governor, after seeing this on a map, announces that this is unfair. "Tennessee," he

---

[1]The United States also restricts our citizens from buying goods from foreigners. For example, we cannot buy sugar freely from the world, where it sells for about half the protected U.S. price. The high U.S. price for sugar is why there is corn syrup, not sugar, in your soft drink!

announces, "is not playing on an even playing field! I demand that Tennessee level itself down to our level using bulldozers! Until we are even and at the same level, Florida will restrict all Tennessee goods from going into Florida." Will this make Florida better off?

No. Florida citizens are being denied all the good deals they were getting before from Tennessee. The deals might be better if, by magic, Tennessee did lower itself. But getting rid of the good deals they were already getting would make Florida worse off. Anyway, where would Tennessee put all that dirt?

Cheap Foreign Labor Will Take Away Our Jobs

Here, the focus again is on jobs rather than on making a good deal. The art of the good deal tells us to buy cheap and sell high. Return to the sun example for the cheapest of deals. The workers replaced by the cheap deal can work elsewhere and we'll have more of all goods.

Suppose there is a nation with extremely low-cost labor and, for that matter, a low cost on everything! This nation can make absolutely every good for, say, half the cost in the United States. Wouldn't this country take away all of our jobs? A more pertinent question is why would this nation ever trade with the United States? Why would it send us boatload after boatload of goods if it wanted nothing in return? The answer is of course it wouldn't. So if it does sell us goods, it must be because it will be buying goods back from us. Jobs would not be destroyed.

SUMMARY OF MAIN POINTS

The following points summarize what we've learned about foreign trade.

Point 1: Trade is mutually beneficial. Both sides profit or they won't trade.

Point 2: Exports are what you sell in exchange for imports. The same is true for nations. International trade is no different than the trades we make every day with each other.

Point 3: The cheaper imports are, the better off a nation is. A smart nation of course would try to get the most imports for a given amount of exports. That would make it best off. That's the best deal. But tariffs work in the opposite way.

THE CURRENT BALANCE AND CAPITAL BALANCE

One of the worries people have about trade deficits is that they incorrectly think that a trade deficit means more dollars are going out of the country (from our buying imports) than are coming back in (from foreigners buying our exports). In fact, this is not the case, because we import and export more than just goods and services. When everything is counted, the dollars going out are matched with the dollars coming in.[2] So there is no need to worry about trade deficits on this account. This complete accounting of dollars in and out is called the *balance-of-payments account*.

---

[2]This is true if foreign governments don't deliberately intervene in foreign trade markets and buy up dollars. This does happen, but usually on a very small scale. But if it becomes a serious problem, our government could print up more money and make up the difference.

The balance-of-payments account has two parts: (1) The *current account,* which keeps track of the goods and services flowing on net out of the United States, and (2) the *capital account,* which keeps track of the physical and financial assets flowing on net into the United States.

At the year's end, the balance of the current account shows the trade in goods and services so that

Balance on trade account = Trade surplus
= Exports – Imports of goods and services

When exports exceed imports, there is a trade surplus. However, if there is a trade deficit (so that imports exceed exports), the trade surplus is negative.

The balance on the capital account shows the trade in assets. If France borrows the money from the United States, it gives us a note that says "I owe you $X." This French IOU is an asset to the United States. Similarly, if a U.S. company buys a French factory, the United States gains a foreign asset. These are examples of imports of assets. On the other hand, if the United States borrows money from other nations, we export our IOUs. If foreigners buy U.S. stocks and bonds, this is also an export of U.S. assets. Like the trade balance, we have:

Balance on capital account = Exports – Imports of assets

The next step is key. We must have

Balance on trade account + Balance on capital account = 0

Why must we have this? Because foreigners are not stupid. If we don't give them goods for their exports, they want our assets (our IOUs)!

Let's see how this works. The United States buys more goods and services from foreigners than it sells from foreigners. We run a trade deficit. In these terms, the balance on the current account is negative. The preceding formula means the balance on the capital account must be positive. We must be exporting more assets than we are importing. That is, we pay for our trade deficit by selling off some of our assets (in the form of stocks, bonds, and U.S. assets such as farms and factories). The dollars spent on all foreign goods (including foreign assets) is just offset by the dollars spent by foreigners on our goods (including our assets). Total dollar spending is unaffected by the trade deficit. No jobs are lost because dollars are going overseas.

Suppose the United States ran a trade surplus, selling more to foreigners than we buy. How do they pay for the difference? By selling off their assets to us. So our current account is positive (exports of goods and services exceed their import) while the capital account is negative (imports of assets exceed their export).

What this says is that the dollars being brought into the United States from the export of all U.S. things (goods and services and assets) equals the dollars being taken out of the United States from the import of all things. Thus, in this broader sense, imports always equal exports. There is no real trade deficit!

Because the trade deficit reflects the excess of buying over selling, it reflects the fact that our nation has to borrow or sell off its assets to pay for the difference. This could be harmful in the long run. So far, it has not been a significant problem.[3] Even if it were a problem, the solution would be to stop our spendthrift habits and increase our savings. Trying to cure the problem of insufficient savings by tariffs and restricting trade is like curing a fever by breaking the thermometer.

---

[3]In particular, if our nation sells stocks and bonds to foreigners and we earn a rate of return that exceeds the interest rate we borrow at, then our nation is better off. This would show up as a trade deficit, yet it reflects a very healthy situation.

WHEN IS TRADE BENEFICIAL TO A NATION?

Trade is the free lunch of economics. With trade, our nation can have more of everything! There are no "trade-offs" or hidden costs. There is a very simple criterion for determining if a nation can be better off with international trade. To understand this criterion, you have to understand that what matters is the relative price of goods, the price of one good divided by the price of another good. The goods that are relevant here are traded goods. Nontraded goods such as the service of fixing a toilet in London are not relevant.

The criterion for benefitting from trade is this. A nation will benefit from trade, that is, it can have more of everything, when the world's relative prices for goods differ from the nation's pretrade relative prices. That's it. A *difference in relative prices* means trade will be beneficial.

Imagine that huge 15-mile-wide spaceships appear over every major city in the world. Instead of mass destruction and really great special effects, the spaceships bring intergalactic trade to our world. The issue is whether our world would be better off with free intergalactic trade.

To analyze this issue, let's make it simple. Suppose there are only two goods—food and clothing. We measure the units of food and the units of clothing so that, prior to the arrival of the spaceships, each costs $100 a unit. That means the relative price of a unit of food is 1.0: One unit of food traded for one unit of clothing. Now suppose the space invaders offer a unit of food for four kirks and one unit of clothing for two kirks. A kirk is their unit of currency, featuring a beautifully rendered portrait of their six-legged, three-eyed supreme leader. The intergalactic relative price of food is 2.0; this means that the price of one unit of food is two units of clothing (work this out now!).

Suppose that, being the intergalactic price, the United States can now buy or sell all the food and clothing it wants at the relative price of 2. What can it do to become better off? Notice that food is now relatively more valuable (the intergalactic relative price being higher than the pretrade price). As shrewd traders, we would want to sell more of the good that's now more highly valued (food) and buy more of the good that's now cheaper (clothing).

Suppose we sell them one unit of food. They pay us 4 kirks. We use these kirks to buy two units of clothing (which cost 2 kirks each). Next, we take the resources that were being used to produce one of the units of clothing and let it be used for making food. Suppose this unit can make one unit of food (this would be the case if the initial prices reflected the true costs of making food and clothing). How have we fared? We now have the same amount of food (having sold one unit and produced another) plus one more unit of clothing! That added unit of clothing is free! It came at no cost!

The trade summarized:

Deal	Food	Clothing
Sell 1 unit of food	−1	
Buy 2 units of clothing		+2
Produce 1 less unit of clothing		−1
Produce 1 more unit of food	+1	
Net effect	0	+1

Note: This assumes that food and clothing both take $100 of resources to produce, so that one less unit of clothing being produced frees $100 of resources that can now be used to produce $100 of food (which is one unit).

Of course, we could have done other things, such as taken the free resources that were producing two units of clothing and used them to produce two units of food. Now we would have the same amount of clothing but one more unit of food. That's what we call a free lunch!

The second trade summarized:

Deal	Food	Clothing
Sell 1 unit of food	−1	
Buy 2 units of clothing		+2
Produce 2 less units of clothing		−2
Produce 2 more units of food	+2	
Net effect	+1	0

How could we get ½ unit more of food and clothing?

Trade summarized:

Deal	Food	Clothing
Sell 1 unit of food	−1	
Buy 2 units of clothing		+2
Produce 1.5 less units of clothing		−1.5
Produce 1.5 more units of food	+1.5	
Net effect	+0.5	+0.5

What if the aliens offer food at 4 kirks but clothing at 8 kirks. Now the relative price of food is 1/2; this means it takes one half unit of clothing to buy 1 unit of food. Now clothing is the relatively more valued good, so we should sell clothing and buy food. As one example, we can sell 1 unit of clothing to the aliens for 8 kirks and buy 2 units of food. We can then take what was used to produce 2 units of food and use them to produce 2 units of clothing. We would then have the same amount of food and 1 more unit of clothing!

The trade summarized:

Deal	Food	Clothing
Sell 1 unit of clothing		−1
Buy 2 units of food	+2	
Produce 2 less units of food	−2	
Produce 2 more units of food		+2
Net effect	0	+1

The point of this exercise is that it does not matter which goods are relatively more expensive and which are relatively cheaper. (Just change their names.) As long as there is a difference between the before-trade prices and the world (or galactic) prices, a nation can have more of everything by trading. Notice that nothing was said about whether the aliens employ cheap labor or if they have any trade restrictions or even if they are giving us the best possible deal. That's because none of this matters. As long as relative prices differ, there are gains to trade!

Why do relative prices differ between nations? The main reason for competitive economies are differences in the relative cost of producing goods. These costs can differ because of (1) differences in the availability of labor, capital, and other resources; (2) differences in tastes and demands for goods; and (3) differences in natural resources.

THE LAW OF COMPARATIVE ADVANTAGE

The law of comparative advantage summarizes the previous sections. It states that a nation will be better off by international trade by exporting those goods that it can produce at a lower relative price than other nations and importing those goods it can buy at a lower relative price than what it would cost itself to produce those goods. That is, buy low and sell high.

Why does the law use the word comparative? Because only the relative advantage matters. A nation could have an absolute disadvantage in each and every good it produces, yet as long as relative prices differ, it will benefit from trade! It is comparative (or relative) advantage that matters!

A simple example illustrates the law of comparative advantage. Suppose that there are units of resources (part labor, capital, and land) that are used to produce goods worldwide. Once again, to keep things simple, assume there are only two goods, food and clothing. Finally, suppose that the United States is worse in producing both food and clothing than the rest of the world. Table 19.1 shows the number of units of resources it takes the United States and the rest of the world (ROW) to produce food and clothing. Note that it takes the United States more resources to produce either good! That means that the United States has an absolute disadvantage in both goods while ROW has the absolute advantage.

TABLE 19.1

Country	Units of Resource Needed To Produce One Unit of Output		Relative Price of Food	Relative Price of Clothing
	FOOD	CLOTHING		
U.S.	6	12	½	2
ROW	3	1	3	⅓

Points to note:

The United States is more inefficient in making food. It takes 6 units of resources in the United States to produce 1 unit of food while it only takes 3 units of resources in the rest of the world.

The United States is more inefficient in making clothing. It takes 12 units of resources in the United States to produce a unit of clothing while it only takes 1 unit of resources in the rest of the world.

The United States has the absolute disadvantage in producing both of these goods.

The relative price of food in the United States reflects its relative cost. Food takes 6 units of resources while clothing costs twice as much, 12 units. So food's relative cost in the United States is ½. Using the same logic, clothing's relative cost is twice that of food. (Note: Relative cost and relative price are the same thing here.)

The United States has the comparative or relative advantage in making food. The U.S. relative price is ½ and the ROW's price is 3. This is the good the United States should sell (export).

The ROW has the comparative advantage in making clothing. The U.S. relative price is 3, which is higher than the ROW's price of ⅓. This is the good the United States should buy (import).

Now we will show how the United States can benefit from trade. Suppose we can buy and sell food at the world's relative price of 3. That is, we can trade 1 unit of food for 3 units of clothing. That means we can sell 1 of food and buy 3 units of clothing.

For each unit of clothing we buy, we can take the 12 units of resources used to produce a unit of clothing and use them to produce 2 units of food (as each unit of food takes 6 units of resources).

Suppose we sell 1 unit of food and buy 3 units of clothing. Then we cut our own production of clothing by 3 units and use the freed resources (36 units of resources) to produce 6 units of food. This will make us better off by 5 units than we had before!

The transaction summarized:

Deal	Food	Clothing
Sell 1 unit of food	−1	
Buy 3 units of clothing		+3
Produce 3 less units of clothing		−3
Produce 6 more units of food	+6	
Net effect	+5	0

Or, after selling 1 unit of food and buying 3 units of clothing, we suppose we produce 1 unit less of clothing. The freed resources allows us to produce 2 more units of food. Now we get more of both goods!

The transaction summarized:

Deal	Food	Clothing
Sell 1 unit of food	−1	
Buy 3 units of clothing		+3
Produce 1 less unit of clothing		−1
Produce 2 more units of food	+2	
Net effect	+1	+2

The terms of trade is the relative price that goods trade at. In this example, the terms of trade is 1 unit of food for 3 units of clothing. If a nation's relative prices before trade differ from the world's terms of trade, then that nation will benefit from trade. In this example, the terms of trade will likely fall between the ROW's price and the U.S. price, or between ½ and 3. At any terms of trade between these two prices, such that it differs from the ROW and the U.S. relative prices, then both the United States and the rest of the world can both get more of all goods from trade.

THE LOWEST OPPORTUNITY COST METHOD OF DOING COMPARATIVE ADVANTAGE PROBLEMS

Saying that country X has a comparative advantage in producing good B is the same thing as saying that country X has the lowest opportunity cost of producing good B. That's why the law of comparative advantage works! It makes sense to produce goods where they have the lowest (opportunity) cost.

A good's opportunity cost is what is given up to get it. Suppose a unit of resource can produce 3 tons of steel or 6 tons of iron. In this case, the opportunity cost of getting 1 ton of steel is 2 tons of iron. The 2 is the ratio of what is given up (here, 6 tons of iron) divided by what is gained (here, 3 tons of steel). That is, to get 1 ton of steel, it is necessary to give up 2 tons of iron. Similarly, the opportunity cost of getting 1 more ton of iron is ½ ton of steel. The ½ is the ratio of what is given up (now 3 tons of steel) divided by what is gained (6 tons of iron).

Let's use the opportunity cost method to solve the two types of international trade problems. We have two countries X and Y, and two goods, A and B.

Problem type 1: We are given the prices of the goods in each country's currency as follows:

Good	Country X	Country Y
A	$6	#5
B	$12	#20

where "#" is the dollar sign for country Y's currency, the yound. Now calculate the opportunity cost of good A (the units of B given up to get 1 unit of A) for both countries:

Good	Country X	Country Y
A	½	¼

Notice now that the opportunity cost of B (the units of A given up to get 1 unit of B) is the inverse of that for good A:

Good	Country X	Country Y
B	2	4

Country Y should produce good A because it has the lowest opportunity cost of producing it (¼ versus X's ½). Country X should produce good B because it has the lowest opportunity cost of producing it (2 versus Y's 4).

Note that the terms of trade must fall between these prices for trade to be mutually beneficial. In this case, the 1 unit of X will trade for between ¼ and ½ units of Y. Alternatively, we can say that 1 unit of Y will trade for between 2 and 4 units of X.

Problem type 2: Here, we're given output/input ratios. Suppose 1 unit of resource (input) produces the following outputs in each of the countries:

Good	Country X	Country Y
A	20	8
B	10	2

Now calculate the opportunity cost, which results from shifting a unit of resource from producing one good to the other. The opportunity costs follow:

Good	Country X	Country Y
A	½	¼
B	2	4

For example, in country X, to gain 20 units of X you have to give up 10 units of B, or a ratio of ½ (= number given up divided by number gained).

Using the lowest opportunity cost method, country X should produce good B and country Y should produce A.

GRAPHING THE GAINS FROM TRADE

It is possible to use graphs to show the benefits of trade between two nations. Some texts skip this section because it adds little to what we've already said. But I include this section in case its material is assigned to you. We begin with a production possibility curve. A production possibility curve shows all the combinations of goods a nation is capable of producing. Suppose there are only two goods, food and clothing. Let us assume that the United States has 240 units of resources and that it takes, as it did above, 6 units of resources to make a unit of food and 12 units of resources to make a unit of clothing. Figure 19.1 illustrates the results on the left. Assume the rest of the world has 60 units of resources and the ability to make 1 unit of food from 3 units of

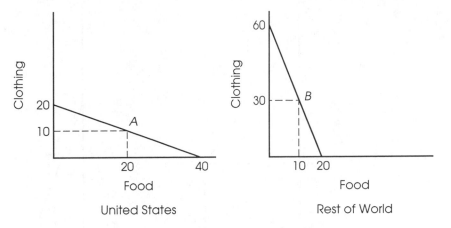

Figure 19.1 Production Possibility Curves

resources and 1 unit of clothing from 1 unit of resource. The result is shown on the right. The points where both consume is shown by points *A* and *B* (these are arbitrarily chosen).

Points to note:

The maximum units of food the United States can produce is 40 units (240/6).
The maximum food the rest of the world can produce is 20 units (= total units of resources divided by resource units used per unit food, or 60/3).
The maximum units of clothing the United States can produce is 20 units (= 240/12). For the rest of the world, it's 60 units (= 60/1).
The absolute slope of the U.S. production function is ½ (absolute slope = rise of 40 divided by run of 20). This is the relative price of food, the good on the horizontal axis. The memory aid is: Put on top the price of the good on the bottom to get the absolute slope. Here, the prices are the cost in resources needed to produce each good. So we have ½ = 6/12.
The absolute slope of the rest of the world production function also equals its relative price of food or 3 (3 = 3/1) or the ratio of the intercepts (= 60/20).
At point *A*, the U.S. produces and consumes 20 units of food and 10 units of clothing. At *B*, the rest of the world consumes 10 units of food and 30 units of clothing.

These observations show the situation before trade. After world trade opens, the terms of trade can fall between a relative price of food of ½ to 3. Let's suppose it turns out to be a relative price of 2 (2 units of clothing for every unit of food). Both still have the original production possibility curves, but they now have the opportunity to trade food for clothing at a one-for-two rate. For the United States, the international price of food (2) is higher than its pretrade price (½), which is the absolute slope of the production possibility curve. The United States will find it cheapest to produce only food, export it, and buy its clothing from the rest of the world. The rest of the world will find the international price of clothing (2) higher than its price (⅓) so that's the good it will produce and sell. The resulting consumption possibility curves due to international trade are shown in Figure 19.2. The new consumption points are shown at points *A´* and *B´*. These two points must be picked so the export of food from the United States matches the import of food from the United States.

Points to note:

The production possibility function still exists. Trade allows both to move to the higher consumption possibility curve (shown by the darker line).
Each country specializes in producing the good it can produce relatively cheaper. (This need not occur if the production possibility curve is curved and convex.) The United

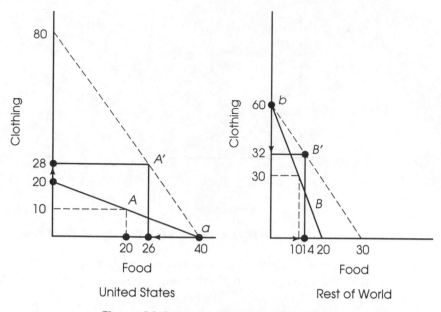

Figure 19.2 Production Possibility Curves

States is at point *a*, producing all food. The rest of the world is at point *b*, producing all clothing. Each is producing the good it has the comparative advantage in.

At point *A´*, the United States consumes 26 units of food. It produces 40 units and exports 14 units.

At point *B´*, the rest of the world consumes 14 units of food. It imports the 14 units from the United States.

The U.S. export of food (14) must equal what the rest of the world imports (14). This is shown by the two arrows on the horizontal axis.

The United States imports 28 units of clothing. It traded 14 units of food to the rest of the world and, at a terms of trade of 2 units of clothing for every unit of food, it got 28 units of clothing back.

The rest of the world produces 60 units of clothing (at point *b*) and exports 28 units to the United States, letting it consume 32 units (at point *B´*).

The U.S. import of food, 28 units, equals the export of food from the rest of the world. This is shown by the arrows on the vertical axis, which must be the same length.

After trade, both countries consume more of both goods. How can this be? How can the United States get more of both goods and yet, at the same time, the rest of the world get more of both goods. Notice that total resources are still the same, yet we now have more of both goods! The answer is that resources have been reallocated to the goods where they have the greatest comparative advantage. Each resource is not necessarily doing what it is best at (because the rest of the world, in this example, does everything better). No, each resource is doing what it does relatively better.

THE BENEFITS OF FREE TRADE USING DEMAND AND SUPPLY CURVES

Figure 19.3 shows the effect of trade before a tariff is imposed. We'll examine as an example the demand and supply for clothing, a good that is produced domestically (that is, within the United States) and also imported from abroad. *DD* is the domestic

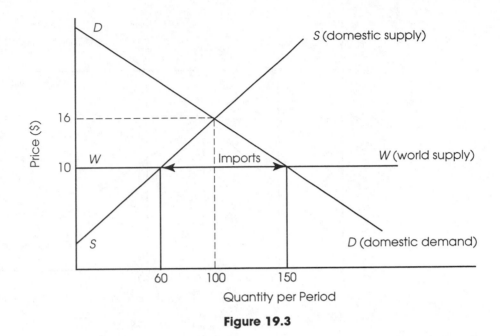

Figure 19.3

demand by U.S. citizens for clothing, and *SS* is the domestic supply for clothing by U.S. manufacturers of clothing. *WW* is the world supply of clothing from foreign manufacturers. We assume the world supply is perfectly elastic at $10. If there were no world trade, the price would be $16, where the domestic demand and supply curves cross at $Q = 100$ units. With world trade, the price is $10 and $Q = 150$, of which 90 units are supplied by imports and 60 units are supplied by domestic producers of clothing.

Points to note:

Without world supply, the price would be set where domestic demand equals domestic supply at $P = \$16$ and $Q = 100$.

With world supply, the price is set where domestic demand equals world supply at $P = \$10$ and $Q = 150$.

Imports equal the difference between domestic demand (150 units) and domestic supply (60). Imports equal 90 units.

Producers are worse off from imports while consumers gain. Overall, consumers gain more than producers lose from the import of goods.

So far, we've only looked at a good that is imported. But any good will become an export if its price is high enough. Suppose in the previous case that the world price of clothing rose to $22? Now the world supply line becomes the world demand line, because the world is ready to buy our clothing at $22 a unit. Figure 19.4 shows the results.

Points to note:

The price rises from $16 before trade to $22 with world trade.

Domestic supply of clothing is 140 units. Domestic demand is 50 units. The difference of 90 units is exported.

In the case of exports, consumers are worse off by world trade while producers are better off. Overall, producers gain more than consumers lose.

Figure 19.5 shows who wins and who loses from international trade on a good that is imported. Note that this part is only discussed in some texts. It is more difficult. Consumers gain area *abcd*, which equals $750. Before free trade, their consumer surplus was area *abe* ($600 = ½ × 100 × $12). After free trade, their consumer surplus is the

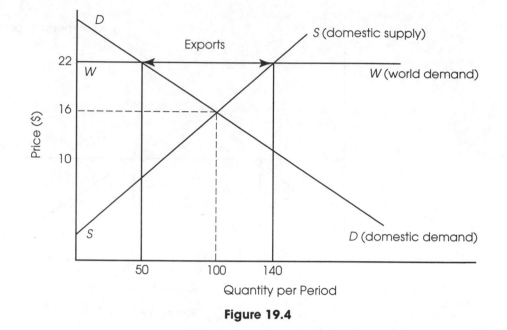

Figure 19.4

bigger area *dce* ($1,350 = ½ × 150 × $18). The difference between these areas is their net gain, area *abcd* ($750 = $1,350 – $600). Another way to get this result follows. The consumer's gain equals (1) the savings of $3 on the units they were buying before free trade (area *abdf*, which equals $600) plus (2) the area that reflects the gain in consumer surplus from the new units they buy (area *bfc*, which equals $150 = ½ × 50 × $6). The total gain is $750.

Domestic producer losses are reflected by the lost profit shown by area *abgd* ($480). Before free trade, their producer surplus was area *abk* ($750 = ½ × 100 x $15). After free trade, their producer surplus is reduced to area *dgk* ($270 = ½ × 60 × $9). Their loss is the difference, equal to area *abgd* ($480 = $750 – $270). Here's another way to get this area. The producer's loss equals (1) the loss of $6 on the units they still are producing (area *ahdg*, which equals $360 = $6 × 60) plus (2) the producer surplus lost on

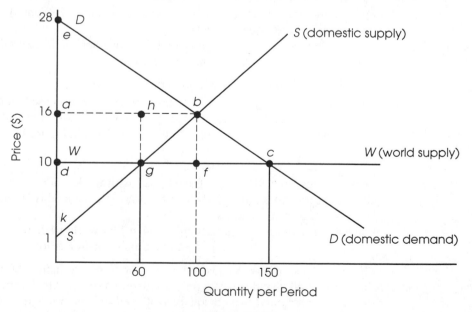

Figure 19.5

the units they are no longer producing, units 60 to 100 (this equals area *ghb*, equaling $120 = ½ × 40 × $6). The sum of these losses is $480.

On net, consumers gain more ($750) than producers lose ($480), making society on net $270. The net social gain is shown by area *gbc*. Before trade, the total surplus (the area between the domestic demand and supply curves) was area *ebk*. After trade, the new surplus is *ecgk*, which takes the old area and adds in the new area between the domestic demand curve and the world supply curve. The net gain is area *gbc*.

THE COST OF A TARIFF

Tariffs are a tax on imports. The main group that benefits are the industries protected from the competition of imports. As a consequence, tariffs can be regarded as an indirect subsidy for inefficient domestic producers. In addition, the government also benefits from the higher taxes. The main group that is harmed by tariffs is consumers. Tariffs and trade restrictions cost each American about $500 a year in the form of higher prices. In addition, industries that export are hurt by tariffs because fewer imports means fewer exports. The costs of tariffs far exceed their benefits. For example, the cost to consumers (in the form of higher prices) of saving one job in most protected industries is close to half a million dollars!

Suppose a tariff of $3 is imposed upon imports (but not on the domestic suppliers). The world supply price to consumers is now $13. The new quantities are shown in Figure 19.6. Demand falls to 125 units. Imports fall to 45 units while domestic supply expands to 80 units.

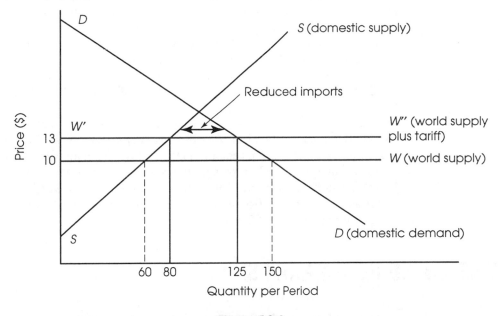

Figure 19.6

Points to note:

The world supply price line shifts up by $3 (the tariff per unit) to $13.
The economy moves to where domestic demand crosses the new world supply curve
    at $13 and $Q = 125$.
Domestic production of clothing goes up from 60 to 80 units.
Imports equal the difference between domestic demand and domestic supply.
Imports equal 45 units ($= 125 - 80$).

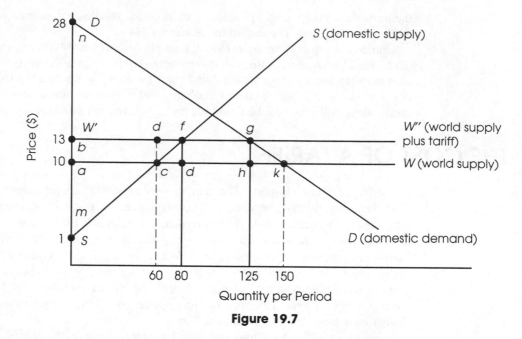

Figure 19.7

How people benefit and are hurt from this tariff is shown in Figure 19.7. This analysis is not in most texts.

The government collects area *dfgh* in taxes (that is, the tariff). This area equals the tariff times the quantity imported. In this case, this equals $135. This tax is a cost to consumers but is a benefit to those the government gives the money to. We thus count this area as neither a net gain nor a loss to the nation.

The gain to domestic producers is the difference between their new producer surplus (area *mbf*) and their free trade producer surplus (area *mac*). The difference is area *acfb* (= $120). This equals (1) the $3 gain on their free trade output (area *abcd*, or $180) plus (2) their added producer surplus and the added 20 units of output, from 60 to 80, which is area *cdf* (= $30).

The loss to domestic consumers is the difference between their free trade consumer surplus (area *ank*) and their new tariff consumer surplus (*bgn*). The difference equals area *abgk* (= $412.50). This equals (1) the $3 lost on the units they still consume after the tariff (area *abgh* = $375) plus (2) the consumer surplus lost on the 25 units they no longer consume, from 125 to 150, which equals area *ghk* (= $37.50).

Producers gain $210 from the tariff while consumers lose $412.50. The net cost to society of the tariff is $202.50.

THE CASE FOR TARIFFS

There are two situations when tariffs can help a nation.

1. Tariffs may improve the nation's terms of trade. If our nation is a monopsony in the world markets, then it might pay it to buy less of some imports. Our nation would be a monopsony if, when it buys more of an import, the world price for this import went up. That means that the marginal cost of another unit of the good is

$$MC \text{ of import} = \text{Price} + \Delta P \times Q \text{ being imported}$$

For example, if the United States imports 1,000 units of wine at $10 and 1,001 units at $10.02, then the marginal cost of the 1,001 units is $30.02 ($10.02 + 0.02

× 1,000). In this case, a tariff of $20 would ensure that U.S. consumers pay the full price of the wine to the nation.

2. Tariffs may help infant industries. Sometimes new industries need help surviving competition. A short-lived and timely tariff might help in this case. This assumes that politicians know which industries do need help and that they'll set the correct tariff. More often than not, the industries getting tariff protection are those that are old and inefficient.

3. Tariffs can be used to get other nations to open their markets. A strategically placed tariff may get other nations to open their markets more to our goods. More often than not, they don't open their markets, and the U.S. consumer gets stuck paying the strategic tariff forever.

All these arguments assume that politicians and bureaucrats are interested in the general welfare of our nation and have the knowledge and ability to act in that interest. In fact, the presence of the power to impose tariffs attracts the political contributions of the most inefficient industries who use the preceding arguments to harm our nation with burdensome tariffs.

QUOTAS

In many cases, governments use quota rates instead of tariffs to limit imports. For example, in Figure 19.8, importers can only import 45 units of clothing.

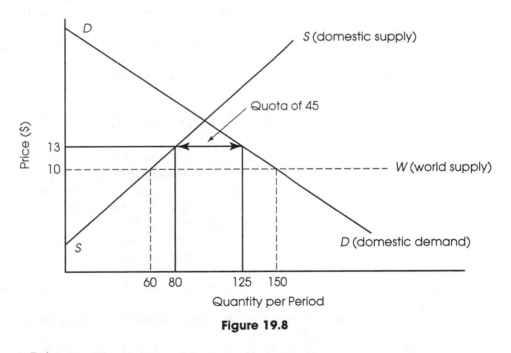

Figure 19.8

Points to note:

With free trade and no quota, the price would be $10, demand would be for 150 units, domestic production would be 60 units, and imports would be 90 units.

The quota limiting imports to 45 units has the effect of raising the price of clothing from its world price of $10 up to $13. Domestic consumption falls to 125 units and domestic production goes up to 80 units. Imports equal 45 units. The same effect would have been achieved with a $3 per unit tariff. (See Figure 19.6.)

The key point to note is that the effects of any quota can be duplicated by some appropriately selected tariff (here, a tariff of $3). The main difference is that (1) with a tariff, the government collects the tax revenues (in this case, it would be $125 = $3 × 45), but (2) with a quota, the foreign producers who sell the imports collect the benefits in the form of a higher price ($125 in added profits from selling the 45 imported units for $3 more than before). Thus, there is usually less opposition to quotas than there is to tariffs.

A STORY

Richard the magician announces that he can convert wheat into cars. He sets up a building in the wheat fields of Iowa and has the farmers bring wheat to him. Then, later, out of the building comes cars. For every $15,000 worth of wheat, he produces one car worth $20,000! The U.S. car manufacturers cry foul. They say he is putting car workers out of business. Richard says, "Yes, but I am employing farmers! Isn't a farmer as good as a car worker?"

Then the car manufacturers accuse him of being unfair, by employing magic. To this, Richard says, "What's fair? We're in a race for the consumer's dollar. In this race, let the consumer decide who wins. That's true fairness."

Failing to defeat Richard, the car manufacturers set about to discover how he does his magic. How does he create cars from wheat? They discover that he ships the wheat to Japan, sells it, and uses the proceeds to buy Japanese cars and bring them into the United States. "This is horrible," they claim! "You're giving car jobs to the Japanese." "No," Richard says. "Nothing has changed. I am giving car jobs to wheat farmers!"

The moral of this story is that the jobs lost to imports are given to those producing exports. The net effect is more goods for our nation.[4]

CRIB NOTES

If a nation's pretrade relative prices differ from world relative prices, then trade will allow a nation to have more of all goods.

Key: Calculate opportunity cost of each good (how many units of other goods have to be given up to get one unit of it). Nation with lowest opportunity cost should produce good.

If two goods, a nation should produce and export good it has lower opportunity cost of producing and produce less and instead import other good.

If two nations, terms of trade for good will be between their opportunity costs.

Problem type one: Two goods, A and B, with pretrade prices and terms of trade.

Opportunity cost of good A = Pretrade price of A/Pretrade price of B.

(Opportunity cost of good A is units of B given up to get 1 A).

Produce and export good A if its opportunity cost < Terms of trade for good A

---

[4]This story is from David Friedman, author of *Hidden Order*, a lively text on economics in everyday life.

Problem Type Two: Two goods, A and B, produce by unit of resource.

Opportunity cost of good A = Amount of B produced by unit/Amount of A produced by unit of resource.

Produce and export good A if its opportunity cost < Terms of trade for good A.

Balance of payment account = Current account + Capital account.

Balance of payment account = 0 if banks don't hold money.

Current account = Exports – Imports of goods and services.

Capital account = Exports – Imports of assets.

Tariff: Tax on imports. Raises price to consumers. Benefit to producers less than cost to consumers.

Quota: Physical limit on imports. Same effect as tariffs except importing firms get benefit of higher price on imports rather than government in the form of tariff revenues.

Review Questions

1. Bob goes to work and gets paid. He then uses his salary to buy goods and services.
   a. What are his imports and exports?
   b. Many people say that Japan should buy the same amount of goods from us as they sell us. This is called *reciprocity*. If this reciprocity doctrine were applied to Bob, what would this imply about Bob?
   c. What is wrong with reciprocity?

2. Joe trades his car for Bill's truck. Both get what they expected. But Joe thinks, "Wow, this truck is worth a whole lot more to me than what that old car was worth!" Does this imply that Bill is worse off?

3. a. When will two nations not benefit from free and open trade?
   b. Some people argue that trade should only take place between equals. How is this statement wrong?

4. Why do most farmers favor free trade?

5. According to the law of comparative advantage, who should produce what goods?

6. The price data for the United States and the alien invaders follows:

	United States	Alien Invaders
Hats	$20	8 kirks
Noisemakers	$5	4 kirks

   a. How can you tell if trade can make both the United States and the aliens better off?
   b. In which good does the United States have the comparative advantage? The aliens?
   c. What are the limits to the possible terms of trade in this example?
   d. How will each party be better off trading?

7. The following shows the domestic demand and domestic supply of wine to the United States. Answer the following questions.

a. If there were no world trade in wine, what would the price of wine be? How much would be sold?

b. If free trade is permitted and the world supply price is $6 a bottle, what will the market price be? How much will be sold? How much will be produced by domestic wine producers? How much will be imported?

c. If a tariff of $2 is imposed on imported wine only, how much will be bought and at what price? How much will be produced by domestic wine producers? How much will be imported?

d. What will happen if the world price of wine goes to $12?

Price($)	Domestic Supply	Domestic Demand
12	18	12
11	16	13
10	14	14
9	12	15
8	10	16
7	8	17
6	6	18
5	4	19
4	2	20

8. How will the following affect the current account and the capital account? How will they affect total domestic spending inside the United States?

    Transaction A: The United States buys a $20,000 car from Japan, and Japan uses the $20,000 to buy a U.S. government bond.

    Transaction B: The United States buys a $20,000 car, and Japan uses the $20,000 to buy a machine from the United States.

    Transaction C: The United States buys a $20,000 car, and Japan uses the $20,000 to buy newly issued stock of a U.S. firm.

9. According to Adam Smith (in *The Wealth of Nations*), "It is the maxim of every prudent master of a family, never to attempt to make at home what will cost him more to make than to buy." How does this apply to free trade?

10. Suppose Santa Claus is real[5] and really does gives toys away for free to all the children of our land. In turn, he asks for nothing but that we be good. A toy manufacturer writes, "Santa Claus is evil! Sure, he may look jolly but in actuality, he is dumping goods on our country below cost and destroying thousands upon thousands of toy making jobs! And if that is not bad enough, he doesn't buy anything from us, so he doesn't even make up for this by creating jobs in our export sector. We demand that the military shoot Santa down and put this so-called do-gooder out of the business of killing American jobs!" Is it true that a real Santa is bad for the United States?

11. Why would a medical doctor employ a gardener when the doctor could do a better job gardening than any gardener?

12. In country A, 1 unit of labor can produce 2 telephones or 4 pencils. In country B, 1 unit of labor can produce 20 telephones or 80 pencils.

---

[5]If you believe Santa is real, then please do not read this statement as implying that Santa is fake. I just wrote it this way because some people actually believe Santa isn't real.

a. In which country does labor have the absolute advantage in producing each good?

b. Which country has the comparative advantage in producing telephones? What is the opportunity cost of the telephone in each?

c. What range will the terms of trade for telephones fall in?

d. Suppose the terms of trade falls halfway between its two limits. Show how each country can have the same number of telephones and more pencils.

13. In question 12, suppose country A has a program that increases the productivity of labor. Suppose labor productivity doubles, so 1 unit of labor can produce 4 telephone or 8 pencils. Is the pencil industry any more competitive than it was before?

14. In Isaac Asimov's famous science fiction series on robots, robots are not allowed on earth because they are so much more productive than humans. If robots were allowed, he argues no one would want to employ a human. Is this correct?

Answers

1. a. When Bob goes to work, he is exporting his services to his employer. The goods and services he buys are imports into his household.

   b. This doctrine says that Bob should buy all his goods and services from his employer. This would, of course, make Bob worse off, because people other than his employer have the goods and services he wants.

   c. Reciprocity eliminates the many indirect trades that money and credit allows us. For example, the United States buys cars from Japan, Japan uses the dollars to buy oil from the Middle East, and the Middle East buys steel from the United States. The United States has a trade deficit with Japan and a trade surplus with the Middle East, yet it all balances out. If we had to have reciprocity with all nations, these mutually advantageous trades could not have taken place.

2. Bill made the trade because he valued the car more than the truck he gave away. Trade is mutually beneficial. In fact, Bill might think he got the better part of the deal also.

3. a. Trade will not take place if both nations have the same relative prices for all tradable goods and services. No differences in relative prices means no trade!

   b. If two nations are equal, they will have equal relative prices. Thus, they will have no gains from trade. Only nations that are unequal will benefit from trade. Thus, the statement is wrong. Trade between equals will never take place. Trade between unequals will make each nation better off.

4. Farmers are one of the major exporters of our nation. Farmers know that fewer imports means fewer exports. If tariffs reduce the sale of imports, then foreigners will not be able to get U.S. dollars they need to buy U.S. farm products. So tariffs mean less imports, and less imports means less business for U.S. farmers.

5. When each country produces the good that it has the lowest relative price of producing, total output will be maximized. Alternatively stated, each good will be produced at the least opportunity cost.

6. a. The relative prices are different, so there is room for mutually beneficial trade. For the United States, the relative price of a hat is 4 (that is, if you buy 1 hat, you have to give up 4 noisemakers). For the aliens, the relative price of a hat is 2 (that is, if an alien buys 1 hat, it must give up 2 noisemakers).

   b. The United States has the comparative advantage in making noisemakers. Noisemakers cost ¼ a hat (while, for aliens, they cost ½ a hat). The aliens have the comparative advantage in making hats. For them hats cost only 2 noisemakers (while for the United States hats cost 4 noisemakers).

    c. The terms of trade for a hat will be between its U.S. price (2) and its alien price (4). So one hat will trade for between 2 and 4 noisemakers.

    d. If the terms of trade fall between 2 and 4 noisemakers for every hat, then both the United States and the aliens can have more hats and noisemakers than before.

7. a. $P = \$10$ and $Q = 14$. All 14 bottles will be produced domestically.

    b. $P = \$6$ (the world supply price) and $Q = 18$ (domestic demand at \$6). At $P = \$6$, domestic supply is 6 units. The difference, 12 bottles, is imported.

    c. $P = \$8$ (the world supply price plus the tariff), $Q = 16$ (domestic demand at \$8). At $P = \$8$, domestic supply is 10 units. Imports equal 6 bottles.

    d. When the world price is \$12, wine will now be *exported* from the United States! At $P = \$12$, domestic demand is 12, and domestic production is 18. The difference (6 bottles) is exported.

8. Transaction A: This increases the trade deficit (the current account goes down by \$20,000) and increases the capital account (the United States exports the U.S. bond, which is an asset to its holder). This will have no effect on domestic spending if the U.S. government spends the \$20,000 (say on bridges or salaries).

   Transaction B: This has no effect on the trade deficit. The current account and the capital account remain unchanged. There is no effect on spending.

   Transaction C: This increases the trade deficit. The current account becomes more negative but the capital account becomes positive. This has no effect on domestic spending if the company issuing the stock spends it (for example, on salary or machinery).

9. No nation should make a good at home that is cheaper to buy abroad. If an import is cheaper to buy than it costs to produce a domestic good, then buy the import. Use the savings (the inputs used to produce the domestic good) to produce those goods that are cheaper to make at home.

10. Economics says Santa is good after all. The people who had toy jobs can now work elsewhere producing even more goods. The total output per person will go up as will per capita income. If Santa did buy from us, then we would not be as well off as when he gave the toys to us free. That's because some of our jobs would have to turn from producing goods for us to producing goods for Santa, reducing the output of goods going to Americans.

11. The doctor's comparative advantage is in medicine. The gardener does not have an absolute advantage in being a gardener, but he does have a comparative advantage in gardening! The doctor is better off doing what she is comparatively better at and employing the gardener to do what the gardener is comparatively better at.

12. a. In country B, labor has the absolute advantage in producing both goods.

    b. Country A has the lower opportunity cost of producing telephones, so it has the comparative advantage in producing telephones. In country A, shifting a unit of labor from producing 2 telephones increases pencil production by 4 pencils. This means that the opportunity cost per telephone in country A is 2 pencils (= 4/2). In country B, the opportunity cost of producing 1 telephone is 4 (= 80/20).

    c. The terms of trade will fall between 2 and 4 pencils for 1 telephone.

    d. The terms of trade would be 3 pencils for 1 telephone.

    Country A will make and export telephones. If it makes 2 more telephones, it can get 6 pencils in return. The resources it takes for it to make 2 more telephones would have otherwise made 4 pencils. So by this trade, it has the same number of telephones but, on net, 2 more pencils than before.

    Country B will make and export pencils. If it makes an additional 80 pencils, it has to give up producing 20 telephones. But it can use 60 of these pencils to buy

20 telephones. On net, it will have the same number of phones and 20 more pencils.

13. No. The opportunity cost of a pencil is the same (½ a telephone). Because this opportunity cost is below country B's opportunity cost for a pencil (which is ¼ a telephone), the pencil industry is still at the same competitive disadvantage as before. Only if labor productivity goes up more in the pencil industry than in the telephone industry would the pencil industry become more competitive. However, at the same time, the telephone industry will become less competitive!

14. Humans may not have the absolute advantage in doing anything, but they must have the comparative advantage in producing some goods. If you think of humans as one nation and robots as another, then trade between these nations will make both better off. Trade is the true foundation of progress.

Glossary

ABSOLUTE ADVANTAGE ability to produce a good with fewer inputs.

ACCOUNTING PROFITS profits ignoring implicit costs. Equals total revenue less explicit costs.

ADDED BUYER EFFECT a lower price for a good attracts new buyers into a market, increasing its quantity demanded.

ALLOCATIVE EFFICIENCY (also termed Pareto efficiency) when no possible trade or reallocation of goods and inputs will make some better off without making others worse off.

ASSETS what people own or what other people owe them.

AVERAGE TAX RATE percent of income paid in taxes.

BACKWARD-BENDING SUPPLY CURVE OF LABOR a curve showing that as real hourly wages go up, workers first supply more and then fewer hours of work.

BALANCE-OF-PAYMENT ACCOUNT account made up of two accounts that keep track of goods, services, and assets flowing in and out of a nation. See also *capital account* and *current account*.

BARTER trade without money.

BILATERAL MONOPOLY market where a monopsony and monopoly deal with each other.

BOND IOU issued by a borrower promising to pay a fixed amount of dollars on specified dates to the holder of the bond.

BREAKEVEN PRICE price at which the firm just covers its costs.

BUSINESSES producers of goods and services.

CAPITAL stock of plants, equipment, inventory, and other resources of production useful for more than one year.

CAPITAL ACCOUNT account keeping track of physical and financial assets flowing on net into a country.

CAPTURE HYPOTHESIS hypothesis that regulatory agencies tend to be "captured" by the industry they regulate and act on the industry's behalf rather than the consumers'.

CARTEL an arrangement among sellers in a market to jointly set price and output.

CARTEL CHEATING PROBLEM all collusive agreements suffer from the tendency of each member to cut its price and take a bigger share of the market.

COASE THEOREM theory that people can get rid of any market failure by bargaining among themselves when transaction costs are low.

COLLUSION attempt, either explicit or implicit, to not compete.

COMPARATIVE ADVANTAGE ability to produce a good at a lower relative cost.

COMPENSATING WAGE DIFFERENTIALS differences in money wages compensating for differences in nonmonetary aspects of work (such as differences in working conditions and fringe benefits).

COMPLEMENTARY INPUTS inputs used closely together. When the price of one goes up, less of both will be used even if output is unchanged.

COMPLEMENTS two goods that go together (such as peanut butter and jelly). When the price of one goes up, the quantity demanded of the other goes down.

CONSTANT-COST INDUSTRY industry with perfectly elastic long-run supply curve.

CONSTANT RETURNS TO SCALE when long-run average total cost stays the same as output expands. Results when a given increase in all inputs increases output in the same proportion.

CONSUMER SURPLUS what consumers are willing to pay for a good minus what they do pay.

CONTROL VARIABLE variable that decision-maker can increase or decrease to get the best net benefit or profit. For example, a control variable for a firm is the output that it produces.

CREDIBLE THREAT threat that in the short run seems irrational (because it harms the person making it) but is credible because it results in long-run profits. An example is a dominant firm's threat to cut its price and drive out of business any competitor charging less than it does.

CROSS ELASTICITY OF DEMAND responsiveness of the quantity demanded to a change in the price of *another* good. Percent change in quantity demanded of a good due to a 1% increase in the price of another good.

CROWDING OUT decreases in private investment spending (which is mainly financed by borrowing) due to increases in government borrowing (that push up interest rates).

CURRENT ACCOUNT account keeping track of goods and services flowing on net out of a country.

DEADWEIGHT LOSS loss to society without any offsetting gains.

DEADWEIGHT LOSS OF A TAX total loss to producers and consumers from a tax minus tax revenues collected. Also termed excess burden of a tax.

DECREASING-COST INDUSTRY an industry with a long-run supply curve that is downward sloping.

DEMAND CURVE any downward-sloping curve that shows a greater quantity of a good demanded at a lower price, provided that other determinants of demand (such as income and prices of other goods) are held constant.

DEPRECIATION decline in the value of an asset over a given time, usually a year. (For calculating national income, depreciation is called the capital consumption allowance.)

DISCOUNT RATE interest rate the Federal Reserve system charges banks that borrow funds from it.

DISCRIMINATION workers not getting the same well-paying jobs or getting less pay than others with the same ability because of their race, sex, or other characteristic not related to productivity.

DISECONOMIES OF SCALE when long-run average total cost goes up as output expands. Results when a given increase in all input results in a smaller than proportional increase in output.

ECONOMIC PROFIT payment in excess of what is necessary to get something done. Economic profit = Total revenue – (Explicit costs + Implicit costs).

ECONOMIC RENT any payment to a factor in excess of its opportunity cost. Also, payment to factor in perfectly inelastic supply.

ECONOMICS study of how people choose among alternative uses of their scarce resources.

ECONOMIES OF SCALE when long-run average total cost falls as output expands. Results when a given increase in all inputs results in a more than proportional increase in output.

EFFICIENCY when people produce all that can be, given their resources. To produce more of one good, an efficient economy must produce less of other goods and is on its production possibility curve.

ELASTIC DEMAND when a given percent increase in price causes a greater percent decrease in the quantity demanded, decreasing total revenue.

ELASTICITY responsiveness of one variable to the change in another, both changes expressed as percents. The elasticity of Q with respect to P is the percent change in Q for every 1% change in P.

EQUILIBRIUM PRICE price at which the quantity demanded equals the quantity sold. Also termed the market clearing price.

EXPLICIT COSTS dollar costs actually paid out.

EXPORTS goods and services sold by domestic citizens to other nations.

FACTOR OF PRODUCTION any input used to produce output (the main factors being land, labor, and capital).

FINAL GOOD good produced for final use and not for resale within the year.

FIXED COSTS costs that neither increase nor decrease as output changes.

FREE GOOD good that is not scarce; good whose supply exceeds demand at a zero price.

FREE-RIDER PROBLEM while everyone benefits from a public good, each tries to be a free rider by not paying for it. As a result, the good may not be supplied in a free market.

FULL WAGE total monetary value of a job (per period); the sum of money wages plus the monetary value of all the nonmonetary aspects of work.

GAME THEORY analysis of small number of players (individuals or organizations) with conflicting interests and whose actions affect one another.

GIFFEN GOOD good whose demand decreases when price goes down. The good must be an inferior good for this to occur.

GRAPH visual presentation of how two variables are related to each other.

HOLD-OUT PROGRAM whenever the consent of a higher percent of people is needed, each person has a greater incentive to hold out his or her consent, with the result that less is achieved.

HOUSEHOLDS owners of all factors in the economy. Households provide the services of labor, land, capital, and ownership to businesses.

HUMAN CAPITAL skills and ability acquired through investment in schooling and on-the-job training.

IMPLICIT COSTS costs incurred because of alternative opportunities given up. For a firm, these include the costs of its owners' time and investment.

IMPORTS goods and services that are bought by domestic citizens and are produced by other nations.

INCOME highest level of sustainable consumption. Income minus consumption equals addition to wealth.

INCOME EFFECT OF A PRICE CHANGE a lower price for a good is like giving consumers more income. Some of this "income" may go for buying more units of the good, increasing its quantity demanded.

INCOME ELASTICITY OF DEMAND percent change in quantity demanded for every 1% change in income.

INCREASING-COST INDUSTRY industry with rising long-run supply curve.

INELASTIC DEMAND when a given percent increase in the price causes a smaller percent decrease in the quantity demanded, increasing total revenue.

INFERIOR GOOD a good that people demand less of when their income goes up.

INFLATIONARY PREMIUM addition to real interest rate to compensate savers for expected loss in purchasing power from inflation.

INNOVATION finding a better way to do something, including a cheaper way to produce a good or a more valued good to produce.

INPUT see *factor of production*.

INTEREST payment for use of funds over a certain period of time.

INVERSE RELATIONSHIP see *negative relationship*.

JOINT PRODUCTS two goods produced together because it is difficult to produce them separately (e.g., leather and beef).

KINKED DEMAND CURVE hypothetical demand curve that an oligopolic firm faces when other firms maintain their price when it raises its price but match its price when it lowers its price.

LABOR FORCE all persons employed or unemployed.

LAFFER CURVE curve showing that as the marginal tax rate increases, total tax revenues first increase and then fall as the marginal rate becomes excessive.

LAW OF COMPARATIVE ADVANTAGE nations are better off when they produce goods they have a comparative advantage in supplying.

LAW OF DEMAND quantity demanded and price are inversely related—more is demanded at a lower price, less at a higher price (other things being equal).

LAW OF DIMINISHING MARGINAL RETURNS after some point, as a firm adds more and more units of an input, the input's marginal physical product diminishes (i.e., it adds less to total output than before).

LAW OF DIMINISHING MARGINAL UTILITY as people consume more of a good in a given period, its marginal utility declines.

LAW OF EQUAL MARGINAL UTILITY PER DOLLAR the highest utility is achieved when the last dollar spent on each good has the same marginal utility.

LAW OF INCREASING RELATIVE COST as more of a good is produced, its opportunity cost rises.

LAW OF SUPPLY quantity supplied and price usually are directly related—more is supplied at a higher price, less at a lower price (other things being equal).

LIABILITIES what people owe others.

LIQUIDITY ease with which an asset (such as a stock or bond) can be converted into cash.

LOGROLLING the trading of votes to get positions favorable only to minority interest groups voted in.

LONG RUN period when firm can change all inputs, including its plant size and equipment. Also, period when firms can enter or exit an industry.

MACROECONOMICS study of the economy as a whole, including the causes of the business cycle, unemployment, and inflation.

MARGINAL ANALYSIS solving economic problems by using small steps and evaluating the costs and benefits of each marginal step.

MARGINAL BENEFIT increase in total benefit due to one more unit of output, labor, or other control variable being increased.

MARGINAL COST addition to total cost due to increasing output by one unit.

MARGINAL FACTOR COST (*MFC*) addition to total cost when one additional unit of an input is employed.

MARGINAL PHYSICAL PRODUCT (*MPP*) addition to total physical output due to an added unit of an input.

MARGINAL PROPENSITY TO SAVE (*MPS*) added savings resulting from $1 more of disposable income.

MARGINAL REVENUE increase in total revenue resulting from additional unit of output.

MARGINAL REVENUE PRODUCT (*MRP*) addition to total revenue when one additional unit of an input (such as labor or capital) is employed.

MARGINAL TAX RATE percent of additional income paid in taxes.

MARGINAL UTILITY addition to total utility from consuming one more unit of a good.

MARGINAL VALUE value of least importance that a unit of a good (or resource) is currently being put to; the loss suffered due to one less unit of the good.

MEDIAN VOTER MODEL when two people are running for office, they will position themselves near the opinions of the median voter.

MICROECONOMICS study of factors determining the relative prices of goods and inputs.

MINIMUM EFFICIENT SCALE level of output where long-run average total cost achieves its minimum.

MONOPOLISTIC COMPETITION market like that of perfect competition except sellers sell a closely related but not identical product.

MONOPOLY only seller of a good with no close substitutes.

MONOPSONY a firm so dominant in a factor market that its hiring decisions affect the input's market price. Faces higher input price as it employs more.

MUTUAL INTERDEPENDENCE when one firm's actions affect another firm's in the same industry significantly, and vice versa.

NATURAL MONOPOLY industry having such large economies of scale that one firm can meet all the demand and still not achieve its most efficient scale.

NEGATIVE EXTERNALITIES activities imposing uncompensated costs upon others. Also termed external diseconomies.

NEGATIVE RELATIONSHIP X and Y are negatively related if when X goes up, Y goes down and vice versa. (Also called an inverse relationship.)

NOMINAL INTEREST RATE actual rate of interest; the extra *money* borrowers have to pay back to lenders, in excess of the loan amount expressed as percent per year of the loan.

NON-PRICE COMPETITION competition between goods on aspects other than price (such as quality and service).

NON-PRICE RATIONING any method of equating supply and demand other than price. Its two main forms are waiting lines and discrimination.

NORMAL GOOD a good that people demand more of when their income goes up.

NORMAL PROFITS long-run accounting profits in an industry, just covering the owner's implicit costs.

OLIGOPOLY market with few sellers and medium to high barriers of entry.

OPPORTUNITY COST value of best alternative that had to be given up in order to undertake a given course of action.

PAYMENT-IN-KIND payment in goods or services rather than in money.

PERFECT COMPETITION whenever there is enough competition that no one seller can raise its price without losing all its customers to other sellers.

PERFECTLY CONTESTABLE MARKETS markets with unimpeded and costless entry and exit of firms.

PERFECT PRICE DISCRIMINATION when seller charges a different price for each unit of the good that's equal to the unit's demand price.

POSITIVE EXTERNALITIES activities creating benefits for others who don't pay for the benefits. Also termed external economies.

POSITIVE RELATIONSHIP X and Y are positively related if when X goes up, Y goes up. And when X goes down, Y goes down.

PRESENT VALUE value of future dollars in terms of what they are worth today. The loan amount one could borrow today and pay back with the future dollars.

PRICE CEILING law imposed by the government prohibiting the price from going above a certain level.

PRICE DISCRIMINATION the selling of the same good at different prices. See also *perfect price discrimination.*

PRICE ELASTICITY OF DEMAND percent change in quantity demanded for every 1% change in price (both percent changes stated as absolute values).

PRICE ELASTICITY OF SUPPLY percent change in quantity supplied for every 1% change in the price.

PRICE FLOOR law imposed by the government prohibiting the price from falling below a certain level.

PRICE SEARCHERS buyers or sellers having large enough shares of a market such that when they buy or sell more, the market price changes.

PRICE TAKERS buyers or sellers whose individual actions have no effect on market price (and thus they "take" the market price as given).

PRIVATE COST cost borne by those producing a good.

PROBLEM OF THE COMMONS abuse of resource when no one owns it and thus no one has an incentive to keep it up.

PRODUCER SURPLUS what producers are paid less their marginal costs.

PRODUCTION POSSIBILITY CURVE graph showing combinations of goods an individual, firm, or an economy is capable of producing. Also termed production possibility frontier.

PROGRESSIVE TAX SYSTEM tax system under which those with higher incomes are subject to higher marginal and average tax rates.

PUBLIC GOOD good whose consumption by one person does not diminish its consumption by others (e.g., national defense).

QUANTITY DEMAND maximum quantity of a good buyers are willing and able to buy at a given price (during a fixed period of time).

QUANTITY SUPPLIED maximum quantity of a good sellers are willing and able to supply at a given price (during a fixed period of time).

QUOTA a limit on the amount of an import.

REAL INTEREST RATE percent increase in purchasing power (i.e., in real goods and services) that borrowers pay back to lenders. Equals the nominal rate of interest minus the expected rate of inflation.

REAL VALUE measure of value removing the effects of inflation. The value of a good (or goods) in terms of their price from some given year (called the base year). Also called value in terms of constant dollars.

REAL WAGE hourly earnings of workers stated in real terms (equals money wage divided by price index).

RELATIVE PRICE Good A's relative price tells how much of good B must be given to get one more unit of good A.

RENT see *economic rent.*

RENT-SEEKING activity costing resources and time with the object of obtaining resources or laws having economic rents; considered socially wasteful because this activity adds nothing to local output.

SCARCITY condition that exists when current resources are inadequate to provide for all of people's wants.

SHIFT IN DEMAND change in demand curve such that a different quantity is demanded at each price. Curves shift only when some variable *other than price* changes. Also called change in demand.

SHORTAGE quantity demanded exceeds quantity supplied (caused by price being below market equilibrium price).

SHORT RUN period when the firm can change (either increasing or decreasing) some but *not all* of its inputs.

SHUTDOWN PRICE price below which a firm shuts down.

SLOPE how much the variable on the vertical (or side) axis changes when the variable on the horizontal (or bottom) axis increases by one unit.

SOCIAL BENEFIT benefit all persons get from a good.

SOCIAL COST cost all persons pay for a good.

SPILL-OVER EFFECT higher union wages causing those losing their jobs in union plants to seek jobs in nonunion plants, forcing nonunion wages down.

SUBSTITUTE INPUTS two inputs that to some degree can replace one another. When price of one goes up, the firm uses more of the other input per unit of output.

SUBSTITUTE PRODUCTS two alternative goods that could be produced with the same (or very similar) set of inputs. (Examples are gasoline and heating oil.)

SUBSTITUTES two goods that compete with each other (such as butter and margarine). When the price of one good goes up, the quantity demanded of the other goes up.

SUBSTITUTION EFFECT OF A PRICE CHANGE a lower relative price means a lower opportunity cost of buying the good, which encourages buyers to buy more of the good (holding real income constant).

SUNK COSTS costs that can't be avoided.

SUPPLY CURVE curve showing relationship between price and quantity of a good that suppliers are willing to supply. Usually upward sloping; the exception is in a decreasing cost industry.

SURPLUS quantity supplied exceeds quantity demanded (caused by price exceeding market equilibrium price).

GLOSSARY

TARIFF tax on imports.

TAX INCIDENCE who actually pays a tax.

TAX SHIFTING shifting tax one pays onto others. For example, firm raising its price shifts tax onto consumers.

THEORY OF PUBLIC CHOICE economic theory of how government acts.

TIEBOUT HYPOTHESIS theory that smaller governments and greater mobility of citizens and firms between cities, states, and nations produce more efficient government.

TOTAL REVENUE total sales (usually per year).

TOTAL SURPLUS excess of the total value of a quantity of a good over its total cost; sum of the difference between demand price and supply price added across all units of a good being bought and produced. Equals the consumer surplus plus the producer surplus.

TOTAL UTILITY total satisfaction derived from consuming goods and services.

TRADE OFF when satisfying *more* of one need means satisfying *less* of another.

TRANSFER PAYMENT payment for which no goods or services are received in return. Examples include gifts and food stamps.

UNITARY DEMAND when a given percent increase in price causes the exact same percent decrease in the quantity demanded, leaving total revenue unchanged.

VALUE ADDED value of a business's output minus its purchases from other businesses.

VALUE-ADDED TAX (VAT) tax on a company's value added.

VARIABLE COST cost of all inputs the firm increases in the short run to produce more.

VOTING PARADOX how a majority will vote on a set of issues can be changed by altering the order issues are presented in.

WAGE-THREAT EFFECT higher union wages causing nonunion employers to also pay higher wages to reduce threat of being unionized.

WEALTH net value of all the assets a person owns (including the value of his or her skills, i.e., the value of all future earnings).

MOVE TO THE HEAD OF YOUR CLASS

THE EASY WAY!

Barron's presents THE EASY WAY SERIES—specially prepared by top educators, it maximizes effective learning, while minimizing the time and effort it takes to raise your grades, brush up on the basics, and build your confidence. Comprehensive and full of clear review examples, **THE EASY WAY SERIES** is your best bet for better grades, quickly!

0-8120-9409-3	**Accounting the Easy Way, 3rd Ed.**—$11.95, Can. $15.95
0-8120-9393-3	**Algebra the Easy Way, 3rd Ed.**—$12.95, Can. $16.95
0-8120-1943-1	**American History the Easy Way, 2nd Ed.**—$11.95, Can. $15.95
0-8120-9134-5	**Anatomy and Physiology the Easy Way**—$13.95, Can. $17.95
0-8120-9410-7	**Arithmetic the Easy Way, 3rd Ed.**—$12.95, Can. $16.95
0-8120-4286-7	**Biology the Easy Way, 2nd Ed.**—$11.95, Can. $15.95
0-8120-4371-5	**Bookkeeping the Easy Way, 2nd Ed.**—$11.95, Can. $15.95
0-8120-4760-5	**Business Law the Easy Way**—$11.95, Can. $15.95
0-8120-4626-9	**Business Letters the Easy Way, 2nd Ed.**—$10.95, Can. $14.50
0-8120-4627-7	**Business Mathematics the Easy Way, 2nd Ed.**—$11.95, Can. $15.95
0-8120-9141-8	**Calculus the Easy Way, 3rd Ed.**—$12.95, Can. $16.95
0-8120-9138-8	**Chemistry the Easy Way, 3rd Ed.**—$12.95, Can. $16.95
0-8120-4253-0	**Computer Programming In Basic the Easy Way, 2nd Ed.**—$9.95, Can. $13.95
0-8120-2800-7	**Computer Programming In Fortran the Easy Way**—$11.95, Can. $15.95
0-8120-2799-X	**Computer Programming In Pascal the Easy Way**—$13.95, Can. $17.95
0-8120-9144-2	**Electronics the Easy Way, 3rd Ed.**—$12.95, Can. $16.95
0-8120-9142-6	**English the Easy Way, 3rd Ed.**—$12.95, Can. $16.95
0-8120-9505-7	**French the Easy Way, 3rd Ed.**—$12.95, Can. $16.95
0-8120-4287-5	**Geometry the Easy Way, 2nd Ed.**—$11.95, Can. $15.95
0-8120-9145-0	**German the Easy Way, 2nd Ed.**—$12.95, Can. $16.95
0-8120-9146-9	**Italian the Easy Way, 2nd Ed.**—$12.95, Can. $16.95
0-8120-9627-4	**Japanese the Easy Way**—$12.95, Can. $16.95
0-8120-9139-6	**Math the Easy Way, 3rd Ed.**—$11.95, Can. $15.95
0-8120-9601-0	**Microeconomics the Easy Way**—$12.95, Can. $16.95
0-8120-4390-1	**Physics the Easy Way, 2nd Ed.**—$11.95, Can. $15.95
0-8120-9412-3	**Spanish the Easy Way, 3rd Ed.**—$12.95, Can. $16.95
0-8120-9143-4	**Spelling the Easy Way, 3rd Ed.**—$11.95, Can. $15.95
0-8120-9392-5	**Statistics the Easy Way, 3rd Ed.**—$11.95, Can. $15.95
0-8120-4389-8	**Trigonometry the Easy Way, 2nd Ed.**—$11.95, Can. $15.95
0-8120-9147-7	**Typing the Easy Way, 3rd Ed.**—$14.95, Can. $19.95
0-8120-4615-3	**Writing the Easy Way, 2nd Ed.**—$11.95, Can. $15.95

Barron's Educational Series, Inc.
250 Wireless Boulevard • Hauppauge, New York 11788
In Canada: Georgetown Book Warehouse • 34 Armstrong Avenue, Georgetown, Ontario L7G 4R9
$ = U.S. Dollars   Can. $ = Canadian Dollars

Prices subject to change without notice. Books may be purchased at your local bookstore, or by mail from Barron's. Enclose check or money order for total amount plus sales tax where applicable and 15% for postage and handling (minimum charge $4.95 U.S. and Canada). All books are paperback editions.

(#45) R2/97